By Alan Alexander, Genevieve Cogman,
Conrad Hubbard and Peter Schaefer

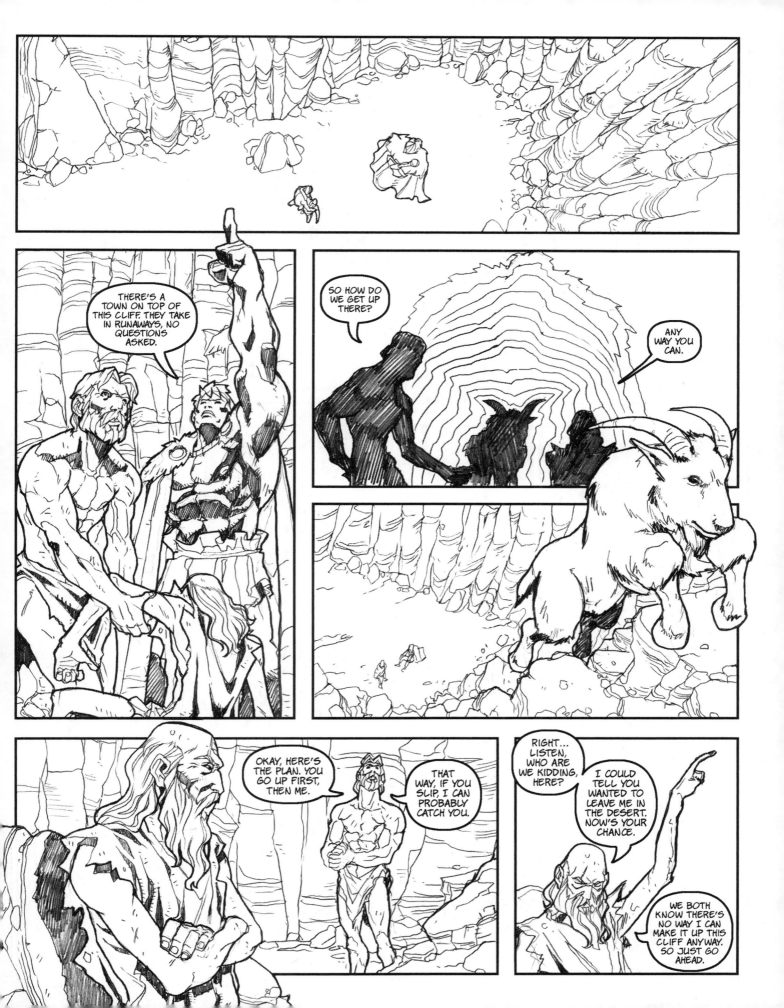

CREDITS

Authors: Alan Alexander, Genevieve Cogman, Conrad Hubbard and Peter Schaefer
Comic Scripter: Carl Bowen
Storyteller Game System Design: Mark Rein•Hagen
Developers: John Chambers and Dean Shomshak
Editor: Scribendi.com
Art Direction and Book Design: Brian Glass
Artists: Ross Campbell, DPI Studios (with Embrio and Jaysin), Andy Hepworth, Saana "Kiyo" Lappalainen, Aaron Nakahara, Pasi Pitkanen, Chris "Satyr" Ready, Andie Tong, UDON (with Evil Annette, Marco Nelor, Joe Ng, Ryan Odagawa and Chris Stevens), Melissa Uran and Long Vo
Cover Art: Imaginary Friends (with Erfan Fajar)
Playtesters: Alan Alexander, John Brozovich, Michael Caposino, Tim Ferguson, Conrad Hubbard, Rachel "Bunnie" Hubbard, Cliff Jackson, Mario Meo, Danielle Newquist, John Newquist, Peter Schaefer, Ryan Smith, Larry Stevens, Joey T., Zachery Walters, Brent Warner

COMING NEXT:

THE BOOKS OF SORCERY, VOL. III — OADENOL'S CODEX

$24.99   160 PAGES

Oadenol's Codex is the guide to the practical application of sorcerous knowledge in the Second Age. From the creation of artifacts to the raising of manses, and from the subtle workings of thaumaturgy to the various naturally occurring miracles of Creation, this third of **Exalted's** Books of Sorcery offer's aspiring geomancers, sorcerer-engineers, thaumaturges and preternaturalists the tools they need to ply their arcane trades. In addition, the book contains a plethora of artifacts, hearthstones, prodigies and manses for players' characters to own or covet and Storytellers to weave into their series.

COMING NEXT IN THIS SERIES:
THE MANUAL OF EXALTED POWER — THE SIDEREALS

$31.99   224 PAGES

Gifted with power by the Five Maidens, the Sidereal Exalted were once the trusted advisors to the Old Realm's Solar masters. Believing the Curse-maddened Lawgivers' irredeemable and unshakably convinced in their moral duty, the Maidens' Chosen persuaded the Dragon-Blooded to rise up and slaughter their masters in order to end the Solars' depredations. Since then, the Sidereals have influenced events behind the scenes in order to safeguard Creation from its myriad of enemies. But with the return of the Solars, the advent of the deathknights, the Dragon-Blooded Realm nearing civil war, the tribes of the Lunars threatening war and the raksha massing for another assault on the shaped world, will the Fivefold Fellowship win the day or will its many sacrifices have been for naught?

WHITE WOLF PUBLISHING

1554 LITTON DR
STONE MOUNTAIN, GA
30083
USA

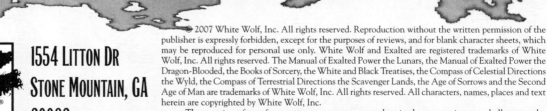

THE MANUAL OF EXALTED POWER
LUNARS™

TABLE OF CONTENTS

INTRODUCTION	12
CHAPTER ONE: THE SILVER PACT	17
CHAPTER TWO: A BETTER WORLD	57
CHAPTER THREE: CHARACTER CREATION	93
CHAPTER FOUR: TRAITS	104
CHAPTER FIVE: CHARMS AND SHAPESHIFTING	124
CHAPTER SIX: THE CASTELESS AND THE CHIMERA	197
CHAPTER SEVEN: STORYTELLING	214

INTRODUCTION

For centuries, they have prowled at the edge of the world. Civilized folk fear them: shapeshifters, war-beasts, the Anathema of the Moon. Sometimes, they walk in human or animal shape and mortals know them not, until they erupt in bestial, murderous rage. Sometimes, they invade the Threshold at the head of rampaging barbarian armies, until Dragon-Blooded heroes drive them back into the Wyld. Warlords, tricksters and destroyers—the enemies of civilization!

That's the story most people in Creation tell if you ask them about Luna's Chosen. Fifteen centuries of propaganda have worked pretty well. The Lunar Exalted themselves, however, tell a very different story.

For centuries, they have prowled at the edge of the world. The creatures of darkness fear them: the border-guards of Creation. Sometimes, they walk among mortals, hidden by animal shapes or illusions, to pursue their foes—then strike, with all the righteous fury at their command. The people beyond the Threshold know them as heroes, honor their leadership—and when their friends make war on civilized folk, why, the Lunar Exalted side with their own. The Realm and its lickspittle vassals are sick: the Lunars take their land to build healthy, new cultures as bulwarks against the Wyld. They are the Stewards, charged by Luna to care for Creation, its people and all life upon it—whether they know it or not. Sometimes, whether they want it or not.

The Dragon-Blooded and their Wyld Hunt have kept the Moonchildren in exile since the great betrayal of the Solar Exalted. The Lunar Exalted, partners and consorts of the Solars, escaped the massacre. First, the Lunar Exalted sought merely to survive. Then, they hoped for revenge. Rage against the usurping Terrestrial Exalted and their Sidereal puppet-masters still burns strong in many Lunar hearts; after all, the Usurpation happened just half a Lunar lifetime ago.

Over the centuries, however, Luna's Chosen have gained other interests, too. They continue to fight horrors out of Chaos, in battles the pampered folk of Creation's heartland never imagine. The Lunar Exalted have built a complex society of their own, spread around Creation's rim. They have even fostered a ring of new cultures outside the Realm's control, from isolated tribes to nascent empires. For every Lunar who yearns for revenge against the Dragon-Blooded, another views the Realm with contempt, as a decaying relic, propped up by the Empress and overdue to fall—and a third Lunar fears that fall. What shall the Outer Horrors do when they realize the Empress no longer can throw them back to the Chaos that spawned them? The Lunar Exalted have prepared for centuries to fight the next great war to save Creation.

As the Deathlords emerge from the Underworld and the Fair Folk muster in the Wyld, the Chosen of Luna know the hour of testing has come. Their former mates, the Solar lords of Creation, live again—but the heroes of the Moon will not depend on them to save the world. In the Time of Tumult, the Lunar Exalted trust only their own strength and cunning, magic and skill to win the future of Creation.

THIS IS NOT A COMPLETE GAME!

Despite its size, **The Manual of Exalted Power—The Lunars** is not a complete game. It is a supplement for White Wolf's **Exalted**, a game about near-divine heroes in a world of high fantasy. The core book describes the Solar Exalted, the Sun-blessed rightful rulers of Creation, reborn into a world that for centuries has hated them as the Solar Anathema, the demonic despots of the First Age. This supplement does not describe the game's various core traits, rules for combat or a complete setting. This supplement just gives in-depth information about the Lunar Exalted, their society, their activities and the rules necessary to create and play Lunar characters. You'll need to consult the **Exalted** core book in order to play.

How To Use This Book

The **Manual of Exalted Power—The Lunars** tells all about the Lunar Exalted, the heroes given power by Luna, second of the great Celestial gods. You can use this book to create an entire series about Luna's Chosen, or create complete, detailed Lunar characters to use in other games as allies or antagonists.

Chapter One: The Silver Pact

This chapter tells the history of the Lunar Exalted from the war against the Primordials to the present. The chapter also describes the factions and customs of the Lunars' chief alliance, the Silver Pact.

Chapter Two: A Better World

This chapter reveals the greatest secret of the Lunar Exalted: the Thousand Streams River, a massive plan to create civilizations that can challenge and replace the Realm. The chapter begins with a discussion of methods for creating and controlling new cultures, then describes four of the Lunars' social experiments.

Chapter Three: Character Creation

This chapter details the rules you need when you create a Lunar Exalted character.

Chapter Four: Traits

This chapter describes the traits unique to Lunar Exalted characters, as well as how existing traits may be applied to Lunar characters.

Chapter Five: Charms and Shapeshifting

This chapter details the protean Charms wielded by the Lunar Exalted, as well as the Knacks that enable them to take the forms of animals, other people and stranger things.

Chapter Six: Casteless and Chimera

This chapter discusses the Casteless, or Lunar Exalted who lack the magical tattoos that stabilize their magical gifts and physical forms. Casteless Lunars run the risk of becoming maddened, ever-changing monsters called chimerae—the most frightening enemies of the Lunar Exalted because they command the same powers.

Chapter Seven: Storytelling

The book's final chapter covers the special needs of storytelling a game about Lunar Exalted characters.

LEXICON

Most of the terms introduced in the **Exalted** core book still apply to the Lunar Exalted. The following terms, however, apply specifically to the Lunar Exalted.

barbarian: A person, usually from a tribal culture, who lives without the customs and appurtenances of city folk and large nations—or at least the customs of the people who use the term.

beastman: The half-human, half-animal progeny of Lunar Exalted unions with humans—or, less often, animals—within the Wyld. Beastmen often serve their progenitor or some other Lunar.

caste: Similar to the other Exalted, Lunars possess different aptitudes and abilities. The three Lunar castes are the following:

Full Moon: The warriors of Luna, masters of physical force, agility, toughness and endurance.

Changing Moon: The tricksters of Luna, masters of social influence, force of personality, persuasion and deceit.

No Moon: The savants of Luna, masters of knowledge, thought, inquiry and the arcane.

Casteless: A Lunar Exalt who has not been fixed into a single set of supernatural aptitudes by magical tattoos.

chimera: A *Casteless* Lunar who loses control of his shapeshifting power and becomes a cunningly crazed, ever-changing monster.

Crossroads Society: A Lunar faction devoted to sorcery, the creation of magical artifacts and other sources of arcane power.

heart's blood: The means by which a Lunar acquires new shapes. The Lunar must kill an animal (or person, or other creature) in a sacred hunt and consume its blood.

Knack: A refinement of the Lunar Exalted's basic power to take the shapes of other creatures.

mate: The one Solar Exalt to whom a Lunar Exalt bears a special, spiritual bond. In the Old Realm, Solar and Lunar mates often did marry, but at least as many were merely friends or partners who found it easy and natural to work together.

Seneschals of the Sun Kings: A Lunar faction that reveres the memory of the Solar Exalted and seeks revenge for their overthrow. The Seneschals are in transition, now that the Solars are no longer dead icons from the distant past.

Silver Pact, the: The collective body of Lunar Exalted who possess a *caste* thanks to their magical moonsilver tattoos, and follow *the Silver Way*. It is not a government, but it does have informal leaders.

Silver Way, the: A somewhat loose code of conduct endorsed by *the Silver Pact*, which details how Lunar

Exalted should treat each other and pursue various long-term goals.

Steward: The ancient epithet of the Lunar Exalted, similar to the Solars' epithet of Lawgivers; now remembered only by the Lunars themselves and their close mortal allies.

Swords of Luna: A Lunar faction devoted to fighting invaders from beyond Creation, especially but not exclusively the Fair Folk.

spirit shape: The first alternate form a Lunar Exalt gains after his Exaltation, an animal that metaphorically expresses some aspect of the Lunar Exalt's personality.

Tell: A physical aspect of a Lunar Exalt's *spirit shape* that manifests in his human form and, to a far more subtle and hard-to-notice degree, in other forms.

Thousand Streams River, the: The Lunars' grand plan to foster new cultures as alternatives to the Realm and its vassals.

true form: A Lunar Exalt has at most three true forms: the human form she was born with, the *spirit shape* she gained at Exaltation and an optional war form that combines aspects of the two. True forms determine the degree to which a Lunar can augment her Physical Attributes, and the Lunar must stay in her true forms once her anima achieves a certain degree of manifestation.

Unblooded: A Lunar Exalt who has not yet learned to take other animal shapes by consuming their *heart's blood*; hence, a novice Lunar, especially one who has not yet been fixed in a *caste*.

war form: A massive and powerful fusion of a Lunar Exalt's human form and *spirit shape*, achieved through the Knack called Deadly Beastman Transformation.

Wardens of Gaia: A Lunar faction that sees its duty as protecting the natural world from humanity, or at least working out mutually beneficial modes of coexistence.

Winding Path, the: A Lunar faction devoted to social manipulation; principal architects of *the Thousand Streams River*.

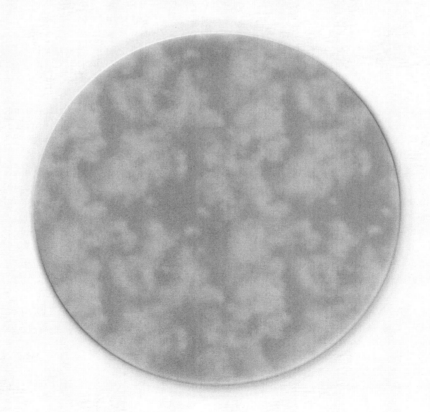

CHAPTER ONE
THE SILVER PACT

To much of Creation, and especially to the Dragon-Blooded, the Lunar Exalted are creatures of nightmare. While humanity has, until recently, enjoyed a long respite from the depredations of the Solar Anathema, the Lunars continued to reincarnate from the Usurpation to the present day. To many Dragon-Blooded, the Lunars *are* the Anathema—twisted, Wyld-tainted monsters that hurl themselves against civilization in barbarous rage.

In truth, the Dragon-Blooded know little about the Lunar Exalted except that they are dangerous. The Dragon-Blooded do not know of the proud pedigree and history of Luna's Chosen. The Dragon-Blooded do not know how many centuries the Lunars held back the denizens of the Wyld before the Dragon-Blooded's precious Empress finally, with stolen weapons, drove Luna's Chosen off. The Dragon-Blooded do not know that for every twisted aberration the Wyld Hunt puts down, a dozen cunning and sophisticated predators walk among the Dragon-Blooded unnoticed. They do not know that many cultures the Realm derides as "barbarian"

belong to an elaborate and systematic attempt to reshape the human race itself. In short, the Dragon-Blooded do not know about the Silver Pact.

In the First Age, the term "Silver Pact" was simply a collective term for all Lunars, in much the same way that "Solar Deliberative" described the collective body of Solars. The Silver Pact never had political power in the same way as the Deliberative; to the extent that any Lunars desired temporal power, they could pursue their agendas in the Lower House of the Deliberative. Rather, First Age Lunars referred to themselves as the Silver Pact when they met together to discuss the wishes of their patron goddess and to trade tales of personal glory.

In the modern era, people outside the Silver Pact—the few who even know it exists—often think of it as some sort of ruling body over Lunar society. Such individuals are misinformed. The Silver Pact consists of all Lunars who have received moonsilver tattoos and been affixed into a single caste. Even if a tattooed Lunar goes years without seeing

another of her kind, any other tattooed Lunar who meets her knows she belongs to the Pact and treats her with the respect her Exaltation deserves. Only the untattooed Casteless and the Wyld-twisted chimerae are denied the protections and considerations of membership in the Silver Pact.

HISTORY

An ancient proverb says, "History is written by the victors." For the Children of Luna, history is written by the survivors. The Lunar Exalted lost much of their ancient lore in their centuries-long exile to the Deep Wyld. Even the Exalted are hard-pressed to endure in that mad realm, let alone fragile diaries and history books. Thus, Lunar history from the Usurpation to the rise of the Scarlet Empire consists mainly of oral traditions that undoubtedly changed over centuries of repetition, to say nothing of the potential for deliberate lies and propaganda having been inserted. Let the listener judge how much of the tale is true. What follows is the history of the Lunar Exalted… as best anyone can recall.

THE CHOSEN OF LUNA

The Incarnae designed their own form of Exaltation according to their needs. To the Solar Exalted, the Unconquered Sun gave the gift of perfection: the capacity to do almost anything as well as it could possibly be done. To the Sidereal Exalted, the Five Maidens gave the gift of destiny, the capacity to make their intentions a part of Fate itself. To the Lunar Exalted, the Fickle Lady gave the gift of change: not just the ability to change their forms according to their desires, but the capacity to change *who* and *what* they were, to adapt to new situations and to evolve to meet any changes in Creation.

Lunar tradition says the Unconquered Sun, as leader of the coup, demanded that his Exalted similarly lead the other Chosen. In response, Luna proposed that each Lunar Exaltation would be emotionally linked to a specific Solar Exaltation, mated to it in fact. The possessors of each would inevitably be drawn to one another; the Lunars would serve the Solars as shieldmates, seconds, bodyguards and even lovers as the case might be. The Unconquered Sun approved of this relationship, since he saw it as a guarantee of loyalty to his own Chosen. Luna smiled secretly at the knowledge that each of her Chosen would be vulnerable to only one Solar… suffering no inherent weakness at all against the other 299.

THE MANY-FACED GODDESS

As with the other Exalted, the Lunars were fashioned to enact the will of their patron deity without actually being slaves to that deity (or else the Primordials could have simply commanded the gods to order their Exalted to surrender). The Fickle Lady, however, is a complicated being—more so than the other Incarnae or most other gods. Both her form and her nature can change with her varied whims; even her gender is not fixed. While she deigns to hold the moon's face

to a constant cycle for the benefit of mortals who depend upon such astrological regularity, no two who encounter Luna describe exactly the same visage or even personality. Indeed, only two features occur among all descriptions of the Silver Goddess: a passionate love for Gaia and, by extension, Creation, and a strong preference for individuals, iconoclasts and outsiders over people who seek always to "fit in." These two characteristics of Luna, above all others, guided her in fashioning her Exalted.

Some people (and gods) think Luna's ever-changing appearance, personality and interests prove she must be crazy. Nevertheless, Luna may have a method to this apparent madness. By diversifying her portfolio of responsibilities across multiple identities, Luna is now worshiped under many different names, often by the same worshipers. In fact, Luna may actually have more mortal worshipers than the Unconquered Sun (though the Celestial Bureaucracy, for obvious reasons, does not tabulate the Essence offerings received by the Incarnae). While Luna receives worship under dozens of names, her most common personae are as follows:

The Bloody Huntress represents Luna in her role as a war Goddess and is usually depicted as the Champion of Gaia. The Bloody Huntress often appears as a stunningly beautiful female in moonsilver armor and carrying a moonsilver long powerbow. Hunter-gatherer tribes chiefly venerate her, and Full Moon Lunars often receive visitations from her at their Exaltations.

The Silver-Horned Watcher is the most frightening aspect of Luna, whom mortals rarely venerate in the modern era. The Watcher represents Luna in her crescent moon aspect, when she provides little light but still looks down from the sky, seeing all that happens in the dark. This aspect is considered a patron of criminals, especially murderers, and of the mad. As the Silver-Horned Watcher, Luna also serves as the god of the Wyld, to the extent that the Celestial Bureaucracy acknowledges anyone as holding that role. In the First Age, the Watcher was the patron of the Waning Moons, although Lunars of all castes prayed for her blessings whenever they entered the Wyld. She is often depicted as either an insane, blood-drenched woman with silver horns and armed with a sickle or simply as a swirling mass of Wyld energy.

The Two-Faced Bride is the form used by Luna in her capacity as a fertility deity. Although called a goddess, the Two-Faced Bride is a hermaphrodite and can assume either male or female appearance. She is also often depicted as in the later stages of pregnancy, regardless of her adopted gender. In the First Age, Waxing Moons often received visitations from the Two-Faced Bride in the shape of an androgynous, pregnant boy.

The Walker at the Crossroads is the most mysterious of Luna's common aspects. She serves as a patron of sorcerers in general and No Moons in particular. The Walker most commonly appears as either an ancient crone or a figure of indeterminate gender completely concealed behind flowing, black veils. No matter how the Walker appears, this aspect of Luna is most commonly encountered at the intersection of roads or paths and always at night.

The White Navigator is a patron of a number of nomadic tribes in the South who depend upon the moon for guidance across the trackless wastes. This aspect of Luna usually appears as a handsome man in silver and white robes. The Navigator is also considered a god of divinely inspired wisdom and is the patron god of hermits and the elderly. During the First Age, the Waxing Moons preferred to worship Luna in her White Navigator aspect.

THE FIRST LUNARS

At the dawn of the Primordial War, Luna Exalted the same kind of people she chooses in the Age of Sorrows. Each Lunar Exaltation seeks out a mortal who rejects attempts

to control her and who pushes herself to excellence, physically, socially or intellectually. Instead of selecting a person to perform some appointed task, the Exaltation simply joins to someone of whom Luna would approve.

Unlike the Exaltations of other Exalted, Lunar Exaltations do not carry an intrinsic caste. Originally, the Exaltation adapted to its host, assuming the properties of the caste most in keeping with the Lunar's nature and interests. Lunars who thrived on using their physical prowess became Full Moons, the mighty warriors whose battle rage made them incredible martial combatants. Mortals who relied chiefly on their intellect became No Moons, wise savants and sorcerers who, together with the Twilight Caste Solars, plumbed the mysteries of Essence for weapons against the Primordials.

In ancient times, the Lunars had three other castes that were lost during the Lunar exile. Lunars who excelled as public speakers and diplomats or who were reverent toward nature became Waxing Moons, the priests and courtiers of Luna, and masters of emotion and connection. Cunning, pragmatic and ruthless Lunars became Half Moons, the military leaders and tacticians who advised the Dawn Caste Solars on strategy. Finally, Lunars who were mischievous, if not outright larcenous, became Waning Moons, Lunar spies and assassins who slipped effortlessly into those places where even a Night Caste Solar could not easily penetrate.

Or at least, that's the story as the No Moon loremasters tell it. Other tales say how the castes were fixed—subversive, almost heretical tales that sprout up every now and then among young Casteless and some of the more lucid chimerae. According to these tales, Luna intended all along for her Chosen to remain Casteless. As a being of constant change herself, she wanted her Exalted to change just as freely. The Lunars of the Old Realm, however, found it frustrating to change castes, which prevented them from growing as powerful in certain areas as their more specialized counterparts among the Solars and Sidereals. And so, filled with hubris, ancient Lunars during their No Moon phase worked great magic upon themselves and gained the power to fix their castes according to their own desires. In doing so, say the stories, the Lunars lost the favor of the Fickle Lady just as the Solars lost the favor of the Unconquered Sun, and both were soon swept from power. In the modern era, virtually no Lunar who has received moonsilver tattoos believes such tales. Or admits it, anyway.

The Principle of Stewardship

Regardless of an individual Lunar's personality or eventual caste, all of Luna's Chosen come from people who possess a strong personal desire to shepherd some aspect of Creation. According to the lorekeepers, Luna's love for Gaia was so great that she would only grant Exaltation to mortals who had already proven their protective instincts. Luna did not wish to create future rulers as the Unconquered Sun did. Rather, she wanted to create champions who could

On the Nature of Stewardship

Conceptually, "stewardship" simply means that a Lunar's Motivation should involve protecting, building and/or improving some specific facet of Creation. The fact that Lunar Exaltations seek out individuals with such Motivations partially explains why the Lunars have not been more active in opposing the Realm these many centuries—Luna simply didn't Exalt people whose Motivations might include "avenge my lover" or "kill all the Dragon-Blooded." She Exalted people whose Motivations might be "protect Creation from the Fair Folk" or "build the Haltan nation into a viable empire" or "guard *The Book of Three Circles* from all who would misuse it."

protect the rulers… if necessary, even from themselves. The Lunars would remind the Solar overlords that the natural world had its own needs and that individual lives and feeling still mattered. In this, Luna sought to balance what she perceived as the cold-blooded and overly analytical advice of the Sidereals. At the same time, Luna wanted to ensure that the Lunars could pursue her agendas (and their own) while still working alongside the Sun's Children. Among the Lunars, this universal protective instinct became known as "the principle of stewardship," and in the First Age, many referred to the Lunar Exalted as "the Stewards."

Most people who used this term undoubtedly thought it referred to the Lunar Exalted in their capacity as seconds to the Solar Exalted. For some Lunars, this became the case. Most Lunars, however, felt a lifelong sense of duty toward something greater than a single Solar or even the Solar Exalted as a whole. To the extent that the Stewards gave their loyalty to the Solar Deliberative, it was because Lunars saw that body as the best means to protect and expand Creation.

The Primordial War

Luna, when designing her proxies for the Primordial War, looked for several characteristics, most notably adaptability, survival instinct and unpredictable cunning. True, the Lunars lacked the Solar capacity for perfection, but the Lunars' Exaltations made them supreme generalists and improvisers.

While the Solars deserved much of the credit for defeating the Primordials, many Lunars served with such distinction that their names became legend throughout the First Age. One-Eyed Therusa became the first to master the shapeshifting Knack called Heart-Theft of the Behemoth, which he used to steal the shapes of Primordials' titanic war-beasts. Ogri Sky-Traveler gave his life to assassinate the White Ram, the guardian of Yu-Shan's gates and the Defining Soul of the Lidless Eyes That Sees, before it could alert the Primordials to the Solars' first surprise attack. Owl-Feathered Princess revealed her invincible White Reaper Form to an army of 10,000 First Circle demons, slaying them all before finally succumbing to her wounds. In the bloody storm of the Primordial War, the Lunars proved their worth again and again, sowing discord and confusion among the enemy through constructive chaos and adapting to changing situations in ways that the methodical Sidereals or the "perfect" Solars never could.

The Dawn of the First Age

After the War ended, the Solars set themselves to governing Creation, while the Incarnae turned to the Games of Divinity. The Solar Deliberative ruled with the support of lower houses manned by the Lunars and Sidereals. If they objected to being denied equal power with their Solar mates, the Lunars never showed it. In fact, the Lunars as a whole seldom took a strong interest in Solar politics. Many Lunars would regret their lack of attention when Solar governance descended into tyranny. At the time, though, the Lunars had different priorities.

The Lunars felt genuinely conflicted over their patron god's withdrawal from Creation's affairs. They were not sure what role they should play. The Lunars began meeting in large groups to debate their collective purpose. They never did agree, but they continued to meet openly throughout the Old Realm, developing philosophies about their place in the world and what stewardship really meant. To signify their intent to remain unified in spite of sincere differences of opinion, Lunar thinkers referred to themselves as the Silver Pact. In time, this name became synonymous with the entire Lunar host. Some of the more paranoid Solars distrusted the very idea of the Silver Pact, but the organization made it plain that it had no political aspirations. Thus, the Deliberative as a whole ignored the Silver Pact.

Officially, Lunars had only two duties during the High First Age: acting as agents of their Solar mates and acting as the agents of Luna. These two duties sometimes conflicted, but never enough to drive a wedge between the Solars and Lunars. Over time, however, this dichotomy caused the Silver Pact to develop five informal factions. These factions never resulted in overt, sectarian strife. They were philosophical outlooks, although some became closer to secret societies. If any other Exalted ever worked with these factions and accepted their philosophies, modern tales do not say.

• **The Crossroads Society** was the smallest faction within the Silver Pact. The faction's membership chiefly consisted of No Moons. According to the Society's lore, the First Age Twilights took it upon themselves to regulate the practice of sorcery among non-Solars, even though the Lunar Bar-Izahd invented the art (see **The White and Black Treatises**, pp. 30-31, for the tale of Bar-Izahd and the Lunar perspective on sorcery's origin). Many Lunar sorcerers chafed under these restrictions, and some even suspected that Adamant Circle Sorcery was not the exclusive birthright of the Solar Exalted but was simply the product of techniques the Solar sorcerers hid from other Exalted.

These Lunar sorcerers founded the Crossroads Society to promote Lunar achievements in sorcery, craftsmanship, medicine and other forms of learning. If they could not precisely equal the Twilights' raw power, the Lunars could excel in other ways. The Crossroads Society was the most secretive Lunar group in the Old Realm, mainly because the most brilliant Lunars were also the first to notice the emerging insanity among the Solar Exalted. The Crossroads Society members recognized that any group of Lunars that challenged Solar dominance might be viewed as a threat. Several Crossroads scholars claim that their forebears made the legendary artifact called the Mantle of Brigid, which allows its wearer to use sorcery spells of a higher level than is normally possible. While most occult historians dismiss such tales, legends associated with the Crossroads Society suggest that some of their number could use Adamant Circle Sorcery through powerful artifacts or other means.

• **The Seneschals of the Sun Kings** consisted of those Lunars who fully accepted the divine right of the Solar Exalted to rule Creation. These Lunars saw themselves as the loyal lieutenants to the Solar rulers (and occasionally, as the power behind the throne). The Seneschals remained loyal both to their individual Solar mates and to the divine mandate of the Solar Deliberative, supporting the Children of the Unconquered Sun as bodyguards, envoys, diplomats and even assassins. Politically, this faction opposed the Winding Path, a rival Lunar faction that did not believe the Solars' divine mandate had no limits. While this opposition usually stayed genial, impetuous Full Moon Seneschals did sometimes assault fellow Lunars who challenged a Solar's wisdom or intentions.

Not all Seneschals were entirely loyal to their mates, though. Many Lunars of this faction became skilled at manipulating their mates into actions of the Lunars' choosing, especially in the waning of the Old Realm when those Solar mates became addled. On the other hand, other Lunars found themselves virtually enslaved to their mates due to the cruelly invasive mind-controlling Charms at the Solars' disposal.

• **The Swords of Luna** accepted stewardship of reality itself and took their place on the front lines of the second great war, the war to expand Creation and defend its frontiers against the Wyld and the Fair Folk. These guardians of the new frontier were often the hardiest Lunars. Most of them came from the Full Moon Caste, warriors eager to pit their strength against that of the howling Wyld. The Swords of Luna welcomed members of all castes, however, so long as they were prepared to walk the razor's edge between reality and madness.

These Lunars developed an extremely martial subculture that valued personal prowess and courage above all other virtues. Many Swords adopted a practice of assigning status and regard based on each Lunar's battle scars. Luna's warriors were not reckless with each other, however. At the fringes of Creation, each Lunar warrior was too valuable to waste on internecine conflict, and so, the Swords developed a system of counting coup as a way to settle their conflicts through ritual, non-lethal combat.

• **The Wardens of Gaia** saw their chief duty as preserving as much of the natural state of Creation as possible, in reverence to Luna's beloved Gaia. The Wardens chiefly appealed to Waxing Moon priests, who brought a strong religious sensibility to their duties. All castes were necessary to preserve Gaia's bounty for the future, however. The Wardens recruited Half Moons to talk the Solars out of chopping down a centuries-old forest to build a new trade road and No Moons to provide cures for diseases that threatened entire species with extinction.

The Wardens also forged close bonds with the little gods of Creation, often speaking for elemental spirit courts that received little respect from the Solars or the Celestial Bureaucracy. As the Old Realm wound down to its bitter conclusion, the Wardens often had to cope with Solar corruption. If a deranged Solar had little concern for the well-being of mortals, he generally cared even less for the plants and animals around him.

• **The Winding Path** was the most politically active faction of Lunars. Dominated by Waning Moons, the Winding Path reasoned that, while the Solars were built for direct action, the Lunars were designed for deception, intrigue and indirect solutions to problems. The Winding Path Lunars worked with the Solar Exalted just as readily as the Seneschals of the Sun King—but in a more circuitous manner, acting as devil's advocates and analyzing a Solar's proposals for all possible outcomes before agreeing with his plan of action. Winding Path Stewards developed reputations as gadflies, agitators and even anarchists as they challenged the Solar way of doing things. The Sun Children found these Lunars thought-provoking or maddening, depending on the individual Solar's temperament.

The greatest philosophical conflicts between the Winding Path Lunars and the other Exalted were about the nature of mortal society. Solars and Sidereals generally believed in a planned, hierarchical society that, in theory, guaranteed everyone a life of ease and safety, but offered mortals little room for advancement. Winding Path Lunars argued that individual mortals should have greater chances to succeed—or fail—on their own merits, following their own interests.

LUNAR VIEWS ON THE FIRST AGE

Modern Lunar Exalted seldom view the Old Realm as a lost paradise. Only a few elders actually date from the High First Age—and all of those from its final centuries when Solar decadence had reached its height. None remember that era fondly. Other elders Exalted between the Usurpation and the Great Contagion, and their views are likewise tainted by the perceived failures of the Shogunate during the Low First Age. While some modern Lunars, mainly Sun King Seneschals,

THE GREAT CURSE

The Silver Pact was and is just as ignorant of the role the Great Curse played in the fall of the Solar Exalted as anyone else in Creation. Some might find this peculiar. Surely, if anyone would notice the onset of madness throughout all Solar society, it would be the Lunars. In fact, many Old Realm Lunars did notice the spreading sickness among their mates, particularly those Lunars who became its victims. They simply drew the wrong conclusion. No one imagined the Primordials could affect Exaltation itself; many Lunars attributed the madness to the Unconquered Sun's decision to grant his Chosen the gift of perfection. The Lunars came to believe that no mortal mind could bear the burden of being a perfect being in an imperfect world, hence the Solars' obsession with removing the perceived flaws in Creation. When confronted by the central paradox of their existence, is it any wonder that so many Solars went mad?

In the modern era, the Silver Pact as a whole has not decided what to do about the returning Solars. A few believe the Solars must inevitably go mad again, but hope the Lunars have a few centuries before then to put contingency plans in motion… for example, establishing a secret body of Lunar assassins to eliminate any Solar who displays overt insanity. As for the Dragon-Bloods and Sidereals, the Lunars simply think their venality and overweening arrogance are widespread character flaws or signs of a sick culture, not signs of any systematic weakness of the breed.

With regard to the Lunars' own Great Curse, Lunars are perfectly aware of their tendency to become bestial in response to certain stimuli, but they simply attribute it to the vagaries of being a Child of Luna. She is a god of madness and change, after all, and if Lunars tend to have moments of apparent madness when exposed to the light of the full moon, then obviously the Fickle Lady wishes it so.

Experienced Lunars often avoid exposure to full moonlight. Some, however, actively seek out exposure to the full moon's rays, and view the cathartic experience of Limit Break as a way to commune with the Goddess despite any negative consequences that ensue. Lunars born of barbarian warrior cultures may even deliberately hold Gatherings on Full Moon nights, referring to the occasional bouts of temporary madness that infect attendees as "Luna's Kiss." No social stigma attaches to Lunars who experience Limit Break during such revelries. In fact, most forms of Limit Break can be seen as a sign of Luna's favor.

Other Lunars may regard colleagues who suffer frequent Limit Break as unreliable or even dangerous, resulting in some degree of social censure. Ironically, though, Compassion-related Limit Flaws inflict the greatest stigma on Lunars. Such Flaws often look like simple cowardice, which is rarely acceptable among the warriors of Luna. See "The Great Curse" on page 121 for more details on Limit Flaws.

hold idealized views of the Old Realm similar to those of modern Solars, most Lunars think the First Age was a time of utter decadence. Lunar social philosophy emphasizes the virtues of personal excellence, independence, veneration of the natural order and rewarding people for what they give to their society. As the elders tell it, the Old Realm's Solars did not hold these ideals.

Rather, the Silver Pact's lore describes an Old Realm where most of humanity lived in indolence. The Solars oversaw every aspect of human life. They regulated the weather to maximize growing seasons, automated factory-cathedrals to reduce the need for laborers and eliminated diseases and other threats to human existence. As the Solars grew in power, if not wisdom, the "Solar utopia" became clear: a world in which no one had to work because the wondrous magic of the Solar Exalted provided for everything mortals needed… everything except a purpose. Of course, the Solar utopia was still a work in progress at the time of the Usurpation. Vast numbers of mortals lived in the muck as peasants while their Exalted lords flew overhead in skyships. Still, the Solar Deliberative promised that, in the fullness of time, everyone in Creation would share in the bounty of Solar rule.

Despite the Lunars' misgivings about Solar hegemony, few Lunars could articulate why the Solar utopia would be a bad thing for anyone. Why wouldn't mortals want peace, health, happiness and freedom from want? What could possibly be bad about paradise? Only in the aftermath of the Usurpation would Lunars realize the flaw in the Solar utopia: It needed the Solar Exalted to maintain it. Remove the Solars, and utopia becomes hell.

THE USURPATION

The Usurpation caught most Lunars unprepared. The Seneschals of the Sun Kings usually found out about it at the exact same time as their doomed mates. After the Usurpation, paranoid, grieving and suspicious Seneschal survivors challenged the loyalty of every other Lunar faction. While no Lunars are known to have actively participated in the Usurpation, rumors spread among the Silver Pact that some Stewards refused to defend their mates. Certainly, some of them didn't seem terribly disappointed by the Solars' fall.

According to some such tales, Sidereals actively, if secretly, courted the Crossroads Society. When this courtship did not bring immediate results, the Sidereals turned to

blackmail, threatening to expose the hidden society of Lunar sorcerers to the wrath of the arrogant and insanely powerful Twilights, or bribery, by promises of occult lore from the libraries of Yu-Shan. Society members who survived the initial purge angrily denied any collaboration with the Usurpation. Privately, though, some Lunar sorcerers seemed rather glad to see the end of Solar hegemony over the mystic arts.

The Swords of Luna were too isolated to assist either side of the Usurpation. The Solars' reckless advance on Creation's rim had spread the group so thinly that the Swords had to devote themselves completely to repelling Wyld incursions. Rather than retreating to the Wyld, the Swords watched as the rest of the Silver Pact came to them. The exhausted warriors could only view the Silver Pact factions as desperately needed reinforcements.

Neither the Winding Path nor the Wardens of Gaia ever joined in the Usurpation. In their hearts, however, many members agreed that Creation could not endure the continued rule of Solars gone mad. By the onset of the Usurpation, most members of the Winding Path were utterly disgusted by the malfeasance and effortless cruelty of the self-styled "Lawgivers." The Wardens of Gaia, for their part, were sickened by Twilight experiments in the unnatural creation of new life, an abomination before Gaia often performed solely for the amusement of jaded Solars.

If any Lunars actively joined in the Usurpation, that secret died with them. Once the Solars were eliminated (along with the most loyal Seneschal mates), the Lunars quickly realized that they were next on the list, regardless of any aid to or assurances from the Sidereals. Dragon-Blooded armies slew any Lunars who did not quickly flee to the edges of Creation.

DIASPORA AND EXILE

Despite the element of surprise, the first wave of the Usurpation killed few Lunar Exalted. Most Lunars had the

THE JADE PRISON

The Sidereals may have hoped to lock Lunar Exaltations in their Jade Prison; if so, the Maidens' Chosen were disappointed. Perhaps the mutable, Wyld-touched Lunar Exaltation defies such confinement; perhaps the Sidereals just couldn't build two prisons, or a prison that held two divine forces at once.

The Lunars themselves never learned about the Jade Prison. They knew only that the Sidereals possessed some unholy means to prevent Solar reincarnation. Lunar Exaltations, however, continued to seek mortal hosts. The Sidereals were forced to rely on brute force instead, creating the first Wyld Hunt to pursue the fleeing Lunars. Indeed, the Wyld Hunt was so named because the Dragon-Blooded had to hunt their Anathema quarry in the Wyld zones where they hid.

good fortune of being far away from Meru, the great capitol city where so many Lawgivers fell to treachery. The great feast that served as a cover for the initial sneak attack was not open to Lunars; perhaps the plotters thought killing the assembled Solars would be hard enough without fighting an equal number of Lunars at the same time. The only Lunars in attendance were the most devoted of Sun King Seneschals. That Lunar faction, once the largest and most prominent, was crippled in one stroke.

One of the few Seneschals to survive that first sneak attack was Perfect Feather, a Waning Moon assassin and sorceress. Neither she nor her beloved spouse, a Dawn Caste general whose name is lost to history, attended the feast. A Sidereal and a phalanx of Dragon-Blooded tried to ambush them; Perfect Feather's mate gave his life to help her escape the deadly trap. Feather avenged her mate by eviscerating the cowardly Sidereal. She could have escaped Meru herself, but she realized that most of her kind did not know what was happening. And so Perfect Feather stayed behind on Mount Meru, hiding from the Dragon-Blooded hordes while she used communication spells to send warnings to as many Lunars as possible. By the time the traitors found and dispatched her, she had warned most of the Silver Pact. While many Lunars wished to stay and fight for their mates, the eldest of the Silver Pact realized the painful truth—that the Solar rule was over. And so, the order was given: flee, to anyplace where the Dragon-Blooded could not follow.

The Lunars planned only to retreat and regroup at the edges of Creation. Their places of power on Creation's rim unquestionably belonged to the Swords of Luna; the survivors hoped they would be safe in those inhospitable regions. Once the slain Solars reincarnated, the Stewards expected to surge back into Creation, rescue their reborn mates and begin the world's re-conquest. Those hopes were soon dashed. The Lawgivers didn't reincarnate, while the Sidereals and Dragon-Blooded soon organized the first Wyld Hunts to hunt the Lunars and the few surviving Solars.

At first, the Wyld Hunt was brutally effective. In those days, the Dragon-Blooded numbered in the hundreds of thousands, and the Sidereals seemed to predict the survivors' every movement, as well as when and where new Lunars would Exalt. For the first time in their collective existence, the peerless hunters of the Lunar Exalted became prey. Within a generation, all of the surviving Solars were laid low, their Essences trapped or destroyed by the Sidereals. Or so the Lunars believed, though rumors of continued Solar Exaltations continued throughout the long exile.

The Lunars, while still free to reincarnate, instead faced death by attrition followed by an eternity of rebirth as ignorant pups, helpless before the Wyld Hunt. They avoided this fate only thanks to the priests of the Waxing Moon Caste who kept their heavenly connections. Initially, all of the Waxing Moons' entreaties to Yu-Shan were ignored. Eventually, a god in the Bureau of Nature, distraught over the Sidereals' perfidy, answered the prayers of a Waxing Moon priest and

The Loom of Fate

The Old Realm Lunars, just as the Solars, knew about the existence of the Loom of Fate. Unfortunately, both the Solars and the Lunars underestimated its potential value. When used to manipulate Fate directly, Sidereal astrology has subtle but far-reaching effects that can influence the destiny of whole nations—but it could affect high-Essence individuals only with great difficulty. Furthermore, the Loom's effects, while remarkable, seemed weak and indirect compared to high-Essence Solar Bureaucracy and Socialize Charms that could affect large population groups. Why tweak and nudge, when you can command?

The Solars and Lunars both missed the fact that the Loom could track individuals according to their destinies. The Celestial Exalted are greater forces of destiny than anyone else in Creation, and an Exalt's destiny only grows more obvious as his permanent Essence increases. As a practical matter, this means the Loom of Fate is very good at predicting the arrival of a high-Essence Exalt at particularly auspicious (or inauspicious) times and places. None of the First Age Lunars ever thought about this facet of the Loom's functioning, largely because none of them ever foresaw a time when they would run for their lives from Sidereal-directed assassination squads.

The deeper a person moves into the Wyld, the less the Loom can track her. Beyond the Middlemarches, a person leaves the Loom's purview completely and does not regain a destiny until she returns to Creation.

Still, while the Loom may mark every sparrow that falls, its Sidereal attendants have limited attention spans. Creation is vast, and a Sidereal who searches for a particular Lunar with no specific idea of where she is could search the Loom for weeks without any luck. In other words, the chances of a Sidereal using the Loom to track a Lunar character and then targeting her with the Wyld Hunt (particularly given the Wyld Hunt's current disarray) are only as good as the Storyteller wants. Of course, a Lunar can make himself noticed through his actions in Creation. A Lunar who kills a mortal in a barroom brawl probably does not much affect the Loom's weave of destinies. When that same Lunar conquers an entire kingdom, on the other hand, the Loom and its watchers notice.

Note, however, that while Lunars can hide from the Loom of Fate within the Wyld, such Lunars are *not* beyond the reach of Fate within the meaning of Sidereal Charms.

revealed the secret of the Sidereals' special knowledge and how to defeat it. For the first time, the elders of the Lunars truly understood how the Sidereal Exalted used the Loom of Fate to track the Lunars across Creation. And so, these Lunars realized that safety from the Wyld Hunt lay in the only place beyond the gaze of the Five-Score Fellowship—someplace outside Fate itself—the Wyld.

The word went out, and one by one, the surviving Lunars fled deeper into the Wyld than most had ever gone before. Sure enough, the Sidereals could no longer perceive the Lunars in the Loom of Fate. History does not record the name of the courageous deity who told the Lunars how to evade Sidereal observation, and the Sidereals themselves never discovered the god's identity, either.

They did, unfortunately, trace the leak to the Bureau of Nature. Lunars believe the enraged Sidereals sent many of that Bureau's ranking gods to their deaths on trumped-up charges. To this day, the Lunar elders say, the petty Sidereal leaders constantly strive to undermine the Bureau of Nature out of fear that it will one day stand with the Lunars against the Sidereals. As for the Lunars, the Sidereals looked deep into the Loom of Fate for any hint of them. Finding none, the Sidereals assumed that the Lunars would meet their end in the Deep Wyld.

The Shogunate

Throughout the Shogunate era, the Lunars were forced to spend much of their time in the Deep Wyld to avoid the Wyld Hunt. Only the most skillful and subtle Lunars could leave the Wyld entirely to learn what was going on Creation. Even these incursions were brief, as Sidereal astrology in those days seemed able to direct the Wyld Hunt against a Lunar within days of entering Creation. As such, the Lunars gained only a cursory understanding of the Shogunate's political structures.

Some facts were clear, however. The great civilization built by the Solars was falling apart, no matter what the Dragon-Blooded insisted. The Terrestrial Exalted, having won Creation, revealed themselves to be totally inadequate at maintaining its glory. Without the capacity to maintain automated factory-cathedrals or to construct sentient artifacts, the Dragon-Blooded enslaved mortals as forced labor, a practice repugnant to the Old Realm Lunars. The Dragon-Blooded massacre of the Solars' artificial life-forms wrought Creation's first large shadowland, Marama's Fell. As a final insult, the Shogunate promulgated a new state religion, one the Lunars found blasphemous on its face. The nascent Immaculate philosophy named the Lunar Exalted (and the dead Solars) "Anathema," demons in human form, while raising the Dragon-Blooded to the level of demigods. The Lunars' rage against the Dragon-Blooded for the Usurpation burned all the hotter. Soon, however, the Stewards faced a new problem much worse than the deficiencies of the Shogunate.

The Breaking of the Castes

Of all the Exalted, the Lunars possessed the most experience with and resistance to the Wyld, but not even the most experienced Steward had ever spent more than a few weeks in the Deep Wyld during a single trip. The exile stretched into years and then decades. About 200 years into the Lunar exile, Ogun Bloody-Tusks, an elder and respected Half Moon, awoke one morning to discover that he had become a Waning Moon. For the first time since his Exaltation, his caste began to shift with the lunar cycle. Other Lunars experienced the same phenomenon. By the fourth century of the Shogunate, this shifting curse had spread to every Lunar in Creation. Even worse, the longer a Lunar spent without a caste, the more prone she became to uncontrolled shapeshifting and even madness. Ogun Bloody-Tusks, the first Lunar to lose his caste to the Wyld, later became the first to be called a chimera, and then the first to be put down by his fellows. The Lunars (secretly aided by allies in the Bureau of Nature) learned of Ogun's reincarnation before the Sidereals and rescued the reborn Lunar before the Wyld Hunt could arrive. However, the Lunars were horrified when the young Exalt, a boy named Uka, could not stabilize his own caste even though he had never been exposed to the Wyld.

Panic nearly spread across the whole of the Silver Pact at this development, which promised the Lunars nothing but inevitable madness, as one by one they all fell to chimerism.

The Lunars could reduce the chance of becoming chimerae by staying out of the Wyld, but that only brought on the butchers of the Wyld Hunt by the thousands. More than 30 Stewards became chimerae, and many more approached that debased state, before a pack of elder sorcerers hit upon a solution. Ironically, while Wyld inflicted the curse of shifting castes, the Wyld also held the possibility of a cure. Experimenting with moonsilver, the Wyld's tendency to turn people into living stories and strange Wyld-shaping techniques stolen from the Fair Folk, the sorcerers found a way to construct a magical identity that could withstand Wyld erosion.

The process first required the Lunar to recite a list of her past accomplishments and proclaim why they should accord her status within a caste. Then, those deeds would be tattooed onto the Lunar's body with pure moonsilver, along with various magical sigils. Once the tattoos were complete, a protected Lunar's caste could resist the Wyld indefinitely. Furthermore, the Lunar also became completely immune not only to Wyld-shaping effects but to all transformative magical effects which targeted her body.

The tattooing process was not perfect. While the sorcerers easily restored the Full Moon and No Moon Caste, the other three original castes were lost to the Wyld and replaced by a new, composite "Changing Moon" Caste.

The Lunars aren't sure why three castes collapsed into one. The most popular theory holds that the full moon and new moon are easily defined conditions. Similarly, the Full Moons and No Moons could establish their caste through acts of physical courage and prowess, or demonstrations of knowledge, cunning and wisdom. The other three castes' phases are all divided—waning, half and waning, leading into the new moon, followed by waxing, half and waxing, leading into the full moon. Meanwhile, the other three castes could not easily display courtly wit, strategic brilliance or daring deceit while out in the Wyld. Consequently, Lunars could more easily fix the two "stable" castes than the three intermediate castes that lack clearly defined boundaries.

A few Lunars think the No Moon sorcerers deliberately collapsed the three castes in order to usurp the Waxing Moons' former role as Luna's priests, as a gambit to increase their own power. Crossroad Society members mock the theory whenever they hear it. Does anyone imagine, they say, that it's *easy* to repair the work of the Incarnae? Luna's Chosen were lucky to emerge from the crisis with three castes. There might have been only one—or their Exaltations might have dissolved completely.

PRIESTS OF LUNA

Prior to the breaking of the castes, all Waxing Moons were automatically considered priests, just as all Zenith Caste Solars and all Sidereals regardless of caste (see **Exalted**, p. 132). As another side effect of the re-forged castes, that facet of Lunar Exaltation somehow found its way into the No Moon Caste instead of the Changing Moon Caste. Thus, in the modern era, all No Moons are considered priests, even though prayer is fundamentally a social action.

BASTIONS AT THE EDGE OF THE WORLD

The Lunar Exalted did not walk alone into exile. As the Shogunate enslaved humanity to serve Dragon-Blooded avarice, the dispossessed were forced to Creation's rim. Thousands of mortals fled to the Wyld itself, risking madness or deformity rather than submit to slavery. The Lunars, who usually skirted the fringes of the Wyld, sometimes found these unfortunates before the Wyld could claim them. Mortals who proved themselves worthy of Lunar respect were permitted to live among the Lunars, who protected the mortals from Wyld predators. In time, small tribes and villages of Wyld-tainted mortals grew, each with a Lunar sponsor. Some Lunars took this sponsorship a step further and began breeding with these tribes within the Wyld. The first results were typical of God-Blooded children. A few Lunars, bored after centuries in the madhouse of the Wyld and curious as to what effect Wyld energies might have on such a mating, tried mating with mortals while wearing the shape of animals.

Astonishingly, such obscene practices bore fruit, and the first beastmen were born. Initially, most Lunars felt disgust at such practices and their progeny. Virtually all Lunars had experimented with changing their gender in order to "see how the other half lived." Many even tasted the forbidden thrill of mating with each other in animal form, or across species, but such liaisons were never allowed to produce issue. As the numbers of beastmen grew, however, their parents argued that perhaps it was time for that particular taboo to be broken. After all, if the Lunars were ever to retake Creation from the Dragon-Blooded, the Lunars would need a strong army at their backs. The beastmen were strong. Furthermore, the beastmen could breed true in Creation, which most Wyld mutants could not. Didn't that show Gaia's approval of these new races? As the centuries passed, a significant number of the Lunars, some more discreetly than others, experimented with breeding beastmen.

Individually, the Lunars were spread across a vast area. Logistics prevented the Silver Pact from meeting as a group, although sorcery did allow for some communication among the leaders. In time, the territories covered by the Lunars and their tribes of beastmen and Wyld mutants stabilized somewhat. Lunars in the West had the greatest freedom of action, since even the Wyld Hunt had trouble patrolling the ocean's depths. Admiral Leviathan became the unquestioned leader of the Western Lunars, and he was the first to introduce beastmen into Creation. At his direction, the pelagothrope tribes of amphibious Wyld mutants, sharkmen, dolphinmen, sealmen and whalemen established territories beneath the Western seas. Most of the pelagothrope tribes established a large hunting ground in the waters northwest of the Blessed Isle. These pelagothropes kept a low profile, acting as the Admiral's eyes and ears in Creation. The direct, God-Blooded children of the great Lunar could even learn Charms to appear as human and spy on their father's behalf. A second, smaller tribe of pelagothropes was sent to the ruins of the sunken First Age city of Luthe, for reasons that Leviathan has never revealed.

Other tribes of beastmen and Wyld mutants followed. The impetuous Uka the Boar created a small tribe of boarmen called the Grondir, which he led into battle against the Wyld Hunt on the frozen tundra 200 miles north of Tzatli. The Wyld Hunt almost exterminated the Grondir and chased Uka back into the Wyld to nurse his wounds and accept the chiding of his elders for his lack of foresight. A few scattered sounders of boarmen still lurk in the woods north of Marama's Fell to the present day, living off the land and occasional banditry. In the East, two First Age Lunars, Silver Python and Rain Deathflyer, bred tribes of snakemen and birdmen, respectively. The two also began a program of drawing mundane animals into the Wyld and mating with them while wearing similar forms. Over several centuries of persistent experimentation, the two succeeded in breeding several species of intelligent animals. These animals were then reintroduced into Creation's forests in small numbers, both to spy for their creators and to breed new populations of intelligent animals that were loyal to the Lunar cause.

In the South, Ingosh Silverclaws and his disciple and lover Tamuz experimented with a small tribe of humans whose Wyld-taint gave them remarkable immunity to heat. The Lunars dubbed these humans the Erzani and attempted to establish them in Creation near the Elemental Pole of Fire. The Erzani settlement took hold, but unfortunately, the mutants' Wyld-taint made them unable to survive in temperatures below 100 degrees. The tribe never moved far from the Southern edges of Creation, since the Erzani found even Gem so bitterly cold that they could not survive for long.

CONFLICTS WITHIN THE WYLD

While moonsilver tattoos made the Lunars invulnerable to the Wyld's reality-twisting power, that chaotic domain still held many dangers. Two threats emerged as especially deadly.

The weakest, though only because of inferior numbers, was the chimerae. Despite the No Moon sorcerers' best efforts, not all of the Lunar exiles received moonsilver tattoos before falling into chimerism. Chimerae invariably turned on their fellow Lunars, as the madness that tore at the chimerae's bodies and minds often gave them a hunger for the flesh of other Exalted. Each chimera also bore a perverse cunning that made it dangerous even to a small pack of Stewards. Worse, whenever a Lunar met her end while in exile, she reincarnated somewhere within Creation. If that new Lunar was neither found and tattooed by a daring Lunar rescue party, nor slain by the Wyld Hunt, then the poor doomed Exalt inevitably became a chimera.

If the chimerae were dangerous because of their power and madness, the Fair Folk, or raksha, were a danger because of vast numbers and an implacable hatred for all shaped existence. Throughout the Old Realm, the Swords of Luna repeatedly warned their fellow Stewards about the menace of these entities from beyond Creation's rim. Only in exile did the Lunars fully experience the soul-searing power of the Fair Folk. Lunars continually skirmished with Fair Folk, who could change not just their shapes, but their entire identities with a thought. The Stewards fought battles of legendary scope against the Ones Beyond, all the more tragic and heroic because no one from within Creation knew how bravely the Lunars fought.

In time, though, the Lunars realized the futility of their position. The Fair Folk didn't just have numerical superiority over Luna's warriors; the Fair Folk had *inexhaustible* numbers. For every goblin, cataphract and behemoth slain, two more could be fashioned from the infinite possibility of that place. The true masters of the Fair Folk were the unshaped god-kings of the raksha, who could not be slain because they lacked any comprehensible existence.

In the eighth century of exile, Changing Moon scouts fought their way through the Deep Wyld with shocking news. The raksha had formed a new army that surrounded all of Creation. The Lunar warriors realized the true horror of their conflict—that every previous battle against the Fair Folk had only been trial runs for the Ones Beyond, sorties to help them understand warfare among the shaped beings of Creation. Shaken but resolute, once more the Lunars sent out warnings to their brethren across Creation, this time urging them to gird themselves for battle against enemies without number who were coming to exterminate the Stewards once and for all. The Lunars needn't have bothered. The Fair Folk did not care about a few hundred Lunars, and something else quite different was coming to kill the Exalted from the opposite direction.

THE AGE OF SORROWS

When the Deathlords unleashed the Great Contagion on Creation, it struck down 90 percent of humanity. The pestilence even reached into the Bordermarches and beyond: the human and beastmen tribes under Lunar protection died just as readily as anyone else. The Lunars, gifted with Celestial Exaltation, fared better than mortals, but even they were shocked at the death toll. And then, the Fair Folk attacked, sweeping past the battered Lunars—ignoring them completely. The true target of the raksha was always Creation itself, a blight upon the perfect chaos of the Wyld that they would remove at all costs.

This was a mistake on the part of the Fair Folk: perhaps the surest way to enrage a Lunar Exalt is to suggest that he doesn't matter, that his *stewardship* doesn't matter. The initial Fair Folk assault swept across the edges of Creation like a tsunami, with the first wave temporarily assuming shapes determined by the elemental alignment of the point of attack. The Shogunate Dragon-Blooded, reduced to a tenth of their former might by the Great Contagion, reeled from the force of the assault. The raksha might have exterminated all of humanity in the first few days of the invasion had not the Lunar Exalted rallied to attack. The surviving elders of the Silver Pact sent flurried messages to Lunars across Creation. From their hidden bolt-holes around Creation's rim, the Lunars struck at the exposed flanks of the Fair Folk army. The daring attack stalled the Fair Folk advance and gave the weakened forces of the Dragon-Blooded a change to regroup.

Almost 100 Lunar Exalted died in order to slow the advance of the Fair Folk, all believing that their cause was hopeless but nevertheless glorious. Incredibly, miraculously, the Lunars' heroic sacrifice paid off. The Dragon-Blood who would become the Scarlet Empress used the extra time bought with Lunar blood to penetrate the Imperial Manse and master its control systems. Today, every school child on the Blessed Isle knows to give thanks to the Scarlet Empress for driving back the Fair Folk hordes. Outside the lorekeepers of the Lunar Exalted, almost no one knows the names of even one Lunar hero who died giving the Scarlet Empress the chance to save the world.

THE NEW DAWN

The Great Contagion and the Fair Folk Invasion in-flicted massive damage on the Lunars, as the Fair Folk did on the rest of Creation. In the aftermath of these calamities, however, the Lunars suddenly had greater freedom of move-ment than any time since the Usurpation. At the height of the Shogunate, the Dragon-Blooded host numbered nearly a million. At the dawn of the Scarlet Empire, only 10,000 or so survived. Likewise, the Sidereals who once sponsored the Wyld Hunt now considered the Fair Folk a much greater threat and focused their power on mopping up the remain-ing raksha forces. After centuries in the wilderness, it was finally time for the Lunars to regroup, compare notes and make plans.

In the 67th year of the Scarlet Empire, the aging but still universally respected Changing Moon Ingosh Silverclaws called for a Great Gathering of all Lunar Exalted from across Creation. Although not all Lunars would leave their personal domains, most felt that the chance for the Silver Pact to meet once again was worth the risk. Two years after Ingosh issued his call, and for the first time since the Usurpation, a majority of the surviving Lunars—187 according to the count, more than half of whom had Exalted since the Contagion—met in a single location, a Wyld zone south of the ancient First Age city of Chiaroscuro in the territory claimed by Tamuz the Wanderer. The elders in attendance were dismayed to learn just how few of their number had survived since the Usurpation. Of the 300 Lunars who walked Creation before

the Usurpation, fewer than 30 had survived, and few of them did so unscathed.

The child prodigy Raksi, youngest of the No Moons at the beginning of the exile, had been driven nearly mad by her experiences in the Wyld. Lilith the Huntress was believed lost to her animal side, perhaps forever. Admiral Leviathan, the eldest Lunar save Ingosh, refused to attend: The Admiral's mysterious obsession with the lost island of Luthe took precedence over his kinship with the Lunar host, although he did send several envoys to observe on his behalf. Ma-Ha-Suchi, once an urbane diplomat renowned for his charm and dashing looks, nearly fell to chimerism before his tattoos were set, and his true form was now a grotesque blend of goat and wolf. Many others had suffered worse fates, with the elders estimating that as many as 40 of the extant Lunars might have become chimera, mainly Lunars reborn since the Contagion.

The Lunars quickly found deep disagreements about what they should do next. The few remaining Seneschals of the Sun King wanted to annihilate the Dragon-Blooded while they were still weakened from the Contagion and then seize power in the name of the Lunars' fallen Solar mates. Members of the Crossroads Society and Swords of Luna shouted down the Seneschals. The members argued that Creation could not withstand another assault by the Fair Folk, which would surely come in the anarchy to follow such an upheaval. More importantly, as the ever-pragmatic Ingosh Silverclaws pointed out, it was by no means certain

that even the assembled might of the Lunars could defeat the forces of the Scarlet Empress, even as weak as they were, so long as she could back them with the First Age weaponry of the Imperial Manse.

Ultimately, the most important question before the Gathering was the one raised by Tamuz, who had followed the ways of the Winding Path during the First Age. Even if the Lunars could defeat the Dragon-Blooded and their Sidereal puppeteers—what then? Could the Lunars quickly and efficiently build a society that could fend off the Fair Folk and the other threats to Creation? Put another way, should the Lunars even try to overthrow the Realm before they had any idea what to put in its place? The Gathering grappled with these questions for weeks before reaching a tentative agreement. Although the Lunars' collective cause was just, the time was not right to bring down the nascent Scarlet Empire. The Empress's power was great, but her reach was relatively short. Luna's Chosen would instead turn their attention to the people at the edges of Dragon-Blooded authority—the isolated and dispossessed tribes who had been reduced to barbarism by the fall of the First Age. Thus was born the great experiment of the Lunar Exalted—the Thousand Streams River.

THE GREAT EXPERIMENT

The Thousand Streams River is the Silver Pact's name for its long-term plan to restructure mortal society so that it can function without the aid of the Dragon-Blooded or indeed any other Exalted beings. The Silver Pact believes the Old Realm failed because the Solars' beneficence made the common folk weak and unable to fend for themselves once the Solars were gone. The Shogunate failed because the Terrestrial Exalted relied upon slave labor to maintain the standard of living enjoyed by the ruling classes. In neither society were people able to perfect themselves as individuals, as Luna would desire. The Solars were gone, the Sidereals were morally bankrupt, and the Dragon-Blooded were venal and incompetent. Only the Children of Luna, purified by their long exile, could lead humanity to find its own destiny. Only they could build a world where a person's destiny was written by his own deeds instead of a magical Loom of Fate.

Except for a few reactionary Sun King Stewards for whom stewardship took a backseat to revenge, the assembled Lunars agreed in principle to work toward a society in which all citizens were respected for their individuality. At the same time, however, this model society would require its citizens to develop their own potential to the utmost in order to participate in the society's bounty. Unfortunately, the Lunars could not agree on how to create this utopia. Thus, the Silver Pact agreed to remain for the time being at the fringes of Creation, acting secretly among the dispossessed tribes at the world's rim. Over the course of mortal generations, the Lunars would build those "barbarian" cultures into viable civilizations that could defy and then replace the Scarlet Empire.

ON THE MEANING OF "BARBARIAN"

This book often uses the term "barbarian" to describe various tribes at the edges of Creation. Although often used as a pejorative term, "barbarian" within the context of **Exalted** has a specific meaning that may or may not be an insult, depending on the speaker. Generally speaking, a barbarian is a member of some culture, typically either a nomadic tribe or an isolated village of hunter-gatherers or subsistence farmers, which does not recognize the ruling authority of the Scarlet Dynasty, the Dragon-Blooded in general or indeed any authority beyond that of village elders, chieftains or shamans. The most chauvinistic Dynasts call Nexus and Chiaroscuro barbarian settlements, but city-dwellers are not usually considered barbarians. Likewise, certain characteristics might be associated with barbarian cultures—illiteracy, the Hundred Gods Heresy, the absence of formal legal systems—but these traits are not universal to barbarian tribes, some of whose customary laws are actually quite civilized when viewed objectively instead of through the lens of Dragon-Blooded superiority.

Thus, a Dynast in Chiaroscuro might consider all Delzahn to be barbarians because even the city-dwelling Delzahn presume to have mortal nobility with a right to rule independent of Exaltation. A Delzahn noble might consider herself and her fellow nobles to be civilized while viewing members of the nomadic Delzahn horde as barbarians. Lunars and some barbarians themselves use the term "barbarian" to identify a particular tribe in exactly the same way as everyone else. They simply see rejection of Dragon-Blooded rule and centralized authority as virtues rather than flaws.

Of course, "several generations" soon turned into "many centuries" as the Lunars greatly underestimated the Empress's political acumen and longevity. Most Stewards at the Gathering expected the Scarlet Empire to collapse within a few more decades. They were quite chagrined to see it continue for another seven-and-a-half centuries.

OTHER GOALS OF THE SILVER PACT

The adoption of the Thousand Stream River was not the only achievement of the Great Gathering. The leaders of the Silver Pact also acknowledged the growing threat of the chimerae, whose numbers had burgeoned in the chaos after the Contagion and the Fair Folk Invasion. The need to kill the chimerae, so their Exaltations could return to Yu-Shan, be purified and seek new hosts again, was one of the few plans to which everyone agreed.

Ironically, to combat this problem, the elders adopted a tactic used by their enemies. The elders announced that when a chimera was slain by a Lunar (or more commonly, a group of Lunars), those who had freed the chimera's Exaltation could present proof of their deed to any Lunar elder and demand a boon from her. The resources of the Lunar elders were and are quite great compared to most newly Exalted Lunars. An elder could supply artifacts, instruction in sorcery and Charms, military support, access to demesnes and manses, and more in exchange for the head of a chimera, and many younger Lunars quickly formed Wyld Packs, not unlike the Wyld Hunts that had pursued their kind for centuries.

Another innovation of the Great Gathering was the mass acceptance of the system for counting coup developed in the First Age by the Swords of Luna. After all the death and destruction the Stewards endured after the Usurpation, it was unthinkable that any Lunar should take the life of another except in the case of chimerae. Too many Lunars had already made the ultimate sacrifice, and too much experience and information was lost with them. Accordingly, counting coup became the practice of the Silver Pact as a whole, and it was expected that when any two Lunars came into conflict, they would settle their differences in non-lethal combat.

Finally, the Lunars agreed that the Silver Pact must devote itself to the rescue and fostering of the Unblooded, the newly Exalted Lunars, dozens of whom had been reborn across Creation after the Fair Folk Invasion. Previously, individual elders had taken it upon themselves to rescue novice Lunars when they Exalted near the elder's territory, but far more Lunars were lost to the Wyld Hunt or to chimerism than were rescued and tattooed. The leaders of the Crossroads Society announced that, henceforth, they would remain in contact, wherever their individual territories were, and that they would watch the stars for signs of new Lunar Exaltations.

While the Crossroad sorcerers lacked the Sidereals' direct connection to the Loom of Fate, many members were skilled at conventional astrology, to say nothing of their spirit allies, their Yu-Shan connections and their ability to seek prophetic visions within the Wyld. The sorcerers pledged to identify newly Exalted Lunars as quickly as possible and magically communicate their locations to the nearest Lunars. The elders conceded that any unfortunate Lunars who Exalted on the Blessed Isle or in Realm-held territories were lost, but through better coordination, they might more frequently rescue people who Exalted throughout the Threshold. To encourage younger packs to risk their lives on behalf of an Unblooded novice, the assembled sorcerers also pledged that the rescued Lunar would have the names of his rescuers scribed into his tattoos, as well as a sigil stating that he owed them a blood-debt. Most of the elders present also announced that, if a new Lunar were brought to them for fostering, they would provide some sort of boon to the rescuing pack.

The philosophers of the various factions also agreed on a universal code of conduct by which Lunar society would judge individual members. A flexible code, the Silver Way, would give individual Lunars wide latitude in their actions but, at the same time, encourage young Lunars to cooperate with their elders through the carrot-and-stick of social recognition and scorn. (See "The Silver Way," on p. 38.)

THE UNBLOODED

The term "Unblooded" (both singular and plural) refers to newly Exalted Lunars who have not yet tasted the Heart's Blood of an animal or human and thus have not learned to take any shape other than their true forms. Lunars also use the term for the Casteless regardless of experience level, with "the blood of Luna" used as a euphemism for liquid moonsilver. Finally, the term is sometimes used as an insult for immature Lunars who made some foolish, avoidable mistake. Uka the Boar was called Unblooded Uka for decades after his disastrous Tzatli campaign.

As a final point, to assuage the concerns of the more paranoid elders in attendance, the Silver Pact agreed to conceal the full extent of the Thousand Streams River from the newly Exalted until each had proven her merit to a group of elders. The Great Experiment would require years of careful discretion, and many elders still had an exaggerated view of the Loom of Fate's capabilities. Conceivably, one wrong move in Creation might give the Sidereal astrologers enough knowledge about the Thousand Streams River to ruin centuries of work.

Consequently, elders who directed the Thousand Streams River spent much of their time in Wyld zones or occluded themselves with powerful Charms to protect them from the eyes of the Sidereals. These elders employed younger Lunars as cat's-paws to hide their true intentions from the Sidereals. The elders offered young packs chances to win renown through feats of daring or courage—feats that would incidentally nudge the elder's pet society in the direction he wished. Over time, this paranoia has decreased (markedly so since the disappearance of the Empress and the near-collapse of the Wyld Hunt). Even today, however, many elders continue to operate through unknowing younger proxies.

Thus has the Silver Pact evolved since the Great Gathering. The mayfly life of the Scarlet Empress surprisingly stretched into centuries, but the elder Lunars found themselves grateful for the extra time: Crafting the perfect society while hiding it from Sidereal manipulation turned out to be harder than anyone at the Great Gathering imagined. (The old Solars made directing nations look so easy….) At the fringes of Creation, barbarians became tribesmen who became civilized city-dwellers… who were then wiped out when their secret Lunar patrons became disenchanted with their way of life. Chimerae rose to become monsters of legend, as terrifying as any behemoth, and were brought

low by either the Wyld Hunt or its Lunar shadow, the Wyld Pack. Fair Folk came and went, most seeking to destroy the Lunars or ensnare them with insane machinations. A few raksha, though, became enamored of shaped existence and dependent on the dreams of mortals. These Fair Folk, whom their fellows regard as traitors, sometimes sought to parlay or even ally with the wary Moonchildren; a few Stewards agreed in exchange for a chance to study their strange magic.

THE TIME OF TUMULT

The last few years have been a time of great change for the Silver Pact, and even for the Children of Luna, some changes are more desirable than others. In RY 762, ancient Ingosh Silverclaws died at the age of 3,189, the most long-lived of any Lunar in recorded history and one of the few ever to die of old age. In his last days, many noted Lunars from across Creation came to his bedside to pay their respects to the architect of the modern Silver Pact. Old Ingosh had one last thing to say, a final warning for those assembled elders. As the tale has spread, while Ingosh took his last breath, his eyes became wide, as if possessed by a sudden vision, and his old Waxing Moon caste mark lit up for the first time since the breaking of the old castes. And then, so the tales say, Ingosh Silverclaws, the last priest of Luna said these words:

The Fickle Lady shows me things, my friends. Terrible things. A time of tumult for all our kind. I see an empty throne and a rotting mountain corpse. An ancient prison throws open its doors, and a plague of locusts who walk like men descends on the land. The dead rise to become gods, and gods fall to become as the dead. A great fire erupts in the South, greater than has ever been seen before. Five score is the number of the dead princes. Two score and ten is the number of the green sun princes who break the world. May the Lady save us all!

And then, Ingosh Silverclaws passed from this life. The assembled elders were shaken by his last words but hoped that they were just the ravings of a dying man, despite their obvious prophetic nature. Six months later, the Empress disappeared. Within the following year, Thorns fell to the Mask of Winters and his corpse-fortress, Juggernaut. The Solars, thought lost for all time, began to return. From the South came the first tales of strange invaders, described by refugees as "locust men." It appeared that, while the Waxing Moons were no more, Luna had one final message for her most faithful priest: The Time of Tumult was at hand.

MEMBERSHIP IN THE SILVER PACT

As a practical matter, a Lunar Exalt becomes a member of the Silver Pact simply by accepting moonsilver tattoos. Since most sensible Lunars immediately recognize the benefits of having a caste, most newly Exalted Lunars join the Silver Pact. There are, however, degrees of membership, and individual Lunars achieve status within the Silver Pact

based primarily on what they give back to it. In the present day, more than two-thirds of all extant Lunars are active members of the Silver Pact, having declared a willingness to cooperate with fellow Pact members against mutual threats (including Wyld Pack hunts), to assist in the rescue and fostering of newly Exalted Lunars and to abide by the principles of the Silver Way.

INITIATION

The initiation process for a new Pact member often begins even before her Exaltation. As soon as word comes of the death of a Lunar Exalt, astrologers of the Crossroads Society begin scanning the heavens for any sign of his reincarnation. Once a horoscope predicts where someone might Exalt, the astrologer sends a magical message to the nearest Lunar whom she considers competent enough to retrieve the Unblooded. Exactly how much competence is required depends on the circumstances. A barbarian who Exalts on the frozen steppes of the Haslanti League can typically be retrieved with little trouble by a small pack or even a single Lunar with less than a half-century of Exaltation. A street urchin who Exalts in the slums of Chiaroscuro—a Realm tributary with a significant Dragon-Blooded presence—might require a retrieval pack of several powerful Lunars, assuming such a rescue can be risked at all.

On the other hand, not all extractions require packs—many Lunars have established cults throughout the Threshold whose members assist "the children of the gods" at the command of their patron. Also, some Lunars consider themselves "urban predators" and establish many contacts even in Realm-dominated cities. One Unblooded was recently rescued by agents of the Guild and then delivered to a Lunar patron in exchange for a *substantial* cash reward. Generally, though, the Silver Pact does not even try to rescue Lunars who Exalt on the Blessed Isle, and rarely do so in tributary domains with large Realm garrisons. In such cases, the young Exalt is left to her own wits and survival instincts. With luck, after she falls to chimerism, she might even kill a few Dragon-Blooded before the Wyld Hunt puts her down.

Ideally, the rescue party makes contact with the new Lunar immediately after her Exaltation and spirits her away to the nearest Wyld zone. More commonly, the rescuers make contact as soon as possible after the Exaltation, once they figure out just who the Unblooded Lunar is. If they have time, they stalk the young Exalt for a few days before making contact, to assess her mental state and minimize the chance for her to reject their offer out of fear or confusion. When finding a new Lunar becomes a race against the Wyld Hunt, the preferred strategy is to draw pursuers away from the young Exalt. For example, one or more Changing Moons in the pack might use their anima powers to manufacture sightings of "Anathema" far away from the Unblooded's true location while other members of the pack spirit her to safety. (Unfortunately, if the pack hasn't identified the new Lunar yet, *she* might follow the false trail as well, hoping to

find "someone like me.") Some Lunars, however, eschew such indirect tactics, particularly Sun King Seneschals who often seize on retrieval missions as a pretext to attack Dragon-Blooded or Sidereals in the Wyld Hunt.

Finally, in some cases, the Unblooded has Exalted too far away for a retrieval pack to make contact but is still, whether through cunning or luck, able to survive and make her way to more accessible territory. Only a rare Lunar indeed, however, can evade the Wyld Hunt for long while burdened with a shifting caste, and only an even rarer one can do so without gaining the telltale mutations of the chimera. In such cases, the retrieval team discreetly monitors the Unblooded for some time before making contact, evaluating her mental and spiritual state. If the pack members agree that she is chimera, they slay her immediately. If the observers decide she can be salvaged, then they make contact and convey her as soon as possible to the pack's sponsor for initiation and tattooing.

IS CHIMERISM INEVITABLE?

The consensus among the Silver Pact is that any Lunar who does not receive moonsilver tattoos *will* become a chimera. Some Casteless may last longer than others, but chimerism is the eventual doom of any Lunar who lacks the protection of the tattoos. In truth, while the risk of chimerism is always great for untattooed Lunars, individual Casteless who are cautious in their habits and who stay away from Wyld zones can avoid becoming chimerae almost indefinitely. Of course, such Casteless do not gain the advantages of formalized caste membership or any of the benefits from joining the Silver Pact that come with it, but some Casteless think the versatility of a shifting caste outweigh its drawbacks. All a Casteless has to do is simply plan his activities around the appropriate "time of the month."

In fact, the number of Casteless has grown slightly since the dawn of the Time of Tumult, in part due to the Cult of Razik, taking one of the names of Luna's aspect as the Silver-Horned Watcher. Founded 20 years ago by a Casteless Lunar named Malik Fenn, the cult preaches that castelessness is the natural state of Lunar existence and that moonsilver tattoos defy the will of the goddess. Although most Silver Pact Lunars would consider Fenn's beliefs heretical, his nearest Lunar elders all happen to be of the Winding Road faction. They agree to leave him alone out of respect for his nonconformity, although they watch him closely for signs of chimerism. They are coming to regret their decision, however, as the charismatic Fenn has persuaded a half-dozen young Lunars to join his cult, decline the tattoos and remain Casteless, despite the risks involved.

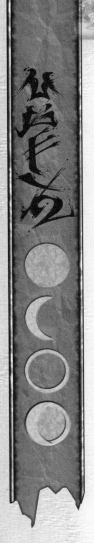

Lunar Tattoos

Once retrieved, the Unblooded is conveyed to an appropriate loremaster. No Moons most often fill this function, but any reasonably respected Lunar who knows the Form-Fixing Method can initiate the Lunar novice. The Charm itself inscribes moonsilver tattoos on the Unblooded's body. In a short period, the tattoos fix the Lunar into one of the three currently existing castes. The actual work of inscribing the tattoos takes several hours and is quite painful. While inscribing the tattoos, the loremaster also questions the new Lunar about her life before Exaltation, both to distract her from the pain of the tattoos and to get a feel for her most probable caste. Once the tattoos are complete, the loremaster immediately subjects the Unblooded to a series of tests designed to show her capacity for mettle, succor, glory, cunning and wisdom—the five traditional characteristics associated with the five ancient castes.

• **Mettle** represents the Lunar's drive to overcome adversity and hardship through unyielding strength and physical endurance. Mettle is the characteristic traditionally associated with the Full Moons who, in the Old Realm, served as champions, bodyguards and shock troops for the Solar Exalted.

• **Succor** represents the Lunar's capacity to form alliances with others, whether animals, mortals, small gods or other Exalted. Succor also represents the Lunar's willingness to seek compromise and to forge alliances through acts of compassion. In the First Age, succor was associated with the Waxing Moons who served as priests of Luna and diplomats to the Spirit Courts. After the breaking of the castes, succor became associated with the Changing Moons who favored persuasive arts.

• **Glory** represents the Lunar's ability to overcome her enemies by any means necessary or available. In the First Age, glory was associated with the generals and tactical geniuses of the Half Moon Caste, who practiced both diplomatic persuasion and outright trickery in devising their stratagems. In the modern era, Glory is associated with the Changing Moons who gravitate toward leadership positions or who rely on personal valor in achieving their goals.

• **Cunning** represents the Lunar's ability to outwit his opponent rather than outfight him. In the First Age, cunning was associated with the Waning Moon Caste, whose members hid behind a veneer of mischief but whose tricks could be educational, deadly or both. In the modern era, cunning is associated with the Changing Moons who prefer to get their way through quick wits, deceit and outright larceny.

• **Wisdom** represents the Lunar's ability to solve problems through reasoning, systematic inquiry, knowledge and forethought. Wisdom is the character trait associated with the sorcerers and savants of the No Moon Caste.

Most loremasters also require Unblooded to stalk and kill at least one animal and to drink its Heart's Blood. Some loremasters have more specific requirements and demand that the novice acquire the Heart's Blood of several animals, most commonly a raptor of some kind and at least one large predator. Tattooed Lunars who complete this portion of the trials are considered "blooded."

An Unblooded is not expected to complete all or even most of her trials. Indeed, some lorekeepers deliberately send their charges on impossible tasks. The purpose of the trials is simply to see how the novice Steward goes about trying to solve each task, whether or not she succeeds. Her actions and thought processes determine her caste. Once the trials are completed, the loremaster adjusts the tattoos, incorporating the deeds the new Lunar performed during her trials into the tattoos' very substance.

The novice Lunar must declare her willingness to serve as a Steward of Luna and select some aspect of Creation—a place, a thing, a concept—that she will defend and shepherd in Luna's name. At last, the Lunar must choose a deed name for herself, one that defines her as a Child of Luna and that her loremaster scribes into her tattoos. Whether the Lunar uses that name exclusively or continues to use her birth name is totally within her discretion. After the Lunar receives a deed name, the Lunar's caste sets itself permanently.

Claw-Speak

To those with the knowledge to see, Lunar tattoos contain a wealth of information about their bearer, including her deed name, her caste, any prior renown she has won and how many blood-debts she has accrued and fulfilled. The tattoos themselves are a combination of occult sigils interwoven with tales of the Lunar's deeds that led to her adoption of her particular caste. To the uninitiated, the tattoos look purely decorative, and devoid of any intelligible writing. In fact, the markings of the tattoos are part of a writing system unique to Lunar society, known as claw-speak. Lunars use this script to convey considerable amounts of information in delicate swirls and cuts that a Lunar can write even with a claw in one of his animal forms. Claw-speak is treated just as any other language for Linguistics purposes, but is taught to non-Lunars only under the most extraordinary circumstances, if ever.

Fostering

Once the new Lunar has been tattooed and properly initiated into a caste, the loremaster instructs her on the past, present and future of the Silver Pact that she has joined. Alternatively, if the loremaster is of a different caste than the student, he may send her to another respected mentor of her caste for fostering. In either case, the Lunar's mentor teaches her the code of the Silver Way and introduces her to other Lunars of the area. If the mentor belongs to one of the five factions, he most likely tries to indoctrinate her into his faction's beliefs and practices.

The initial stages of Lunar fostering also typically include an intensive period of combat and survival training. While the Full Moons are considered the preeminent warriors of the Silver Pact, all Lunars are expected to fight in these demanding times: even the most scholarly and introverted No Moon must know at least one form of combat. The fostering period continues until the young Lunar has achieved sufficient expertise to justify releasing her to her own devices, assuming she does not wish to remain with her mentor any longer.

THE BENEFITS OF FOSTERING

Mechanically, the effects of fostering mean that any Lunar character with a caste begins play with at least one dot in Survival and at least one dot in one of the combat Abilities (Archery, Martial Arts, Melee or Thrown). Starting Lunar characters also usually begin play with at least one Background dot in Mentor or Reputation. Tattooed Lunar characters who begin play without either of these Backgrounds are assumed to have completed their fostering but have done nothing other Lunars found impressive and did not encourage their teacher to continue advising and assisting them.

GATHERINGS

The Great Gathering of RY 69 was the largest assembly of Lunar Exalted in a single location since before the Usurpation. The logistics of that meeting were daunting and required Ingosh Silverclaws to call the Gathering a full two years in advance. Since that time, the Silver Pact has not met en masse, but individual elders routinely call lesser conclaves simply referred to as Gatherings. In these meetings, every interested Lunar within a geographic area is invited to discuss some question of mutual concern. Topics of Gatherings include developments among the Dragon-Blooded or Fair Folk, rumors about Deathlord activity, new information about the returning Solar Exalted or virtually anything that the hosting elder believes important enough to disseminate among his fellow Stewards.

A Grand Meet is a larger and more social form of Gathering. Grand Meets occur in each of the four cardinal directions every 50 years during the autumn equinox (which typically falls during the first week of Ascending Wood). The oldest Lunar within that quarter of Creation serves as host. In the past, Grand Meets gave Lunars of all ages a chance to become acquainted, for Lunars of different factions to argue about the rightness of their respective approaches and for the lorekeepers of the Silver Pact to trade information.

Mentors of newly tattooed Lunars often send their young students to Gatherings in the elders' place, most commonly

STORYTELLING A GATHERING

A Gathering is generally a mix of court intrigue and drunken hooliganism, with occasional ritual combat over imagined slights thrown in. There is little in the way of any formal agenda. On the first night, the host of the Gathering typically throws a feast for the guests, followed by some type of social event to occupy the younger Lunars (combat, hunts, sing-alongs, orgies, whatever), while the Lunars who have gained the host's respect quietly meet to discuss whatever the real agenda is.

On the next day, the host typically holds some sort of general meeting to discuss any pressing matters of concern to the Silver Pact as a whole, such as Deathlord or Wyld Hunt activities, rumors regarding Solars or Fair Folk or chimera sightings. In this manner, the host rarely has to ask any guests to investigate such matters, because young Lunars eager to prove themselves regularly volunteer for the most dangerous jobs. Often, the host invites a younger Lunar who has succeeded in such a dangerous mission to report her findings to the assembled group. In this way, not only do the Lunars gain important information from the most direct source, but a heroic young Lunar gains the accolades of the group, potentially improving her Reputation and thereby her usefulness to the host. The Changing Moon Lunar Anja Silverclaws recently achieved considerable recognition from her peers for her time spent spying on the activities of the Mask of Winters.

When the players' characters are young Lunars with little experience thrown into the aggressive and complex world of a Silver Pact Gathering, the storytelling possibilities are endless.

The Challenge: The character, who is being fostered by a famous but reclusive Lunar, has been sent to represent his mentor at a Gathering. Another Lunar who is fostered by a rival of the character's mentor finds some pretext to challenge the character to ritual combat, thinking that if she gains a blood-debt over the character, she can compel him to reveal his mentor's plans and perhaps even spoil them in some way. Of course, as the challenged party, the character has the right to set the terms of the combat—but terms that favor him too obviously might lose him status among the other Lunars. How does he respond? Systems for counting coup are described on page 41.

Romance in the Air: The character meets another Lunar whom he finds highly attractive. The other Lunar reciprocates his attraction, or at least seems to, but is she what she appears to be, in any sense of the word?

Pack Formation: The character meets other Lunars with similar levels of experience who want to form a pack to seek out and slay a chimera rumored to prowl relatively nearby. If the character hits it off with the others, they might invite him to join their group (an excellent way to introduce characters to each other and get them involved in the plot). Or perhaps the young pack snubs the character, and he decides to assemble a pack of his own to achieve the same objective. Then, the two packs race to see who can reach the chimera first (assuming either pack can kill the deadly beast).

Headhunting: The character has achieved some degree of Reputation, to the point that a powerful elder approaches the character with an offer of mentoring. The character might seriously consider the advantages of working for such a formidable Lunar, although obviously there will be strings attached. But what if the character already has a mentor? How does she react if the character spurns her for a more influential patron?

when the mentor is an elder who remains paranoid about the Sidereals and the Loom of Fate. The student gains an opportunity to meet his fellow Lunars in a (relatively) controlled environment. If he can bring back plenty of information without giving too much away, he might improve his standing in his mentor's eyes. On the other hand, a mentor with a particularly foolish or naïve student may well fill his head with deliberate misinformation so that even if he gives away too much, the elder's rivals gain nothing in the exchange—to say nothing of any Sidereals, masters of their own forms of disguise and deception, who may pump the student for information.

THE SILVER WAY

Since the Great Gathering, the Lunars have regarded the doctrine known as the Silver Way as their chief code of conduct. In keeping with the fluid nature of Lunar society, however, each tenet of the Silver Way is remarkably broad in its scope, so much so that people outside the Silver Pact might question why the Lunars bothered to set rules at all. The truth is that the Silver Way, while expressing principles the Lunars hold dear, is very much the product of a committee. Specifically, the Silver Way forms a compromise among five different factions of Lunars, some of which had mutually exclusive views on how Lunars should behave. More importantly, the Lunars are creatures of change, and no fixed set of statutes could ever cope with the endless variety of Lunar existence, either inside or outside of the Wyld. As such, the Silver Way is open to varying interpretations, depending on the Lunar. The general principles of the Silver Way are as follows.

Never Flee; Never Surrender

The Lunars are intrinsically a martial people. Even the most introverted No Moon has at least as much combat skill as the average civilian Dynast, and most Lunars can slay a Dragon-Blooded soldier with ease. In the Old Realm, not every Lunar needed to fight. The terror of the Usurpation and the long exile changed their attitude. Once, the Lunars had to flee because an enemy caught them unprepared for battle. That will never happen again.

The first principle of the Silver Way expresses this principle of combat readiness. Of course, "Never Flee; Never Surrender" oversimplifies the Lunar view of combat. The Great Gathering chose this language to placate the Seneschals of the Sun King who were still spoiling for a rematch with the Dragon-Blooded and the Sidereals. "Never Flee" does not exclude the possibility of tactical withdrawals, although a Lunar whose army is completely routed will lose much face if the result happened because of careless planning or foolish strategies. "Never Surrender" seems like a pointless admonition given that a Lunar who surrenders to his enemy most likely dies a few seconds later. Dragon-Bloods do not take "Anathema" prisoners.

In fact, "Never Flee; Never Surrender" refers not to individual battles or conflicts, but to the war for Creation. The Silver Pact holds that the Sidereals and Dragon-Blooded did not defeat the Lunars during the Usurpation. Rather, the Stewards made a tactical retreat due to the enemies' superior numbers, logistics and surprise. The Lunars survived. When the Lunars were slain, their Exaltations still found new hosts. Accordingly, the Lunars' enemies merely won a battle but not the war.

Younger Lunars often mock that interpretation of events, though rarely to the faces of Sun King Seneschals. The usurpers drove the Lunars from Creation and kept them out for 15 centuries. Didn't the Sidereals defeat the Lunars just as completely as the Solars? Such a question betrays the inexperience of someone new to Exaltation. Lunars live for millennia. At the time of the Usurpation, a few elders among the Lunars still remembered the Primordial War. Today, scores of Lunars are older than the Scarlet Empress. What matters is that the Lunars never gave up, and now that the Empress is gone, now that their ancient allies have returned and their enemies are in disarray, the war for Creation must turn in the Silver Pact's favor.

Viewed within this context, "Never Flee; Never Surrender" means two things. First, the humiliation of either a rout or a total defeat is an unacceptable waste of resources unfitting for a Steward. Accordingly, only a foolish Lunar rushes to battle against an obviously superior force. Uka the Boar did so centuries ago, and his defeat still shames him. Uka would have better served the Silver Pact by shepherding his Grondir boarmen and building them into a truly unstoppable force instead of striking before he was prepared. Second, Lunars must never take their eyes off their ultimate

goals: the rescue of Creation from the Dragon-Blooded and their Sidereal puppet-masters, and the building of a perfect society for the future, in whatever form it may take.

Repay Your Debts

The phrase "Repay Your Debts" carries a hidden meaning. The words left unspoken are "To Other Lunars." Individual Lunars may or may not consider themselves ethically obligated to follow oaths given to non-Lunars or repay favors to them. This principle refers to the blood-debt, a social convention that has kept the Lunars united for centuries when they might have fallen to infighting and territorial disputes. Simply stated, whenever a Lunar accepts a blood-debt owed to another Lunar (or has one forced upon her), she is expected to defer to that Lunar's position on minor matters or else satisfy the debt by performing some task of the debt-holder's choice.

A number of situations can lead to one Steward owing a blood-debt to another. First, every Lunar who is rescued by a Wyld Pack after his Exaltation owes a blood-debt to the leader of the pack that rescued him. He does not typically owe a debt to the lorekeeper who tattooed him, since every member of the Silver Pact has an obligation to tattoo the Unblooded without recompense. However, a lorekeeper of the same caste as the Unblooded frequently offers an extended period of fostering (and greater access to training and resources) in exchange for a blood-debt.

Finally, when two Lunars come into conflict and settle things by counting coup, the loser is obligated not only to defer to the winner on whatever point led to the conflict, but also to accept a blood-debt. Officially, this blood-debt compensates for the winner's refusal to slay the loser, which would customarily be his right in trial by combat. More practically, this tradition ensures that aggressive young Lunars out to prove themselves refrain from constantly challenging their betters in hopes of gaining prestige. The price a novice Lunar pays for fighting more experienced Lunars is an ever-increasing set of obligations, some of which may be quite dangerous.

When the appropriate conditions for accepting a blood-debt are met, the tattoos of the Lunar accepting the debt temporarily become fluid, allowing the debt-holder to draw a small circle on the debtor's flesh. The mark quickly fills in with moonsilver and becomes a part of the Lunar's tattoos. Two conditions must be met before the tattoos can be so altered: The debtor must freely agree to accept the debt, and the debt must be in exchange for some service or gift from the debt-holder. Sparing the life of a defeated enemy is one such service. On the other hand, if the would-be debt-holder tries using unnatural mental influence to *force* a Lunar to accept a debt, the tattoos themselves refuse to change their markings. Likewise, blood-debts are magically enforced only among Lunars, and the tattoos do not alter to denote a debt owed to anyone else. That doesn't mean that a Lunar cannot swear an oath to repay a debt to a Solar,

for example. It just means that the Lunar can't change his tattoos to reflect that debt.

Once the blood-debt has been accepted and carved into the tattoos, the debt-holder may demand a service on the spot, or he may hold the debt in reserve for some future need. He cannot "transfer" the debt as if it were a marker, but he can inform the debtor that she may perform some task for a third party and the debt-holder will consider the debt fulfilled. Once the debt has been fulfilled, the debt-holder can again alter the tattoos, this time by drawing a single line through the ring that represents that debt. The line also fills in with moonsilver, signifying that the debt no longer exists.

Blood-debts carry no social stigma, though having a large number of outstanding debts marks a Lunar as impetuous and perhaps immature to challenge so many superior opponents in such a short time. There is a significant social penalty, however, for becoming an *oath-breaker*. A Lunar becomes an oath-breaker when the Lunar expressly refuses to perform an obligation owed to the debt-holder that is within the Lunar's capability, or else when the Lunar attacks the debt-holder. In the former case, Lunars sometimes become oath-breakers rather than perform some obligation that they find morally unacceptable. Examples might include betraying an ally into the debt-holder's hands, murdering some innocent person or performing acts of bestiality at the debt-holder's behest when doing so violates the Lunar's own code of conduct. Attacking a debt-holder rarely happens, and most commonly occurs when a Lunar has become unwillingly indebted to someone he actively despises.

In either case, the entire circle representing the debt fills in with moonsilver to become a solid silver disk representing the broken oath. Most Stewards feel a natural distrust for oath-breakers, and an oath-breaker mark can only be removed when the debt-holder (or her reincarnated self, if she was slain) forgives the debtor for the breach and names some other service the oath-breaker can perform. Only an extremely magnanimous Lunar is likely to do so, however. Elder Stewards often take the blood-debt so seriously that they hold the debtor's breach over him for centuries, if not the rest of his life.

A rarer and more serious form of blood-debt is the *life-debt* acquired when one Lunar saves another from certain death at considerable risk to herself. For example, an Unblooded usually incurs a blood-debt to the leader of the pack that retrieved him. However, if a member of the pack died during the course of the retrieval, the Unblooded might be required to swear a life-debt instead, to acknowledge the pack's greater sacrifice. As another example, any Lunar might feel obligated to accept a life-debt to another Steward who rescued her from certain death when the rescuer was not obliged to do so or when the rescuer was a much younger and less experienced Lunar.

A life-debt imposes a greater level of obligation. The tattoos represent the life-debt by three concentric circles. The debtor must perform three major tasks of the debt-holder's choosing, with each successful task resulting in one slash through the circles. After three slashes (like an asterisk), the debt is fulfilled. Instead, the debtor can choose to follow the debt-holder and serve him for a year and a day, at the conclusion of which the debt is fulfilled. Finally, saving the life of the debt-holder may satisfy the debt.

If the holder of a blood-debt dies before the debt can be fulfilled, the debt becomes null and void. Any Lunar automatically knows when the Steward who holds her debt has died, and she can then mark out the debt herself as if it were fulfilled. If the holder of a life-debt dies, however, the debt carries through to the dead Lunar's next incarnation. Debtors who owe a life-debt to a deceased Lunar often insist on leading the pack that rescues his reincarnation. Doing so extinguishes the life-debt automatically.

BE JUST AND GENEROUS TO THOSE BENEATH YOU

This provision lies at the core of the Thousand Streams River. The Incarnae chose their Exalted to lead the rest of humanity and show them the way to a better life. The Sidereals and Dragon-Blooded betrayed their duty, and while the Solars may yet reclaim their divine mandate of old, they have a long way to go to regain their power—and a longer way before being forgiven by some Stewards. When the Great Experiment is complete, however, humanity will forge its own destiny, free from the whims of the Exalted. In the meantime, Lunars must bear the burden of guiding their chosen territories and peoples.

Just as a good alpha leads to a strong pack, so must a Lunar patron demonstrate justice and compassion in her dealings with any tribe she takes under her patronage. The Silver Pact seeks to guide mortals toward a better way of life: When a Lunar becomes a tyrant over her chosen territory, it may fall to her fellow Lunars to show her the error of her ways. Assuming they can, of course. Few Lunars in the modern Age have shown as much cruelty and tyranny as Raksi, Queen of Fangs, but unfortunately, even fewer Lunars could challenge someone of her raw power. In other words, shorn of all flowery language, "Be Just and Generous to Those Beneath You" can also be expressed as, "Be nice to your followers or don't count on our support when they turn on you." The wisest elders point to the lesson of the

Usurpation and the ancient defeat of the Primordials: No matter how powerful you are, or how thoroughly you oppress your subjects, *they can kill you.*

Of course, any social stigma attached to mistreating one's subordinates does not apply to one's enemies. While many Moonchildren would blanch at how a Lunar such as Ma-Ha-Suchi tortures and mutilates the Realm soldiers that fall into his hands, none would accuse him of being unjust or ungenerous in doing so. The Silver Pact asks no quarter from its enemies, and gives none in return.

Finally, this provision of the Silver Way affects the relationship between a blood-debtor and his debt-holder. The Silver Way does not give any real guidelines on what sorts of tasks a Lunar may assign as repayment for a particular debt. However, Lunar leaders frown on a debt-holder who assigns obviously suicidal tasks or deliberately humiliating ones just because she takes a dislike to her debtor. A debtor who feels that the debt-holder misuses the blood-debt relationship in a deliberately malicious or pointless manner that does not support the goals of the Silver Pact can petition any Lunar more respected than the debt-holder and state his case.

If the Lunar agrees that the task demanded is either hopelessly suicidal or else a malicious waste of the debtor's time, the Lunar may intercede with the debt-holder and try to persuade her to change the conditions imposed. Failing that, he can challenge the debt-holder to trial by combat, with the winner taking on the original blood-debt plus an additional debt from the loser. Most debt-holders typically agree to a more reasonable repayment on the debt rather than risk losing it outright and owing a debt to a more powerful Lunar.

SLAY NOT YOUR BROTHERS AND SISTERS

This provision of the Silver Way began as a custom the Swords of Luna faction adopted long before the Usurpation. Throughout the Old Realm, the Solars (as any reasonably sensible rulers) restricted duels between Exalted. After all, an Exalt with several centuries of experience was obviously more useful for society than one who had recently Exalted. Accordingly, the Solar Deliberative passed laws that effectively banned dueling among the Exalted. At the frontiers of civilization, however, Lunars were rarely in a position to be punished for anything, let alone a death-duel with a fellow Lunar in which the killing might arguably have been in self-defense.

Accordingly, at some point during the First Age, Lunars of the Silver Pact adopted a system of ritual combat known as "counting coup." When two Lunars disagreed so seriously that the argument threatened unit cohesion at Creation's rim, they were expected to settle the issue through combat. It wouldn't prove who was right, but it would prove whom the unit needed more, and so whom the other Lunars would support. The challenged party could set the specific terms of the fight—only melee weapons, only to first blood, only while shapeshifted into certain forms—but, generally, counting

coup resulted in the best warrior winning. This also had the beneficial effect of encouraging every Lunar to develop his fighting skills to their peak.

After the Great Gathering, counting coup became an accepted and indeed required part of the Silver Way. The Lunar Exalted had suffered catastrophic losses during the Great Contagion and the Fair Folk Invasion. The last thing the Silver Pact needed was for Lunars to fall into the sort of internecine warfare that had already weakened the Scarlet Empress and her rivals at Lookshy. Accordingly, counting coup was not merely made part of the Silver Way, but also part of the tattoos themselves. Thanks to modifications made to the tattooing process by the Crossroads Society, the tattoos actually form a part of ritual combat.

In practice, counting coup works as follows: When two Lunars come into conflict, either side may challenge the other to combat. The challenged party retains the right to set any conditions she wants on the battle. Accordingly, canny Lunars often try to goad the other Stewards into challenging them first. If conflict looks inevitable but neither party will formally issue the challenge, the higher-ranking Lunar (as defined by their relative Reputations) can "interpret" the other Lunar's remarks as a challenge and then claim the right to set conditions for combat herself. Once the challenge has been declared, the tattoos of both combatants start to glow. Once the winner has been declared, either through the loser's submission or through the winner achieving some predefined victory condition, the winner's tattoos cease to glow but the loser's continue to do so. The winner can then draw a circle on the loser's skin with his finger to denote the existence of a blood-debt. From that point, the loser is obligated both to repay the blood-debt and to concede whatever issue prompted the dispute in the first place. Failure to concede the disputed point marks the loser as an oath-breaker just a surely as refusal to fulfill the blood-debt. Accordingly, the battle effectively ends the dispute unless the loser feels so strongly about his position that he accepts the scorn of the entire Silver Pact to continue his course.

As a final note, counting coup does not always take the form of physical combat. This is the most common form—and few Lunars object if the challenged party calls for any form of one-on-one combat—but the challenged party may choose some other form of competition, such as an archery competition, a hunt, a race over difficult terrain or even a card game. The only requirement is that the challenger must have at least a sporting chance. Other Lunars would consider it bad form, for example, for a witty and sophisticated Changing Moon to require a brutish Full Moon challenger to defeat the Changing Moon in a contest of epic poetry writing. On the other hand, challenges between Changing Moons often turn on skills such as public speaking, performing or even seeing who can seduce the most mortals in a given night, while rival No Moons may often resolve their differences through sorcery battles, riddle contests or obscure strategy games.

In some rare instances, two Lunars come into conflict so violently and completely that one or both will not settle for a blood-debt from the loser. If the winner slays her defeated opponent, the winner may or may not suffer loss of Reputation, depending on the circumstances and on who knows what she did. Nothing in the tattoos themselves can mark one Lunar as the slayer of another. If any Lunar witnesses agree that her cause was just, most Stewards simply consider the matter closed. Indeed, while slaying a defeated Lunar enemy is considered bad form, no Lunar is *entitled* to keep his life. Anyone who can't defend himself against a determined killer probably got what he deserved.

On the other hand, a Lunar who makes it a practice to slay his rivals in ritual combat may well represent a divisive danger to the Silver Pact as a whole. In such cases, an elder who becomes aware of a killing and considers it unjustified may intercede and personally challenge the killer to ritual combat. Upon the elder's victory, she then decides whether to accept a blood-debt and force the killer into some form of penance, or else put him down like the rabid dog he seems to be. Of course, to enforce such a rough justice, the elder must actually defeat her opponent—and since the challenged party chooses the nature of the battle, most elders do not lightly put their lives on the line.

DEFEND WHAT IS YOURS

The polestar of the Silver Way lies in the four words "Defend What Is Yours." Even the Casteless feel the need, the compulsion, that is the principle of stewardship. As all Moonchildren realize, Luna chose each of them to guard and nurture some part of her beloved's Creation, whether it is the tiniest village or the greatest nation, a horde of beastmen or a single mystical tome. The Silver Pact agrees that, by working together, all Lunars find it easier to fulfill their own duties of stewardship. Nevertheless, all Lunars agree that if they must choose between stewardship and getting along, the role of the Steward must come first.

In short, the Silver Way grants each Lunar the right and the freedom to defend her chosen object of stewardship by any means she deems necessary. If the holder of a blood-debt commands her to harm what she would protect, she may defy the command and her tattoos will not mark her as an oath-breaker. If she slays outright another Lunar who threatens what she would nurture, no shame falls upon her. If her duty of stewardship carries her into the heart of a metropolis or even into the domain of the enemy, no Lunar will gainsay her decision to follow her destiny. This is the blessing and the burden of stewardship. All Lunars must defend what is theirs, no matter where that duty takes them.

The urge toward stewardship is connected to the concept of territory. Most Lunars (just as most humans) are social, but individual Lunars typically have a strong territorial instinct. A Lunar who becomes the patron of a barbarian tribe as part of the Thousand Streams River undoubtedly wants to exclude other Exalted who may disturb her work. Another Moonchild might simply wish to return to the tribe or city that birthed him, settle old scores and take over. A third Chosen of Luna might simply seek solitude to develop her own skills and puissance. The Silver Pact places great emphasis on the right of each Lunar to possess and control his territory, and a number of Lunar Charms serve to announce a Lunar's territorial borders and alert him to any intruders.

On the other hand, no Lunar is entitled to a territory she is not strong enough to keep. Absent preexisting vows of mutual protection or some personal agenda, a Lunar seldom comes to the aid of a neighbor who finds himself attacked in his own domain. Indeed, a Lunar neighbor may cheerfully expand her territory into that of a younger, less experienced Moonchild if she judges that he cannot defend what is his. Luna fashioned her Chosen as warriors for Gaia, not arbiters of property disputes.

FACTIONS OF THE SILVER PACT

The divisions within the Silver Pact exist just as they have since the First Age. As before, there is no internecine conflict among the different factions. Indeed, a Lunar can join more than one. For example, nothing prevents a mighty Full Moon warrior who fights against the Wyld as a Sword of Luna from also studying sorcery with the Crossroads Society. Knowledge of magic might help the Full Moon fight the Fair Folk or chimerae, while his combat mastery might help the Society members defend their mystical secrets from thieves. Only the Sun King Seneschals typically exclude members of other factions from their activities, and vice versa. The Seneschals favor the outright return of Solar rule. The other factions, and most especially the Winding Path, would prefer almost anything else.

THE CROSSROADS SOCIETY

The modern Crossroads Society remains primarily a No Moon enterprise, but accepts any Lunar who wants to learn sorcery, artifact creation or other arcane arts. The Society is a profoundly paranoid and secretive organization that resembles a mystery cult: New members must complete progressively higher levels of initiation before they learn the more sensitive information. Indeed, outsiders seldom know just who is a member of the Crossroads Society. Leading Moonchild sorcerers don't bother hiding their membership, of course; it is obvious and assumed. Other Society members obscure their identities behind masks, illusions and false identities. The Society's reasons for such obfuscation are partly philosophical and partly practical. Philosophically, the lonely art of sorcery demands hard work and great care from its practitioners, and the Society wishes to discourage Lunars who want to master magic just for glory or fame. At the same time, the Society prefers candidates whose intellect and cunning warrant inclusion in this most intelligent and cunning of fraternities. Accordingly, figuring out who belongs to the Crossroads Society is often part of the Society's initiation process.

INITIATION

Initiation into the Crossroads Society closely tracks the five trials necessary for initiation into the practice of Terrestrial sorcery itself, each tailored to fit both the specific needs of the Society member mentoring the initiate and the Lunars' approach to magic. The first trial, humility, often takes the form of forcing the young Lunar to confront his own intellectual deficiencies. Because so many Lunars come from less civilized regions and less affluent classes, quite a few Society candidates are poorly educated, if not totally illiterate. Even though much of Lunar sorcery is an oral tradition, the Crossroads Society still values literacy, including fluency in Old Realm. For initiates into the Society, the trial of humility often means being forced through remedial schooling, sometimes alongside small children, somewhere in the mentor's territory.

The second trial, tutelage, begins once the student masters basic academics, as only then can master and student discuss the intricacies of sorcery. At this phase of initiation, the young Lunar formally becomes an apprentice to the master sorcerer. He accompanies her everywhere, serving her as needed and accepts whatever lessons on the occult arts the master chooses to impart.

The remaining three trials—the journey, the fear and the sacrifice—are often combined into a single terrifying ordeal. The apprentice, having mastered all the mundane occult knowledge his master could impart, journeys into the Deep Wyld on a spirit quest to open himself up to magic. The mentor's instructions are clear: Go into the Wyld, and do not return until you become a sorcerer or accept that you never will. Few young Lunars have ever been in the Deep Wyld for long, let alone by themselves, and the Fair Folk are

always eager to taste the fear of a new visitor. The Lunar must grapple with such enemies by himself, as well as whatever mind-bending wonders and horrors the Wyld reveals to him. As the Moonchild roams among burning giraffes that dance across diamond savannahs and the clouds sing arias about his greatest shames, he seeks the secret that reveals how to bend Creation to his will.

The spirit quest traditionally lasts for 40 days and 40 nights, though time rarely stays consistent within the Wyld. During the last night, if the Lunar has not abandoned his quest, he receives a visitation. Most Society members think the visitor is Luna in her Walker at the Crossroads aspect. Some say it is Luna in her Silver-Horned Watcher aspect. A few whisper that it is the Wyld itself. Whatever the being is, it invariably asks the same question, "What do you have to offer?" This is the trial of sacrifice, and a wrong answer by a foolish apprentice might leave him mad, tainted by the Wyld despite his tattoos, or simply lost forever. A more astute answer might be to offer up whatever the Lunar seeks to steward. In any case, those who have the wit to escape with their minds, bodies and souls intact will return as both sorcerers and initiates of the first degree of the Crossroads Society.

THE JASMINE GEMS OF MISHIKO

Crossroads Society members usually teach apprentices one-on-one, but they do have a sorcerous academy, of sorts. Five magical gems, when brought together, apparently summon the spirit of Mishiko, the daughter of Bar-Izahd, whom the Moonchildren claim as the First Sorcerer. Mishiko provides guidance through the initiatory ordeals of sorcery. The Crossroads Society views Mishiko as a supplemental tutor rather than competition—mostly because the five sorcerers who guard the gems for five-year terms usually belong to the Society. These gems are among the Society's greatest treasures… and exactly who guards them is one of the Society's greatest secrets. See **The White and Black Treatises**, pages 30-32, for more information about Mishiko.

SOCIETY RANKS

The Crossroads Society has three degrees. The first degree is open to any Lunar who has learned to cast Terrestrial Circle Sorcery by any means. Initiation into the second degree requires a period of service to any Lunar who is already at least a second-degree member. This apprenticeship period lasts until the Lunar masters five Terrestrial spells, has learned to perform astrology at the Adept level (see **Exalted**, pp. 137-138) and has learned the Form-Fixing Method to confer moonsilver tattoos. During second-degree apprenticeship, the Lunar is often called upon to accompany packs sent to rescue

Unblooded. The young sorcerer is not expected to tattoo the Unblooded herself, even if she knows the Charm. In rare cases, however, such as when the Unblooded faces serious danger of becoming a chimera, the apprentice is authorized to fix the novice Lunar's caste herself in the nearest Wyld zone. Once the initiate masters the requisite arts and Charms and has assisted in at least one retrieval or chimera-hunting mission, she accepts a blood-debt from her mentor and becomes a second-degree member.

The third and final degree of membership requires an additional period of apprenticeship, this time to a Society member who has mastered Celestial Circle Sorcery. Although the Lunar can abandon her quest at any time, the period of apprenticeship otherwise lasts until she achieves her own initiation into Celestial Circle Sorcery. The apprentice must also master several Charms dealing with thought, knowledge, mystical perception or crafting artifacts. Once the apprentice meets these requirements, her master sends her once again into the Wyld for a spirit quest. This quest has only one trial—sacrifice—and the Lunar must spend 40 days and 40 nights in the Wyld contemplating what she can give away now that will satisfy the visitor who comes to meet her.

GOALS OF THE CROSSROADS SOCIETY

In the modern era, the Crossroads Society continues to seek lost sorcerous knowledge and First Age technologies. With the return of the Solars, the Society has become more aggressive in its search for lost knowledge. The Society members are fully prepared to compete with Twilight Castes for control of such resources. The Lunar mystics claim they suffered under the yoke of Twilight arrogance once before. They will not do so again.

Unfortunately, their greatest strength is also their greatest frustration. Raksi, the Queen of Fangs, is a No Moon elder and a nominal member of the Society. She controls the First Age city of Sperimin, the Sixfold Spire that was Sperimin's great sorcerous academy and the legendary *Book of Three Circles*, the foremost record of First Age sorcery in existence. Unfortunately, any Society member who seeks access to this knowledge must accede to the insane Raksi's whims if he wants to study the *Book* for even an hour. Few among even the most committed savants can stomach a diet of human babies for the time it takes to master even a single Celestial Circle spell.

Members of the Society, beyond expanding their knowledge of sorcery, also seek to gain influence over the rest of the Silver Pact, primarily by making themselves indispensable. As well as training new sorcerers, the Society also holds most of the First Age technical knowledge available to the Lunar Exalted. Crossroads members provide their fellow Lunars with technical know-how on subjects such as manse construction and warstrider maintenance… in return for "future considerations."

The Crossroads Society is nearly the exclusive source for astrological insights among the Silver Pact. The Society has always said that locating newly Exalted Lunars is a duty its members perform without any thought of reward for their work. Of course, that doesn't mean the Society members would *turn down* any reward that might come their way. And as long as the Society is the only body that can predict new Exaltations, who is to complain if individual Society members give allies in the Silver Pact first pick at the new recruits, in exchange for the occasional side benefits (or even to know, for that matter)?

THE SENESCHALS OF THE SUN KINGS

The Sun King Seneschals are the smallest of the modern factions, but as the returning Solars have made their presence felt, this faction has quietly become the fastest growing one. The faction suffered far greater casualties during the Usurpation than any of the others due to individual Seneschals' refusal to abandon their mates. During the exile, the few survivors could only recruit new Lunars through tales of the fallen glories of the First Age. Most young Lunars, however, saw the Solars as a relic of the past who would most likely never return. While the Dragon-Blooded were clearly an enemy, the Stewards had to fight them for immediate and concrete reasons, rather than to avenge a centuries-old betrayal. Thus, the twin pillars of Sun King philosophy—veneration of the Solar Exalted and revenge on the traitorous Dragon-Blooded—had little relevance for modern Lunars. Indeed, when Seneschals experimented in the creation of new societies, they typically took direct control of territories in the Wyld and the far Threshold, ruling openly as god-kings in the manner of their former mates. Some Seneschals even thought they were pretty good at it. A few even dreamed that someday a Lunar Deliberative could rule Creation and restore ancient glories.

That has all changed. The Solars returned with all their former glory (if not yet their former power), and the Scarlet Empress, the heart of Dragon-Blooded society, vanished. The Seneschals took the return of the Solars, almost simultaneous with the Empress's disappearance, as proof that the faction was right all along and that the Solars are destined for victory. Young Lunars who encounter the returned Solars with all their burgeoning power are often forced to agree. Whether they deserve such authority or not, the Lawgivers unquestionably seem to bear the mantle of divine authority.

As for the Dragon-Blooded, the Seneschals don't know any more about why the Empress disappeared than anyone else, but they have no shortage of conspiracy theories. Most of these involve her assassination by a returning Night Caste or perhaps even a heroic Lunar. Likewise, the official story from the faction is that no one freed the Solars from whatever trap contained them for 15 centuries. Rather, the Solar Exaltations freed themselves to return "in Creation's greatest hour of need."

In many ways, the Sun King Seneschals function as a loosely organized cult. The closest thing to centralized leadership consists of an ad hoc council of Lunar elders. Ironically,

SELF-TAUGHT SORCERERS

While the Crossroads Society offers reliable training in sorcery, a would-be Lunar sorcerer can also draw upon the Salinan Working. This mystical endeavor infused the precepts of sorcery into Creation itself so that Essence-channelers could initiate themselves and learn sorcery simply through enlightened observation of the world around them. Lunar sorcerers helped the Twilight Caste master Salina develop her mystical school. No wonder, then, that Lunars easily learn sorcery through mystical contemplation and spontaneous ordeals. The Society tries to recruit self-initiated Lunars through the promise of access to its accumulated spells and lore—but not every sorcerer accedes. Lunar society includes many independent sorcerers as well.

none of them are actually old enough to remember a First Age Solar. The eldest of the council, Swims in Shadows, predates the Great Contagion by only a decade, yet he speaks on behalf of his mentor, Leviathan, and so, the elder's words carry great weight.

INITIATION

Initiation into the Sun King Seneschals usually begins at the same time as initiation into the Silver Pact, since the majority of the Seneschals are inducted into the faction's cult-like structure by the Lunars who fostered them; they never know any other approach to Lunar Exaltation. The novice Lunars hear tales of the Old Realm, where Solars and Lunars ruled Creation as mates, Lawgiver and Steward—tales subtly augmented with the supernatural charisma of a Lunar storyteller. Seneschal mentors encourage their fosterlings to think of themselves as one-half of a whole being, with their respective mates essential to becoming complete. Consequently, before the return of the Solar Exalted, the initial training period could be viewed as the process of becoming worthy to marry someone the initiate would never meet.

After several years of training, young Seneschals reach the second stage of initiation, when the elder Seneschals consider the younger ones worthy of hearing the whole truth of the Usurpation. The Seneschal versions of the story emphasize the treachery and brutality of the Terrestrial and Sidereal Exalted and, to a lesser extent, the malfeasance of other factions that placed selfish interests above protecting their mates and thus preserving Creation's rightful order. Once a mentor believes he has prepared a novice Lunar to reject false teachings from other Lunars and to view the Dragon-Blooded as the enemies of all right-thinking beings, he sends her out to seek her destiny.

Until recently, most such Seneschal destinies fit into two categories. Some young Seneschals began their own experiments in the Thousand Streams River, usually in the form

of a rabidly anti-Imperial society. Others launched directly into conflict with the hated Dragon-Blooded by staging attacks on Realm holdings. A good deal of the Realm's picture of barbarian invaders burning civilization to the ground at the behest of mad Anathema leaders comes from activities of the Sun King Seneschals. Since the return of the Solars, however, many young Seneschals set forth to seek their mates and assist them however possible, whether as follower, mentor or ally.

Many… but not all. Despite the obvious appearance of the Sun King Seneschals as a Solar-worshiping personality cult, many of its older members recognize that Solar rule had its flaws, although such minor imperfections certainly did not warrant the Usurpation. These leaders believe that, while Solars should undoubtedly rule, it would be best if they took advice from Lunars… exclusively. For the Solars' own good, of course, and the good of Creation.

The members of this cabal work to advance Solars who show suitable "appreciation" for Lunar benefactors. These Seneschals also watch for young Lunars who might see through the façade of uncritical devotion, as well as for any who might be cunning enough to embrace the cabal's hidden cause.

GOALS OF THE SENESCHALS OF THE SUN KINGS

The faction's goals are simple: find their former mates, help them (and the rest of the returning Solars) however possible and stand by their side as the Solars take their rightful place as the rulers of Creation. As a corollary to these goals, most Sun King Seneschals believe that a Solar renaissance will begin with the destruction of the Scarlet Empire. Radical members would even seek the complete extermination of the Dragon-Blooded in revenge for the Usurpation and for what these Seneschals see as 1,500 years of darkness. Consequently, the faction spends an inordinate amount of time plotting strikes and counterattacks against Realm legions.

THE SWORDS OF LUNA

The Swords of Luna stand, as they always have, at the frontier of the world. These Lunars have little to do with the Thousand Streams River. Instead, the Swords of Luna concentrate their power on preparing for the Fair Folk incursion these Lunars suspect may come any day. Over the last few centuries, however, some of the Swords of Luna have had non-violent encounters with the Fair Folk. These Lunars learned that some of the raksha developed an affinity for shape and rather enjoy living in Creation. A few of the Changing Moons have even formed tentative alliances with Fair Folk who fear their unshaped brethren from deeper in the Wyld. More importantly, the No Moons among the Swords of Luna have learned much about the nature of the Fair Folk, and some have even learned how to use some of their eldritch wonders.

THE CULT OF THE ILLUMINATED

The Seneschals know that a few Solars receive training and material support from an obscure religious order called the Cult of the Illuminated. Thus far, however, the faction knows little about the Cult. Some Lunars have encountered the Cult and become concerned about its potential to mislead naïve, young Solars. The Lunars suggest infiltrating the Cult in order to influence its direction and make certain that it serves the Solars (and the Lunars) instead of the other way around.

The Lunars have no idea that the Cult of the Illuminated is a Sidereal front dedicated to finding Solars and, from the Lunar perspective, brainwashing them into ruling according to Sidereal philosophy. Once the Seneschals discover the truth about the Cult, however—and especially the Cult's occasional tendency to capture newly Exalted Lunars and brainwash them as pets—the Seneschals will almost certainly go to war with the Cult in order to determine who shall set the course for the Solars' return to power.

INITIATION

Compared to the other factions, initiation into the Swords of Luna is daringly simple. Go into the Wyld, find something bigger than you are, kill it and bring back its head to any member of the faction. A Lunar who accomplishes that much gets inducted into the faction at the lowest level. Thereafter, advancement depends almost entirely on how well she can fight, either against Wyld creatures or against her fellow Swords in ritual combat.

GOALS OF THE SWORDS OF LUNA

For most Swords of Luna, defending Creation against the Fair Folk trumps all other objectives. This includes the Thousand Streams River—as the Swords put it, you can't create a better world if the Ones Beyond destroy it—and the few Sword experiments in that area involve creating martial societies to wage war against the Fair Folk. The elder Swords still remember the hordes of shapeless Wyld horrors sweeping across the borders of Creation. The Swords' leaders believe the Ones Beyond may try again, once they learn that Creation's geomantic defenses no longer have a wielder. Consequently, the faction's primary goal is to prepare for a second Fair Folk Invasion. To that end, the faction pursues several tactical approaches.

Many faction members also join the Crossroads Society. These battle-sorcerers endlessly research ancient tomes in search of lore pertaining to the reality generators and jade obelisks the Old Realm Solars used to push back the boundaries of Creation and stabilize the Wyld.

The Swords of Luna have also engaged in extended breeding programs. Only the Wardens of Gaia exceed the Swords in the breeding of beastmen and Wyld mutants. But where the Wardens seek to build a perfect society through eugenics, the Swords want only to construct an army of Wyld-resistant shock troops to counterbalance the raksha's hobgoblin hordes.

The Swords aggressively pursue research into the Wyld itself. On occasion, they have obtained Fair Folk artifacts and turned them against their creators. Sometimes the Swords steal these artifacts; sometimes shaped Fair Folk trade them for protection from stronger raksha nobles and less tolerant Lunars.

Faction members who are subtle enough to penetrate into Dragon-Blooded territories search for information on the Realm Defense Grid—specifically about how to locate and activate the remote control stations supposedly dotted around the Threshold. Daring Swords suggest that if the Realm completely falls apart, a strike force of Lunars might reach the Imperial Manse and take control of it themselves… if they know how it works.

After the Seneschals of the Sun Kings, the Swords of Luna is the faction most ready to form alliances with the Solar Exalted. The Swords may have doubts about Solar rule, but one thing is clear—no force in Creation has ever been as effective against the Wyld and the Fair Folk as the First Age Solars.

The Wardens of Gaia

During the First Age, the Wardens of Gaia focused their attention on the natural world that was Gaia's bounty. After the Fair Folk Invasion, the Wardens had to reconsider the relationship between natural life and the unnatural effects of Wyld mutation. Too many of Gaia's creatures had been transformed into mutants just to write them off as abominations to slay. Many of the Lunars themselves bore marks of Wyld mutation due to their failure to repair their caste marks in a timely manner. The Wardens of Gaia usually perform their Thousand Streams River experiments among barbarian tribes who have felt the Wyld's touch, either in the form of Wyld mutations or through the machinations of the Lunars themselves. The Wardens lead the other Stewards in controlled breeding among their beastmen children. Even among fully human tribes, though, the Wardens of Gaia work to build societies based on the hunter-gatherer model, while they undermine agrarian or urban societies.

Initiation

The Wardens of Gaia recruit most of their prospective members from Lunars who came from "barbarian" cultures. A great many Changing Moons of this faction study to become shamans and ambassadors to the spirit courts. Initiation consists of an extensive course in guerilla warfare, spirit lore and Wyld mysticism.

SHAMANISM

Gods exist for everything in Creation, from physical objects to abstract concepts. All of these gods respond to prayer. When a particular religion in Creation is described as "shamanistic," the term specifically refers to a *direct* worship of *local* spirits that bypasses the Celestial and Terrestrial Bureaucracies. The term also invokes the idea of the "shaman," an individual chosen by the gods to speak on their behalf, as opposed to rigid, clerical hierarchies such as the Immaculate Order, which presumes to enforce the will of the Dragon-Blooded on the gods themselves.

Shamanistic cultures don't pay much attention to divine bureaucracies or the great gods who represent concepts such as beauty or justice. Such gods mean little to a barbarian struggling to survive in the wilderness or a farmer worried that a storm may destroy his crops. Rather, shamanistic cultures worship gods *who help* and ignore gods who don't. The people value local gods, particularly local territorial gods. The barbarian doesn't worship a "god of war": He worships the god who personally blesses his axe or spear. The farmer doesn't worship a "god of weather": He worships the god who turns aside a hailstorm.

The shaman, for his part, acts as a diplomat who negotiates with these local spirits. He is a priest (as defined on p. 132 of **Exalted**), but he may well deliver his prayers (and the prayers of his tribe) to the god in person. His value to his tribe depends on what boons he can persuade the local gods to grant the tribe. When a barbarian village suffers three straight droughts despite the local shaman's best efforts, it is most likely time to get a new shaman.

Among the Lunars, shamanism primarily represents a political approach to dealing with the gods of both Yu-Shan and Creation. A Lunar shaman can approach a local god as an equal, if not a superior, and offer the worship of hundreds or even thousands of barbarians in exchange for the god's favor. Because this worship bypasses the Celestial Bureaucracy, the local god gains far more Essence from his worshipers than he otherwise might, since no other gods take a cut of his worship. And because a Celestial Exalt facilitated the arrangement, the local god even gains a measure of protection from a Celestial audit. Everybody wins—except for the Immaculate Order, of course.

The faction has four highly informal levels of membership. A Son or Daughter of Gaia is a new recruit who does not yet know much about the ways of the Wardens and whom an older member fosters. A Brother or Sister has completed the first stages of initiation. Attaining this level of membership requires significant knowledge of Wyld lore, religion, military tactics and combat skills. A Mother or Father has successfully bred one or more beastmen, Wyld mutants or intelligent animals capable of breeding true. A Grandfather or Grandmother has created an entire race of such creatures—an entirely new species loyal to the Warden's needs but able to sustain itself without the Warden's active supervision.

GOALS OF THE WARDENS OF GAIA

The Wardens of Gaia have always favored barbarian cultures, and other societies that live close to nature, over what others would call "civilization." Since the Great Contagion, however, the faction has become somewhat radicalized. The most extremist members of the faction would level every city in Creation if they could and force the entire human population to live as hunter-gatherers. Some of those Lunars may eventually try to achieve that goal: They have formed a loose alliance with Amoth City-Smiter, the God of Ruins and a high-ranking deity in Yu-Shan. Barbarian tribes guided by these Wardens invariably raze the cities they conquer to the ground, leaving behind just enough rubble for Amoth's stature to grow. Ma-Ha-Suchi leads this sub-faction of the Wardens and continually makes elaborate plans to lead his armies across Creation in a swath of destruction. Unfortunately, perhaps, most civilized folk get their ideas about Moonchildren from such radical Wardens of Gaia, who live down to every scare-story told by the Immaculate Order.

The more moderate wing of the Wardens still opposes conventional urban life but is willing to try merging the idea of city-dwelling with veneration of nature. Silver Python and Rain Deathflyer lead this wing of the faction. They receive great respect for their activities with the Haltan Republic, an arboreal society that lives in harmony with the intelligent animals of the Haltan Forest. Even Silver Python and Rain Deathflyer, however, must follow the central tenet of the Wardens of Gaia: "That which is worthy of life shall live." Accordingly, the two plan to withdraw their protection from Halta and see if it can survive on its own.

While few Warden experiments have borne as much fruit as Halta, many do show intriguing potential. Three hundred miles south of Rathess, for instance, a No Moon savant called Blue Kachina seeks to blend the characteristics of humans and army ants to create a collective intelligence in which each individual literally is a part of the entire society.

THE WINDING PATH

The Winding Path is currently the largest of the five factions. This faction pays the most attention to the needs of human beings (instead of sorcery, the Wyld, beastmen or ancient grudges). Since most young Lunars still view themselves as humans given a gift of power, young Lunars find the Winding Path more accessible than the other four groups. Also, the elders of the faction strive to stay abreast of the contemporary mortal society; this appeals to young Lunars who view many elders as relics of the ancient past.

In contrast, Lunars who meet the Winding Path's de facto leader Tamuz are astonished to learn that he predates the Usurpation, for he seems more at home in the modern world than many Lunars who are only a few centuries old.

INITIATION

As one might expect for a faction devoted to misdirection and devil's advocacy, a potential recruit to the Winding Path might not know he's been recruited until after his initiation. The faction doesn't care much about ceremonies: A Steward joins the Winding Path when she agrees with its ideas, works toward its goals and gains the respect of other members.

The Winding Path has a close relationship with the Crossroads Society: The Winding Path's experiments often result in technologically advanced societies that respect the value of scholars and sorcerers. Accordingly, the Crossroads Society frequently gives respected Winding Path Lunars "first pick" of Unblooded, particularly when one Exalts in or around a Threshold city.

The Winding Path welcomes urbanized recruits. These Exalted learn to infiltrate and manipulate urban cultures much more easily than the typical, illiterate barbarian. The vagaries of Exaltation, however, seem to choose Lunars from among barbarian cultures somewhat more readily than from urban cultures. The Winding Path does not hesitate to recruit from barbarian-born Lunars when one demonstrates intelligence and discretion. Regardless of the Lunar's social background, the Winding Path looks for subtlety and cunning, and those traits can appear in mortals from any culture.

When a Winding Path member targets a young Lunar for recruitment, the recruiter typically sends the young Lunar on a series of missions designed to challenge his skills at infiltration, misdirection and manipulation. If the recruit comes from an uneducated background (very common, even for urbanized Lunars), the recruiter makes continued aid and support conditional on the novice Lunar's willingness to overcome these deficiencies. While the masterminds of the Winding Path make use of any young Lunars in their schemes, the elders do not reveal the full scope of their activities to those who cannot at least read, write and function in civilized society. Conversely, when a Lunar comes from a more civilized background, Winding Path mentors demand that the potential recruit learn to operate among barbarian raiders, simple farmers and other "uncivilized" folk—and to like them.

Lunars at the lowest level of Winding Path initiation are referred to as "agents," and an agent typically spends years or even decades working for a Winding Path elder. Many elders of this faction show an almost insane paranoia about the reach of Sidereal astrology, and some refuse to leave their havens in the Wyld. Instead, they send young Lunar agents as their proxies to achieve some objective—to assassinate a particular mortal leader, to arrange the marriage between two feuding houses, to fake a "miracle" for a religious cult under the elder's sway. The agent is never told outright what

long-term goal each mission is supposed to advance. This is actually the true Winding Path initiation.

True membership (in terms of actually knowing what is going on) only goes to Lunars who can figure the truth out for themselves. When the agent can confront her mentor with the true reason for the missions she has performed, only then does the mentor acknowledge her as wise enough to join the Winding Path. At that point, the new initiate often transfers to another Winding Path for specialized training in covert action, astrology evasion and politics. The faction tries to match initiates with senior members who hold similar views on the Thousand Streams River. Once the initiate masters whatever her mentor decides to teach, she can leave if she wants to begin her own experiment in society-building. Many do not, however. Often, the long years of apprenticeship win the apprentice over completely to her mentor's vision. Rather than leave to pursue her own experiments, she continues to assist with the mentor's. No stigma is attached to either decision.

GOALS OF THE WINDING PATH

The Winding Path is obsessed with the Thousand Streams River to the exclusion of all other agendas. As the faction that first proposed the project, the Winding Path assumes responsibility for overseeing the project as a whole—sometimes to the point of conflict with other Lunars whose experiments diverge too far from Winding Path ideals. In particular, a few of the more aggressive Winding Path Lunars discreetly sabotage experimental societies where Lunar patrons rule openly as god-kings. Winding Path Lunars also wreck societies that rely too heavily on Wyld mutations at the expense of purebred mortals. Certainly, a Lunar could easily forge a functional society according to her desires within the Wyld, but doing so is a meaningless exercise if the benefits of that society cannot be replicated among normal humans. Such sabotage is usually undertaken by an individual elder with particularly strong viewpoints on the Thousand Streams River and an equally strong conviction that the society he attacks is an affront to it.

Members of the Winding Path usually reject the rustic approach of the Wardens of Gaia. Instead, most Winding Path Stewards favor moving barbarians from a nomadic existence to a more structured, urbanized society while keeping certain barbarian values. Most members of the Winding Path regard venerable Tamuz as their leader because of his success at maneuvering the Delzahn horde's noble class into ruling Chiaroscuro while keeping the bulk of the Delzahn as pastoral nomads.

THE SILVER FACTION

For all the successes of the Winding Path, the faction has one secret whose exposure could make its members pariahs among the Silver Pact. Several centuries ago, three Sidereal Exalted approached leading members of the Winding Path under a flag of truce. These Sidereals presented evidence of

how they had discovered some of the less subtle facets of the Thousand Streams River—and then concealed them from their fellow Chosen of the Maidens.

These Sidereals, who called themselves the "Silver Faction," claimed that they regretted their role in the Usurpation. More importantly, they claimed to agree philosophically with the goals of the Silver Pact in forming a new model for society that does not require Exalted god-kings in order to function. The Silver Faction and the Winding Path elders tentatively agreed to share information and to cooperate. While the Winding Path elders who know about the Silver Faction still do not entirely trust it, the benefits of expanded connections within Yu-Shan made the alliance worth the risk.

Thus far, the Silver Faction has helped run interference for Lunars whose activities might otherwise draw down the Wyld Hunt. The Silver Faction Sidereals have also smuggled several Lunars into Yu-Shan, allowing them access to several high-ranking gods, including Amoth City-Smiter and other influential gods at the Bureau of Nature. The Sidereals have even smuggled a few Unblooded off the Blessed Isle, though the Silver Faction made it clear that these were extraordinary cases: It has neither the resources to perform such rescue operations very often nor the political capital to survive exposure if the other Sidereals discovered the Silver Faction's activities.

According to the Silver Faction members, Sidereal society as a whole is virtually dominated by an authoritarian "Bronze Faction" that has secretly controlled the Scarlet Empire for centuries. The Bronze Faction includes the very same Sidereals who orchestrated the Usurpation. In one of the more recent meetings between the Winding Path and the Silver Faction, an impulsive young Full Moon committed a major faux pas by offering to assassinate members of the Bronze Faction. The Silver Faction delegates were horrified by the very suggestion of murdering their fellow Sidereals… for the most part. After the meeting ended, one of the Sidereal delegates was observed talking privately with the very same Full Moon who had made the suggestion.

OTHERS

The combined factions comprise just over half of the Silver Pact. The remaining Lunars belong to the Silver Pact because they all possess moonsilver tattoos, they all revere Luna and Gaia and they accept some obligation of stewardship, even if it is stewardship of something as small as a single Nexus neighborhood (as in the case of Seven Devils Clever). They all agree on the need to rescue newly Exalted Lunars and to slay chimerae wherever necessary. Beyond those core beliefs, however, unaligned Lunars each pursue their own paths through Exaltation. Most of these unaligned Lunars have some affinity for one or more of the existing factions but refuse to be drawn into faction politics. Furthermore, many of them are quite young—more than a third of all Lunars are less than a century old, and only a handful have lived more than a millennium. Many of the younger Lunars maintain social contacts from before their Exaltations. They value their connections to their former lives too much to care about the Silver Pact's grand schemes for the whole of Creation.

THE PACK

For Lunars, the "pack" structure is a relatively new phenomenon. Unlike Solars, who naturally gravitated toward "perfect circles" with one member of each caste, the First Age Lunars never felt any particular compulsion to form small social groups. Any alliances among small groups of Lunars happened for short periods to achieve specific goals. (Of course, the Lunar mates of Solar circle members could hardly avoid frequent contact and working together. The Lunars merely did not consider themselves part of a distinct, long-term group.) Most likely, this disdain for long-term alliances was a natural result of Lunar Exaltation. Luna selected champions who prized individuality and personal strength, and a wolf pack in which every member considered himself an alpha was hardly an efficient social unit.

The idea of pack relationships did not become commonplace in the Silver Pact until after the Great Gathering. By that time, most Lunars were quite young (relatively speaking), while most real power in Lunar society lay with the elders, each of whom was more than a match for even a handful of young Lunars. Despite the elders' personal power, however, they were too few to handle all the business of the Silver Pact. The survivors of the Contagion and Invasion began encouraging young, inexperienced Lunars to form small, short-term packs to achieve various objectives. Most packs were and are brief alliances, but some of them become so successful that their members stay together, the benefits of pack membership outweighing the Lunar instinct for individuality.

Unlike Solar circles, in which each Exalt typically has a set role within the group based on her caste, the members of Lunar packs contribute in whatever way seems best to them. In the most successful packs, the leader is whichever member shows the best leadership qualities *for achieving the goals of the pack*. Since packs can pursue many different goals, Stewards of any caste can lead packs. Many packs have martial goals, and so, the members follow the Lunar who has the best tactical instincts, at least in combat situations. On the other hand, a pack sent on a reconnaissance mission might defer to its most cunning Changing Moon. A pack sent to retrieve an Unblooded Lunar might follow whichever member knows the most about that territory. Indeed, a pack might rotate its leadership among whichever Moonchild possesses the greatest skills for each particular mission. In time, though, many packs settle on the member who most consistently demonstrates leadership qualities and good judgment in all areas as their permanent leader, with the pack member she trusts the most serving as her lieutenant.

While perfect circles have five members by definition, packs can be of any size. They usually have between three and eight members, depending on the pack's needs. Larger packs have more warriors for fighting but must also spread the glory of the pack's successes more thinly. While most packs have a relatively even distribution of castes, some specialized packs do not. In particular, the Crossroads Society sponsors several exploration packs that recover lost First Age artifacts and mystical lore; and their members are mostly No Moons. Also, a Lunar can join multiple packs, at least for a short time. For example, a No Moon sorcerer who belongs to an exploratory pack might provide sorcerous muscle for another pack sent to retrieve an Unblooded, or a Changing Moon who has experience in dealing with a Fair Folk court might be asked to assist a reconnaissance pack scouting that area. In general, however, if a Lunar devotes himself to a pack, he does so only to one pack at a time.

Some particularly successful packs, invariably one in which the members have become very close friends, decide to strengthen their alliance and form a sworn brotherhood. Doing so requires the pack to find a Lunar sorcerer who can perform the Terrestrial Circle Spell Sworn Brothers' Oath (see **The Manual of Exalted Power—The Dragon-Blooded**, pp. 122-123). This spell supernaturally augments the packs' existing sense of internal loyalty. Sworn brotherhoods are most common among packs associated with the Swords of Gaia who have fought together for years and who forge their bonds in blood.

Packs usually form among young Lunars, and there are no records or stories of any packs operating before the Great Contagion. Indeed, the elders Silver Python and Rain Deathflyer are considered eccentric because the two of them work so closely together without coming into conflict.

COMBAT PACKS

Combat packs are groups of Lunars formed to complete some military objective. The Swords of Luna often form combat packs to attack Fair Folk targets in the Wyld, while elder Seneschals of the Sun Kings often sponsor combat packs to sabotage and assassinate Dragon-Blooded throughout the Threshold. One elder in the West retains the services of an aquatic combat pack to harry the fleet of the Deathlord called the Silver Prince. Combat packs frequently continue to work together after they dispatch the enemy they were called together to fight: military service, even ad hoc military service such as a combat pack, tends to form a powerful bond among those who serve together. A number of combat packs are famous among the Silver Pact for their internal loyalty as

well as their body count. Combat packs primarily consist of Full Moons and Changing Moons. No Moons who belong to combat packs typically specialize in combat sorcery, as well as esoteric combat skills such as warstrider maintenance.

CONQUEST PACKS

While a combat pack exists to fight some enemy as part of a military objective, a conquest pack fights for glory and plunder—to conquer, but not to rule. Conquest packs move around from target to target, and they may raise barbarian armies to sack the cities of Creation. This type of pack usually consists of novice Lunars who Exalted in particularly rough barbarian societies and who view the benefits of Exaltation as tools for killing enemies and taking their stuff, rather than for building some type of utopia. In many ways, conquest packs represent the stereotype of Lunar war packs, particularly among the Dragon-Blooded, who typically assume that all Lunars are rampaging barbarians. Ma-Ha-Suchi sponsors several conquest packs. One such, the quartet of Lunars who lead the mercenary company called the Claw-Strider Battalion, has sacked more than a dozen villages and towns throughout the Republic of Chaya.

EXPERIMENTAL PACKS

An experimental pack consists of young Lunars who wish to participate in the Thousand Streams River but who lack the personal skill and experience to start a social experiment on their own. Instead, a group of Lunars who share a common philosophy join forces, allowing them to manipulate and control a much larger area than each could manage individually. Not many experimental packs have formed; most Lunars find it too difficult to agree on the subtleties of the Thousand Streams River ever to share power over an experiment. The most prominent experimental pack in Creation is the Thousand Fangs, which consists of seven Lunars under the leadership of a 300-year-old Full Moon called Red Sky Hyena. Twenty years ago, the Thousand Fangs conquered the Erzani Wyld mutants (see p. 30) and forged them into a military dictatorship. Today, the Thousand Fangs Total Control Zone is still under the pack's control, but the Lunars struggle with constant uprisings among the Erzani resistance.

RECONNAISSANCE PACKS

Reconnaissance packs, also called scout packs, are small Lunar groups whose members specialize in stealth and observation. The Silver Pact frequently forms such packs to investigate potential threats. In recent years, Lunar elders sent several reconnaissance packs to investigate the plans of the Mask of Winters. None of those packs could stay in Thorns very long, though the lone spy Anja Silverclaws successfully penetrated the Deathlord's security several months ago. By succeeding where these packs failed, she shamed several Lunars of greater experience and may well have made some enemies. Another prominent reconnaissance pack is the trio known as the Raiton Brotherhood, which offered its services

to the Bull of the North as part of his campaign. Secretly, the Raiton Brotherhood also spies on the Bull on behalf of an alliance of Sun King Seneschals who ponder the best way to approach the Bull and guide him to greatness.

RETRIEVAL PACKS

These packs set forth to retrieve Unblooded Lunars and convey them to the Wyld for tattooing. Retrieval packs are typically short-term alliances whose members care more about the rewards than in establishing new friendships, although some packs have been so successful that they remained together. The leader of a retrieval pack is entitled to a blood-oath from any Unblooded the pack successfully rescues, but all the members of the pack receive boons from the elder who called on the pack. Any Lunars can and do join retrieval packs, but they usually include at least one No Moon who knows the Form-Fixing Method.

WYLD PACKS

These packs perform one of the saddest—and most frightening—duties known to Luna's Chosen: hunting and killing chimerae. Retrieval packs may become Wyld Packs if a Casteless Lunar has fallen to that state before the packs can find her. Other Wyld Packs set out to kill Lunars who became chimerae long ago.

LUMINARIES FROM THE FIRST AGE

Fifteen centuries have passed since the Usurpation, a long stretch of time even for the Lunar Exalted. Whether through the Usurpation, the Great Contagion, the Fair Folk Invasion or simply the relentless march of time, the number of Stewards born in the First Age has dropped to roughly a dozen. Some of these ancient worthies remain in the Deep Wyld, where they manipulate events in Creation through proxies. Others move among Creation like ghosts, obscured by powerful Charms and Wyld magic beyond the ken of their younger compatriots. Listed below are a few elders who dwell more openly in Creation and who are perhaps most likely to make the acquaintance of an Exalted hero, for good or ill.

LEVIATHAN

Several hundred miles west of Abalone and several thousand feet straight down lives a beast of terrifying might. Ancient Leviathan, who wears the form of a killer whale magnified into the size of a behemoth, is one of the oldest beings in Creation. He is also one of Creation's largest predators and certainly one of its most dangerous. In the Old Realm, Leviathan was a Full Moon military officer who rose to the rank of admiral, one of the few non-Solars to do so. His stewardship covered the entire Western Ocean; its waters were one of only three things he ever loved. The second was the Eclipse Caste Admiral Kendak Arkadi, the supreme commander of the Solar Navy, who was Leviathan's Solar mate and boon companion for centuries. The third, unfortunately, was Arkadi's wife

Amyana, Queen of Luthe and the Zenith Caste regional governor for the Western Archipelago.

Leviathan's decades-long illicit affair with Amyana tore at the great Lunar, as his passion for the Zenith Caste queen conflicted with his supernaturally imposed loyalty to Arkadi. This conflict came to a head during the Usurpation, when Leviathan received nearly simultaneous calls for help from both Amyana and Arkadi… and chose to answer Amyana's. Leviathan was too late to save either his friend or his lover from Dragon-Blooded mutineers, but to this day, his choice gnaws at him. Before dying, Amyana deliberately sank the floating city of Luthe to the ocean's floor to keep it out of Dragon-Blooded hands. To avenge both Amyana and Arkadi, Leviathan activated a self-destruct protocol that sank most of the ships in his own fleet, crippling the usurpers' ability to patrol the seas. Then, Leviathan turned his attention to the few Dragon-Blooded survivors of Luthe's fall, devouring them whole in his cetacean form.

Today, the Admiral waits beneath the Western Ocean, near the city that has obsessed him for untold centuries. Even his closest disciples do not know what he hopes to accomplish there. If, occasionally, lights from sunken Luthe blink on and off in response to the glow of his tattoos, no one but Leviathan knows what they represent. The Great Whale communicates with the Silver Pact only through younger surrogates. Indeed, Leviathan has not walked on dry land since the Usurpation and has not taken on any form save that of a gigantic orca since before the Contagion. Despite his seclusion, he fully supports the Thousand Streams River, having personally introduced tribes of whalemen and pelagothropes into Creation.

In the First Age, Leviathan was a prominent Sun King Seneschal. In the modern era, that faction still considers him a de facto leader, if only for his cold and implacable hatred for all Dragon-Blooded. Despite this, Leviathan rarely takes any authoritative role in the faction, although he regularly summons the aquatic Lunars of the West to discuss developing issues and he readily teaches his disciples what he knows of the First Age. Of Luthe, however, he says only that, the last time he walked on two legs, he entered the fallen city and left his moonsilver trident, Islebreaker, sitting on an empty throne. Exactly whom Leviathan reserves that throne for is a secret he keeps to himself.

LILITH

It is a testament to the versatility of Lunar Exaltation that a Waning Moon, whose caste was associated with stealth and misdirection, became one of the deadliest hand-to-hand combatants Creation has ever seen. Lilith is a peerless spy and infiltrator as befits a Changing Moon, but she also remains one of Creation's greatest non-Sidereal martial artists. Lunars who hear her tale are surprised, then, that this deadly combatant meekly accepted abuse and near-torture at the hands of her own husband. When they met, Desus of the Eclipse Caste was a witty gallant who matched her trick for

trick. Centuries later, he became a crazed sadist armed with mind-bending Charms.

In the First Age, Lilith supported the Sun King Seneschals. Her fellow travelers in that faction saw her loyalty to her mate as merely an acceptance of the natural order of things. If any Seneschals ever noticed that Lilith bore more wounds from "relaxing" with her mate than she ever did after battles, no one ever found it socially proper to mention it. And so, Lilith suffered for centuries, cursed with undeniable passion and implacable hatred for the same man. When the Usurpation came and Lilith saw her mate die before her eyes, her response was an earthshaking howl that somehow combined unutterable grief and indescribable joy. Then, she fled into the Wyld and gave herself to the beast within her, becoming an animal in mind as well as body.

Only the merest luck saved Lilith from becoming a chimera. Old allies among the No Moons, loathe to put down such a peerless warrior, captured her and worked to restore her mind, even as they forced the tattoos upon her. No trials were necessary for Lilith, whose renown was already legendary. When they finished their work, the No Moons released Lilith to her fate. She fled further into the Wyld, sparing a look to her saviors that could have been either gratitude or contempt.

In the centuries since, Lilith moved into and out of Creation at her whim. Her skills at stealth remain unsurpassed; no Wyld Hunt ever interfered with her passage through Creation. Unfortunately, her forays did no good for other Lunars. Only with the return of the Solars has Lilith snapped from her centuries-long reverie. Rumors spread among the Lunars of the Northeast—Lilith is on the move, the Owl Woman has met the Mammoth Avatar, Golden-Eyed Jorst was torn asunder by a moonsilver-clad warrior of ancient power.

Thus far, Lilith has not deigned to meet her fellow Lunars, least of all any members of the Sun King Seneschals. While the Seneschals themselves still claim her as a member (if only to exploit her legendary reputation), the leaders of this faction wonder exactly what Lilith shall do about the returning Solars. For yet another rumor says that Lilith spent months pursuing the heir to her former mate's Exaltation, and none can say what will happen when she finds him. Not even Lilith herself.

MA-HA-SUCHI

Ma-Ha-Suchi came as close as any Lunar ever has to becoming a chimera without actually falling into that debased state. In the First Age, Ma-Ha-Suchi was a diplomat of the Waxing Moon Caste and also a proud man whose striking good looks almost justified his vanity. This legendary womanizer (although he did not limit his affections to women) was dubbed "the Wolf with the Red Roses." Neither Ma-Ha-Suchi's elegant, lupine form nor his suave disposition survived the exile into the Wyld. Ma-Ha-Suchi was among the first affected by the breaking of the castes and afflicted by a host of Wyld mutations and mental aberrations, the most

prominent of which was the permanent adoption of cloven hooves and goat horns in all of his true forms.

Today, the ancient Lunar is consumed with self-loathing for his grotesque appearance. He projects his hatred on the rest of Creation. As a particularly obsessed Warden of Gaia, Ma-Ha-Suchi takes inordinate pleasure in his elaborate breeding experiments. He lives surrounded by an army of beastmen who also blend wolf and goat traits. In the recesses of his fevered mind, Ma-Ha-Suchi considers whether his children might someday become a viable replacement for all of humanity. They are so much prettier, after all.

Ma-Ha-Suchi also feels an obsessive hatred for the Dragon-Blooded, whom he blames for his forced exile into the Wyld. He takes almost any chance to combat the Terrestrial armies and inflicts grotesque tortures upon capture Dragon-Blooded. Not all of Ma-Ha-Suchi's breeding activities have the goal of producing beastmen, after all. Worst of all, his hatred for Dragon-Blooded is becoming a hatred of all humanity. He regularly directs his beastmen army, among the largest beastman populations in Creation, to cull nearby human settlements. To his thinking, if such settlements cannot defend themselves, they are not fit to survive and deserve extermination.

His actions have not gone unnoticed. Already, a Solar hero confronted Ma-Ha-Suchi and tried to reason with him. The Lunar easily defeated the neophyte hero and sent him away, beaten and humiliated. Word of this reached nearby Lunars, who have become concerned about the elder's activities. No Lunar benefits from outright conflict between the returning Solars and the Silver Pact. Winding Path Lunars sometimes wonder whether Ma-Ha-Suchi seeks to build a society of beastmen or simply a rampaging army of nihilistic destruction. More importantly, some Lunars now wonder whether Ma-Ha-Suchi was really saved from becoming a chimera after all or whether they have merely allowed a Wyld-tainted monster free reign in their councils.

RAIN DEATHFLYER AND SILVER PYTHON

Somewhat unusually for Lunars and virtually unheard of for elders of any age, Rain Deathflyer and Silver Python are partners in the Thousand Streams River. Rain Deathflyer, a mighty hawk-aspected warrior, has the distinction of being the "youngest" elder who dates back to the Old Realm. He Exalted at barely 20 years old after his predecessor was slain during the Usurpation. Just a few months later, he entered the Wyld in the company of Silver Python, the Serpent Queen, an experienced Lunar some 200 years his senior who rescued him from the nascent Wyld Hunt and taught him the ways of the Silver Pact.

Over the centuries of exile, the student-mentor relationship evolved into a close friendship interspersed with occasional sexual dalliances. Silver Python changes gender every 20 years as a way to commune with the Fickle Lady, and Rain Deathflyer has made love to the Serpent Queen in her female form. However, he remains stubbornly squeamish about homosexuality (despite having engaged in bestiality) and has never responded to Silver Python's advances while she wore a male form, a quirk she finds endlessly amusing. For her part, the Serpent Queen claims she cannot remember whether she was born female or male, and Rain Deathflyer insists on viewing her as female regardless of the form she wears. Regardless of their unusual relationship, the pair acts like an old married couple. They often complete each other's sentences.

Centuries ago, the two attended the Great Gathering together. They became among the first Lunars to experiment with society-building. Today, many Lunars see the Republic of Halta as a model of how a Thousand Streams River experiment should be conducted. Surprisingly, considering the urbanized culture they fashioned, neither of the two No Moons belongs to the Winding Path. Rather, they are Wardens of Gaia who strove to create a nation in which humans recognize the importance of nature's bounty in all things. For the most part, they succeeded. But the two Lunars are also considered quite moderate for Wardens, and both of them have great respect for the ideals of the Winding Path. Accordingly, they have no problem with the Haltan Republic becoming far more "civilized" than any other Warden experiment. As with all Warden experiments, Halta will either survive or die, settling the question of its viability one way or the other. That said, Rain Deathflyer is the more emotional and humane of the two, and he has a much stronger attachment to Halta than Silver Python, who has grown increasingly detached and capricious over the centuries. If Halta does fall, it may well drive a wedge between the two despite everything they have accomplished together.

Although both Rain Deathflyer and Silver Python are No Moons, neither interacts much with the Crossroads Society, and both have only minimal skill at sorcery. However, both Lunars are geniuses at biology and sociology. Each has bred a stable beastman line whose members are far more intelligent and civilized than most extant beastman species. Also, each has successfully bred dozens of intelligent animal species and introduced them to Creation.

RAKSI, QUEEN OF FANGS

The Child Raksi, as she was once known, bore a singular distinction in the Old Realm: At the age of 13, Raksi became the youngest person ever to Exalt as a Lunar. Despite her youth, Raksi was a prodigy among the No Moons. By her 16th year, she had already learned Celestial sorcery. Unfortunately, the Usurpation began a few months later.

The journey into the Wyld exposed the Child Raksi to horrors. The Wyld has a way of showing things that no one, least of all a rather naïve young sorceress, should be made to see. Raksi endured for centuries, struggling to ignore the voices that whispered unendurable truths in her head, the

music that the Wyld sang with color and smell instead of sound, the shapeless lovers who came to Raksi in the night to tempt her with impossible pleasures. Then, one day, her caste broke, and so did her mind.

Raksi's Wyld flaws are not so immediately noticeable as Ma-Ha-Suchi's. Oh, she does have fingers that bend backwards when she doesn't pay attention. And, of course, her human true form still has the body of a nubile, 16-year-old girl who will never flower into full womanhood. It's her more subtle flaws that most Lunars pretend to ignore: her preference for the succulent taste of human flesh, the joy she takes from breeding apemen to worship her as a goddess, her burning hatred for anything she finds beautiful.

Despite her madness, or possibly because of it, Raksi became one of the preeminent sorcerers of the Silver Pact. She helped fashion the first tattoos, and she remains the foremost Lunar sorcerer in Creation. When the Fair Folk Invasion ended and the Lunars reentered Creation, Raksi did not hesitate on her course of action. The few inhabitants of Sperimin, decimated by Contagion and Invasion alike, were no match for the hordes of apemen who descended on the city led by a gigantic she-ape clad in moonsilver armor with talons of brass. Sperimin fell within hours. Seven centuries later, Raksi still rules its ruins. Her beastmen, far more ape than human, continue to breed amongst themselves but have no purpose save to protect the city and worship its queen. Today, Raksi, the Queen of Fangs, has rechristened Sperimin as Mahalanka, "the City of a Thousand Golden Delights," although those delights are for Raksi alone.

Raksi knows about the Silver Pact and the Thousand Streams River, but she does not concern herself with them. Her initiation into Celestial sorcery left Raksi with one overriding purpose in life—to master the arts of Solar Circle Sorcery. To her, nothing else matters; her studies of The Book of Three Circles consume her attention. She believes that some day she can find a way to cast Solar spells. Utterly mad, she meditates on the duality of her Lunar existence, maintaining the form of a perfect, innocent princess while engaging in the most vulgar and rapacious deeds. She enjoys torturing male captives while wearing the shape of the captive's mother. When the victim begs for death, she laughs even harder.

The Crossroads Society considers Raksi a de facto member. While she cares nothing for its politics, she often invites young Lunar sorcerers to her domain to study… if they have the stomach for it. Raksi lords her magical acumen over would-be apprentices, and she lets no one read from the fabled Book of Three Circles unless she considers the reader as inhuman as herself. During her exile, the Wyld had much to show Raksi, and she, in turn, has so much to share with her fellow Lunars.

TAMUZ

During the First Age, Tamuz was a military commander of the Half Moon Caste, as well as mate and husband to a powerful Twilight Queen named Chiara who ruled over vast

Southern territories. Tamuz had a natural sense of duty and obligation to his mate, but it was not a loving relationship. The arrogant, manipulative and petty Chiara forced Tamuz to give up his military career to help her govern a domain too large for the feckless queen to rule by herself. Tamuz, a Winding Path philosopher, often disagreed vehemently with Chiara on her authoritarian rule. The Lunar also, as he delicately put it, "did not care for the company of women." Ironically, considering the friction between the two mates, Chiara most likely saved Tamuz's life by forbidding him to accompany her to Meru for the great feast when the Usurpation began. When Tamuz learned of his mate's death, he felt relief as much as anything else. He left for the Wyld immediately, stopping only to rendezvous with his mentor and secret lover, Ingosh Silverclaws.

Tamuz was more fortunate than most Lunars in that, after the breaking of the castes, he never suffered from any effects of chimerism. He helped Ingosh organize the Great Gathering and devise the Silver Way. For his own part in the Thousand Streams River, Tamuz chose the Delzahn Horde, a large nation of nomads that roamed the deserts south of Chiaroscuro.

Today, Tamuz moves like a shadow among the Delzahn tribes, whispering a word here, a suggestion there, an encouragement to Delzahn fitness to rule all around. The most prestigious member of the Winding Path has spent centuries building the Delzahn Empire into a working society. Although he is remarkably clearheaded for a Lunar of his age, Tamuz has several blind spots in his views of the Delzahn. He ignores the overtly misogynist nature of Delzahn sexual relations, an indirect reflection of Tamuz's negative feelings about his former wife and about women in general.

The Delzahn experiment is perhaps the only Thousand Streams River experiment to function as a Realm tributary, a situation Tamuz deliberately created so his experiment could flourish under the very noses of the enemy. After centuries of careful waiting, however, events may soon force Tamuz to take a more direct approach than he would prefer. True, the Empress is gone, and within a few centuries, the Delzahns might expel the Dragon-Blooded entirely, but Tamuz fears to wait much longer. Specifically, he fears the coming of a Solar Exalt bearing Chiara's Exaltation, driven by destiny to seek out and conquer her former domain—and destroy all of Tamuz's work.

Affairs of the heart increasingly distract Tamuz. He recently learned that Ingosh Silverclaws' Exaltation has reincarnated as a young woman who calls herself Anja Silverclaws. Anja dwells far to the east near the city of Thorns, where she spies on the Mask of Winters and relays what she learns to her allies among the Marukani. At times, Tamuz wonders if he has any obligation, out of respect for old Ingosh, to assist Anja or even to deter her from such dangerous pursuits. What Tamuz does not acknowledge, even to himself, is that he also wonders whether he could love Silverclaws the woman as much as Silverclaws the man.

CHAPTER TWO
A BETTER WORLD

When they saw the post-Usurpation, Contagion-shattered remains of Creation, gnawed by the invading Wyld and reeling from the loss of so much First Age technology that had supported it, the Stewards agreed they should do something. Those few Lunars who survived all the catastrophes were Exalted of great age and power. They had the strength to drive an entire people to change and the cunning to shape them to suit their wishes. And this, ultimately, was what the Lunars decided that they would do.

Without their god-king rulers, the great kingdoms of the First Age had proven unable to support themselves. When famine, disease, war and the Wyld hit them, they collapsed. If Creation was to rebuild itself, it needed functioning societies and nations. A tree with diseased roots must fall. Similarly, a political system or nation whose foundations were corrupt or weak would fail at the time of trial. Humanity could no longer rely on the matchless power of the Solar Exalted, the foresight of the treacherous Sidereals, the numbers of the Dragon-Blooded

or even—most galling of all—the valor and care of the Lunars themselves. The new nations would have to stand by themselves, and remain healthy.

This time, the Lunars would create something *better*. They called it the Thousand Streams River, in hopes that all the different nations the Lunars planned to grow would all contribute to Creation, mingling their strengths and each providing different gifts to a renewed world.

The natural spread of opinions as to what was actually "best" for a society was countered by the sheer immensity of Creation and the lack of experienced Lunars. Creation still held more than enough territory for the Stewards to spread out and choose an area of their own. Just as shepherds of their flocks, or gardeners weeding their plots, the Stewards could pick nations on the borders of Creation and choose a future path for their chosen people. Subtly or obviously, gently or lethally, the Lunars could direct a nation into prosperity and into whatever traits they thought might encourage survival and growth. And if the nation failed,

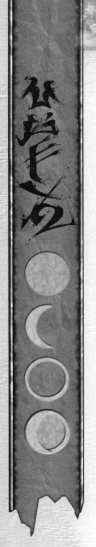

or if their ideas proved unworkable—well, time to tear it down and start again.

The logical place for these activities lay toward the edge of Creation. The Scarlet Empire could not enforce its will so far from the Blessed Isle. Lack of Dragon-Blooded rule permitted social change within a few mortal generations. The Lunars could easily see if a new concept worked or not: Did a nation function well, or did the seeds of decay or internal disruption already germinate? They could decide whether to continue a promising line of work, or discard it on the spot rather than waste further time with it.

Dozens of unnumbered nations and tribes have flourished briefly under the Lunars' tutelage and guidance, and then vanished. Some have prospered and grown to become thriving nations, such as Halta or the Haslanti League. A few grew briefly to become nightmares, corrupted by the Wyld or other influences, and were stamped out by the Lunars themselves. Few now remember the brief kingdom of the Keredar, with their slaves and their dueling, or the lands of the Trasti, overtaken by Wyld corruption and madness, or the tribes of Larros, drowned by the mountain lakes and by their own lusts and weakness.

The Lunars still argue how they should judge their pet projects: which are most effective, and which deserve to survive? An ancient Lunar Exalt has a very different perspective from a mortal human. Tribes and societies flourish today that think they are doing well and will exist for centuries yet, but which their Lunar patrons already mark for culling and removal. But also, whatever thrives deserves to thrive, by nature's own judgment. A Lunar may ignore morals and customs in favor of raw strength, and seek only to understand why the society succeeded. Time, and the Lunar Exalted, will have the final word.

MOLDING SOCIETIES

Luna's Chosen have a number of ways to affect mortal beliefs and change societies. These range from the blatant ("Do as I command or die horribly") to the subtle ("See how we prosper with this new custom"). They include the theological ("The gods have spoken!"), the physical ("The floods have destroyed the new town") and that old cliché of reward and punishment—the carrot and the stick.

Sometimes, Lunars take care to avoid obvious interference, choosing to conceal themselves and work from behind the scenes. They may want to evade the notice of other Exalted. The Lunar in question may feel that her people may learn obedience to herself, rather than whatever lesson the Lunar wants to impart. At other times, Stewards adopt the roles of god, heroes or even their true identities as Exalted of Luna, stepping forward to tell the people what they should do and how they should do it.

The Haltan Republic offers an example of subtle manipulation. By now, most Lunar Exalted know that the elders Rain Deathflyer and Silver Python live in Halta and guide its growth, with the Haltans themselves unaware

of the Lunars' presence. The famous pair move subtly, adjusting public opinion and issuing their suggestions via allied deities, or using junior Lunars as pawns. On the negative side, the elders must be careful about what can be traced back to them (even by other Lunars), and they are restricted in their public actions. On the positive side, Halta develops under the impression that its achievements are all its own, which gives the people a great feeling of independence and vigor.

The Haslanti League, on the other hand, gives an example of obvious manipulation. Here, the Lunar Arvida openly took the Haslan tribes under her guidance and gave them laws and inspiration. Later on, after her death, the Lunar Gerd Marrow-Eater led them in battle against the occupying forces of the Guild and handed down a system of government before vanishing from human sight. This overt manipulation can attract the attention of other Exalted, or can backfire if the people see themselves as somehow rebelling against an evil oppressor or a false deity. The Lunar Ten Stripes has encountered just such a backlash in her disastrous experiment on the island of Simenare.

MANIPULATIONS

Here are some of the methods that Lunars use to direct the evolution of a society or a nation. Some manipulations are general and can be used to direct a course of action. Others act to reward desired behavior (the carrot) or inhibit undesired behavior (the stick). Lunars prefer to use a combination of all three. A minor problem associated with using rewards, of course, is that they carry the threat of dependency on the Lunar—whether the people know it or not—which defeats the purpose of the Thousand Streams River

DISCOVERY

Someone discovers a treasure trove from the First Age that contains useful items, scrolls of knowledge, ancient laws or similar things that can shape a nascent society or provide assistance to a growing one. For instance, a tribe that's just settled down to practice agriculture might find an ancient guide to crop rotation and farm management. This allows a Lunar to push his society one "technological" step forward, while allowing the people to think that they have made the discovery and chose to exploit it themselves. Arranging a discovery often works better than simply handing new techniques and items over to members of the group, since the people get the added benefit of feeling that they achieved any triumphs themselves. Actually putting this into action requires finding or forging the appropriate materials, tools, documents or whatever the people are supposed discover, then setting the scene and allowing members of the group to stumble across it in a natural-seeming way.

Example: When the Haslanti League began exploring the Great Ice, a group of Haslans entered the tombs of ancient chieftains. (Some explorers claimed that the Haslans received guidance from their shamans' dreams.) They found examples of First Age iceships with steel outriggers and the plans for air boats. This allowed them to build their own iceships to take advantage of the Great Ice, and later to build air boats and form the Haslanti Wind Fleet. Members of the Twisted Stone Conclave arranged the discovery by planting the artifacts; they also persuaded several totem-spirits to provide guiding dreams for the shamans in case the explorers failed to find the tombs.

Problems: Sometimes, in spite of all the care that the Lunar takes to provide useful items or information, the humans refuse to use it. They may reject the discovery on religious grounds, on superstitious grounds or just simply because the people don't trust it. An isolated discoverer or discoverers may also try to make off with the find and sell it to the Guild or a scavenger lord for personal gain. Finally, the group's infrastructure may simply not support widespread reproduction of these items, if the people lack sufficient resources or labor. A Lunar must make sure her chosen people can *use* a discovery.

DIVINE INTERVENTION: THE DIRECT APPROACH

The Lunar presents himself as a god and demands that the people bow down and obey him. Once they are suitably cowed, he provides them with new commandments and guides them in the proper paths.

Example: The Lunar Exalt Arvida presented herself to the Haslans as an actual deity and commanded them to remain in harmony with the wilderness and to avoid building cities and towns.

Problems: A people who already have strong faith in one or several deities may not wish to embrace a new deity, particularly one that demands extreme changes to their way of life. Likewise, the deities themselves may object to a Lunar claiming equal rank with them, demanding worship or taking their own believers in a new direction.

DIVINE INTERVENTION: THE INDIRECT APPROACH

The Lunar persuades the gods of the people in question to provide new commandments to the people, guide them in new paths, order them to obey a new leader (of the Lunar's choosing) or take some other course of action. Bribery, alliances, gifts and the slaying of enemies are all excellent ways for the Lunar to obtain a god's co-operation. Threats and intimidation are also possible, but the Lunar should bear in mind that, if the nation rises and grows

SATYR

strong, so, too, will the patron god. At that point, it would be a bad idea to have the patron god as an enemy.

Example: The Lunar Exalts Rain Deathflyer and Silver Python maintain a good relationship with Caltia, patron of Halta. While she would not take any action that would harm Halta, she is open to carefully presented requests about actions that she should take or opinions that she should state.

Problems: A patron god will not advocate a course of action that seems likely to detract from her worship, harm her people or lower the numbers of those who worship her. Also, the patron god may not wish to listen to the Lunar's requests once she considers herself powerful and important enough to ignore him.

IMPERSONATION

Given a Lunar's shapechanging gifts, it's possible to take the place of a respected member of the group in order to issue commands or guide them. Alternatively, a Lunar can impersonate a young member of the group, rise "naturally" to leadership and guide matters from there. A Lunar can even impersonate (and even actually have been) a famous hero or legend, returned from death to lead his people once more to glory.

Example: While establishing Delzahn society, Tamuz created the myth of the Kha-Khan. He now considers playing the role of the Kha-Khan "finally returned" in order to exercise a more direct control over the Delzahn tribes.

Problems: If the Lunar assumes someone else's role, his imposture may be spotted due to a lack of information or a mistake in relationships. If he pretends to be an ancient hero who has returned—even if he is that hero!—then skeptics may claim that he's a fake. Even true believers may become doubtful if they see anything out of place. Also, one pretender can open the way to others. What if *another* impersonator takes the role over later, or uses it to support his own fakery?

ORDERS

The Lunar can simply step forward, introduce himself as an Exalted of Luna and explain that the group of people must now do what she says. She may sweeten this with promised rewards ("You shall be under the guidance of Luna herself and prosper as never before!"), use threats ("But those who try to leave shall die horribly!") or both. This method has the virtue of simplicity and may work well with very primitive tribal folk. It is less likely to work on more developed groups, or ones who feel particularly attached to their current ruler, laws or customs.

Example: The Lunar Ten Stripes did this on the island of Simenare, claiming leadership by virtue of her Exaltation and then giving orders to all and sundry. Through a combination of bribes to local leaders and using spirits and siaka to keep the island cut off and affect the fishing, she was able to hold power.

Problems: For obvious reasons, this works badly with people who believe that all Lunars are Anathema—or, more usually, that all Exalted who are not Dragon-Blooded are Anathema, even if they couldn't give the precise details. It can also become dangerous if the Lunar's presence becomes known outside the nation's borders, and the Wyld Hunt or Sidereals come to investigate. And what if the people simply refuse to obey? The Lunar must abandon the project or carry out some of her threats—which may leave the people chastened and obedient, but also leaves them resentful… *dangerously* resentful. As the Usurpation proved, many weaker people acting together *can* kill a god-king.

THE WYLD

People touched by the Wyld can be forced into stereotyped beliefs and behaviors far more reliably than normal humans. Once the Lunar has properly conditioned her chosen subjects, she can then steer them out of the Wyld to conquer or otherwise assimilate another culture, in hopes that the implanted customs survive and spread. It's a convenient shortcut for impatient experimenters.

Example: While in the early stages of their work on Halta, Rain Deathflyer tried mingling some Wyld-conditioned tribes with the nascent population in order to speed up their dependence on pets and their living in the trees.

Problems: This method relies on people who are often insane, who might simply destroy the target culture (or be destroyed) instead of merging with it. They might even excite public opinion *against* the desired customs simply because they're the customs practiced by the lunatic invaders. Also, Wyld barbarian invasions attract notice from the Realm, Threshold nations, Sidereals and others… not to mention that other barbarians or Fair Folk can use such attacks as openings for their own invasions.

POSITIVE REINFORCEMENT: CROPS, CLIMATE, HERDS AND HUNTING

This method rewards the populace for a particular sort of behavior—for instance, instituting new farming practices, setting new boundaries, honoring the gods in a new way or changing social rules. It usually convinces the people that the gods favor their current course of action and encourages them to continue it. While this can be done openly (the Lunar appears, praises the people's actions and summons up good weather or bountiful food in a dramatic way), it usually works better as a more subtle course of action. Lunars can easily contact local petty gods and spirits to arrange good weather, good hunting and good crops, or maybe even have Charms and spells to do the job themselves.

Example: In the West, the Lunar Ten Stripes is on good terms with a number of local storm mothers and spirit courts. When she sees that her island of Simenare obeys her laws thoroughly, she arranges good winds and good fishing for the boats going out to sea.

Problems: Too much reliance on this can mean that perfectly good weather or hunting is regarded as divine favor when, in fact, it isn't or, equally, that bad weather or hunting are treated as divine disapproval when they aren't. Also, local spirits won't always want to help. They may have their own superiors to whom to answer. And finally, today's special reward becomes tomorrow's entitlement: People don't stay grateful and can be annoyingly quick to take good crops and good fortune for granted.

POSITIVE REINFORCEMENT: GENERAL FORTUNE

This relates to a particular person, usually an important one, rather than the whole community. If the Lunar arranges for this person to prosper, then he will favor whatever new arrangements led to his prosperity. This can be overt (a private meeting, a promise that he will do well if he goes along with a certain course of action and then prosperity) or covert (so that it seems to be a natural progression from the new laws or customs to the increased cash flow or goods). A Lunar usually takes this course of action with pivotal figures in a community, rather than the everyday hunter or herder—though positive reinforcement can, occasionally, provide a good object lesson for a totally random and average tribesman to show an unexpected profit. For instance, a random hunter who obeys new hunting strictures might come back with a full load of furs, serving as an example to all. The actual prosperity can be arranged via Charms, spells, success at trading or other manipulations.

Example: The first Queen of Halta ruled wisely and well. Rain Deathflyer and Silver Python saw to it that she was blessed by particularly intelligent animal companions and regularly favored by divine rainbows, prosperous fields and so on.

Problems: Sometimes a human accepts the prosperity and then goes back to the old customs, thus negating the example. (Of course, this apostasy then makes him a good target for negative reinforcement.) Also, one man's prosperity could leak over onto his neighbors' fields or goods, thus diluting the example, especially if they have opposing views. And there is always the possibility that his aggrieved neighbors who are doing worse than him may decide that he's somehow stolen their good fortune and kill him for it.

POSITIVE REINFORCEMENT: MILITARY SUPERIORITY

If the humans follow the new rules and customs, they are rewarded by victory over their enemies. A Lunar can arrange this overtly, by leading the mortals into battle or providing additional forces such as animals or beastmen, or covertly, by secretly advising generals and shamans or weakening the enemy beforehand so that they crack easily. It's a very convenient carrot, since at some point any group must defend itself against exterior forces or want to attack its neighbors.

Example: When the Haslanti League rose up against the Guild, the Lunar Gerd Marrow-Eater led the Haslans in battle three times, but left them to win the fourth and final battle themselves. They won all four times. This not only confirmed Gerd's status as semidivine war leader and lawgiver, but also gave the Haslans confidence that if they followed his ways, they would conquer even without him there to lead them.

Problems: The group's current war leaders may claim credit for winning the victory, finding some justification to explain why it is due to them rather than to the new customs or strategies that the group has adopted. Gods may also claim the credit, or shamans on behalf of the gods. There is also the possibility of losing the battle or war, which can be taken as a very bad omen indeed.

POSITIVE REINFORCEMENT: TRADE AND PROSPERITY

It's not only healthy for a nation to have good trading relationships with its neighbors; it also promotes happiness and vigor in the nation itself. All but the most self-sufficient nations find it useful to import luxuries (unless a Lunar deliberately aims for absolute self-sufficiency in his project). Increased trade and affordable luxuries help a nation not only accept, but believe that it's on the right course. A full belly and a bit of wealth help the mind rest easily in its current tracks. Lunars can improve commerce by secretly keeping the roads clear and guarding merchant convoys or by using contacts (human, Exalted, spirit or divine) in other countries to encourage positive trade. Also, trade lets a Lunar bring in new customs or tools, by examples or purchase, or allows a Lunar patron to test his culture by seeing if its customs diffuse outward.

Example: Halta does magnificently in trade. Halta has herbs and drugs to offer that can be found nowhere else in the world. And it's all (as Silver Python and Rain Deathflyer take care to subtly remind the Haltans) the product of their respect for the natural world, their good relationships with primitive tribes and their hard work and animal assistants. Proof positive that the system works. Haltan customs also diffuse outward to neighboring tribes that start by trading with it and end by adopting the culture wholesale.

Problems: The biggest problem is the Guild. As it did in the lands now known as the Haslanti League, it will move in on any possible trading opportunity and endeavor to twist it to its personal profit. This is a potential hazard of opening any trade routes. Even without the Guild, there's always the possibility of the Lunar's chosen group not doing as well in trade as it might: bandits can hit convoys, exchange rates may fluctuate, goods may be worth more or less depending on climate and harvests. Also, trade can bring in ideas that the Lunar doesn't want.

NEGATIVE REINFORCEMENT:
ASSASSINATION

Sometimes, it's easiest to remove a troublemaker who's speaking out against the Lunar's chosen laws, customs or leaders, or otherwise being awkward. The Lunar doesn't have to be subtle. If she is currently presenting herself as a divine figure, then smiting the offender with divine wrath or tearing him limb from limb and nailing his parts to the posts of the temple or throwing him off the top of a palace are all good ways to demonstrate why you shouldn't argue with gods. If the Lunar desires subtlety, however, then the offender might simply perish in a way suitable to his misdeeds. For instance, an erring hunter might be found torn to death by wild beasts, or a woman who complained about the treaties with the Fair Folk could turn up having clearly violated those same treaties and then suffered for it.

Example: On the island of Simenare, while it was still in a stage of transitional government, two mayors spoke out against the new laws. They were found the next day on the beach, in pieces, having been mauled to death by siaka. Public opposition lowered for a while.

Problems: The person who dies can become a popular martyr and actually incite further opposition to the Lunar's will. This becomes particularly awkward if the Lunar killed a troublemaker in public or in a way that can be traced back to her.

NEGATIVE REINFORCEMENT:
CROPS, CLIMATE, HERDS AND HUNTING

This punishment affects the whole community. Crops fail, the weather is bad, the wild game goes away…. It's the flip side of positive community reinforcement through good weather, crops and hunting. Lunars can arrange this sort of thing through Charms, sorcery and spirit allies. Prolonged misfortune may convince any community that its people have somehow offended local deities or spirits and that the people need to make amends. Negative reinforcement can punish the group for inappropriate behavior or soften them up before introducing some new law or custom. Then, the Lunar rewards adherence to a new custom with a sudden change for the better. This punishment can also persuade a group to move elsewhere—maybe bringing two tribes together in the hope of merging their cultural strengths.

Example: In the Haltan jungle, prolonged and persistent rain is not necessarily unnatural, but it can be extremely depressing and awkward for a village subjected to it. The tree village of Setsu engaged in heavy trade with the Guild and considered inviting it to open an outpost. After Silver Python arranged a month's persistent rain, neither the Guild nor the village of Setsu was interested any longer—and the village celebrated the Guild's departure with rather desperate festivities in the hope that the rain would finally stop.

Problems: Sometimes, local spirits won't cooperate or even work against the Lunar to protect the community.

Also, sometimes, the community won't take the hint and assumes that these are divine trials to test the people's resolve or simply natural phenomena they must endure. Even worse, the people might not realize *which* activity provoked their punishment and try to please the gods by casting out all "newfangled customs." The Lunar's chosen people may also simply give up and leave their homeland en masse, in search of a better life somewhere else.

NEGATIVE REINFORCEMENT:
GENERAL MISFORTUNE

One doesn't have to kill a man to make a public example of him. Long-term misfortune and poverty not only provide a healthy and obvious showcase of why one should obey the customs (or the gods or the Lunar) but also keep on providing the example and give the rest of the group someone else to look down on and despise. Best of all, if the victim publicly mends his ways, the Lunar can shower him with good fortune and wealth, thus rubbing the point in. A Lunar can engineer this personally or through agents (human, animal or divine), but should do it subtly. The point is to demonstrate that nature itself is set against this person, rather than the Lunar.

Example: In the early days of Halta, some people didn't want to use animal pets to work the forest, preferring to do everything themselves. This was partly because they did not want to spend time and goods worshipping the animal avatars. Not only did these people not prosper as well as their fellow Haltans who had pets to assist them, but the people who didn't use pets did noticeably worse than anyone would expect. Their crops rotted on the tree, their water was brackish, their roofs sprang leaks, and other minor problems multiplied until their lives were miseries.

Problems: As with assassination, sometimes this kind of thing can make the victim into a popular martyr, and his dogged example of resistance sway opinion in his favor. It's also important that the Lunar not be caught engineering the victim's problems, and preferably not even be suspected of doing so. If the public realizes that some outsider caused the victim's troubles, then again popular opinion probably turn toward the victim and away from the Lunar and her chosen cause.

PUTTING IT TOGETHER

One benefit of the Silver Pact's cooperation is that elder Lunars are often willing to give younger Lunars a few useful hints and pointers before they attempt their own contribution to the Thousand Streams River. In exchange for future favors or respect, an elder may even provide a younger Moonchild with useful tools, a well-situated target population, helpful spirits, an introduction to a patron god and similar benefits.

Older and younger Lunars can also work together to their mutual advantage. Younger Lunars serve as figureheads, enforcers and agents who can clear up isolated problems

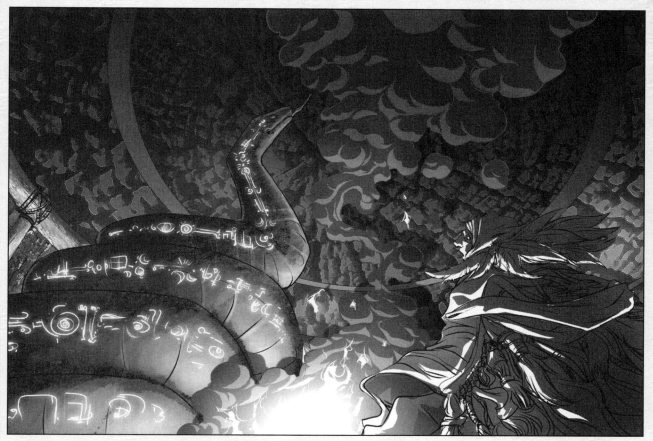

in the territory while the older Lunar keeps an eye on the capital or on particularly important figures. The younger Lunar gains experience and has the benefit of advice and protection from a mentor who can deal with problems such as the Realm, the Sidereals or other situations that young Lunars generally cannot yet handle on their own. Older Lunars are also better at knowing when to cut their losses and give up on a society or when to take violent action before a situation gets out of hand—or when *not* to take action, which can often be more difficult.

A Lunar's attempts to shape a society often follow this pattern:

RESEARCH

Identify the target population, their territory, their gods, their laws and customs and their habitat. It's best to work with a group who are currently dispossessed from their previous territory, unhappy in some way or otherwise in difficulties. A completely happy population that is thriving, prosperous and content with its gods has no reason to change its ways, and will resist attempts to make it do so. (And a nation that's achieved all this while remaining independent of the Realm is clearly doing something right in any case and deserves study to find out how it managed it.) A Lunar can despoil and lay waste to an established nation or tribe in order to build it up again in the desired direction, and this has been done, but it

means fighting against its gods when they're in a position of power, and risking doing more damage than can the Lunar can repair later.

ESTABLISHMENT

Whether by divine interference, divine impersonation, personal charisma, subtle suggestions or other methods, the Lunar imparts guidance to his chosen people on how they should live. This may be obvious and straightforward—the equivalent of handing a set of commandments to a prophet on the mountainside—or it may be subtle, with slow suggestions spaced out over decades and filtered through shamans, dream-readers, chieftains and warriors.

MAINTENANCE

Once the Lunar lays down the guidelines and promulgates them through the group, he has to ensure that it keeps working. Some Lunars like to stand back at this point and leave the experiment to mature on its own. They feel that interference would be counter-productive or would cause the humans to become too reliant on the Lunars' protection and guidance. Others prefer to work from behind the scenes, giving the occasional nudge when they feel it becomes necessary. They can use the various positive and negative reinforcement techniques to nudge the humans into staying in line, keeping an eye on how the society progresses in person or through spies.

EVALUATION

There comes a point where the Lunar organizing the experiment has to decide if it is worth continuing or not, and if she can actually call it a success. While some Lunars keep working on tribes and societies for centuries, and have yet to decide that the project is complete, others can recognize success or failure within a century. Also, some Lunar Exalted might feel that a society has already started on the path to collapse and might as well be discarded on the spot. Others Stewards might think they can save the experiment with a bit of effort, and pursue a course of vigorous maintenance and remodeling. A collapsing society may still possess useful traits that the Lunar wants to pass on to a successor culture: apparent failure or conquest may simply be the next step in a Lunar's long-term plan.

Finally, different Lunars hold different ideas about what constitutes a success. One Moonchild might require a fully self-sufficient society that can survive even if all its bordering nations fall apart, and defend itself against their attacks while holding firm to traditional customs and honoring its gods. Another Steward might want a fluid, malleable group of people who can adapt and survive anywhere, city or wilderness; they might even live on the road and never claim a territory of their own. It all depends on the Lunar's criteria for the experiment. The mortals themselves may think that they live in a perfectly adequate society and never imagine that their secret Lunar patron considers them a waste of time and trash to discard.

FINISH

If an experiment fails, the Lunar patron can leave it to destroy itself. Some Lunars find that watching a nation fall apart gives them useful information for their next experiment. And if a culture doesn't fall apart, but simply wasn't what its patron wanted, then other Lunars may still consider it a useful addition to the Thousand Streams River.

Other Lunars prefer to clean up after themselves, especially if their pet nation is likely to cause widespread trouble before disintegrating. The Lunar can assassinate the nation's leaders, strike down its priests, disable its infrastructure and so on. This is felt to be simple good manners if the group of mortals is close to another Lunar's experiment or to territory or people whom another Lunar considers important. In RY 535, for instance, the young Lunar Tail-Flashing Serpent was severely reprimanded by her elders in the Silver Pact for abandoning a tribe she had sought to culture in imitation of the Haltan Republic. Instead, the tribe developed a dependence on drugs and stimulants, and gave the Guild an entry into the whole region. The tribe moved north and staged several raids on Halta before being put down, causing Halta's two Lunar protectors some mild inconvenience.

On the other hand, if the Lunar decides his experiment is a success, he can leave it to grow further on its own. (However, most Lunars with successes do keep track of them and are likely to intervene if exterior forces threaten an otherwise functioning nation.) The Threshold contains several noteworthy successes from the Thousand Streams River… and equally noteworthy failures.

SIMENARE

Simenare is an island in the archipelagoes of the Southwest, but safely to the north of the Lintha pirates. A hundred years ago, the Lunar Ten Stripes decided to use Simenare as the site for an extremely violent cultural experiment. A Fair Folk raid had recently stripped away most of the islanders' menfolk; the few men left behind had difficulty handling the remaining fishing-boats, and due to the West's cultural strictures, the women could not help them. Ten Stripes decided to repopulate the island with a mixture of new inhabitants, in an attempt to infuse a hybrid vigor into Simenare and see how the gender roles would rebalance if given the opportunity. Since Simenare was known as a frequent target of the raksha (when known at all), few came there to trade, and Ten Stripes felt sure of reasonable privacy.

The island is currently an uncomfortable mix of people, with native islanders, shipwrecked sailors, several rescued Lintha orphans, some traveling merchants and even a few refugees from the Skullstone Archipelago. Ten Stripes preached the virtues of hospitality and help to the needy, mutual cooperation and all tasks being available to anyone who wants to undertake them. She fights centuries

TYPE OF EXPERIMENT

Simenare is a recent experiment by a comparatively young Lunar. The experiment is failing. Ten Stripes introduced too many random factors and cannot control the resulting mix, which constantly threatens to dissolve into open anarchy. Several neighboring islands also watch Simenare and are held back only by fear of Ten Stripes' powers. The moment Ten Stripes relaxes her grip on the island, Simenare's society will fall apart violently. Ten Stripes wanted to create an egalitarian society, with everyone willing to turn his hand to any task, unconstrained by gender, age or anything other than ability. She tried to impose this vision by force.

Ten Stripes introduced herself openly as a Lunar and gave direct orders to the inhabitants of the island, enforcing her will through a mixture of fear and bribery. While she can command the local spirits and divinities, their relationship with her depends strictly on results. If Simenare falls apart or the people perish, the little gods will turn against Ten Stripes to save as many of their worshippers as they can. The people gain no great benefits from her presence and view her as a tyrant rather than as a benevolent leader.

of tradition and multiple prejudices, and unfortunately, she is losing.

THE BEGINNINGS OF SIMENARE

Simenare is an island similar to many in the West, originally settled by fishers from the Wavecrest Archipelago in the Low First Age. With a land area of about 50 square miles, generally fertile land and good fishing nearby, the island's inhabitants could fend for themselves. The three small towns were each governed by a five-yearly elected (female) mayor, and a council of the three mayors ruled the island as a whole. However, few policy decisions were ever required. Simenare was fertile but not overly prosperous, was not situated in a convenient place for military action and was not worth enough to be targeted by the Guild. The island's main problem consisted of attacks by a nearby raksha Freehold, but as long as the islanders remembered to wear their charms and observe sensible precautions, only the truly foolish were lost.

While Simenare technically swore allegiance to the Wavecrest Archipelago, in practice, the island had little to do with its parent islands. It had no volcanoes to worry about, no valuable tribute to offer and insufficient military strength to contribute soldiers. Both sides accepted a token understanding. Simenare did, however, have the same general morals and principles as Wavecrest; in particular, women were forbidden to participate in seagoing ventures, but governed the land-based craft industries and agriculture. Men were sailors, traders, fishermen, divers and couriers; women were blacksmiths, shopkeepers, merchants, cooks and farmers.

Simenare was mercifully free of Wyld zones as well as volcanoes, and the islanders let worship of Wavecrest's volcano gods lapse. Instead, the islanders honored the small gods of the local seas, the earth's fertility and Shennim, the patron deity of the island itself. Shennim is a very minor god, just as the island is a minor island, but he did provide the occasional bit of assistance to islanders, who worshipped him mainly as a protector against the Fair Folk.

Daily life on Simenare went undisturbed for centuries. Although the Guild visited occasionally, it didn't bother to use the island as a trade hub or to subjugate it; Simenare just wasn't important enough. Simultaneously, the island was just far north enough to stay out of the orbit of the Lintha and too small to attract the Realm's interest. The people of Simenare lived content, having no reason to consider changing their ways.

Over the years, however, the Fair Folk in the Freehold nearby had grown increasingly hungry. The few souls they claimed were mere specks in their constant need for nourishment. Anahima, Queen of the Freehold, led her assembled raksha in a raid that she intended to keep them well fed for months, if not years. They called up unexpectedly large shoals of fish in order to bait the island's fishermen into sailing out to catch the fish. Then, the raksha sang up a storm, shattering most of the boats and drowning or capturing nine out of 10 of Seminare's fishermen, dragging them down into the depths.

The few men who returned home told a horrible story of Fair Folk, storm, sinking ships and wholesale destruction. The island faced starvation: The people had not enough men left to man the fishing fleet and sustain regular catches, while the actions of the Fair Folk showed that they intended to use the islanders as a larder. Perhaps the islanders could send to Wavecrest and ask for help, but would Wavecrest bother to respond? And would the Fair Folk even let a ship pass in the first place?

Ten Stripes arrived like the answer to their prayers. As night fell, she came walking out of the sea, glorious and beautiful, with tiger-striped hair flowing down her back and a shark's pointed teeth in her mouth. She promised that if the islanders obeyed her, she would keep them safe from the Fair Folk and see to it that they were fed and prosperous. If the islanders turned against her, then she would leave them to the raksha and would summon up the sea to drown the island and all who lived on it.

The people of Simenare fell to their knees and vowed obedience.

THE NEW ORDER

Ten Stripes promised that new men would come to Simenare. In the meantime, however, all must set their hands to whatever tasks were needed to survive. She promised that the gods would guide her in selecting which women should assist with the fishing. She herself would see to it that fish filled the nets and would destroy the Fair Folk. Divine omens (thunder from a clear sky, flights of colorful birds and earthquake rumblings) and good weather displayed themselves as she spoke. Ten Stripes also declared that from now on, Simenare would receive all shipwrecked travelers into its population and that they would learn the ways of the island and become good islanders.

TEN STRIPES AND OPPORTUNITY

Ten Stripes watched a number of islands for several years, looking for a suitable opportunity to implement her plans. She saw the Fair Folk massing for a raid and could have warned the people of Simenare. She didn't. Whether or not they survived did not matter to her; they were just another group of mortals. If they were weakened afterward, however, they would form a suitable breeding population for her experiment. Either way, she lost nothing.

When Ten Stripes spoke to the people of Simenare later, she told them how much she grieved for the loss of their menfolk and how she would have saved them if only she could have arrived in time.

Popular opinion was mixed. The people of Simenare were still in shock and had begun to feel the loss of their fathers, sons, husbands and brothers—but the gender divisions for labor were so deeply embedded that even divine command could not make the new order acceptable. While all the islanders approved of the destruction of the Fair Folk and could accept (with reservations) the idea of taking in shipwreck survivors, no islanders totally trusted their new leader. In many ways, they were too civilized for her to easily imprint herself on them as their new ruler. They had grown accustomed to elections and councils, and had lost the need for immediate response to the necessities of the wilderness.

However, enough women declared themselves willing to work on the boats, and enough men grudgingly accepted the women's presence. The fishing fleet of Simenare could set sail once more, albeit at one-fourth its former strength. Those ships with women on board stayed close to shore, and the women took on menial roles, since they lacked the skill for more advanced sailing tasks.

No ships arrived from Wavecrest, from the Guild or from anywhere else during the three months after Ten Stripes' appearance. Some of the more cynical islanders took this as ominous.

Meanwhile, Ten Stripes attacked the raksha Freehold. She called on siaka-spirits and other dangerous ocean-spirits to assist her. She was, at the time, a comparatively young Lunar and could not inflict as much damage as she wanted. Ten Stripes did kill a number of noble raksha and dueled with Queen Anahima herself. The two agreed on a truce: Anahima kept the prisoners she had already taken but promised to refrain from all attacks on the people of Simenare. She insisted in return that the people of Simenare should all bear a particular tattoo, so that the Fair Folk could recognize the islanders.

Ten Stripes agreed and left the Freehold without retrieving the prisoners. When she returned to Simenare, she said that the Fair Folk had already killed all their men, but that she had won safety for the islanders in exchange for them all bearing the tattoo. Only Shennim knew the truth.

Cultural Mixing

Two years later, a few dozen merchants from the traveling Denzik fleet washed up on the shores of Simenare. This was not by accident. Ten Stripes waited for a single ship from a Denzik convoy to sail within range, and then led some whales to smash holes in the ship's hull and push the ship to Simenare. When the merchants washed up on the beach, they were pleasantly surprised by the native hospitality and the generous welcome they received. Learning that the island's ruler was a manifest Lunar Anathema came as a less pleasant surprise.

Ten Stripes decreed that the Denzik merchants could not leave Simenare. They would stay and marry among the locals, though the merchants might choose their trade

Divine Support

Ten Stripes was wise enough to pay proper respect to Shennim, even though he was only a petty god. She promised that he would continue to receive proper worship and sacrifices, and that as the number of people on the island rose, so, too, would his power. Shennim had his doubts, but he was weak and had little choice. His divine manifestation in his temple formally approved of Ten Stripes, declaring her a savior who had come to the island in its hour of need.

The Lunar did not take the time to be as polite to other local spirits. She ordered them to obey her and used Charms—or simple force—when they failed to comply.

as they wished. The outraged Denzik merchants, who had expected to return to their native fleet—or at least to a more civilized island—demanded transport to Wavecrest.

All three of the island's mayors—Debela, Manedha and Arshana—had fallen in with Ten Stripes' plans to a servile degree, fearing that she would replace them if they spoke against her. When the three mayors realized that the Denzik merchants were plotting to escape, the mayors arrested them for unspecified "crimes against the lady Ten Stripes" and cut the tendons in their legs, crippling them for life. The Denzik then had to take sedentary jobs. Most became tradesmen, another function normally assigned to women on the island, which further confused gender lines. However, the men were far from fully accepted and harbored a strong resentment against the island and its leader.

Two popular farmers—Luicel and Vivefra—publicly disagreed with Ten Stripes, saying that the Denzik should

Outside Communications

Ten Stripes easily cut Simenare off from the outside world. Even when responsibilities elsewhere took her from the island, she could leave spirit allies behind to spy on the islanders. Ten Stripes also directed ally siaka-spirits to attack any incoming ships from outside and to attack the islanders themselves if they sailed more than a certain distance from Simenare.

Guild ships presented a greater problem. They sailed in convoys and would have been investigated if they all sank and kept on sinking. She permitted Guild groups to visit the island, but ensured that they met one of her loyal mayors and restricted the other islanders' contact with the Guildsmen. The Denzik castaways were not allowed anywhere near the Guild merchants.

have been allowed to go home and even gifted with additional presents as a sign of good faith. The two women were found the next morning on the beach, apparently mauled to death by siaka. The islanders quickly took the hint and instantly declared absolute loyalty to Ten Stripes.

THE NEW DISORDER

After 20 years, the island's society had split into three divisions: the "normal" men, the "normal" women and a third group consisting of the Denzik merchants and the women who served on board ships. The first two groups looked down on the third. Even those few women who became Tya (holding technical male status in return for celibacy) felt contempt for the land-bound Denzik men and the seagoing women.

The Denzik also brought a new concept with them. One believed in the Immaculate faith. During his time with the Denzik fleet, his fellows saw his faith as a mild eccentricity, pardonable in a good merchant. Now that he and the others found themselves trapped and crippled on a lonely island ruled by a Lunar, his faith found firm ground, and the other Denzik began to share it.

THE IMMACULATE REBELLION

Fifty years after Ten Stripes came to Simenare, the islanders rebelled against her rule. All the mayors by now were her hand-picked toadies. Anyone who openly disagreed with her decisions was found dead the next morning or suffered from apparently natural misfortunes such as bad fishing or poor crops. Shennim grew uneasy, sensing that worship was being diverted from his own believers to some other target, but could not identify what or where. Ten Stripes paid little attention to Shennim's complaints, however, and thought that her experiment proceeded as well as could be expected. She spent much of her time back on the mainland, supervising the breeding of several groups of tiger-beastmen whom she intended to use as her next project.

Meanwhile on Simenare, the Immaculate cult spread from the Denzik merchants to others on the island. Without the benefit of actual guidance from Immaculate monks, the Denzik's faith deviated from the original precepts and became a folk religion. The Simenarean faithful didn't know the complex philosophies and mangled or simplified the rituals, but in their prayers, they cursed the evil Anathema and honored the virtuous Dragons, whom the Simenareans saw as ultimate, pure forces of nature. (Naturally, this far in the West, they considered the Dragon of Water the most important.)

This faith spread among both the traditionalist and the "lower-class" factions. To the traditionalists, it offered a "purer," higher way of thinking, while among the Denzik and the women viewed as lower-class, it became a faith of defiance, revenge and bloody rebellion, just as the Dragon-Blooded had risen up against the Anathema.

When Ten Stripes next returned to the island, a small conspiracy plotted to murder her. This group of 50 men and women, chiefly composed of descendants of the Denzik and the women who had first gone to work on the boats, intended to kill their oppressor and free themselves to leave the island. They reached an arrangement with co-religionists among the traditionalist islanders, who promised to help the conspirators by staging a huge feast to distract Ten Stripes, assassinating her sycophant mayors and providing the ships by which the conspirators would leave Simenare. The island would then return to the customs of the past.

The group, led by one Ameras Hookbone, poisoned their spears, harpoons and the wine Ten Stripes was given with extracts taken from lethal jellyfish and spiked stonefish. The assassins managed to take Ten Stripes by surprise and inflicted serious wounds on her while she struggled with the poison, but she survived through the use of Charms. Ten Stripes slew them in the guise of a great tiger and then ravened up and down the island, traveling from one end of it to another in a single night, screaming for blood and crying out for merciless vengeance on all traitors.

Some of the surviving conspirators killed themselves that night. Others tried to escape in one of the fishing boats, but Ten Stripes' siaka slew them when they reached her boundary. Their colleagues among the traditionalists pretended innocence and were first in line to hunt down conspirators the next morning. Ameras's head ornamented Shennim's shrine, and his skull still perches on a pillar there to this day.

Considering the matter later, Ten Stripes actually viewed this as an excellent sign of cultural dynamism and ability to cooperate. Although she was mortified (and would certainly not tell other Lunars) that the islanders had managed to injure her, and that they had *dared* to rebel against her, the fact that she had produced a group of people who could almost kill a Lunar was a positive step forward.

Of course, Ten Stripes made several bloody examples over the next few weeks, and thoroughly re-established her authority. She discovered the ongoing Immaculate beliefs. After publicly shattering the hidden shrines and the altar tablets of the worshippers, she demanded that they recant their faith in front of their fellow islanders or perish on the spot at her hand. Most of them chose to recant… or at least pretend to.

The Immaculate faith was not wiped out on the island. The faith went even deeper underground, and its adherents began to pray with real fervor. This also opened the way for other beliefs: Once the islanders had consciously abandoned the tradition of centuries, they were open to new possibilities.

New Blood: The Lintha Slaves

Three decades later, Ten Stripes decided that her experiment did not go as well as she had hoped. Despite the regular additions of shipwrecked sailors to the population, the people remained stubborn and obdurate. Many only obeyed her orders grudgingly, and she needed force and terror to keep her few truly fervent (or sycophantic) followers in power. In order to bring in a group who would be unquestionably loyal to her, she decided to wreck a Lintha slave ship. She noted their patrol and trade routes, and at one point, they came within a few days of Simenare. A mixed group of slaves who attained freedom under her guidance would, she convinced herself, become both grateful and loyal to her and would help stabilize the island's population and weaken the traditionalists.

Public Repression and Consequences

Ten Stripes demonstrated her youth and inexperience by making a bad situation worse. Most of the people of Simenare obeyed her out of fear; very few did so from any hope of reward. The general population of the island kept on with their daily life and saw her more and more as a cruel oppressor who gave them nothing and killed anyone who dared to speak against her. Adherence to the old customs and ways became a form of principled rebellion. The islanders quickly forgot her assistance against the Fair Folk or even suspected that she might have been in league with them.

Older, wiser Lunars would have found a way to put down the rebellion that didn't so obviously leave her as the main tyrant and the target of everyone's hatred. Some Lunars would have framed the conspirators as guilty of other crimes as well—being in league with the Fair Folk, for instance, or Yozi worship—and have roused public opinion against them. Other Lunars would have made a public show of "letting the god of the island judge the traitors" while having previously arranged the verdict with the god before any trial took place. A really perceptive Lunar would have noticed the trouble brewing beforehand and made concessions such as allowing the truly unhappy group to leave the island on a couple of ships. (Whether or not they would have ever reached land again is a different question.)

Techniques of pure terror and reward only work on the most primitive populations. On a group with well-developed ideas and traditions of its own, public repression and confinement are more likely to rouse direct resentment and calcify public feeling against the Lunar. If the people have some outside notions to give them a standard of comparison—such as the Denziks' accounts of life beyond the island and their Immaculate faith—the people are even less likely to submit. They *know* there's something better.

A month later, Ten Stripes crept aboard the Lintha ship *Bone Osprey* by night and slaughtered the captain and crew without mercy. She spared only a few Lintha children whom she felt could be re-educated. Drugging the slaves to keep them docile and calling wind and water elementals to her aid, she drove the ship to Simenare and let the ship beach itself. The islanders came out and were glad enough, simply from natural human kindness, to care for the slaves and help them recover. Few people wanted to adopt the Lintha orphans, but either from a desire to please Ten Stripes, or from a desire to avoid her wrath, enough families volunteered to take in a single child and help them grow into "normal" islanders.

The children were bad seeds. They had already sucked in Yozi worship at their mothers' breasts and sought revenge on Ten Stripes as well as an eventual return to the Lintha stronghold of Bluehaven. The little vipers quickly realized how the islanders hated Ten Stripes and began to spread their poison in the appropriate ears, whispering about how the *true* gods could bring her down and restore the way things ought to be. The children chose the underclass of sea-going women and land-bound men—by now, generations removed from the first sailors and Denzik merchants, but still despised—as their targets, spreading murmurs of rebellion and Yozi adoration while growing up as apparently grateful islanders.

Importing Random Factors

Older Lunars, when working on a particular group of people, are very careful about admitting outsiders and other random factors to their chosen nucleus tribe. Ideas are like weeds; they take root unexpectedly, spread surprisingly fast and can become impossible to root out. Wise Lunars make sure that their people are already well rooted in their faith and customs, and stamp out anything that might threaten the community gestalt. An older Lunar would never have allowed the Lintha children to live in the first place. Tainted stock should be cut out rather than permitted to breed.

What's more, no sensible Lunar would have even considered importing potential Yozi worshippers in the first place. Older Lunars still remember the tales of the Primordial War as something that happened to their immediate ancestors, but to younger Lunars, the Primordial War is simply another story of the distant past, and Yozi worship can seem no more pernicious than any other cult that demands human sacrifice—ugly, but less unusual in the further Threshold than one might think.

Recent Events and Current Status

The three current mayors are Ten Siaka, Amadocens and Lethia. Ten Siaka was named in homage to Ten Stripes and is a fervent loyalist, utterly convinced by the Lunar's charisma. She is strong-willed and determined, but bad at judging people around her. Ten Siaka's town is a hotbed of treachery whose inhabitants levered her into the role of mayor to please Ten Stripes and make it less likely that she would notice their own plotting. Amadocens is a traditionalist man who doesn't want his job, doesn't want Ten Stripes on the island and just wants everything back the way his grandparents told him it used to be. He gained his position through competence, but yearns for the day that he can hand it over to a worthy female and go back to sailing, the way that men are supposed to. Lethia is thoroughly tainted by the Lintha cults but cunning enough to present herself as a Ten Stripes loyalist and orthodox tribeswoman in public. The fields of her farm are freshened with blood sacrifices.

The island holds about 3,000 inhabitants. It is fruitful for its size, and the local fishing is good. About 2,000 of the islanders live in the three main port towns, with the remaining 1,000 scattered across the island in small homesteads or villages. The fishing boats go out daily, but Simenare lacks any genuine fleet or any warships; Ten Stripes does not permit the islanders to build them. Similarly, the island has no standing army, though the islanders train daily with harpoon and trident, and the mayors possess honor guards. Each mayor handles law and order in his own part of the island. All cases of life and death go to Ten Stripes (and are held for her judgment if she is away from the island), but lesser matters are left to the mayors' own judgment. Punishments range from beatings to mutilation and confiscation of property.

Shennim himself, the god of Simenare, despairs of his people. He knows how many of them merely mouth prayers when they come to worship, and he can feel the hollowness in their words. But he no longer has the strength to fight Ten Stripes openly, if indeed he ever did.

The three main factions on the island at the moment are the Loyalists, the Traditionalists and the Aware. The Loyalists serve Ten Stripes faithfully, whether through fear, ambition or genuine belief. They comprise about 10 percent of the population, but are backed by Ten Stripes herself. Ten Siaka is their most public representative, with backing from Gantens, a fishing captain with a fanatically loyal crew who enjoys the power he has.

The Traditionalists want to return to the old ways, with the men at sea and the women on land. About 60 percent of the population holds this view. Some still worship Shennim, but others believe in a version of the Immaculate faith. Amadocens is their effective leader, though they have no definite organization or plans for the future.

The Aware are the Yozi worshippers and make up the remaining 30 percent of the population. Led by Lethia, they plan to spread their faith further through Simenare, then assassinate Ten Stripes, enslave the other islanders, regain contact with the Lintha pirates and become a Lintha outpost in the region. The Aware regard the Lintha as the "Chosen people" of their baleful gods. Some of the Loyalists and Traditionalists know the island has a third faction that doesn't seem in accord with either of their views, but members of the Aware are good at masquerading as Loyalists or Traditionalists as the situation requires.

OPINIONS ON THE EXPERIMENT

Ten Stripes herself has finally realized that her experiment failed. Her stubbornness kept her at the project for decades after other Lunars would have finished it, but even she now accepts that her manufactured society just doesn't work. Instead of integrating with mutual respect, the people with traditional roles despise the people with non-traditional roles, and the culture is breaking apart under the strain. Equally, the ideas on trade introduced by the Denzik merchants—and the Immaculate faith in particular—have introduced stresses to Simenare that Ten Stripes did not anticipate. The whole place is on the brink of revolution, and she must become more and more autocratic and brutal to maintain her authority, making public examples of offenders.

The Simenareans' behavior disgusts Ten Stripes (after all she did for them!) so much that she is likely to disappear one day, never to return, and let the island fall apart. The result may surprise her. Without her to keep order, a short and vicious civil war is likely to follow, leaving the "underclass" in control. At that point, the islanders probably descend into open Yozi worship and incorporate piracy into their way of life. Should Simenare manage to send emissaries so far, the Lintha pirates will be glad to adopt the island as a distant base and even send colonists to help repopulate it. The agreement with the local Fair Folk also holds as long as the people of Simenare retain their tattoos, allowing the islanders to remain immune to the raksha's depredations. At that point, Simenare becomes a positive danger to all sailors nearby and a cancerous node dangerously near to the Wavecrest Archipelago.

THE DELZAHN AND CHIAROSCURO

Chiaroscuro is the largest and oldest city in the South, lying in the fertile coastal belt along the Inland Sea. During the First Age, Chiaroscuro was the South's largest and most prosperous port. At the height of the First Age, the city supported a population of more than 20 million, handling trade from the South, East and Southeast. During the Usurpation, however, Chiaroscuro suffered vast destruction. A number of the city's magnificent towers lie in ruin, and rubble fills many streets. Caravans of stinking camels and dusty horses plod down roads of blood-red glass. Although many towers have fallen, the city and the regions around it still boast almost a million inhabitants.

Chiaroscuro is ruled by the Tri-Khan, the hereditary leader of the nomadic Delzahn tribes, who first re-inhabited the city in RY 211. The Delzahn are a divided people, a group of nomadic tribes who have to an extent become city-dwellers. They rule the city with an adroit hand, managing trade agreements and political deals that leave them a Realm tributary in law and an independent city in reality. Now, the remaining nomads look down on their fat, city-dwelling cousins who rely on bodyguards to maintain their honor. Meanwhile, the city-dwelling Delzahn maintain their grip on the city as they would handle the reins of a camel, with elegance and deftness, and pity their country cousins who lack appreciation of the city's trade, power and refinements.

TYPE OF EXPERIMENT

The Delzahn were (and to an extent still are) a set of nomadic tribes, camel-herders and hunters, a warrior culture with a great contempt for those who cannot defend themselves. The First Age Lunar Tamuz saw their raw potential and also saw the unfulfilled, unexploited, still viable city of Chiaroscuro. He felt that the two could combine to create a thriving whole, retaining the dynamism and honor of the nomads while teaching them civilized ways and re-cultivating the city back into growth again. He united the three tribes of the Delzahn and led them to conquer the city, but instead of looting it, he dominated it and left his people in command of it. Tamuz hoped to create a people who could be as virile and strong inside a city as outside it, civilized yet forceful and independent. And so, he transplanted one culture into a radically different setting and set out to help the people flourish.

As the centuries passed, the city-dwellers and their nomadic cousins have slowly grown apart. While custom and bloodlines still bind them together, and the occasional subtle intervention by Tamuz himself reminds them of their shared roots, more and more they look down upon each other. As the population of Chiaroscuro grows, farmers and traders from the city encroach upon the Delzahn's traditional pastures, forcing the city-dwelling Delzahn to take sides and driving the nomads further away from the city itself. If Tamuz wishes to reunite the two parts of his experiment before they break their ties completely, he may need to act soon. War threatens this region, as it does all of Creation, and war may come as a uniting factor, or as the final, divisive straw that breaks the camel's back.

The Kha-Khan

Delzahn religion emphasizes sky-worship. Twisted memories of the Old Realm's religion form part of the liturgy, including the propitiation of spirits and fragments of Exalted lore. The fusion with the Immaculate faith emphasizes the primacy of the Dragon-Blooded, but most shamans keep old stories of the Celestial Exalted alive because the shamans fear what may happen if they ignore the powers of the skies. And symbolizing that power is the Kha-Khan, King of Kings: the Rider on the Winds, the Chosen of the Moon, Descended from the Night Sky, the Lord Who Will Come Again. To the sound of the drum and the rattle of brass pipes, as the dust-filled desert winds blow the sand into great, heaping dunes, the shamans dance and prophesy his return in blind trances.

Delzahn prophecies predict the coming of the Kha-Khan, sent from Heaven to unite the horde once more. Nomadic storytellers say that Tamas Khan was the last Kha-Khan. Being merely mortal, the ruler of Chiaroscuro does not claim his ancestor's title, and so, he merely calls himself the Tri-Khan, the lord of three tribes, rather than the Khan of Khans. The nomads of the South await the return of their prophesied leader, and prepare the way with their constant raids.

The Coming of the Delzahn

In RY 210, the great Tamas Khan united the three tribes of the Delzahn nation on the Plain of Wind-Scattered Bones and led them to loot Chiaroscuro. At that time, the city still lay in the ruins of its fall from the First Age. Chiaroscuro was a scrabbling collection of tents pitched among the stumps of glorious glass towers, ruled only by the occasional warlord or by squabbling gangs. No single power could hold it against the constant contenders from all directions. Even in rubble, the city sat at the gateway to the coast and the intersection of the trade routes, and its port remained largely intact. Chiaroscuro was too great a prize to leave unmolested, but equally, it was too great a prize for any particular leader to retain for more than a few years.

When mystics and shamans among the Delzahn began speaking of a prophesied figure called the Kha-Khan who would unite the tribes into one people, few listened at first. But the word spread from tribe to tribe like a desert storm, coming to a dozen different places and a dozen different shamans at once. All the spirit world seemed aflame with it. When the prophesied figure appeared, stronger than any man, more skilled than any warrior and a better leader than any of the khans, he gained the Delzahn's respect with ease. Though it took years to bring the scattered tribes together

and to form them into a single social group, he had a prize to lure them with: the wealth of Chiaroscuro.

Tamuz used a proxy to impersonate the promised Kha-Khan, thus remaining behind the scenes and able to manipulate the Delzahn people more subtly. His proxy, a young Lunar who took the name of Tamas Khan, was a competent Lunar warrior but aware of his own inexperience at scheming and large-scale politics. More to the point, the young Tamas Khan knew he could not cope with Realm interference or Sidereal opposition. He was glad to work with the older Tamuz and learn from the experience.

The Delzahn Horde took Chiaroscuro with almost insulting ease. The city simply didn't have the manpower to resist it. The warlord ruling it at the time, Saiz Ellendar, mustered his troops and called on his nearby allies for assistance. The allies in question looked at the Delzahn Horde and defaulted, deciding to make their own deals with Tamas Khan after he sacked Chiaroscuro. The merchants had already fled, and the remaining rabble left in the city were hardly worth the spears they could carry. Most hid.

The Delzahn Horde moved in slowly. First the Delzahn took the outlying farms, then the outer walls (too damaged for a small force to defend) and then thrust through to the heart of the city to destroy Saiz Ellendar's own troops. Tamas Khan himself slew Saiz in a very public and dramatic duel. Grandmother Bright's district was spared; the streets flared

up and barred it away, and Tamas Khan ordered that nobody interfere with a holy place that the spirits themselves were clearly protecting. (Tamuz had made a private deal earlier with Grandmother Bright, goddess of Chiaroscuro, who was interested in stable rule for the city.)

The next step was far more difficult than simply sacking Chiaroscuro. Tamuz had to persuade the Delzahn to settle the city and use Chiaroscuro as more than just a target for raids.

CHIAROSCURO, THE DELZAHN CITY

Any barbarian horde includes a few people ready to enjoy the luxuries of civilization and surrender their nomadic ways in return for power, pleasure and obedient slaves. Tamuz deftly selected nomads who were also men of reasonable principle and who seemed unlikely to destroy the city's economy in the pursuit of pleasure. Many were older men, who wanted to settle down under conditions of comfort, knowing that their sons would continue to ride the desert and carry on the old traditions. Others were younger nomads who knew they would never rise to power in the tribes and saw this as a quick way to gain status. Some brought their wives and families, while others took new wives from among the inhabitants of Chiaroscuro.

Tamas Khan used his divine authority to state that Chiaroscuro would become the center of the Delzahn Empire. With Tamuz's help from behind the scenes, he chose people to remain behind and rule the city who had the inclination and ability to do so. Then, he led the remaining horde back out to the surrounding territory to dispose of Saiz Ellendar's previous allies and any remaining local warlords, thus removing them from the immediate temptation to plunder the city.

One of Tamas Khan's first moves, after establishing Delzahn rule over Chiaroscuro, was to call in the Guild. However, the Delzahn were still very much in control; Tamas Khan held raw authority in his hands, honed to an edge by his recent capture of the city, and those Delzahn who occupied it were no less proud or warlike than their nomadic kin. The Guild entered under good trade terms, but was only permitted to bring set numbers of guards and did not at that point have a share in the ruling authority. (As usual with the Guild, that didn't last long.)

Chiaroscuro quickly rose from its glass-strewn ashes. With Tamas Khan and the Delzahn firmly in power, the city became more stable than it had been in 200 years. What was more, Tamas Khan quickly established it as a tributary of the Realm. This offended many Delzahn, but Tamas Khan (with help from Tamuz) spoke powerfully of the advantages of powerful allies, that there was no shame in acknowledging the Realm's might and that a small payment in tribute would enable them to enjoy the great riches of Chiaroscuro until the end of time. He assuaged Delzahn pride to some degree by calling the tribute a *gift*, from one mighty empire to another—not submission, but a partnership.

THE END OF TAMAS KHAN

The Delzahn have many legends but few definite accounts of Tamas Khan's death. The general agreement is that a visiting force of Immaculate monks from the Realm discovered some great evil, and their great king joined them to pursue it into the Wyld, where he slew it. However, Tamas Khan took great wounds in the fight himself, and he withdrew to Heaven to heal himself. The story always ends with a prophecy that the Kha-Khan will return again when his people need him and that he will unite them once more.

AFTER THE KHA-KHAN: EXPANSION

Although Tamas Khan returned to Heaven (as was generally believed), he left behind wives, children, family and orders for a regency. The aging general Agyar Enies took power per the instructions Tamas Khan had left behind. Although the Delzahn mourned the Kha-Khan's departure, they agreed he made a wise choice in heir. Agyar Enies rebuilt a standing army that could defend a city rather than one suitable to the open plain. He also instituted the current tax system, which did a great deal to reconcile the Delzahn occupiers to city life. He also received the first, rather small, Dragon-Blooded representation. The Empress had been mollified by Tamas Khan's willing submission as a tributary—and had urgent wars elsewhere (such as Lookshy)—so she allotted Chiaroscuro a strictly nominal garrison. Future Tri-Khans kept that garrison to more or less its original limits.

The Delzahn quickly settled into their new roles as the aristocracy of Chiaroscuro, with the Tri-Khan and the ruling family at the top, the nobles below them, the Delzahn commoners below that and everyone else, however rich or powerful, after that. The system continues to this day. The Delzahn emphasis on kinship confers noble status on anyone who can trace a direct line to a member of the royal family. All members of these noble lineages receive special privileges, ranging from a share in the tax revenues to the right to duel or race camels within the city. Given

EXALTED INTERFERENCE

The Sidereals took only a couple of decades to notice Lunar activity in the South that might threaten the Scarlet Empire. They might have realized it faster, but Tamas Khan avoided performing obviously Lunar feats, while Tamuz stayed well behind the scenes. By the time the Wyld Hunt arrived at Chiaroscuro (which, as a Realm tributary, had to cooperate with the Immaculates), the Delzahn were well established.

Following Tamuz's instructions, Tamas Khan engaged the Wyld Hunt and then withdrew to the Wyld, where, with Tamuz's help, Tamas convincingly faked his own death. The Sidereals then withdrew, assuming they had purged the Delzahn of Anathema influence. The Sidereals allowed stories of the Kha-Khan's mythic end to filter back into general usage, since they preferred the legend to any suggestions that the Delzahn's greatest hero might have been Anathema.

Bronze Faction Sidereals permit some level of Lunar (or even Solar) interference in areas verging on the Wyld, but they pay attention when it happens in areas close to the Realm or that threaten Realm influence, satrap provinces or tributaries. Of course, this was more true in the past, when their resources were not so tightly stretched. The Solars, and the Deathlords, represent a more immediate threat than comparatively subdued Lunars working with isolated tribes. The Lunars do their best to encourage this attitude.

the extent of the royal clan, almost one in six Delzahn are now nobles of some degree; at the current date, Chiaroscuro currently holds more than 40,000.

The tax system is quite simple and wholly predatory. Every ship and every caravan that docks at or enters the city must pay a cut to the nobles. Of course, every tax collector takes a cut as well—generally as much as he believes he can keep without angering the royal family. Consumer pressure keeps the taxes within limits, however, because each merchant or ship captain may pay her taxes to any tax collector she wishes. The sight of several tax collectors bargaining with the captain of a wealthy fleet as to who can offer him the best tax rate is possibly unique to Chiaroscuro.

As Chiaroscuro flourished, so, too, did the farmlands around it, forcing the nomadic tribes to move further outward. Agyar Enies, and the Tri-Khans after him, wanted to keep Chiaroscuro reasonably self-supporting and not too reliant on imported food. This widened the gap between nomadic and city Delzahn, exacerbated by the fact that the nomads could no longer raid the farmers without reprisals from the city.

THE KHA-KHAN CULT

Tamas Khan departed after his faked death, richly rewarded by the elder Lunar; Tamuz remained behind to manipulate the Delzahn Empire. He did so through secretive cults that venerated the Kha-Khan and, indirectly, Tamuz himself. Many of the Tri-Khan's own family and other powerful Delzahn belonged to these cults, making it easy for Tamuz to keep a firm grip on the reins of power. In some cases, he sent dreams to the priests of the cults, and they passed on his messages. Other times, he used spells and Charms to manipulate them like puppets while they prophesied in trances. On rare occasions, Tamuz had gods and elementals manifest to bring messages "from the Kha-Khan in his palace beyond the winds," but he reserved this for important occasions, in order to preserve the sense of importance.

When the Immaculate Order sent missionaries to Chiaroscuro, shortly after the arrival of the Realm garrison, Tamuz feared that they might reduce or pervert his cults. However, between native influences and the fact that the Immaculate faith's dogma was less firmly developed then than it is now, a weird heterodoxy formed that became more or less acceptable to all concerned. The Delzahn people accepted that spirit worship was a de facto veneration of the Immaculate Dragons, who joined the general religious iconography of the region. This only reinforced the Kha-Khan cults, promoting the image of him as descending from Heaven and now adding that he came "with the blessing of the Dragons." More recent Immaculate monks have had absolutely no success leading the population away from these mingled, pitifully heretical beliefs.

Tamuz himself did not expect this particular mingling of beliefs, but lost no time exploiting it, delivering appropriate visions to his chosen priests and adding draconic images to altars and ritual phrases. Other Lunars are divided between those who applaud his opportunism (usually those who saw the Immaculate faith arise, and realize how much of a sham it is) and those, for example, the Sun King Seneschals, who disapprove of this sort of tampering.

None of this growth came easily. Chiaroscuro expanded under a constant state of tension, with the Delzahn slowly adapting their customs to city life, the Guild struggling to expand its power, the Realm garrison trying to get a foothold in local government and the common people simply struggling to survive.

NOMADIC DELZAHN

On the plains, the Delzahn continually travel across the deserts and savannas. A child can easily handle a

camel by his fifth birthday. Horsemanship comes next. A Delzahn receives his own steed as the formal beginning of adulthood. The young nomad rides alone for three days, contemplating the open savanna while the tribe moves on, and the rider must catch up with them afterward. Men return to the tribe with fresh meat from the hunt; women return with a poem.

The Delzahn hold that a man's honor lies in his deeds and ancestry rather than his appearance. By custom, therefore, all Delzahn men wear veils of brightly colored cloth whose embroidered patterns declare their lineage and personal glories. When traveling, Delzahn men wear white or dun-colored robes against the sun. In contrast, the Delzahn believe that a woman's only true asset is her beauty. All women go bare-faced, and unmarried women in search of husbands typically wear light, gauzy clothes designed to display their bodies.

Women and men have strictly divided roles among the Delzahn. Women should gather food and tend to the tribe's possessions and their family's lineage, while the men engage in war and hunting. The tradition of Dereth grants exceptions to these roles. Dereth are men and women who formally choose to live as the opposite gender, and are treated as such legally and ritualistically. They must wear a gray sash or veil at all times to signify their status.

A tribe measures its wealth by the number of animals it owns. A local orkhan owns all the tribe's possessions but allows each family to tend its own herd. Above the orkhans of each sept are the khans, each of whom claims dominion over a dozen or so septs through rights conferred by lineage and ritual combat.

Though the Tri-Khan remains the high leader of the Delzahn, the horde is far from unified. The khans out on the savannas and desert technically admit his authority and submit to his rulings, but with more and more resentment. They see the degeneration and softness of their profit-seeking urban brethren, and the way that they themselves are forced out of their traditional lands and raided for slaves who are then *sold*. Bad feeling grows, and the nomadic Delzahn are ripe for a charismatic leader—in one direction or another.

URBAN DELZAHN

Although some of the Delzahn descendants have lost their taste for war and travel, the traditions of the Delzahn remain strong in Chiaroscuro. Slavery is legal within the city, and the urban Delzahn even raid their nomadic cousins to provide the large number of slaves that aristocrats keep as trophies. The raids hone mounted fighting skills and are a part of Delzahn tradition, so they often result in the nobility taking more prisoners than they can comfortably support. Excess slaves are given as gifts or sold in Chiaroscuro's markets. Raiding other tribes for slaves—including other Delzahn tribes—is an old and accepted part of Delzahn tradition. As such raids become a significant source of supply to the

Chiaroscuro slave trade, they also increase the contention between the nomadic and urban Delzahn.

Many Delzahn nobles honor their nomadic ancestors by regularly staging hunts. Mounted on swift, fine-boned horses and sturdy camels, the nobles and their guards ride off in search of sand lions and golden-horned desert antelopes. (In some cases, the animals are rounded up beforehand and released into the territory where the hunt takes place.) These hunts are also military exercises and serve to hone the skills of the excellent Delzahn cavalry.

Fights often erupt in the streets of Chiaroscuro, provoked by the highly elaborate Delzahn dueling code. Many young Delzahn men (or female Dereth), especially those from noble houses, watch for the most insignificant slights as a chance to prove their dueling prowess. Most duels end at first blood or when one combatant is driven out of the dueling circle, but death and maiming occur with regularity. Duels over jealousy or accusations of dishonor are often to the death.

RECENT EVENTS AND CURRENT STATUS

The Delzahn Empire is strong, and Chiaroscuro with it. The many little wars that plague Creation do not impede the flow of trade or reduce the need for goods and slaves. The Delzahn nomads stay busy with tiny border wars and intrusions on the edges of their territory. The current Tri-Khan, Yejouj Khan, is an intelligent man in his 50s who controls the Empire as smoothly as he still does his horses. (He also attends one of the Kha-Khan mystery cults, allowing Tamuz to pass on suggestions and advice at crucial moments.) Yejouj Khan's direct heir, Semanos, is experienced and smart, but far from a match for his father—as both Realm and Guild have noticed.

The Chiaroscuran navy is a well-drilled force numbering 512 ships, commanded by Admiral Nares. The navy hunts pirates, guards the waters and frequently escorts

THE GRAFTED CULTURE

The urban Delzahn need constant care and attention to stop them slipping into the ways of decadence and luxury. Tamuz's strongest allies in this are custom and pride: Custom keeps the Delzahn families raiding and hunting, while pride provokes individual Delzahn to dueling and other glory-seeking practices. His human agents play on interfamily feuds to give the urban Delzahn a target to fight against—each other.

Tamuz must work constantly to maintain the urban Delzahn where they are. On one side, they risk becoming too civilized, abandoning their warlike traditions or forgetting their ancestors. On the other, they risk abandoning the city to return to the plains, to the glories of open warfare and riding as they wish under the free sky. (And, indeed, many young Delzahn do this every year and return to the tribes.) Tamuz has worked on families as a whole, removing overly permissive heads of families where necessary or providing visions to reactionaries to stop them from returning wholesale to the desert. In both cases, he keeps them in the city to maintain its vigor and continue its growth. Tamuz is very much a gardener who cares for his bushes and flowers, and who allows them free growth within their particular plots, but mercilessly cuts away any attempt to spread outside those areas.

In general, Tamuz's modifications to Delzahn culture have been subtle and secretive. He influenced major figures (usually senior members of Delzahn families) and worked through them to shape the general populace. Some of his targets received "divine" direction through the Kha-Khan cults or were sent dreams and visions to prompt particular courses of action. His human or younger Lunar agents manipulated other people through bribery, threats and impersonation. Tamuz prefers to work through proxies. His human agents usually believe he is someone else: a senior Delzahn minister, a high-ranking army general, a member of the secret service or even occasionally a Realm spy or Immaculate monk.

Tamuz even conducts his experiment under the direct gaze of the Realm and the Guild, taking useful elements from both, rather than hiding on the borders of Creation like other experiments. Other Lunars admire his secrecy and elegance of design. They not only respect his ability to guide the population so discreetly, but also his facility in doing it under constant inspection from the Realm. The fact that Tamuz managed to twist the Immaculate faith into further support for the legend of the Kha-Khan is viewed as particular artistry; other Lunars only wish they could do as well.

Guild ships into and out of port. Although the navy technically lies under the Tri-Khan's command, the navy commanders know that their true allegiance lies with the Guild. They would perform almost any favor for its local syndics. The army stationed in and around Chiaroscuro, on the other hand, is Delzahn to the bone. The cavalry in particular is loyal to the Tri-Khan alone, rather than to the Guild. The further parts of the Delzahn Horde feel greater loyalty to their own orkhans and khans than to the distant Tri-Khan. While they would unite with their urban brethren against invaders, the day may come when they consider sacking Chiaroscuro themselves, as the Kha-Khan did long ago.

Although the Tri-Khan appears to obey the Realm's commands, somehow those commands never seem to keep the Delzahn from doing exactly as they please. Chiaroscuro remains open to any and all visitors. Deathknights, Fair Folk, spirits, outcastes and any other beings may trade or even settle here. Of course, anyone who uses his powers to disrupt commerce or cause trouble will swiftly face a well-armed squad of town guardsmen, or even a Wyld Hunt composed of the local Dragon-Blooded and Immaculate representatives. The balance of power in Chiaroscuro is delicate, and upsetting it is extremely dangerous.

POLITICS AND THE REALM

Chiaroscuro's vast port is so important that, in the Realm's own interests, the city *should* be a virtual puppet of the Realm. So far, the Tri-Khans (with prompting from Tamuz) have managed to maintain the Delzahn Empire's independence. Tri-Khans tactfully receive Immaculate missionaries with every possible hope for their success, they accept a Dragon-Blooded garrison (though also keep it small), and they stress the need to keep the Delzahn in power rather than have the area degenerate into a mess of warring states.

Now that the Empress has disappeared, Tri-Khan Yejouj must play the various Great Houses against each other. He has done away with the more powerful of his Dragon-Blooded minders, either murdering them or arranging their withdrawal. A few of the weaker Dynasts are allowed to stay, but Yejouj distracts them with mercantile opportunities, pleasures, vices or conflicts with each other. He also covertly offers assistance to the Realm's many regional enemies, including factions in Harborhead, counting on the trouble they cause to distract the Realm even further from his demonstrably peaceful and well-ruled fiefdom.

In addition, the Tri-Khan has close ties with the Guild. In return for the ability to buy and sell any goods without restriction, the Guild uses its considerable power to help keep Chiaroscuro free from domination by the Realm. In Chiaroscuro, anyone may buy and sell whatever she wishes. While some commodities are best dealt with discreetly, the Tri-Khan and his nobles prohibit no sales and deny no one entrance.

OPINIONS ON THE EXPERIMENT

Tamuz is well pleased with the Delzahn experiment, but he views it as far from concluded. He looks for some way to reunite the two branches of the Delzahn, either through time or through the return of the Kha-Khan—and he may no longer have the centuries required to do it smoothly and subtly. While he could easily assume the position of Kha-Khan and reunite the nation, doing so might attract the Realm's attention far too early—indeed, might even give the Realm a convenient and nearby target to unite *itself* against. Timing is clearly key here, and Tamuz watches current events and changes in the Delzahn Empire with a hawk-like eye.

THE HASLANTI LEAGUE

The Haslanti League is a confederation of nine city-states and about 150 semi-nomadic tribes. Each city-state runs its own affairs, but League members cooperate on matters of economic development, foreign policy and

military operations. The Lunars do not deny their role in the League's history; they guided the tribes that originated the League, led them in rebellion against the Guild and even today watch over them and aid them against Fair Folk incursions and threats from the Wyld.

The League occupies a rough, bitter land with harsh weather and strictly limited areas of verdure and agricultural production. However, the land has bred some of the toughest people in the world, and the Lunars recognize that fact. They have come back to this experiment again and again, as a smith returning iron to the anvil, to help forge a League that slowly struggles to its feet and grows to adulthood.

BEGINNINGS: ARVIDA OF THE CRESCENT EYE

About 400 years ago, the southern and eastern shores of the White Sea were home to about 200 tribes of loosely linked herding peoples. In the extreme Northeast, the Haslanesh hunter-gatherers followed wild mammoth herds. In the south, the Haslanahsa herded domesticated reindeer, and the Haslanosha herded domesticated elk. The three people spoke a common language, and they shared many cultural norms, including shamanism and several important totem-spirits.

These three tribal groupings shared a common origin. They descended from exiles from one of the northernmost cities of the First Age—Tzatli—and the territories around it. When the city fell in the Shogunate's ruin, its people fled into the wilderness. Thousands upon thousands died in the snow, from the attacks of predators, from exposure and from simple despair. Only the strongest survived the horrors of those frozen marches. Yet, a few people possessed or developed survival skills and taught these to the others. From these survivors grew the three barbarian peoples.

The "gods" who watched over the tribes included a Lunar Exalt of the First Age, Arvida of the Crescent Eye. From the time of Tzatli's fall, Arvida acted as a terrible, wild patron to all three Haslan tribes and claimed all their territory as her own. Their legends ascribed 99 forms to her and told how she struck down mammoths with a single blow or drove herds of reindeer and elk in terror at the sound of a single footfall. The Haslan called her Bear Woman and worshipped her in terrified awe.

Arvida was a Full Moon Lunar, proud and passionate, who saw the barbarian tribes of the north as more vibrant and more alive than the hand-fed, petty, city-bred fools at the end of the First Age. She took on the mantle of a goddess to lead the newly formed tribes. They were still young, without the weight of tradition that some of the other tribes carried, ready to listen to her words. She taught them the ways of survival and ordered them not to build cities or towns but to live in harmony with the wilds around them: to hunt, fish and farm while avoiding the sins of the Shogunate and before.

However, Arvida's open actions attracted the Realm's attention. She was a very public Anathema, making little attempt to conceal her nature. Old Realm and Shogunate documents recorded her name. A specially briefed and equipped Wyld Hunt, with Sidereal assistance, set out to bring her down. After a hunt that lasted eight years, she was killed in the spring of RY 412.

THE ORPHANED TRIBES

Arvida's death traumatized the tribes. News of her passing spread swiftly (indeed, as though carried by the winds themselves), coupled with disbelief. Many members of the tribes refused to accept the truth, while others despaired and fell into compacts with the Fair Folk or succumbed to the Wyld. Madness gripped the Haslan people for more than 100 years. Their shamans went through a long period of obsession with the Wyld, with spirits and with other Exalts—anyone who would answer their pleas and offer them guidance. Chiefs and whole families destroyed themselves through berserk vendettas in which they murdered and raided each other for decades. Families and kinship lines were wiped out completely.

A number of observing Lunars took this as proof that Arvida's experiment had failed. Her influence had not strengthened the Haslan, but weakened them. They pointed at the disintegration of tribal society, the willingness to embrace unhealthy forces such as the Wyld or the Fair Folk, the sheer madness that gripped so many of her people. Some Lunars argued for a simple coup de grâce, to finish the poor fools off quickly and mercifully. Other Stewards felt that

the Haslans should receive a last chance. If they could pull themselves out of their pit, then indeed they might deserve consideration. But if they failed, then small loss.

RECOVERY

Over the next 150 years, many of the tribes slipped back and forth between hunting and gathering, nomadic herding and settled farming. The damage done during the time of madness warped many traditions and shook many firm beliefs. While the traveling herders still looked down to an extent on the settled farmers, and vice versa, the sheer degree of scorn ebbed. Boundaries between tribes blurred as families took whatever lifestyle seemed useful. But the original beliefs that Arvida had sowed among them still remained, deep-rooted: Build no cities, make no towns, but live in harmony with the wilderness.

The climate grew slowly warmer, and it became possible to camp in one place for extended periods of time, even with thousands of elk or reindeer to tend. While tribes who depended on mammoths had to keep moving to follow their herds, the Haslanosha and the Haslanahsa settled down to some degree in the greenfields where food was plentiful and relatively easy to collect. Other folk colonized the emeralds and acted as go-betweens for the settled groups and those who still migrated.

THE FOUR CAMPS

Four of these semi-permanent camps became particularly important as trade centers, religious precincts and meeting-places. As more Haslan settled in these camps or made regular visits, the Lunars again grew interested. Gerd Marrow-Eater was most prominent, but Elcithe Avalanche-Dancer, Merian Whitecrow and Flintbeak Nightingale aided him. The Haslan had indeed proven that they could overcome their weakness and grow strong. While they did not develop entirely upon the lines that Arvida intended, they still showed promise. The four Lunars, none of them very old, chose to assist the Haslans by disposing of Fair Folk marauders on their borders, but the Moonchildren agreed that the tribes should advance at their own pace.

Then, the Guild arrived.

CORRUPTION AND CIVILIZATION: THE GUILD

The Guild first approached the tribes in RY 500 through the Four Camps, which had become meeting-places for foreign traders. Over the next 50 years, the Guild grew to dominate the tribes. By providing iron tools, weapons and other luxury goods—and of course, addictive drugs—the Guild stripped the Haslan tribes of substantial wealth. The Four Camps became larger, more prosperous and more permanent… with permanent garrisons of Guild mercenaries. The lands around the Four Camps were colonized for agriculture and pastureland, and the property passed from Haslan natives to Guildsmen. Even more of an insult to the teachings of Arvida, the Guild introduced slaves to the region as miners and demanded tribute in amber, ivory, woolen cloth and leather.

The tribes resented both the presence and the arrogance of the Guild merchant princes. For their part, the Guild officials bribed tribal leaders to advance Guild agendas and tried to coax concessions from whole regions at once. The Guild officials also encouraged intertribal warfare to increase the slave population, sometimes going so far as to fake attacks and raids in order to incite hostilities.

The tribes felt increasingly trapped. By now, the Guild had brought in sufficient troops and slaves to garrison the Four Camps and many of the larger greenfields, and held the trade routes in a firm grip. The tribes themselves lost their best warriors to internecine warfare, or had their strongest members and best crafters taken as slaves. The tribes' finest goods departed as tribute. They were weakened even further than they had been by the madness of the previous century, poisoned and then leeched upon by the minions of "civilization."

At the same time, the Guild's expeditions delved deeply into the Great Ice in search of the now-legendary Tzatli. In doing so, the Guild unwittingly sowed the seeds of its own undoing. While they did not find the First Age treasures they sought, the expeditions introduced the Haslan porters and guides to the Great Ice. Other Haslan tribes headed north when Guild-protected herders, miners and taxmen pushed them out of the best lands along the White Sea's southern coast. Guild officials showed up at a summer encampment in search of tribute to find the tribe gone, the reindeer scattered or given to other herds and no tribute to be had.

All of this began to form a new group among the Haslan, a group of people who could survive on the Great Ice.

The Great Ice

A coat of ice and snow ranging from a few feet to more than 50 feet thick lies over all the land north of the White Sea. Pack ice covers the sea itself, and freezes solid for half the year. To an outsider, this frozen land seems barren and useless. To the trained Haslanti eye, the land brims with opportunity.

Mining and fishing are the major preoccupations on the Great Ice. Rocky islets in the White Sea yield amethysts, topaz, amber, turquoise and diamonds. Crevasses in the ice can catch silt and wind-blown seeds, forming emeralds, which become refuges for people working on the snow plains—hunters, prospectors and the like. Iceships and their crews harvest fish, whales, walruses, seals and other bounties from the sea. The Great Ice is a vital part of the Haslanti League.

A Rare, Secret Intervention

Merian Whitecrow gave the Haslan one of Arvida's last secrets. In the guise of dream quests, he guided Haslan shamans to caves and other hidden sites where Arvida concealed First Age ice yachts. These vessels were designed with science and craft beyond the abilities of the Haslan, such as outriggers fitted with steel blades for skating over the ice. The tribes took these finds as a sign of destiny, copied the designs using their own materials and left their herds behind to travel out onto the ice, looking for a home beyond the Guild's reach. The Lunars also gave the Haslan the secrets of the air boats that would later become such a feature of the Haslanti League. At this time, the Haslan people had no way to build them. They had the idea, though, and stored the designs for later use—already beginning to envisage a future without the Guild.

A New Beginning: Meeting at Twisted Stone

Active and passive resistance to Guild arrogance and taxation increased, from hiding their best animals when Guildsmen came for tribute to iceship piracy against Guild caravans. New income and food supplies came from the Great Ice. Emerald by emerald, greenfield by greenfield, the Haslan drove the Guild out of the Haslan territory. Without habitable bases, the Guild had no way to bring in troops and hold the ground. By RY 580, the Guild was confined to the Four Camps and a few minor trading centers along the coast.

At last, chiefs and shamans of 40 different tribes received messages to meet at the Lighthouse of Twisted Stone, a lonely point east of the camp of Icehome, where an ancient and broken beacon of the First Age overlooked the White Sea. Tribal leaders came on horses, reindeer and elk, by iceship

Lunars and the Guild

Why did the Lunars not take action against the Guild at an early stage? The Lunars had the power to kill the Guild's representatives and block the Guild from Haslan territory. Had they done so, they could have avoided much painful bloodshed later on.

The Guild's oppression, however, forced the Haslan people to explore the Great Ice and welded them together into the Haslanti League. Some Lunars argue that the Guild served a necessary purpose in this case; others, that the Haslans eventually would have taken the same steps on their own. The question is still under debate among Lunars who care about the more theoretical aspects of the Thousand Streams River.

and skis, wondering at the summons but eager to learn what they might do. To their surprise, a living god awaited them at the Lighthouse of Twisted Stone.

The Lunar Exalt named Gerd Marrow-Eater, a No Moon Caste of proven wisdom and strategy, had summoned them all. Youthful but strong, he seemed to them as Arvida reborn, able to take the shape of the eagle, the wolf, the whale, the bear, the elk and the reindeer. And each time he did so, the avatars of the animal spirits came and bowed down before him, showing him respect and acknowledging his power. The shamans saw this and declared him worthy of allegiance and obedience. Likewise, all day he defeated the mightiest champions of the gathered Haslans. He killed none of them, though he took the smallest finger of each warrior's left hand.

The War of Independence

Gerd Marrow-Eater demanded that the tribes take council together. He raised their passions with a speech in which he declared that the Guild pushed the tribes too hard, forced civilized ways upon then, turned them into nothing but slaves. But the Haslanahsa and the Haslanosha were 100 times more numerous than the Guild! The land was theirs! Once the tribes united, neither the Guild nor the Realm nor any power in Creation could take the North from them. They could form a covenant that would merge all that was best from settlers and herders, fishers and miners, a union that would hold the North forever.

Gerd's speech drove the tribes into a passion of fury and enthusiasm. The chiefs appealed to him to lead them to victory against the Guild and its mercenaries. The Lunar consented to lead them three times, but three times only. After that, he would advise and guide them and send others to help them. Yet, Gerd said, the best victory would be won by the Haslan tribes for themselves. For three days, the two Haslan peoples argued between themselves, setting

HASLANTI SOCIETY: PHYSICAL AND MYSTICAL

The Haslanti possess a deeply mystical culture. They worship their ancestors, the avatars of the animals, and the gods of fate and dream. But their society is also very much founded on physical strength: simple battle against other human beings, struggles against the elements, mastering of herdstock and ice-fishers and all the other tribal duties that demand a healthy body to go with the healthy soul. The group of Lunars who called themselves the Twisted Stone Conclave didn't want to give undue power to either the shamans or the warriors while helping the tribes break free of the Guild's hold. Gerd Marrow-Eater had to impress and dominate the Haslans both physically and mystically.

Gerd could have taken full authority and led the tribes without a single voice raised in dissent, but he and his fellows didn't want this. It would only have made the tribes dependent again, as in Arvida's day. They could all too easily imagine another catastrophic collapse if the Lunar's presence was removed, crushing the tribes' spirit of independence and exploration, however benevolent Gerd's leadership.

out terms for a covenant that would stand as long as did the North itself. Haslanahsa and Haslanosha merged to form the Haslanti League.

And the Haslanti League went to war.

Gerd insisted that the tribes unite themselves before he would lead them, and the chiefs obeyed. Word went out to the furthest wanderers on the Great Ice, across the wide plains, into every emerald and greenfield, and secretly into the Four Camps, whispered from Haslanti to Haslanti when the Guildsmen could not hear. It was an idea whose time had come. Everyone hated the Guild; everyone saw the advantages of joining together to expel the Guild. The League spread, and every tribe agreed to it, and waited for the call to battle.

In RY 583, Gerd did as he promised. With greater and greater audacity, he led the Haslanti three times against one of the Four Camps, and conquered them. Chiefs and shamans begged Gerd to stay and lead them to capture the fourth and largest Camp, Icehome, but Gerd refused. He claimed that he had other obligations, and that if a god helped the Haslanti to victory, then the Haslanti territory would not be a land suited to mortals. (In fact, the Twisted Stone Conclave had agreed that for this last campaign, the Haslanti must stand or fall by their own merits.) Instead, he helped the war leaders plan how to take Icehome, then set three chiefs, one from each region, to direct the attack.

POLITICAL STRUCTURE: THE COUNCIL OF OLIGARCHS

Despite their wishes to leave the Haslanti to develop in peace, members of the Twisted Stone Conclave thought it wise to give them at least a few guidelines toward governing the League. The Twisted Stone Conclave had already noticed fractures forming during the war against the Guild, as the settled tribes, the herders and the fishers all sought to protect their own interests. Gerd made two very basic suggestions: a council of 12 (had 12 chiefs not fallen, he would have found a similarly dramatic way to make the point) and the basic principle of discussion before conflict. From there, Haslanti government mostly evolved from tribal customary law.

This developed into the Council of Oligarchs, a group of 12 delegates elected from the local assemblies. Beneath the Council are the 36 district assemblies, at which all citizens are entitled to attend and speak, and that conduct all legislative business for the League as a whole. An Oligarch must be over the age of 45, native born to the League, have served as an arbitrator in at least 10 disputes each worth at least one talent of silver and be nominated by her home district to a council seat and elected by acclaim at the relevant assemblies. The Council of Oligarchs acts as the interpreter of the League's laws. The Council functions as the high court for all the districts, towns and tribes of the Haslanti. Technically, the League is led by the Archon, a six-year post for a retired Oligarch, but in practice, the Council of Oligarchs makes the decisions and interprets the laws.

The long and bloody battle lasted 12 days. A dozen chiefs and countless warriors died in the fighting, streaming down the walls of the greenfield and then ascending to the Citadel. When they had finally fought their way to the heart of Icehome and stood in triumph, Gerd waited for them atop the hill of the Citadel. He stretched out a hand, indicating all the territory from White Sea to farmland to the tundra beyond. "You lost twelve chiefs," he said, "so your nation will always have twelve chiefs to sit in council and judgment. As long as you talk out your difficulties first, before you fight, everything you can see from here, and more, shall belong to the League of the Haslanti forever." With these words, he vanished from mortal view.

WAR, PEACE AND AIR BOATS: THE LEAGUE SPREADS

The League's sudden and powerful emergence in the North greatly alarmed Gethamane, Whitewall and even the Realm's client nations all the way south to the Inland Sea. Rightly judging that the landscape and people would be difficult to conquer, the Scarlet Empress sent a large delegation of the Immaculate Order north. She believed that gods or spirits lay behind the League's appearance, and that it would be best to put down the divinities responsible. At the same time, the Guild pressured Gethamane to close itself to products from the League, and enlisted Cherak and Sijan in a boycott of Northern goods.

Both efforts failed. The Immaculate Order never succeeded in hunting down Gerd and actually did the League a service by humbling a number of predatory spirits, small gods and Fair Folk. Many tribes, suddenly released from difficult rites and harsh spirit rulership, petitioned to join the League, thus actively strengthening the confederation. While the Haslanti League could not crack Gethamane and take its trade routes, it could occupy the surrounding territory and block the Guild's caravans. (Gethamane walked a complicated tightrope of claimed neutrality and quiet favors to both sides.) Eventually, Gethamane publicly relented, and the Guild had to accept limited trading privileges in Haslanti lands in exchange for acknowledging the League's political and economic independence.

The League developed its modern military during the Gethamane War, copying First Age gliders and air boats from the plans passed down for more than a century, adapted to human-powered, Second Age technology. Ironically, much of the technical skills for manufacturing gliders and air boats was built on the foundations left behind by the Guild. The Wind Fleet is now the core of the Haslanti armed forces.

THE WIND FLEET

The Wind Fleet of air boats is the pride of the Haslanti League and a demonstration of the North's ingenuity. Other nations may rely on Hearthstones and Essence, but the Haslanti air boats rely on rendered whale oil or kerosene, and the skills and courage of pilot and crew.

However, the League also has some larger airships powered by First Age Essence devices salvaged from Tzatli. These are kept in reserve and not used indiscriminately—partly because of their great value, and partly because there is very little hope of repairing their power sources if they should be damaged or break down.

LUNAR OVERSIGHT

While Gerd Marrow-Eater may have vanished from human eyes, the Twisted Stone Conclave still maintains a hold on the Haslanti people. The gods select the Archon of the Council of Oligarchs; in this case, the "gods" are the Twisted Stone Conclave, a number of totem-animal avatars, and the Haslanti Ennead (the nine gods of Ice, Fate and Dream who are the particular patrons of the Haslanti League).

The Lunars do not hold any direct positions in the military. The grand-nephew of one of the Twisted Stone Conclave, General Bjorn Varjnison, is the overall commander of the League army and militia, though. He passes on information or meddles in Haslanti affairs on the Lunars' suggestion. Similarly, the Lunars maintain an agent on the Grandmothers, the directors and operation board of the Ears of the North, the Haslanti spy agency. Since the agency's founding, at least one of the Grandmothers has been a Lunar of the No Moon Caste. The present Lunar, Keen-Eyed Snowcat, is a mere 86 and Haslanti-born herself. Her responsibility is not so much to direct the Grandmothers as to conceal them from other prying eyes and ears in the North.

WYLD STORMS

In RY 674, Wyld storms began to blow through Haslanti territory, continuing on and off for the next 50 years. Whether through the actions of the Fair Folk, or simply due to the weakening of Creation's borders, several large and once-stable pockets of the Wyld drifted around Haslanti territory, driven by the wind. Everything changed where they passed. Islands appeared in the White Sea. Frozen fog closed around farmlands and left them miles away when it cleared. Tundra bloomed with unnatural plant life. New predators stalked the land. Dozens of tribes simply vanished.

The Twisted Stone Conclave acted. Not only did these Wyld storms interfere with an extremely promising experiment, dispersing it was their duty as Stewards. Some of the Lunars entered large Wyldfogs and dissipated them. Other Lunars froze other Wyldfogs in place until the natural forces of Creation could stabilize them and restore the natural order. The Lunar called Flintbeak Nightingale dispersed one such cloud in RY 726, only five miles from Icehome. She refused to accept the thanks of the city and would not agree to enter it so that they could celebrate her victory and pay her homage. The Haslanti in general have very positive attitudes toward Lunars, though (to the great irritation of the Immaculate Order and the Realm). This extends to Solars as well to some degree. From the Haslanti's limited experience of Lawgivers, they seem to a sort of second-best Lunar, powerful in combat but clearly handicapped through their inability to change shape.

RECENT EVENTS AND CURRENT STATUS

Since the close of the Wyldfog War (as the Haslanti call it), a new spirit of innovation and exploration has taken hold among the Haslanti. Explorers have followed ancient songlines backwards to the buried city of Tzatli (rediscovered in RY 731), while the League itself ponders new alliances and expansion. The Haslanti maintain their barbarian roots, with even fourth-generation settlers taking a few weeks each year to travel across the tundra or to journey on the Great Ice. Children are fostered out by tradition to kinsmen who live and work elsewhere in the League, thus continually binding together all the different branches—farmers, herders, fishers and miners—and reminding them what they owe one another.

OPINIONS ON THE EXPERIMENT

As far as the Twisted Stone Conclave is concerned—and most Lunars would agree—the Haslanti League is a success. Gerd Marrow-Eater himself has grown bored with the League, having built a functional society and now wanting to do something else. The rest of the Twisted Stone Conclave maintains their interest. They see potential for further development, possibly involving spreading Haslanti customs and behavior further south. The Lunars have perhaps grown too fond of their pet project and are unwilling to let it go.

While the League is a success in Lunar terms, outside events may overtake it, and its own expansion could bring trouble down upon it. No one could have predicted the Bull of the North's rise: neither the Oligarchs nor the Twisted Stone Conclave can gauge his full intentions. Likewise, the League's air fleet operates at full extension and cannot afford any significant damage or loss of ships without curtailing its operations. The League may yet fall, but if it does, it will be because exterior forces bring it down. With its firm foundations and with occasional Lunar guidance, the League is likely to remain sturdy for centuries to come.

HALTA

Haltan legends tell that as the Contagion ravaged the cities of the world, many people not yet infected fled into the deep forests, seeking to isolate themselves from the dying masses of humanity. To avoid the bands of marauding hobgoblins and Wyld-tainted animals that wandered the forests of the East, these people learned the ways of the forest and became adept at hiding in the trees when enemies came near. After a few decades spent in this desperate fashion, beneficent gods took pity and helped these refugees, teaching them how to live in the trees and make full use of the forest's great bounty.

This is the tale of Halta the bountiful, the generous, the gracious giver of life, and her wise inhabitants who live in harmony with nature and work together to achieve a living, beautiful land. And just as with many such happy tales, on closer inspection, it's not as pretty as it looked; as

TYPE OF EXPERIMENT

In Halta, the Lunars very carefully prepared the ground before the experiment began. Silver Python and Rain Deathflyer arranged divine patronage, located fertile land, dealt with nearby barbarians and spread the Lunars' own concepts of suitable government and tradition among the people. Then, the Lunars drew back and let the humans get on with their lives, only intervening in moments of extreme urgency, but guarding the borders and keeping the experiment unpolluted.

This sort of methodology can result in a well-balanced political and social system, since the humans have mostly developed it themselves and worked out the problems and snags along the way. On the other hand, a society thus sheltered from many problems of the outside world can become like a hothouse flower. It thrives while protected and isolated, but wilts without that constant nurturing. When a once-isolated society must interact with the rest of Creation, moral and cultural standards may deteriorate, wartime necessities may alter the social system and physical damage may harm the living and social systems the society depends upon. Halta remains untested.

with swans, where the bird floats serenely on the water, but below paddles desperately to keep afloat.

After the Usurpation, some Lunars fled to the easternmost edge of the Great Redwood Forest. Centuries later, mortal refugees from the Great Contagion and Fair Folk Invasion took the same path. Two Stewards, Rain Deathflyer and Silver Python, took pity on the human refugees and taught them to live high up in the trees, using the forest's great natural bounty to allow them to thrive and prosper.

The two Lunars were among the advocates of the Thousand Streams River. When the Lunars saw the desperate refugees struggling to survive but oblivious to the food around them, they saw an ideal group of specimens for an experiment—but they also felt pity for the weary, hungry, desperate mortals. The Lunars thought they could create a people that embodied the strength and self-reliance of barbarians together with the learning and organization found in civilized lands. The Lunars hoped they could create a land where beastmen would be accepted as fellow citizens, where everyday respect for the gods would be a natural part of life and where humans would live in harmony with the natural world around them, creating rather than despoiling.

The Lunars dreamed of a perfect society. Balanced, harmonious, rational, in touch with its roots, vital, growing; in all ways, the two Lunars thought, the opposite of the brutal, bureaucratic Shogunate. The two Lunars knew what they wanted, and they set out to make it.

RAW FOREST: THE BEGINNINGS

The humans were innocents in the wilderness. They needed guidance, strength and safety. The question of food was a minor one. The forest held many forms of food that could easily be gathered by any human who knew what they looked like, however weak or unable to hunt. The first real step of building Halta involved staying alive in the face of Fair Folk, Wyld-tainted barbarians and still-human barbarian tribes, and indeed, preventing the refugees from becoming savages themselves, as the strongest among them survived by bullying and robbing the weak.

The Fair Folk were silent during this period, and the human inhabitants of Halta could only be grateful for it. Though they did thrive, and surprisingly quickly, the republic's famous tree-cities lay far in the future. The inhabitants were still poor, scrambling semi-barbarians, trying to stay alive.

Rain Deathflyer dealt with the barbarians and Wyld barbarians rapidly and practically. He appeared to them under the guise of a forest-spirit or protective deity and forbade them to harm "his chosen people" under penalty of death. When barbarians disobeyed, he slew them in the form of a giant hawk, leaving their mutilated bodies as messages to their tribes. Once the barbarians not only obeyed him but also sought to propitiate him, he led chosen warriors and shamans to meet the refugees and to teach them the

BEHIND THE SCENES

It was essential, Silver Python felt, to prepare the ground first. Even the best of seeds could not flourish where the earth was barren or where they would be eaten before growing. The Lunars needed a nourishing environment to produce their society. Rain Deathflyer dealt with the barbarians, while she dealt with the spirits, gods and Fair Folk, arranging patronages, or at least temporary truces.

The Fair Folk were the most difficult to handle. Even given her skills at negotiation and her surpassing prowess, Silver Python could not persuade the local Fair Folk to sign a definite treaty of non-aggression. All three of the local Fair Folk monarchs—Yseult, Slulura and Marika—refused to bind themselves to any treaty that would hinder their depredations. In the end, Silver Python promised that in return for a truce of 100 years, she and Rain Deathflyer would allow the humans to negotiate their own pacts with the Fair Folk without interfering. The Fair Folk gleefully agreed, already envisaging a free harvest of dreams and souls.

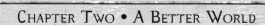

local ways of hunting and gathering. The Steward arranged marriages between the more peaceful local tribes and the newcomers, and the various communities began to share languages and beliefs.

The three Forest Rulers of the East, Arilak, Caltia and Jorst dwell in a delicate balance: Arilak the Unseen holds dominion over all the jungles and tropical forests in the East and Southeast, while Caltia the Eternal commands the East and Northeast's evergreen woods and Golden-Eyed Jorst controls the entire East where deciduous trees hold sway. Via spirit intermediaries, and then in person, Silver Python approached Caltia the Eternal. Silver Python pointed out the benefits of a thriving, growing population who would revere Caltia in particular and strengthen her among the trio of Forest Rulers. Caltia was quick to see the potential advantages and agreed to provide protection in

THE BEASTMEN OF HALTA

While the two main types of beastmen in Halta are hawkmen and snakemen, other types do exist. Some descend from previous tribes of beastmen dating back to the Contagion or from communities that seek a better life in Halta. A few new forms of beastmen came from Halta's own breeding programs. While no one likes to discuss it in public, the attempts to produce more intelligent and skilful animals sometimes result in new forms of beastmen as well, or creatures who can interbreed with humans. Such creatures tend to fall outside the limits of Haltan acceptance and often flee into the Wyld to form new communities. Some remain peaceful, but others become degenerate savages, bandits preying on travelers and nearby settlements. In isolated communities far to the East, beastmen and ordinary Haltans occasionally marry, but their children never find a place outside those remote villages.

The Haltans certainly tolerate beastmen, but still consider them both fearsome and inhuman. Even if the two Lunars achieved their aim of a society where beastmen can live next to humans, it is far from a harmonious commingling of races. Humans and beastmen stay as separate as oil and water in Halta and have no wish to bring their communities closer together.

This partial failure of their plan disappoints Rain Deathflyer and Silver Python. The diversion of beastmen into particular areas of society is far from being the free contribution of both peoples that they anticipated. Beastmen have become too rarefied, too taboo, for everyday work and casual labor. The Lunars see no immediate way of remedying this, however.

return for worship and to watch over this new nation—assuming that the people obeyed her precepts and revered hunters, of course. Similarly, avatars of animal-spirits (hawks, monkeys and several others) agreed to let their creatures assist the humans in return for regular offerings and good treatment.

THE BIRTH OF CIVILIZATION

With the theological and practical groundwork done, the new Haltan nation began to grow. One of the biggest developments was the tradition of the Test of Survival, which still endures to this day. When Haltan children come of age, between 12 and 16, all go into the forest alone for two full weeks. They make this journey with nothing more than clothes, a knife, a blanket, flint and steel and one full waterskin. At the end of this time, they must return with either an animal they have killed or a rare plant they have harvested. Youths who cannot succeed in either task must remain in the wilderness until they have done so. All Haltan children who wish to become legal adults must pass this test.

Another feature of Haltan life that began early in the nation's history was the toleration of beastmen. Before the Usurpation, many Solars and Lunars created personal pets, breeding stock, armies, assassins and other minions who were part-human, part-other. The Dragon-Blooded slew many beastmen who fell defending their masters, exterminated others as potential threats or drove them into the Wyld. In the Lunars' long exile at Creation's rim, some Lunars bred beastmen as subjects or potential warriors against the Dragon-Blooded. When Creation shrank in the Fair Folk invasion, all these part-humans fled from the advancing Wyld or were lost to chaos.

Many of these part-humans took refuge in the Eastern forests. Some formed tribes of their own. Others mingled with human groups and took on particular duties, winning acceptance by their deeds on the battlefield or by the authority of the animal avatars whom they spoke for. The Haltan people tolerated the beastmen by divine (or rather Lunar) command and assimilated them to a degree, but beastmen lived in particular districts rather than mingling with the human population, and took on particular tasks, usually becoming warriors, doctors or shaman-priests. They are, in a sense, excluded upward: prestigious, but not loved.

GROWTH AND THE GODS

The concept of meritocracy and upward expansion germinated like a seed in the nascent Halta. Citizens came to believe that it should be possible for anyone, of any birth, to rise to a station suited to his or her merits. Suddenly, people were exchanging new ideas—new ways of breeding animals, of cultivating plants, of building in the treetops. The tree cities began to take form, slowly expanding from villages, just as the nation itself began to spread its wings and take form. There was no prejudice; there was simply opportunity.

Even the gods approved. The blessing of Caltia herself clearly lay on people who followed her ways, who honored the forest and made good use of their opportunities, and who strove to expand and increase. Ill luck, frequently fatal, lay on those who tried to limit her worship out of loyalty to other gods.

PREVIOUS DEITIES

The gods of the refugees, weakened and impoverished as they were, did not want to lose their few remaining worshippers. However, the gods had little choice: They were not strong enough to challenge Caltia, and they no longer had the backing in Yu-Shan to lodge a formal complaint; given that their former nations were shattered, they were weakened and many other deities took advantage of the turmoil in Creation to increase the number of their own worshippers. The gods had to accept their losses and endure their diminished status as best they could.

A few survive to this day as minor forest spirits, worshipped by single villages and barely surviving, forgotten to Creation at large. Dremnos, Lord of Stone, once patron of 100 cities, is now reduced to guarding and protecting a small hamlet of inbred, traditionalist stonecutters. Lohath, Veil of Dawn, once a handmaiden of the Unconquered Sun, now guides the hands of a few maidens as they spin and is grateful for their pitiful prayers. Some of these petty gods bear a significant grudge toward Caltia or remember their glory days when thousands bowed down to them and prayers murmured sweetly in their ears. Should someone offer them a chance to regain worshippers and rise in power again, these gods would be glad to take it.

Some of the refugees chose to spread out into allied areas, forming their own small communities, preserving their previous gods or adopting new local ones. Even if they paid due respect to Caltia, they felt greater loyalty to their particular patron. A few such small kingdoms survive to this day as client states of the Haltan Republic; Bloody River is the most notable, and is ruled by a harsh triumvirate of local gods who demand prayers several times a day even from the smallest children.

The Lunars permitted these secondary deities, so long as the Lunars did not lose too many people from their growing nation. It was, after all, to the Lunars' advantage to propitiate local small deities and forest spirits. Anyone who pressed too hard for another god's worship at Caltia's expense, however, tended to suffer lethal "accidents."

INTO THE TREES

The community also discovered a common enemy and thrived on it. Caltia had long been on bad terms with Golden-Eyed Jorst, the lord of the East's deciduous trees. Their mutual dislike echoed in constant, low-level strife between the areas of the land where they each were strong. Now that Caltia's worshippers had risen in number, so did Jorst's animosity toward her. His Linowan followers began to pick off the refugees or kidnap them to absorb them into his own people. The Haltans naturally objected. The common enemy helped the refugees blend together to become a single nation. War with the Linowans became part of Haltan culture, part of Haltan life. They had always been a nation at war; they would always be a nation at war.

The Haltans adopted the barbarians' habit of living in the trees, and while their dwellings in no way compared to the mighty cities that would be raised later, above-ground travel became the norm. Many Haltans (the nation had by now begun to call itself the Republic of Halta) began to look down on "mere" ground-level travel as something restricted to the very young, the infirm or the incapable. Widespread use of Young Monkey Tea (a local herbal mixture that is a mild muscle relaxant) resulted in children who were physically more flexible than their parents and who grew up with tree-climbing as a way of life.

A few generations after the Lunars began their experiment, they were satisfied with the results. The people were blended, thriving, vigorous and beginning to spread outward, with a common foe to battle against and a healthy devotion to their protective deities. It was time to turn rustic villagers into a great nation.

THE FAIR FOLK: TREATY AND COMPROMISE

A hundred years after Silver Python's agreement with the Fair Folk, in RY 281, the raksha rose from their Freeholds and began to seize captives from the human population once more. Queen Chaltra Amritsa and her Council sent messages that they were prepared to negotiate, and the Fair Folk responded, already gloating over the many victims they would glean from these pitiful humans.

Silver Python had promised she would not help the Haltans form their own pact with the Fair Folk. She never promised to deny the Haltans *other* help. When Chaltra Amritsa sat down to negotiate, an avatar of Caltia and a powerful woodland-spirit called a forest walker stood behind her. Under the threat of wholesale divine retribution, with the gods turning the wrath of the entire forest against them, the Fair Folk hammered out terms.

In the end, the realities of forest life made it fairly straightforward to reach an agreement that neither side particularly liked, but that both could live with. The mortals sought safety in the trees; the Fair Folk preferred to hunt on the ground. They agreed that any mortal or animal who touched the forest floor was fair game, but that if the individual could climb a tree, she was safe. People above could

lower ropes or come down to the forest floor, but could not attack the Fair Folk from up in the trees. Finally, all Fair Folk had to ask permission from the local Haltan leaders before climbing up into the trees and would be fully subject to Haltan laws and customs while they remained.

Further clauses dealt with protection against attack by the Linowan, and codicils in future years included agreements over trade. However, the basics were clear and well-defined. It set a precedent for Haltan-Fair Folk interaction that enabled a surprising degree of trade and peaceful commerce—and mutual military assistance—over the years.

THE EVOLUTION OF GOVERNMENT

The Haltan crown has always been a hereditary matriarchy. This goes back to the days when the refugees first stumbled into the jungles of Halta and has not changed since. However, after two sequential weak queens (Mathriel, in RY 253, and Sarielde, in RY 267), it became acceptable for the queen to choose her heir from among all her close relatives, rather than simply her daughters. As the decades passed, the customs grew for the queen to consult the Council of Nobles in the process and to step down while still in her prime, rather than ruling into her old age. This began simply as appointing a successor when the queen reached 40, in case of illness or death in battle. Over time, this became a full handover of power, with the old queen acting as advisor to the new monarch. The consultation with the Council of Nobles continued until the Council was expected to select the queen, rather than the queen herself, and a number of queens of Halta have bitterly resented this.

Haltans now accept as law that the Council of Nobles chooses all new queens from among the previous queen's close relatives, including her children, nieces, younger cousins and second cousins. When the queen turns 40, or possibly earlier, the Council of Nobles assembles and consults with the queen to decide upon her heir. The queen herself has no choice in the matter, though the Council does listen to her advice.

The Council of Nobles began as a collection of tribal elders. As time went by, it became formalized into a group of people, each of whom held responsibility for a different fiefdom in Halta. Finally (and this took more than a century to implement fully), the nobles became dependent on a vote from the residents of their district. The election became a triennial event, resulting in the downgrading of some nobles and the upgrading of others, and even the revocation of some nobles' status or the appointment of completely new nobles. The Council itself grew in importance as Halta expanded, since the queen had to delegate more and trust the word of advisors from regions she did not know personally.

Actually becoming a noble involves rigorous competition. Prospective nobles must demonstrate their competence at everything from knowledge of Haltan history and law to public speaking and animal handling. The nobles themselves prefer new members who have actually fought against the

Linowan, but almost a third of all nobles have never done so—particularly in the provinces furthest from the Linowan border. Deputies decide the results of the initial competitions, but the assembled Council of Nobles votes on the final selection of new aristocrats. These competitions take place every three years in Chanta. Competing is free, but only native-born Haltans can become nobles. By tradition, the Council reserves a few dozen of its 500 seats specifically for intelligent animals.

Under the Council, the Haltan government has three large departments. The Department of Halta administers justice, collects taxes and directs public-works projects. The shaman-priests control the Department of Religious and Natural Affairs, which governs both Haltan relations with the gods and Fair Folk and with their sacred forest. Arborists in this department must approve all significant alterations made to living trees. The third division is the Department of Warfare, which controls the Haltan Guard and the elite commandos. Though fully independent in matters of war, the Department of Warfare must loan surplus troops to the Department of Halta, which uses them to perform almost all public works in the nation.

NON-SUCCESSION CRISIS

The most dramatic step toward the current bureaucracy came in RY 450, when the current Queen Kalenen attempted to circumvent the Council of Nobles and seize sole authority. She was 38 years old and knew that soon she would have to choose a successor. Firmly believing that none of her relatives could match her abilities, she secretly arranged with members of the Department of Warfare to stage provocations and fake atrocities along the Haltan-Linowan border. Kalenen planned to whip up fury among the Haltans and launch full-scale strikes on the Linowan, with Fair Folk backing; she intended to pay the Fair Folk in Linowan prisoners. With Halta in a state of active war, as opposed to passive border-guarding, Kalenen calculated that she could call on the Council of Nobles to continue her reign for a few years longer, rather than crown a new and inexperienced monarch. And once the precedent was set, she intended to hold the throne until she died.

She succeeded. What's more, she succeeded dramatically, riding on a wave of public acclaim as the queen who virtuously sacrificed herself to her duty, holding the throne in the face of the Linowan enemy, selflessly overriding the weight of law and custom for the greater good. (The Lunars in the background decided to let her reign for a few decades more, to see what it did to Haltan society, and whether it was worth pursuing in the future.)

Several years later, the scheme fell apart when a group of young nobles and commandos investigated the border strife, and temporarily set aside their differences with the Linowans to find the true culprit. They traced the historical evidence back to the Department of Warfare and, from there, to the queen. With the aid of spirit allies, and some

beastmen and intelligent animals marginalized by the sidelining of the Council and the postponement of regular elections, they proved that the queen had arranged the border flare-ups. Some Fair Folk also testified—not out of any interest in justice or the welfare of Halta, but because in their twisted minds they considered it a dramatic and appropriate thing to do.

Queen Kalenen was tried, sentenced and took poison before she could be thrown from the tallest tree in the capital. The Council of Nobles resumed its usual functions

SOMETIMES, THINGS GET COMPLICATED

The current Haltan bureaucratic system is far more complex than Rain Deathflyer and Silver Python originally planned. They imagined separate fiefdoms, each contributing a member to a Council, with the people of the fiefdom having the right to depose their chosen representative through duels or other confrontations. The whole business of casting ballots to approve a noble's performance leaves the Lunars unconvinced. Their unease has been exacerbated by the fact that many nobles hold elaborate festivals before the populace rates their performance, and use food, drink, entertainment and often outright bribery to win positive votes. Still, it's not *too* far from tribal customs of leaders selected by popular acclamation.

The two Lunars are more annoyed and disturbed by the bureaucracy itself. As Halta grew, its burgeoning population, local traders and nobles found that old tribal customs just didn't cover new situations of law and commerce. For a while, they just made stuff up, some of which worked and some of which didn't. And then, someone found a stash of ancient books in a ruined Manse, including a Shogunate manual of civil-service administration. The Haltans changed a lot of what they found in the book, but they still built a civil-service bureaucracy.

Rain Deathflyer and Silver Python didn't plant those books. Sometimes, people find long-lost knowledge all by themselves.

Unfortunately, dismantling the current political and bureaucratic systems would be difficult. The best way of doing so might be a major war that allowed the Haltan crown to assume absolute power and simplify matters. The two Lunars ponder this as a possibility, especially given the current military situation, but equally don't want to risk Halta falling apart in the middle of a war or losing the other cultural traits they value. After all, what if absolute monarchy *didn't* eradicate the civil service, but merely co-opted it?

and became, if anything, more regular in its customs and bureaucracy. While the Haltan group who foiled the plot entered history as saviors of the nation, their collaboration with the Linowans was left out of the stories. As far as standard folklore has it, the Haltan group worked with Fair Folk, beastmen, spirits and animals to save the Republic, thus emphasizing Halta's mingled and cooperative nature.

FROM BEASTMEN TO ANIMALS: HALTAN CITIZENS

Halta is one of the few nations that accept intelligent animals as full citizens. To be precise, any person or creature born inside Halta and capable of both rational thought and communication is considered a citizen of the Republic of Halta, whether human, beastman, baboon, giant spider, reptile or other creature.

This acceptance of animals as Haltan citizens did not occur overnight. It happened because of decades spent working alongside animals who evinced human intelligence and direct signs from the avatars of the animal spirits that they wanted their creatures to enjoy rights equal to humans. Caltia herself declared her support for this just and righteous law, since "All those who can hunt, let them hunt; all those who can flee, let them flee." Her servants among the forest walkers interpreted this gnomic statement as a direct command to accept the law. The Hawk God Yesryk, Seris the Avatar of Serpents and other, lesser patrons of animals also all spoke in favor of the law from their shrines. With

a certain amount of complaint and dissension, the Haltans eventually obeyed.

As the years passed, and it became clear that they were not going to be outnumbered by a huge flood of intelligent animal life, the Haltans became more comfortable about their new fellow citizens. In fact, animal citizens became acknowledged and accepted in a way that beastmen still have not. Animal citizens live among humans, work together with humans and are the friends of humans, while beastmen still find themselves marginalized into particular jobs or districts of town and treated with awe or fear.

THE CITIES AMONG THE TREES

With the assistance of plant spirits and forest walkers, the Haltans slowly developed the small, treetop villages of the barbarians into great tree-cities that echoed the glories of the First Age in their size and beauty. Water-vines carry and circulate water around the cities. Great bridges link the trees and cities. The trees offer fruits and nuts, and other cultivated plants grow on the ground or in gardens in the sky. The whole Haltan forest has become a human-worked miracle of arboriculture. The Haltans do not need to go down to the ground if they do not want to, ever.

Small Haltan towns and villages are all built on the same plan. They consist of a collection of between three and 100 dwelling platforms, each of which houses between two dozen and 100 people or holds a similar number of shops

and other services. In the smaller settlements, all of the platforms may be built in the same cluster of three or four trees, each platform lying only five or six yards above the one below it. In areas where fear of dangerous animals or Linowan raids is high, villagers build wooden stockades around the individual platforms.

Small towns have populations of between 300 and several thousand people (of all species), while the major cities have populations exceeding 10,000. The biggest cities are composed of redwoods hundreds of feet tall, each bearing eight to 10 platforms at various heights. Counterweighted elevators (pulled by trained forest baboons), branches and rope bridges allow passage between the different platforms of the city. The platforms themselves consist of networks of long, narrow branches woven together so closely that they are watertight, supported by the dense underbranches of the trees.

BEHIND THE SCENES

For once, the Lunars had nothing to do with the Haltans' achievement. They merely encouraged the humans to work with the forest spirits, then stood back and let them get on with it. The Lunars didn't design the forest cities at all. Rain Deathflyer is personally extremely proud of this.

OUTSIDE INTERFERENCE

Throughout its history, Halta endured very little interference from other Lunars, or indeed from other Exalts at all. The Realm has mostly been content to trade with it or to fund Linowan aggression but avoid personal involvement. After all, Halta is a long way from the Blessed Isle. Other Lunars avoided the area and held back their personal barbarian tribes out of respect for Silver Python and Rain Deathflyer's work. These days, Halta covers so wide a territory that it can swallow up invading barbarian tribes and assimilate them while barely noticing them.

Young Lunars occasionally enter the area to train under the two elder Lunars, or simply seek territory of their own. Arr-D'gado, who claims the Proving Ground to the north, keeps to his own territory and does not interfere in general Haltan affairs, only in those who trespass on his land. The Last Hunter of Xaal, a refugee from the lands of Raksi, Queen of Fangs, acquired the manse of Xaal through service to Rain Deathflyer and Silver Python. They agreed to let him hold the area if he dealt with the Dragon-Blooded currently occupying it. The Last Hunter of Xaal now keeps to a 10-mile territory around the manse, rarely leaving it for the last three centuries.

Halta is an untouched, pristine plum. Exalts of all types are beginning to realize this.

CURRENT STATUS

Halta is currently under the rule of Queen Chaltra Evamal, who is 39 years old and on the brink of passing her crown to her successor. The country is allied to the Bull of the North, and provided soldiers for his war, but has also suffered for it. As the Bull expands his own nascent empire, Halta, too, may be drawn deeper into conflict. Many generals, seeing the recent destruction of the city of Fallen Lapis, urge the queen and the nobles to pull out of the alliance. Others encourage it as an unparalleled opportunity to destroy the Linowan menace once and for all. Currently, debate is deadlocked, while both sides seek powerful allies. Celestial Exalted are courted, the shaman-priests negotiate

BEHIND THE SCENES

The Lunars recruited support from the animal avatars in part through the Lunars' promise to breed intelligent animals, who would achieve full citizenship in their growing nation. While the Lunars could see the avatars' reasoning, the Lunars also knew how difficult it would be to persuade the forming Halta to accept this. People throughout Creation love their pets or use animals in their work, from sheepdogs to fishing cormorants, but accept animals as actual people?

The Lunars' first step was to get a few isolated specimens of intelligent animals accepted as citizens. It was easy to arrange a few accidents in which intelligent animals helped rescue the victims or cases in which intelligent animals helped feed or support isolated homesteads and tribes threatened by famine, raksha or Wyld-twisted barbarians. Most Haltans kept animals for work or as pets; some Haltans were even prepared to acknowledge a degree of intelligence. When these heroic specimens began to speak and ask for civil rights, it caused widespread disturbance, but not the level of panic that might otherwise have resulted. Many Haltans were prepared to accept that the occasional monkey or serpent or baboon might be as worthy of respect as their fellow human beings.

The next step was to formulate a law granting Haltan citizenship to all those who were born in the forest and who could express rational thought. Targeted assassination would have been actively unhelpful in getting the law passed or affecting public opinion: It would only have roused suspicion against the animal population. Instead, the Lunars put their weight on the theological lever. Caltia spoke, and the people complied.

with gods and raksha, and the Republic of Halta is in a state of mild turmoil as both nobles and commoners face the possibility of all-out war for dominance in the Northeast of Creation.

OPINIONS ON THE EXPERIMENT

Halta is a complicated ecosystem of a country. Because of its natural resources, Halta can support a complex civilization with a high degree of cooperation, law and government, combining self-sufficiency with exterior trade. Halta flourishes like an orchid on the bark of a tropical tree, rare and precious and beautiful, yet dependent on a number of substrata that it barely acknowledges to exist. The people of Halta have grown entitled. They live in a country of plenty, and feelings of superiority have grown along with it. The typical Haltan sees other nations who mistreat their animals, squander or ignore their natural resources and labor under conditions of slavery or serfdom. In his heart of hearts, he wonders why they just can't all manage as well as he does. He enjoys a good life because his ancestors made good decisions—but he does not know the hidden hands behind those choices.

The Haltans take their treaties with the Fair Folk for granted and now see the raksha as just another natural hazard. Some Haltans even view the raksha as a useful resource Halta can draw upon for soldiers and crafters in time of need, rather than as a potential threat to the kingdom. Few Haltans realize just how little the Fair Folk like or trust anyone in a human way. The Fair Folk cannot break their sworn word, but if someone showed them a way around the treaty, many of them would raven across the country, devouring dreams and souls. Likewise, the Haltans view the barbarian tribes of the Wyld and the Far East as no threat, simply because they have never attacked in strength. They do not know that this is due to a courtesy agreement between Lunars. Haltans have not planned for a large-scale barbarian attack in centuries, because they have not needed to.

Rain Deathflyer and Silver Python are almost convinced that their experiment succeeded. Almost. They believe that the only remaining step is to test it. They will let the Haltans choose whether to join the Bull of the North, the Realm, the Scavenger Lands or stand apart. The Lunars will let other Lunars invade with their barbarians, if they want. The two will draw back and see if Halta can survive without their protection, their boundary lines and their guidance. If not, then the Republic of Halta does not deserve to survive in any case.

And even if Halta fails in a crisis, Rain Deathflyer and Silver Python know they have bred something new in Creation. The arboreal cities, partnerships with sentient animals and other customs have value and will endure. Waves of refugees will spread these seeds to other societies, where they may flourish, growing a new cycle of experiments. The Thousand Streams River flows on.

THE RIVER HAS NO END

For this is the final secret of the Thousand Streams River—the enigma that baffles even the wisest Sidereals and most everyone else who hears of it, even if a Winding Road theorist such as Tamuz tries to explain it, slowly and clearly. *The River has no end*. The Great Experiment is *never* complete.

Indeed, quite a few Lunars themselves do not grasp this point. They imagine that someday, one of their experiments—Halta, perhaps, the Delzahn, the Haslanti or some civilization yet unborn—will rise to replace the Realm. Or that some fusion of civilizations will do so… and then, the New Realm will cover Creation as the Old Realm did, a changeless and perfect utopia.

If the Fickle Lady teaches one great truth, however, it is change. Nothing stays the same forever. Any "New Realm" would inevitably corrupt itself or encounter some threat it did not know how to counter. Therefore, there must never be another all-encompassing world empire, just a patchwork of states of various sizes, rising and falling, growing and dying, *evolving*, each—with luck—contributing something new and good to the cultures and countries that come after it.

In the Time of Tumult, however, all the experiments are in danger. Creation itself faces a time of testing. The Stewards know that soon they must fight for their lives, and everyone else's, if they hope to see a better world. Or any world at all.

CHAPTER THREE
CHARACTER CREATION

The host of Lunars includes a greater number of old and powerful Exalted than almost any other group in Creation. Only the Sidereals can boast more centuries of experience, and many elder Lunars would say the long lives of the senior Chosen of the Maidens were dearly bought by the sacrifices of the Children of the Moon.

Despite the existence of Lunar society over vast ages, and the millennia of influence from its eldest members, the Children of Luna are among the most dynamic of the Exalted. While the Dynastic Dragon-Blooded built a single stasis-bound society stratified around the Scarlet Empress, the Lunars constructed at least a half-dozen vibrant new civilizations. As the Solar Essences lay helplessly bound within the Jade Prison, the Lunars waged a war against the Fair Folk. Whereas the Sidereals ensconce themselves ever deeper within the Bureau of Destiny in Yu-Shan, the Lunars make new inroads with the Bureau of Seasons and the Bureau of Nature due to their impressive recoveries of swathes of Creation lost to the Wyld.

The Silver Pact has always included a high proportion of relatively young, inexperienced Exalts. Perhaps because of their intimate connection with the Fickle Goddess, the Lunars tend to push their limitations more than other Exalted. Constant defiance of the odds leads to a greater casualty rate than that of other Celestials, and thus, more Lunars perish and are reborn. Perhaps Lunars owe their dynamism to this steady influx of new blood; perhaps it comes as a side effect of their protean nature. Whatever the reason, until the sudden release of the Solar Essences five years ago, most novice Celestial Exalts were Lunars.

Although they are not as numerous as the returning Lawgivers, many young Lunar Exalted have arisen in recent years, inheriting the Exaltations of victims of the Wyld Hunt, the war against the Fair Folk and the violence of the Time of Tumult. These new Lunar heroes enter an age of sorrows, shaken by the rebirth of god-kings, sickened by the consuming darkness of the Underworld and encircled by the chaos at the edge of Creation. Such are the characters you'll create. How will they shape the world?

WHO ARE THE LUNARS?

The Lunar Exalted are the Stewards of Creation. When they fought against the forebears of the gods during the Primordial War, this was perhaps most clear. Preparing for the war, Luna forged her Chosen with an eye toward defending the Essence of the world, since it was inextricably tied to her Primordial lover Gaia. The Silver Lady realized that the fighting might destroy the very Creation they hoped to gain, and she endeavored to instill a persistent defense against this possibility within the hearts of her Exalted.

The Lawgivers sought to co-opt this role later in the later First Age, but they did not completely succeed. Some Lunars never completely accepted Solar rule, and even those who did often resisted Solar domination better than the rest of Creation. Most Children of the Moon still considered their stewardship to extend from Luna, however much the Solars might have manipulated the Lunars to the contrary.

In the Time of Tumult, the claims of stewardship are as varied as the Lunars themselves. Raksi has become queen of the ruined City of Sorcerers and custodian of the priceless *Book of Three Circles*. Tamuz leads a handful of tribes in the South and secretly considers the mighty Delzahn of Chiaroscuro his personal ward. Younger Lunars, such as Seven Devils Clever, might initially protect a single crime-ridden neighborhood in Nexus, but the goals of the Exalted cannot stay so small for long.

Many of the eldest Lunars feel some degree of duty to defend the entire world against the omnipresent threat of dissolution by the Wyld and invasion by the Fair Folk. As such, the Lunars claim vast territories at the edges of Creation or near unstable Bordermarches. Younger Lunars often try to act in a similar role, if only because the Silver Pact encourages its members to join in defense against the Wyld. Nonetheless, the Pact has never managed to unite every one of the Children of the Moon, and Lunar Exalted can be found in nearly any quarter of the world. From the dismal swamps of the Southwest to the halls of the Haslanti Oligarchs, the Silver Lady's Chosen win renown as mighty warriors or remain unknown due to their cunning. Only the Blessed Isle remains free of their presence, for smart young Lunars are quick to leave if they can, and foolish ones perish at the hands of the Wyld Hunt.

CREATING A LUNAR CHARACTER

This chapter provides the rules you need to create Lunar characters. The process is similar to that of creating a Solar according to the core **Exalted** rules. However, the Children of the Moon differ from their Solar brethren in many areas. These steps walk you through the rules and help you create an interesting Lunar character.

STEP ONE: CHARACTER CONCEPT

Coming up with an interesting and playable character concept is the first and most important step in creating an **Exalted** character. Before filling in a single dot on your character sheet, think of someone you would like to play. You can start with a few words that describe who your character is, such as "wise shaman" or "bloodthirsty warlord." This gives you the basic kernel of a character, which grows into a full character as you add detail to her. Naturally, as you explore the character you create, this concept becomes more complex, interesting and refined. You might expand your concept to be, "A wise shaman whose life is dedicated to protecting her homeland in the great Eastern forests from the depredations of the Wyld and greedy wood spirits alike" or "An escaped slave who returned to his people and became a bloodthirsty warlord and leads them in revenge upon his onetime captors."

A roleplaying game is a cooperative effort to have fun: You are one of a group of people playing an awesome game of imagination together, rather than a competition playing *Go Fish* with a deck of cards. Because the game is a shared activity, make sure that your character is interesting and playable *within* the group. Presumably, when you play with other players, your character will occupy an approximately equal share of the story. If your character is interesting to you, but bores the other four players (for example) in your group, then you are going to bore your friends to death one-fifth of the time they want to spend having fun. Also, you need a concept you can actually play within the scope of the series your Storyteller means to help you explore. If you choose to create a "bloodthirsty warlord," but your Storyteller wants to spin a fantastic tale of spiritual quests to unite the gods and people of one of the directions of Creation, you may find yourself sidelined by the story or excluded by your fellow players' characters. Worse yet, you might simply derail the game entirely and make yourself and your fellow players miserable.

HOMELAND

The world of **Exalted** is a huge place, filled with an amazing variety of cultures. Where your character was born or raised will shape her personality in innumerable ways. The Lunar Essence chooses to Exalt an individual who is both a proven survivor and who feels a deep-felt desire to watch over something bigger than himself. Often, this results in the Exaltation of heroic members of one of the mighty barbarian tribes, due to their finely honed survival skills and strong defensive attachment to their people. The Stewards of Luna find that their patron favors the indomitable spirit of the untamed tribesman, and this esteem is widely reflected in Lunar Exaltation. Such is not always the case, however.

While the Lunar Exaltation arguably hearkens closest to the original state of humanity when the Exalted Essences were formed, the Exaltation does not ignore the hardened survivors found within the heart of civilization. Many Lunars come from the tribes of the Eastern forests, Southern deserts, Western islands or Northern wastes, but some of the Moonchildren arise from broken neighborhoods in metropolitan cesspools such as Nexus. Is the social structure of the street gang so dissimilar from that of the wilderness tribe? Many of the Chosen of the Silver Lady vehemently oppose the spreading blight of urban decadence, while others embrace the thriving masses of humanity.

Does your character come from the tree-climbing Haltan Nation? Or does she stride the sands of the Southern deserts? What does she think of her icewalker ancestors and their totem-spirit? Can she overcome the dominant prejudices of the Silver Pact and prove that her Nexus heritage is no sign of weakness? Pick your character's native culture and look at the traditions she has learned for a lifetime. See **Exalted**, pages 49-67, for an overview of the regions of Creation and the people who inhabit them—and don't be afraid to suggest your own background cultures to your Storyteller. The core book only describes a few of the major cultures.

If your character comes from some place remote from the series' starting location, then you should work that into your backstory as well. Why did the character leave? Does anyone pursue? Did the travel happen before or after Exaltation? Why did the Exalt come to the area she now inhabits? Was she drawn by a fragmentary memory from her Exaltation's previous life? Did her mentor ask her to perform some mission in the region? Does the character ever regret her decision to leave her homeland? Establishing the reasons for traveling 1,000 miles from home lend more depth and believability to a character than just randomly declaring, "My character traveled from the isles of the West to the city of Nexus." Given that such a character is likely to draw extra atten-

tion specifically because she looks out of place, the reasons should be worth the added complications.

CASTE

Just as all of the Celestial Exalted, the Lunars are divided into different castes. The Lunars were designed as potent weapons in the war against the Primordials. Because the Incarnae knew that the imperishable nature of the Exalted required that they serve some long-term purpose—long after the Primordials' defeat—each caste fulfills a role envisioned by the Silver Lady. The mighty Full Moon Caste reigned supreme among Lunar warriors, while the No Moon Caste guarded the secret wisdom of their Fickle Mistress.

Misfortune led to near-destruction of the Lunar castes by the chaos of the Wyld. Only by implanting magical tattoos could the Lunars salvage some remnant of the ancient caste system. Nevertheless, three of the ancient castes were shattered beyond repair—Waxing Moons, Half Moons and Waning Moons—and even the most powerful Lunar sorcerers could not recover them. Instead, they pieced together fragments of the three and created the amalgamated Changing Moon Caste.

Each Lunar begins without any caste at all. Those known as the Casteless spend their Exalted lives shifting from one caste-like state to the next as surely as the eternal phases of the moon. Given their close connections to the Wyld, this is a dangerous state of being in the Time of Tumult. Most Moon Chosen eventually meet elder Lunars who convince them to accept the Wyld-suppressing tattoos and fix their caste. Once branded, the Lunar gains protection from the Wyld and becomes a member of the Full Moon, Changing Moon or No Moon Caste.

More details on the individual castes, and the Casteless, are found in Chapter Four: Traits. Choose the caste that you feel best fits your character concept, or have him remain Casteless if that seems like a more suitable choice for your concept. If you are not sure which caste best matches your concept, you might speak to your Storyteller about starting the series Casteless with an eye toward gaining a caste once your character's actions lead you to an answer.

SPIRIT SHAPE

Upon Exaltation, the Chosen of the Moon gains a second shape, which she can assume as readily as her natural human form (see p. 127 in Chapter Five: Charms and Shapeshifting for details). Known as the spirit shape, this form is that of a specific animal representing the Lunar's inner nature and personality. A majestic warrior might acquire a sleek jaguar as his spirit shape, while a crafty street urchin takes the iconic shape of a sly fox.

The spirit shape of a specific Lunar is unique and personal. Two different Lunars might both have a wolf as their spirit shapes. The bloodthirsty warlord may assume a massive, red-maned lupine form, while the hardy Northern shaman takes the shape of a lean, white winter wolf. Barring the use of Charms or shapeshifting, the warlord's wolf-shape is unique to him, a distinctive, individual example of the red-maned wolf. As a consummate shapeshifter, the warlord might devour the Heart's Blood of other wolves and steal their shapes as well. Only his personal spirit shape is one of his true forms, however.

Choose a single, specific animal you consider totemic to your Lunar character. Try to describe this spirit shape with the same care you give to your character's human form. What are the distinguishing characteristics of your second shape? Does your winter wolf have eyes as blue as the Northern sky on a clear day? Does your fox form's fur have a darker undercoat that seems to give it a faintly purple shading?

THE TELL

Luna moves through the sky, ever-changing in her glory. Yet, she is always the moon. So it is for the Lunar Exalted: Whatever form they might take, their Essence stays the same. Each Moonchild possesses a singular characteristic known as a Tell, which marks her in some way regardless of what shape she might assume. Though the Tell may express itself differently depending on the Lunar's current form, the fundamental signature of the Tell does not change. Some Lunar elders believe the Tell is essential to holding together their protean forms, and certainly, the moonsilver tattoos used by the Silver Pact incorporate the Tell into their designs.

Choose a Tell that represents your spirit shape and will appear in some manner throughout your shapeshifting. Many Tells appear white or silver in color. If your second shape is that of a snowy owl, you might have a fine mantle of down upon your shoulders in human form. In every other form, your character might show mottled marks reminiscent of an owl's feathers. For complete rules on the Tell, see Chapter Five: Charms and Shapeshifting (p. 130).

MOTIVATION

Motivation is a short description of your character's primary goal. It's what drives your character to go out and be a hero, and is partly why Luna chose your character for Exaltation. The Motivations of Lunar Exalted are larger than life and bigger than mere mortals can hope to achieve. Most Lunar Motivations incorporate or shape their vision of stewardship.

Examples of Lunar Motivations might include becoming the greatest admiral in history, restoring the lost castes of Lunar Exaltation, reclaiming the swathes of Creation lost to the Wyld or building an impenetrable wall to defend them, or conquering the Realm and installing oneself as the Silver Empress.

Create a Motivation for your character that is suitably epic in scope and fitting to her concept. See **Exalted**, page 88, for more information about choosing, playing or changing character Motivations.

STEP TWO: ATTRIBUTES

The Lunar Exaltation produces a tremendous increase in inherent and instinctual Traits. Just as any Celestial Essence, the Exaltation chooses a host who is already superior and enhances the person to near-divine status.

As with all characters, Lunar characters start with one dot in each Attribute before you assign any other dots. Unless subjected to tragic disaster within a series, a character always has at least one dot in every Attribute.

In keeping with your character concept, decide how you want to assign your Attribute dots among Physical, Social and Mental Attributes. Pick one Attribute set to be primary, one to be secondary and one to be tertiary.

Physical: Strength, Dexterity, Stamina
Social: Charisma, Manipulation, Appearance
Mental: Perception, Intelligence, Wits
(For a full explanation of Attributes, see **Exalted**, p. 101.)

A Lunar Exalt has eight dots to divide among her primary Attributes, six to assign to secondary Attributes and four dots to invest in tertiary Attributes.

Lunars have an affinity for the Attributes that their castes favor. These affinities are called Caste Attributes. A character increases those particular Attributes with greater ease than the others (i.e., dots in those Attributes are less expensive to buy with bonus or experience points).

- **Full Moon Attributes** are related to speed and might: Strength, Dexterity, Stamina.
- **Changing Moon Attributes** deal with beauty and social interaction: Charisma, Manipulation, Appearance.
- **No Moon Attributes** describe reasoning and understanding: Perception, Intelligence, Wits.

In addition, a Lunar with a caste has an affinity with one more Attribute. This is called a Favored Attribute and provides the same reduction in cost as a Caste Attribute. You cannot choose a Caste Attribute as your Favored Attribute, but you may choose any one of the other six Attributes.

Due to a caste Lunar's wider range of Attribute affinities, a stronger connection to Luna and the presumed mentoring (however brief) from an elder Lunar capable of fixing her caste, a caste Lunar also gains one additional dot she may place in one of her Caste or Favored Attributes.

Casteless Lunars do *not* have Caste Attributes. However, due to their fluctuating Lunar anima, they receive *two* Favored Attributes. You cannot choose to Favor the same Attribute twice, but you may choose any two of the nine Attributes as Favored. If you plan to gain a caste during play, then think about which caste you might desire. A Casteless Lunar may only join a caste for which one of her Favored Attributes is a Caste Attribute. A Casteless Lunar does not get the additional Attribute dot, and a Casteless who gains a caste during play does not automatically gain one either (although she might spend Experience to gain points, as usual).

A player may not assign more than five total dots to any Attribute, including the original dot.

STEP THREE: ABILITIES

A Lunar Exalted gains 25 dots to assign to her Abilities. Lunars are natural survivors, and combined with the animal instincts they gain from their spirit shape, this gives them an affinity for the Survival Ability. All Lunars receive Survival as a Favored Ability. In addition, as heroic figures, Lunar Exalted get to choose one additional Favored Ability. Dots in these Abilities are less expensive to buy with both bonus and experience points.

Since Favored Abilities represent something your character knows well enough to have some talent, you must assign at least one dot to each Favored Ability. You cannot get a double cost reduction by choosing Survival again as a Favored Ability. A Favored Ability may only be gained once. For more on Favored Abilities, see **Exalted**, page 74. You may not assign more than three dots to any Ability unless you buy the extra dots with bonus points. Even with bonus points, you may not total more than five dots for any single Ability.

Lunars who belong to the Silver Pact must also have at least one dot in their choice of Archery, Martial Arts, Melee or Thrown. Additional requirements may apply if the Lunar belongs to one of the factions within the Silver Pact. See Chapter One: The Silver Pact for each faction's minimum requirements.

SPECIALTIES

Don't forget to consider specialties, which can be bought at any appropriate time with either bonus points (at character creation) or experience points (once play begins). A specialty represents a narrowly focused area of expertise within one of your Abilities. You don't have to take any specialties, but they can help define your character's Abilities.

For more on specialties, see **Exalted**, page 74.

STEP FOUR: ADVANTAGES

Advantages describe the magical abilities possessed by the Lunar Exalts, as well as their "place" in the world, their passions and extremes.

BACKGROUNDS

Backgrounds measure such things as a character's wealth, social connections and fame (or infamy). See pages 106-112 in Chapter Four: Traits for explanations of these advantages.

Similar to Solars, Lunar Exalts gain seven dots to assign among their Backgrounds, though their choices differ somewhat. Backgrounds should tie into your character concepts, as defined in Step One. No Background can be raised above three dots without the use of bonus points. Buying the fourth or fifth dot of a Background with bonus points costs more than buying the first, second or third dot. See the "Bonus Point Costs" table, page 103.

KNACKS

Just as their namesake, the Lunars are consummate shapeshifters. Although they possess Charms—as all Exalted do—the Lunars' trademark is their power to move from one form to the next as surely as the faces of the moon. They call their unique shapeshifting powers Knacks. The most talented Children of the Moon can slip from the world of man to beast in the blink of an eye, and transform into an amazing variety of creatures. Lunar warriors often learn to assume a monstrous war form, half-man and half-beast. With mastery of their shapes, the Chosen of the Moon can speed across the sky as birds, swim the ocean depths as great orcas or smash through walls as mighty yeddim. Stealthy Lunars might creep into a fortress as tiny mice or silently glide over the walls on the wings of snowy owls.

The range of tricks a Lunar can perform with her innate ability to shift forms is controlled by her mastery of the Knacks. Each Knack has varying prerequisites, according to its potency and the difficulty in mastering it. As a starting character, you receive eight choices, which may be used to select Charms or Knacks. Thus, you might choose to have four Charms and four Knacks for your character, or six Charms and two Knacks or any other legal combination. You must choose at least one Knack and four Charms, however. For details on the Knacks, see their section in Chapter Five: Charms and Shapeshifting, starting on page 131.

CHARMS

Charms are the numerous mystical powers of Luna's Chosen that do not relate directly to shapeshifting. Lunar Charms are divided according to which Attribute they augment or draw upon, though sometimes the relevant Attribute for such magic can surprise the uninitiated.

Lunars start with eight choices that they may use to select Charms or Knacks. As noted under the Knacks section, a Lunar can split these eight choices in a number of ways, taking any legal combination of Knacks and Charms that adds up to eight choices. The Lunar must select at least four Charms and at least one Knack, however. In addition, the first Charms that the Lunar selects, up to four total, must come from the character's Caste or Favored

Attributes (see Chapter Five: Charms and Shapeshifting, starting on p. 126). Although the Casteless don't have the specialized power of a Full Moon, Changing Moon or No Moon, they excel in their Favored Attributes. If a Lunar chooses five or more Charms, then the additional Charms, beyond the first four, may fall outside of her Caste or Favored Attributes.

VIRTUES

Lunar Exalted start with one free dot in all four Virtues and get five additional dots to assign. No Virtue may be higher than three dots unless the player spends bonus points.

Choose one Virtue with at least three dots rating as your primary—this Virtue is the root of your character's Virtue Flaw. See pages 121-123 of Chapter Four: Traits, for rules on Limit Breaks and a list of sample Virtue Flaws. See also **Exalted**, page 102, for more information about Virtues. Choose your Virtues and Virtue Flaw to be consistent with your character concept.

STEP FIVE: FINISHING TOUCHES

Here, you determine your character's final Traits and finish rounding her out.

WILLPOWER

Add your character's two highest Virtue ratings for her initial Willpower. You can increase Willpower to no higher than 8 with bonus points. Only characters with two Virtues at 4 or higher may begin the game with a Willpower above 8. See **Exalted**, page 115, for complete rules on Willpower.

INTIMACIES

Intimacies are things that your character cares about on a meaningful level. You may choose a number of Intimacies equal to your character's dots of Compassion. See **Exalted**, page 90, for complete rules about Intimacies.

ESSENCE

Lunar Exalted begin with an Essence rating of 2. You can raise this value with bonus points, but characters may not start the game with an Essence above 3.

A Lunar's Personal Essence pool equals the sum of the character's permanent Essence, plus twice her Willpower.

A Lunar's Peripheral Essence pool equals the sum of four times the character's Essence, plus twice her Willpower, plus four times her highest Virtue.

HEALTH LEVELS

Lunar Exalts possess seven health levels, just as any mortal: one -0 level, two -1, two -2, a -4 and one Incapacitated health level. Lunars gain a choice of two -1 or four -2 additional health levels for every purchase of Ox-Body Technique (a Stamina Charm found on p. 156). A character may purchase Ox-Body Technique as many times as she has dots of Stamina.

BONUS POINTS

Assign bonus points to help you fine-tune your character to fit your concept. Raising Abilities, Backgrounds or Virtues above 3, or raising Essence above 2, at character creation, requires you to use bonus points.

You have 15 bonus points to spend. For a complete list of Traits and their bonus point cost, see p. 103 for the "Bonus Points Cost" chart.

THE SPARK OF LIFE

If you merely throw together a bunch of rules choices that revolve around a single core concept, you really don't have much in the way of a character. A character should have a personality, with hopes and dreams. If she is to be a truly epic hero, there should probably be some things wrong with her, too. **Exalted**, pages 77-79, gives you lots of ideas to help you bring life to your character. What does she look like? What people matter to her? What was her life like before her Exaltation? Look at the questions there, and see how many you can answer. Each answer supplies another interesting detail of your character.

Your character is one of the Chosen of Luna. Although your character is a proven survivor, some greater destiny calls out from within her soul. As Luna feels love for Gaia, so your character feels some strong sense of stewardship toward something. What does she feel that she protects? Does she do this solely for personal reasons, or does she believe that she is a caretaker on some greater power's behalf?

What about her shapeshifting ability? Does she seek to understand the beings she becomes? Or is it merely a tool to an end? Does she seek to preserve some aspect of the wounded and dying? Or does she consume the Heart's Blood of any being that strikes her fancy?

The more thought you put into your character, the greater depth she is likely to contain. Don't worry about every little detail, though. **Exalted** is a cooperative storytelling game, and some of the greatest moments happen within the game when you discover something about your character through interaction rather than a scripted backstory.

WYLD MUTATIONS

With your Storyteller's permission, your character can begin play with special, nonhuman features and intrinsic abilities. These might be actual Wyld mutations gained from excessive shapeshifting before your Lunar character received her tattoos—she almost became a chimera. A character could also gain mutations because she spent time in the Wyld before her Exaltation, or because she came from a race or tribe that possesses such features from birth, such as beastmen or various Wyld barbarians.

You can buy these special Traits with bonus points, and *only* with bonus points: one for a pox, two for an affliction, four for a blight and six for an abomination. At the Storyteller's option, entirely negative mutations supply extra bonus points (1 for a deficiency, 2 for a debility, 4 for a deformity)—but these points may *only* be spent on further, positive mutations. Players cannot spend them on anything else.

See **The Compass of Celestial Directions: The Wyld** for more information about playing mutant characters. This is a special option, and not all Storytellers may want to allow it.

OR EVEN WORSE...

As a further optional rule, the Storyteller may declare that any positive mutations a character gains (from the Wyld, or from the spontaneous mutations the Casteless may suffer) must be paid for by "pre-spending" future experience. In this case, poxes, afflictions, blights and abominations cost experience points equal to twice their bonus point cost. If you use this optional rule, be sure to tell your players about it in advance.

Character Creation Summary

Caste Lunars

• Step One: Character Concept

Choose your concept, caste and Motivation.

Note caste's anima powers. Note spirit shape and Tell.

• Step Two: Choosing Attributes

Note that all nine Attributes start with one dot automatically.

Prioritize your Attribute categories: Physical (Strength, Dexterity, Stamina), Social (Charisma, Manipulation, Appearance) and Mental (Perception, Intelligence, Wits). You have 8 dots to assign to your primary Attribute category, 6 to assign to your secondary group and 4 to place in the tertiary category.

Choose Physical Attributes: Strength, Dexterity, Stamina.

Choose Social Attributes: Charisma, Manipulation, Appearance

Choose Mental Attributes: Perception, Intelligence, Wits

Record Caste Attributes (3). Full Moon (Strength, Dexterity and Stamina), Changing Moons (Charisma, Manipulation and Appearance), No Moons (Perception, Intelligence and Wits).

Select Favored Attribute (1). A caste Lunar may choose a single additional Attribute to be Favored. You cannot choose to Favor an Attribute that is already a Caste Attribute.

You gain one additional Attribute dot that you may assign to one of your Caste or Favored Attributes.

• Step Three: Choosing Abilities

Note Survival as Favored Ability.

Select one additional Favored Ability (may not be Survival).

Choose Abilities (25—at least one must be from each Favored Ability; none may start higher than 3 without spending bonus points).

Silver Pact Lunars must have a minimum of two dots in Survival *and* one dot in Archery, Martial Arts, Melee or Thrown.

• Step Four: Select Advantages

Choose Backgrounds (7—none may be higher than 3 without spending bonus points), 8 Lunar Charms or Knacks (at least 4 Charms and 1 Knack, up to 4 Charms must come from Caste or Favored Attributes), Virtues (5—none may be higher than 3 without spending bonus points) and Virtue Flaw.

• Step Five: Finishing Touches

Record Essence (2), Willpower (the sum of the character's two highest Virtues), Personal Essence pool (Essence + [Willpower x 2]), Peripheral Essence pool ([Essence x 4] + [Willpower x 2] + [highest Virtue x 4]) and health levels (7 + any gained from Charms).

• Bonus Points

You may spend bonus points (15) at any point in character creation. Bonus point costs may be found on page 103.

Castes

- **Full Moon:** Deadly warriors who survive via speed and strength.

  Caste Attributes: Strength, Dexterity, Stamina

  Anima Powers: May double leaping distance and movement speed. Doubles Strength rating for purposes of feats of strength.

- **Changing Moon:** Cunning agents who survive through guile and subtlety.

  Caste Attributes: Charisma, Manipulation, Appearance

  Anima Powers: May appear as a person known to the Lunar for one scene. Gains Essence dice to actions assisted by trustworthiness of chosen image.

- **No Moon:** Wise mystics who survive due to their intellect and ancient lore.

  Caste Attributes: Perception, Intelligence, Wits

  Anima Powers: May reduce the mote cost of all Occult-related actions (whether Charm or spell) taken for the remainder of the scene. Also gains an obscuring aura of shadows.

Motivation

Choose a driving and epic goal for your character.

Virtues

Compassion—Empathy and forgiveness.

Conviction—Determination and emotional fortitude.

Temperance—Mental clarity and self-control.

Valor—Courage and bravery.

Intimacies

May choose a number of Intimacies equal to character's Compassion.

Backgrounds

- **Allies**—Aides and friends who help in tasks.
- **Artifact**—Wondrous devices of the First Age.
- **Backing**—Standing and rank in an organization of power and influence.
- **Contacts**—Information sources and people in useful places.
- **Cult**—Mortals who worship you.
- **Familiar**—An animal companion.
- **Followers**—Mortals who look to you for leadership.
- **Heart's Blood**—The shapes of animals and men that you may take.
- **Influence**—Your pull in the world around you.
- **Manse**—A place of power and Essence.
- **Mentor**—A teacher and instructor.
- **Reputation**—Your renown in society.
- **Resources**—Material goods and money.
- **Solar Bond**—A supernatural connection to your Solar mate.
- **Tattoo Artifact**—An artifact of power worked into the very substance of the Lunar's tattoos.

CHARACTER CREATION SUMMARY

CASTELESS LUNARS

• STEP ONE: CHARACTER CONCEPT

Determine why your character has not had her caste fixed. Choose concept and Motivation. Note spirit shape and Tell.

• STEP TWO: CHOOSING ATTRIBUTES

Note that all nine Attributes start with one dot automatically before you assign any.

Prioritize your Attribute categories: Physical (Strength, Dexterity, Stamina), Social (Charisma, Manipulation, Appearance) and Mental (Perception, Intelligence, Wits). You have 8 dots to assign to your primary Attribute category, 6 to assign to your secondary group and 4 to place in the tertiary category.

Choose Physical Attributes: Strength, Dexterity, Stamina.

Choose Social Attributes: Charisma, Manipulation, Appearance

Choose Mental Attributes: Perception, Intelligence, Wits

Select Favored Attributes (2). You may not choose the same Attribute more than once. Casteless Lunars do **not** possess Caste Attributes.

• STEP THREE: CHOOSING ABILITIES

Note Survival as Favored Ability.

Choose one more Favored Ability (may not be Survival).

Choose Abilities (25—at least 1 must be from each Favored Ability; none may start higher than 3 without spending bonus points).

• STEP FOUR: SELECT ADVANTAGES

Choose Backgrounds (7—none may be higher than 3 without spending bonus points), 8 Lunar Charms or Knacks (at least 1 Knack and 1 Charm, up to 4 Charms must come from Favored Attributes), Virtues (5—none may be higher than 3 without spending bonus points) and Virtue Flaw.

• STEP FIVE: FINISHING TOUCHES

Record Essence (2), Willpower (the sum of the character's two highest Virtues), Personal Essence pool (Essence + [Willpower x 2]), Peripheral Essence pool ([Essence x 4] + [Willpower x 2] + [highest Virtue x 4]) and health levels (7 + any gained from Charms).

• BONUS POINTS

You may spend bonus points at any point in character creation. Bonus point costs may be found on the table below.

CASTE

The Casteless do not possess a caste.

MOTIVATION

Choose a driving and epic goal for your character.

VIRTUES

Same as for caste Lunars.

INTIMACIES

May choose a number of Intimacies equal to your character's Compassion.

BACKGROUNDS

- **Allies**—Aides and friends who help in tasks.
- **Artifact**—Wondrous devices of the First Age.
- **Backing**—Standing and rank in an organization of power and influence.
- **Contacts**—Information sources and people in useful places.
- **Cult**—Mortals who worship you.
- **Familiar**—An animal companion.
- **Followers**—Mortals who look to you for leadership.
- **Heart's Blood**—The shapes of animals and men that you may take.
- **Influence**—Your pull in the world around you.
- **Manse**—A place of power and Essence.
- **Mentor**—A teacher and instructor.
- **Reputation**—Your renown in society.
- **Resources**—Material goods and money.
- **Solar Bond**—A supernatural connection to your Solar mate.
- **Taboo**—Culturally significant behavior that helps protect a Casteless Lunar from the Wyld.

BONUS POINT COSTS

Trait	Cost
Attribute	4 (3 if a Caste or Favored Attribute)
Ability	2 (1 if a Favored Ability)
Background	1 (2 if the Background is being raised above 3)
Specialty	1 (2 per 1 if Favored Ability)
Virtue	3
Willpower	2
Intimacies	3 to increase starting Intimacies to (Willpower + Compassion).
Essence	10
Charms	7 (5 if Favored or Caste Attribute)
Knacks	6

Most of the Traits used by Lunars are identical to the ones used in **Exalted**. Virtues, Abilities, Attributes, Willpower, Essence and the like are all handled identically, or nearly so. For the rules governing these traits, see the relevant portions of **Exalted,** particularly the Traits chapter (see **Exalted**, p. 88).

EXPANDED BACKGROUNDS

The last 15 centuries have not been kind to the Chosen of Luna. They have not fully recovered their ancient glories from the havoc wrought by the Usurpation, the Great Contagion, the subsequent massive Fair Folk invasion, the collapse of Creation's borders and constant pursuit by the Wyld Hunt.

Nonetheless, at least eight ancient Lunars remain from the First Age and a handful of small social groups yet exist that embody different Lunar ideals. The dominant group among these is the Silver Pact, and its members manage to save a respectable portion of new Exalts from the Wyld

Hunt. These young Moonchildren are often already popular heroes among their own people, and being inducted into their Lunar heritage by its most powerful icons only tends to expand their place in the world. Despite the most strenuous efforts of the Realm, the Stewards can gain both friends and power.

ALTERED BACKGROUNDS

The nature of Lunar society requires redefinition of certain Background traits. Lunar Exalts have access to the following Backgrounds from the **Exalted** core book: Allies, Artifact, Backing, Contacts, Cult, Familiar, Followers, Influence, Manse, Mentor and Resources. Except as described below, existing Backgrounds work just as they do in **Exalted**, pages 110-114.

ALLIES

For the most part, the Allies Background works for Lunar Exalted the same as for Solars. Some Moonchildren have allied with the new incarnations of their Solar mates from the First Age, however, and such an ally should be represented as one dot higher than normal due to their innate mystical bond (see p. 20 for a description of this bond). Most Silver Pact members can claim one or more fellow Lunars as allies. Some Lunars may even forge an alliance with one of the powerful animal totem gods popular with various Threshold tribes.

ARTIFACT

Occult savants know about the protean properties of moonsilver, but few artificers have reason to exploit the potential of the most mutable of the magical materials. Lunars may attune to wondrous devices composed of other materials, but only at the risk of hampering the mercurial flexibility of their forms. The Lunar Exalted favor moonsilver artifacts because these items can change shape along with their owners. Indeed, many older Chosen of the Moon regard the use of moonsilver as the exclusive right of their kind. These elders tend to take a dim view of anyone else possessing moonsilver artifacts and may seize such items for themselves or to pass on to young Lunar protégés. Aside from the special benefits of moonsilver, the Artifact Background works as described in **Exalted** page 111.

SATYR

BACKING

As portrayed in **Exalted**, page 111, this Background represents standing and rank in an organization of power and influence. The five factions jointly comprising the Silver Pact wield the greatest influence over Lunar society. Each faction is at least philosophically led by one or more elder Lunars, and if their personal presence does not suffice to convince other Lunars to follow them, their mastery of such things as the secret of moonsilver tattoo manufacture often does. A Lunar Exalted who wants support from the political factions of Lunar society should assign Backing dots to one or more of these five factions: the Crossroad Society, the Seneschals of the Sun Kings, the Swords of Luna, the Wardens of Gaia and the Winding Path. Lunars who belong to the Silver Pact must have a minimum of one dot in Archery, Martial Arts, Melee or Thrown. Members of the individual factions may need to meet additional requirements described in Chapter One: The Silver Pact. A starting Lunar cannot possess more than four total dots (combined) of Backing in the separate Silver Pact factions.

The Realm and the Wyld Hunt have gone to great lengths to stymie the power of the Lunars in Creation. Having more than three dots in non-Silver Pact Backing is particularly rare, and players may only choose four or five dots with Storyteller permission. Even if the Storyteller's plans allow for such exceptional ratings, characters must pay double the usual cost for the fourth and fifth dot of Backing outside of the Silver Pact (i.e., the fourth and fifth dot costs four bonus points each). This increased cost does not apply to Backing gained during the course of play.

CULT

This Background works as noted in **Exalted**, page 112. Despite the valiant efforts of the Wyld Hunt, Lunar Exalted are better established than the newly returned Solars, and thus may start a series with a Cult rating of up to three dots. This Background should not be taken lightly: the player must work with the Storyteller to establish the reasons for the religious devotion her character receives.

FAMILIAR

Lunar Exalted use the same rules for the Familiar Background as found on page 112 of **Exalted**. Their innate spirit shape, however, somewhat limits Stewards in their choices of familiar. Most familiars are of the same type of creature as the Lunar's spirit shape. A Child of the Moon who takes the shape of the winter wolf as her animal true form probably seeks out a wolf as her familiar. The Lunar may have a familiar of some type the Storyteller, at her sole discretion, deems compatible with the Lunar's spirit shape. If the Storyteller decides that ravens, for example, are suitable due to their dependent habit of following wolves around in order to feed upon the leavings of their kills, then she might allow a character whose spirit shape is that of a wolf to have a raven familiar. A rabbit, on the other hand, would be terrified by the wolf-form; trying to keep such a familiar just wouldn't work out.

FOLLOWERS

Lunars use the rules for the Followers Background found on page 112 of **Exalted**. Although they can become powerful leaders, however, the Children of the Moon do not gain such powerful, supernatural leadership qualities as the Solar Exalted. Starting characters must pay double the usual cost for the fourth and fifth dot of Followers (i.e., the fourth and fifth dot costs four bonus points each), assuming that the Storyteller allows starting Lunar characters to begin with such a massive following in the face of Realm suppression. This increased cost does not apply to followers gained during the course of play. Followers are most likely human, but some Lunars may favor beastmen instead or have followers of both sorts. If a breed of beastmen is superior to humankind, the Storyteller might consider reducing the total number of followers granted by this Background.

INFLUENCE

The Wyld Hunt has not succeeded in its efforts to eliminate all of the Lunar Anathema. Nonetheless, its constant depredations have forced all but the most powerful Lunars to limit their exposure or face potential destruction. As such, starting Lunar characters must pay double the usual cost for the fourth and fifth dot of Influence (i.e., the fourth and fifth dots cost four bonus points each). This increased cost does not apply to Influence gained during the course of play. Players should ask the Storyteller before assuming that more than three dots are possible, however, and be prepared to provide an explanation how their characters gained such influence, yet has escaped the Wyld Hunt's notice.

FOLLOWERS VERSUS COMMAND

Storytellers who wish to allow the option might let Lunar characters use the Command Background from **Manual of Exalted Power—The Dragon-Blooded**. The primary differences between Command and Followers are issues of resources and control. The Command Background assumes that the character leads troops through the authority of a greater power. Thus, she does not have unrestricted control over her soldiers. On the other hand, she is not solely responsible for the upkeep of these troops, either. The Followers Background assumes that the character uses her own Resources, Backing or Influence to support her following. This usually results in greater loyalty, unfettered by obligations to another authority, accompanied by the responsibility of being the primary sponsor of the Followers in question. If the Storyteller allows Command, the fourth and fifth dot of this Background cost double for a starting Lunar, as with the Followers Background.

A Lunar leading a war band composed of ferocious barbarians who are loyal to her should take Followers. A Moonchild who serves the Tri-Khan, and leads a band of Delzahn warriors in the name of Chiaroscuro, might take Command with the Storyteller's permission. If the Storyteller doesn't want to use this option, the Followers Background can still represent these warriors. The difference between the two Backgrounds is significant, but it is also subtle enough to allow for interpretation.

MANSE

The Manse Background works as described in **Exalted**. Lunars do not have the massive infrastructure of the Realm to support the caretaking of their manses. Because of this, most of their manses are in out-of-the-way locations chosen where their isolation makes them easier to defend… or just because a Lunar can't hold a well-known manse without attracting the wrong sort of attention. Lunar Exalted particularly favor manses attuned to Lunar Essence, though the majority of Creation's manses are of elemental aspect.

MENTOR

Rare is the Silver Pact member who lacks a mentor, and an elder Lunar mentor is a powerful teacher indeed. If your character belongs to the Silver Pact, yet has no Mentor rating, explain why he became estranged from the elder who tattooed him and/or trained him. Does the elder who invested so much time and effort feel betrayed? Did the elder turn the tutelage of her protégé over to one of her earlier students? Or have the great deeds of the independent young Lunar simply made him a potential rival, too dangerous to aid any further? Has the character's mentor simply moved to another part of Creation?

NEW BACKGROUNDS

In addition to the Backgrounds presented in **Exalted**, the Children of the Moon can choose from several additional Backgrounds.

HEART'S BLOOD

Gifted with the protean nature of their patron goddess, the Children of the Moon can take the form of any animal whose Heart's Blood they have consumed in a ritual hunt. The hunt is instinctive to the Lunar, occurring to her as part of her Favored Survival Ability. Though the Casteless naturally seek out the Heart's Blood of their prey, the Silver Pact encourages training to refine the ritual in honor of the Silver Lady. See pages 128-129 for more details on the ritual hunt. Once a Moonchild has properly devoured the Heart's Blood of a suitable entity, she possesses the knowledge of its unique shape. This Background represents the catalog of shapes the Lunar has mastered over her lifetime.

Not all shapes possess equal value, however. Once you claim the shape of one raven, you don't gain much benefit from also claiming the shape of a different raven. On the other hand, if you consumed the Heart's Blood of Wisdom of Eyes, the ancient raven who has scavenged the lands of the wolf beastmen for 100 years, his specific form would be significant. A sign from a Lunar disguised as Wisdom of Eyes might manipulate tribal shamans or even move them to war. Similarly, consuming the Heart's Blood of a red cardinal doesn't provide any new functions, but its bright scarlet form is significantly different from that of the raven. The Heart's Blood Background, therefore, represents the number of *distinctly different* forms a Lunar can assume.

A form may be different because it's from a new species, as in the case of the cardinal and the raven. The ritual hunt presents enough inconvenience that Moonchildren seldom bother collecting species after slightly different species, however.

A form may also differ because it is a distinct individual: Something about the particular animal sets it apart from others of its kind, as in the case of Wisdom of Eyes or the satrap's favorite hunting dog (which she can tell apart from other dogs of that breed).

Humans always count as distinctly different forms. So do beastmen, Fair Folk and other sentient creatures (assuming a Lunar can take their forms at all). If a Lunar can take the form of Wyld-altered creatures, each mutated animal counts as a distinctly different form as well.

See Chapter Five: Charms and Shapeshifting, pages 128-129, for restrictions upon which Heart's Blood shapes a character may gain. Generally, any creature from the size of a housecat to a moose is open for ritual hunt, but a Lunar must possess particular Knacks to gain other shapes. For instance, Humble Mouse Shape is necessary before mastering

REGIONAL WILDLIFE

The North contains arctic animals, including herd animals such as elk and mammoths, owls and other birds of prey, hares, foxes, polar bears and saber-toothed cats.

The Northeast is home to animals found in evergreen forests, including elk, wild horses and other herd animals, big cats and wolves, large bears and birds of prey such as eagles and falcons.

The East contains temperate forests, which hold predators ranging from large weasels to tyrant lizards, herd animals such as horses, wild goat and deer, and numerous large rodents. There are also swamps containing alligators, large carnivorous turtles, rodents and snakes.

The Southeast contains savannas where herd animals such as aurochs, antelope, and elephants are hunted by dangerous predators such as big cats, wild dogs, hyenas and vipers. Rainforests are also prevalent, containing big cats, large insects and arachnids, enormous snakes and wild boar.

The South is largely desert, home to lizards, snakes and camels. Red-tailed hawks and roadrunners hunt various species of sand-dwelling rodents and spiders. One of the largest beasts to roam the area is the furnace rhino, a creature which feeds on mineral-rich soil and sports metal-alloy armor plates and jagged horns imbued with one of the magical materials.

The Southwest runs the gamut from coastal lands to brackish swamp to forested mountains. Elephants, crocodiles and tigers are among the largest creatures here. The animal population also includes numerous species of apes, colorful birds and large rodents.

The West is a great ocean filled with sharks, dolphins, giant squid, whales and other marine life. The region's numerous islands are home to sea birds, snakes, large rodents and occasionally larger beasts such as wild boar or the lizards known as tomb beasts.

The Northwest is a cold arctic sea with rocky coastlines, home to whales, seals and walruses. Inland, there are wild goats, elk and polar bears.

The Blessed Isle is largely tamed, with most of its beasts being domesticated animals such as cows, goats and llama. Sparsely inhabited areas are home to birds of prey, mountain goats, foxes, weasels and large rodents. Occasionally, Dynasts seed an area with a small stock of dangerous predators so they may be hunted for sport. Rarer, but well-known, animals include hearth cats, firemane horses and scarlet cranes.

Urban areas rarely suffer the presence of larger wildlife. Instead, they are home to vermin such as wild cats and dogs, large rats and other rodents, small birds, vipers, monkeys, huge insects and scavengers that feed on the waste of humankind.

the form of a mouse, while Towering Beast Form is required before mastering the shape of a yeddim. Prey's Skin Disguise is required before mastering the shape of an individual human being. The Lunar's initial human form, her spirit shape and any unique forms explicitly granted by Knacks do not count toward this Background.

X   You have only your true forms—your human shape and your spirit shape. Why do you shun the ritual hunt of Luna?

-     1-3 additional, distinct forms
- •   4-10 additional, distinct forms
- • • •   11-20 additional, distinct forms
- • • • •   21-40 additional, distinct forms
- • • • • •   41+ additional, distinct forms

REPUTATION

Lunar society is widespread and sometimes disjointed. Nevertheless, the Children of the Moon are few in number. Provided that they survive the Wyld Hunt and other dangers, the long-lived Lunar Exalted eventually learn of each other, if only by reputation.

A Steward's deeds give other Lunars an idea what to expect from her in the future. This reputation might be positive or negative (or both), and it affects the way others view the character. The reputation might not even be true: A sorcerer who ruthlessly guards a horde of magic might be renowned as a cannibal simply because she abides the presence of predatory beastmen who bolster her defenses. The five traditional merits associated with the faces of Luna are mettle, succor, glory, cunning and wisdom. Many Lunars actively seek to gain renown for one or more of these. In the First Age, Lunar society bequeathed titles of respect upon its members, based upon their renown, or "face." Such matters are often politic, and such titles are far from universal in the Time of Tumult, but earning titles of reputation is a sure way to gain the notice of elder Lunars who still respect such traditions. Informal reputations simply measure the degree to which other Lunars (and their associates) view a character as meritorious, or at least formidable.

In situations the Storyteller deems appropriate, a player may add her character's Reputation rating to her dice pool when making Social rolls. In situations in which the reputation is a liability, the player subtracts an equal number of dice.

X   Urrach-ya, "The Nonperson"
You have yet to make a reputation for yourself.

-     Nain-ya, "The Kin"
Your performance during your trials was considered impressive.
- •   Uf-ya, "The Honored"
You have begun to make a name for yourself among one or more factions within the Pact.
- • •   Ikth-ya, "The Respected"
Your deeds are such that many of the elders have heard your name.

- • • •   Murr-ya, "The Revered"
Tales of your exploits have spread throughout the Silver Pact, and there are those within the Threshold who fear your name.
- • • • •   Shahan-ya, "The Greatest"
The elders of the Silver Pact expect you to help reshape the world. Your legend is known throughout Creation.

SOLAR BOND

While refining the Essences of her Chosen, Luna agreed to instill an innate bond within each Lunar, tying that Exalt's Essence to that of a single Solar. Thus, each of the 300 Moonchildren was mystically associated with one of the 300 Solars as surely as day is paired with night. Whether by design, happenstance or personal interaction, different Lunars formed bonds with Solars with varied degrees of strength. Ma-Ha-Suchi says he scarcely grieved when his spouse was murdered, though his subsequent headlong plunge into the Wyld suggests he harbored feelings he would not admit. Lilith remained with her First Age spouse Desus despite physical abuse that sometimes shattered her bones, but no one can say whether she stayed because of her Solar Bond or the supernatural mental influence of her mate. Whatever the individual relationship might have been, these bonds still exist. As the Solars return to Creation, the Children of the Moon find they cannot ignore their ancient bonds.

For the default rules of the basic Solar-Lunar bond, see page 20. Dots in the Solar Bond Background indicate a stronger relationship than suggested by the standard rules. Lunars who were intimately connected to their Solar partners could tap into unexpected strength when defending their companions. Each dot of Solar Bond gives the Lunar two dice in her Solar Bond pool. Her player may assign one or more of these dice to any action undertaken with the deliberate purpose of aiding the Solar to whom the Lunar is bonded. Each die may be used once per story, and this dice pool refreshes at the end of every story.

In addition, each dot of Solar Bond adds one to the Lunar's Mental Defense Value whenever a social attack might cause her to act against her bonded Solar. Conversely, each dot of the Solar Bond Background reduces the Lunar's Mental Defense Value by one whenever her actions go against her bonded Solar. This bonus or penalty stacks with the default Intimacy created by the Lunar's bond with the Solar.

X   Your bond to a Solar mate exists, but you struggle to resist it.

-     You feel a strong mystical connection to your Solar associate.
- •   You are drawn to your Solar partner, and her influence is difficult to resist.
- • •   You can scarcely help being the greatest of friends or most faithful of lovers to your Solar companion—even if you hate her.
- • • •   Your First Age incarnation died staunchly defending your mate, despite her madness.

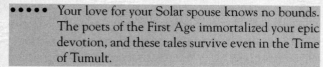

••••• Your love for your Solar spouse knows no bounds. The poets of the First Age immortalized your epic devotion, and these tales survive even in the Time of Tumult.

TABOO

A taboo is a special form of worship practiced by shamans or tribal cultures. People subject to taboos must do or not do certain things out of deference to the traditions of their patron spirit. Taboos can often be quite burdensome: this struggle in the name of the patron grants the god Essence. For some Lunars, this is merely a point of cultural interest. However, Casteless Lunars who hail from a society that practices strong taboos can find that their tradition of controlled behavior helps them resist Wyld taint. Children of the Moon who already bear moonsilver tattoos need no such help, and thus may reserve their respect (or lack thereof) for taboos to whatever individual bargains they might pursue with tribal gods.

Examples of minor taboos include never killing an albino animal or never eating pork, while a moderate taboo might demand that the Lunar never touch the dead outside of a battle, or never touch the shadow of any priest or shaman. A serious taboo might require the Casteless only to eat food prepared in a certain way, while a severe one could mean never shedding the blood of an honorable enemy, or remaining strictly vegetarian (forget about collecting Heart's Blood).

For a Casteless Lunar, each dot in the Taboo Background reduces the total number of dice involved in each of her Wyld Taint rolls. This reduction may result in a dice pool of zero, in which case no roll occurs. If the Lunar ever violates one of her taboos, she loses its benefits until she spends one month engaged in ritual purification or similar behavior, and her player succeeds at a (Charisma + Lore) roll with a difficulty equal to

the rating of the broken taboo. Breaking a minor taboo when you possess Taboo 5 probably only reduces its rating to 4, while violating a severe taboo would demand a month's time and a difficulty 5 roll to recover any use of the Background.

X   The superstitions of the tribes mean nothing to you.
•   You honor a couple of minor taboos.
••   You respect at least one moderate taboo and a handful of minor ones.
•••   You abide by at least one serious taboo and a few lesser restrictions.
••••   You bear the burden of a severe taboo and a number of lesser rules.
•••••   You suffer at least two severe taboos whose restrictions sometimes seem contradictory.

TATTOO ARTIFACT

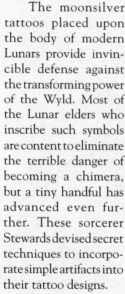

The moonsilver tattoos placed upon the body of modern Lunars provide invincible defense against the transforming power of the Wyld. Most of the Lunar elders who inscribe such symbols are content to eliminate the terrible danger of becoming a chimera, but a tiny handful has advanced even further. These sorcerer Stewards devised secret techniques to incorporate simple artifacts into their tattoo designs.

Every set of these special tattoos is an artifact composed of moonsilver. The sorcerer who inscribes the tattoo artifact embeds additional elements that mimic the form of the desired artifact. Such designs are limited to artifacts the Storyteller deems appropriate to include in a tattoo design. Endlessly repeating whorls of moonsilver covering the Lunar's chest, abdomen, shoulders and back might confer the benefits of an artifact chain shirt. Cylindrical designs around her forearms and wrists might form hearthstone bracers. An intricate inset pattern might serve as a hearthstone amulet. See **Exalted**, pages 380-391, for examples of artifacts.

A tattoo artifact has the advantage that no one can steal it from the character. Short of death, few forces could possibly deprive a Lunar of use of her tattoo artifacts. On the other hand, the Lunar must permanently attune to tattoo artifact. Any Essence normally committed must stay committed forever. Unlike the rest of a Lunar's moonsilver tattoos, a tattoo artifact cannot be hidden by shapechanging Knacks or Charms unless such powers explicitly allow the Lunar to hide her artifacts as well. If a supernatural effect hides a Lunar's moonsilver tattoos, but cannot hide her artifacts, then the rest of her tattoos become invisible except for the specific designs that compose her tattoo artifact. A Steward bearing a pair of hearthstone bracers as a tattoo artifact might still bear moonsilver designs upon her forearms but nowhere else should she manage to hide her caste-fixing tattoos.

Tattoo artifacts cannot reproduce medium or heavier armor. They also may not create external weapons: A moonsilver design encompassing the Lunar's entire hand might qualify for a smashfist, but there is no way to create a tattoo artifact daiklave. An artifact with no attunement cost may not be a tattoo artifact. A tattoo artifact cannot duplicate magitech items with a repair rating (such as those found in **Books of Sorcery Volume 1: Wonders of the Lost Age**). Storytellers should feel free to disallow tattoo versions of other artifacts, if they can't see a simple way the artifact could be represented by a design on a person's body.

This Background is not available to Casteless Lunar characters. Unless the Storyteller decides to allow some special exception, a Lunar who already has moonsilver tattoos cannot add a tattoo artifact. The design must have been incorporated into her original caste-fixing.

Other Traits

Linguistics (Claw-Speak)

Most animals possess some means of marking their territory—and humanity is no stranger to the idea, either. Many mortal tribes leave signatures carved into trees or stones along the borders of their lands. Long ago, the Silver Pact developed a system of symbols that can be drawn using claws, beaks or antlers as well as a human hand and an ink brush. This secret code enables the Pact to leave warnings for their fellow Lunars, convey messages or record a specific event at a particular place. Silver Pact members do not teach this secret language to anyone they don't trust. A character with at least one dot invested in a Lunar Mentor or some Backing in a Silver Pact faction, and at least Lore 1, may use one of her dots of Linguistics to learn claw-speak.

Caste

Just as the Solar Exalted are divided into castes, so do the Lunars have different duties, roles and innate predispositions. In the First Age, the Moonchildren had five castes, which arguably mirrored those of the Lawgivers. Just as all of the Exalted, Lunars were designed to serve as warriors against the Primordials, but the Silver Lady loved Gaia and thus designed her children to act as protectors and stewards of Creation. After the Usurpation, the Lunars fled to the edges of the world and fought to hold back the Wyld even as the defenses of the Old Realm were lost to treachery and rebellion. Unfortunately, the unbridled chaos of the Wyld warped their Exaltations in unforeseen ways. In the Time of Tumult, only three castes remain, and some unfortunate Moonchildren remain Casteless.

Since the Usurpation, the Immaculate Order has taught that the Lunar Exalted are demons called Anathema, though of a variety more bestial than the Solars. The Order has names for the surviving castes of the Lunar Anathema, and most civilized people only know these names for the three Lunar castes. Although the Order's Sidereal masters know about the existence of Casteless Lunars, the Sidereals see no benefit to introducing such confusion into the Realm's mythology. A Silver Pact initiate knows herself as a Full Moon Caste, but if others learn of her power they think of her as one of the Frenzied.

Anima Effects

All castes of Lunar Exalted can channel Essence directly through their animas to produce magical effects. Every Lunar Exalted can use her caste's anima power without special training.

In addition, any Lunar Exalt can spend a single mote of Essence to:

• Cause her caste mark and tattoos to glow brightly for a scene (as if the character has spent four to seven motes of Peripheral Essence).

• Cause her anima to glow brightly enough to read by for a scene (as if the character has spent eight to 10 motes of Peripheral Essence).

• Cause her Tell to become unmistakable and impossible to miss for a Tell.

• Know the precise day of the lunar month, the phase of the moon and the time of day for the rest of the scene.

FULL MOON CASTE

The Children of Luna say that the full moon shines brightest in the sky when the Wyld becomes strongest, for then is the might of Luna most dearly needed to keep Creation from washing away like a sandcastle before the tide. In this endlessly recurring time of danger, Luna displays all of her power and glory, and so do the Children of the Burning Moon. As Stewards of Creation, the Full Moons stalk the night to destroy its enemies through brute force and quicksilver speed. When the next day dawns, the broken bodies of Creation's foes litter the ground. The blood of the fallen may frighten the children of Gaia, but they shall remain safe for another month. Some Exalted scholars question this claim, drawing a connection between Luna's protean nature with the amorphous chaos of the Wyld. Whatever the truth of the matter, no one can doubt that the Full Moons are the greatest warriors of the Silver Pact.

The Usurpation divided the warriors of the Full Moon Caste. Those who felt strong loyalty to their Solar partners stood by their sides and fought against the treacherous onslaught of the Dragon-Blooded or led frenzied campaigns of bloody revenge upon hearing of the ambush in Meru.

The rest realized that the chaos of the Realm threatened to open the borders of Creation to the ravening forces of the Wyld, and they rushed to fill the gap.

Lunars of the Full Moon Caste are stronger, faster and hardier, their intrinsic physical might unparalleled amongst the Exalted. Strong as an ox, swift as an asp and enduring as a camel, the Full Moons carry the battle to the foes of Creation and prevail through physical prowess. Few beings in Creation can stand before one of the Full Moon Caste in single combat. Young Lunars often depend heavily upon their physical superiority and favor a style of combat that makes the most of their natural talents. Elder Lunars achieve a fluid mastery of their fighting techniques, smoothly shifting tactics and shapes as they seize upon their enemies' weaknesses.

Trials: A Lunar of the Full Moon Caste excels at her trials through direct action. She faces dangerous beasts and defeats them through might of arm or speed of blade. She makes long treks through uninhabitable wastelands, and completes ritual hunts without tiring. Whatever the challenge, the Full Moon conquers it with her immense strength, lightning reflexes or unflagging endurance. If she shows promise in another area, the elders note it with interest, but tradition demands that her natural predilections not be ignored.

Spirit Shapes: Full Moons favor animals known for their great strength and endurance, or for their speed and agility. Bears, great cats and aurochs are common, as are serpents and large birds of prey.

Anima Banner: The anima of a Full Moon Caste Lunar shines with a steady glow of soft white or silver light. Greater expenditures of Essence increase the intensity. Once their banners become iconic, the banner displays abstract or realistic images of their spirit shape.

Anima Effects: Full Moons may spend five motes of Essence to double their speed and leaping distances for a scene. The Full Moon also doubles her Strength for the purpose of feats of strength. This effect stacks with other increases, but only by adding a factor equal to the original value, not continuing to multiply by two. A Lunar who increases her running speed twice moves at three times her normal speed, not four.

Whenever the Lunar has 11 or more motes of Peripheral Essence active, this Anima Effect activates automatically without cost.

THE FRENZIED

The Realm's histories tell how these Anathema sought the power of great beasts and went mad. By the light of the moon, these feral lunatics ripped out the hearts of their hapless foes and drank their blood. When faced with the might of the Dragon-Blooded Host, the maniacs fled into the wilderness. The Wyld Hunt pursued and destroyed them, but sometimes, the foul patrons of the Anathema drive one their servants mad, and the hunt for the Frenzied must begin anew.

Caste Attributes: Members of the Full Moon Caste excel in physical might, agility and endurance. They possess a natural affinity for the Attributes of Strength, Dexterity and Stamina.

Associations: The season of summer, the element of fire, the color white, the Maiden of Battles

Sobriquets: Children of the Burning Moon, Silver Blades, Luna's Warriors, Nightfangs, the Frenzied (derogatory)

Concepts: Former pitfighter, barbarian warrior queen, urban gang leader, ruthless pirate, orphaned farmboy, hunter of abominations, relentless guerrilla, martial arts sifu

I HAVE NEVER FOUND CHAINS TOO STRONG FOR ME TO BREAK. HOW STRONG ARE YOUR NECKS?

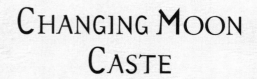

Changing Moon Caste

The Children of Luna say that the changing moon shifts in the sky as Luna demonstrates her waxing beauty, her sway over creatures of light and dark, and her mastery of deception and misdirection. If the Full Moons defend the body of Creation, then the Changing Moons protect the hearts and souls of the children of Gaia. A Child of the Shifting Moon trusts in her ability to convince other beings to do whatever is necessary, whether through guile or raw animal magnetism. Her enemies cannot be sure of whatever they see with their own eyes.

Before the Usurpation, there was no Changing Moon Caste. During the First Age, three now-lost castes existed: the Waxing Moons, the Half Moons and the Waning Moons. So varied were these Lunar Exalted that it is difficult to generalize about their reactions to the treachery of the Dragon-Blooded. Many felt closer to the Solars than did other Moonchildren, and therefore suffered their loss most keenly. Others are said to have been all too familiar with the growing madness of the Children of the Sun, and all too happy to assist in their destruction.

Members of the Changing Moon Caste are magnetic, slick and sexy. Amongst the Lunar Exalted, the Children of the Shifting Moon become the greatest spies, assassins and leaders. Few beings in Creation can resist the carnal allure of a Lunar seductress or navigate the shifting words of a Lunar diplomat. As Stewards of Creation, Changing Moons use misdirection and persuasion to defend their charges. Trusted guards may mysteriously disappear or abruptly change their loyalties, and disorganized war bands may suddenly display cunning tactics. The foes of Creation can scarcely predict what will greet them when the next day dawns.

Trials: A Lunar of the Changing Moon Caste excels at her trials through animal magnetism, persuasion or deceit. She might defeat her foes through trickery or even beguile them into friendliness. She can impress fickle spirits with charm and rival the Fair Folk for grace. Whatever the challenge, the Changing Moon conquers it with personal charisma, slippery tricks or stunning attraction. Traditions are less established for this caste, and sometimes, it seems that the elders choose it for a young Lunar simply because nothing else seems to fit.

Spirit Shapes: Changing Moons favor animals adored for their beauty or grace. Great cats, birds of prey and serpents are common, as are animals whose luxurious fur, skin or feathers are sought by hunters.

Anima Banner: The anima of a Changing Moon is a shifting prism of bright silver light and dark blue or purple shadow, with flickers of other colors. Greater expenditures of Essence intensify the colors, and the patterns shift faster. Once one's banner becomes iconic, it displays abstract or realistic images of the Lunar's spirit shape.

Anima Effects: A Changing Moon can spend 10 motes of Essence to craft an illusion that allows him to appear as any one person he knows. This trick lasts for a scene, and comes complete with voice and smells. The imagery is accompanied by the perception of trustworthiness, lending bonus dice equal to the character's permanent Essence to any social action that such an aura assists. If the Lunar's anima banner activates at any level, however, its light pierces the illusion, and his tattoos may become visible. This dispels the illusion, but bathes the Changing Moon in an array of ever-shifting shadows and silver light that make him difficult to see clearly. Add the Lunar's Essence to the difficulty of any effort to discern his identity by sight, assuming that the investigator did not see him before the activation of his anima banner.

Once the Lunar expends 11 or more motes of Peripheral Essence, this anima effect activates automatically without cost. Since the Changing Moon's anima banner is active at this point, the anima effect automatically results in shifting light and shadows.

THE TRICKSTERS

Ancient records speak of Anathema who clad their bodies within lies. These craven creatures would lurk on the edges of the wild, slipping into cities and villages to seduce loyal husbands, devour them and lay their bestial seed within unsuspecting wives. Fortunately, the righteous Dragon-Blooded drove out these Tricksters and their beastman fosterlings. It is said that some fled into the forsaken shadowlands of Marama's Fell, where their treacherous ways led to infighting and slaughter.

Caste Attributes: Members of the Changing Moon Caste excel at the use of personal charm or guile. They possess a natural affinity for the Attributes of Charisma, Manipulation and Appearance.

Associations: The season of spring, the element of air, the color purple, the Maiden of Serenity

Sobriquets: Children of the Shifting Moon, Silver Mirrors, Luna's Courtiers, Night-thieves, the Tricksters (derogatory)

Concepts: Escaped slave, bandit lord, former prostitute, cunning ambassador, seductive assassin, king of thieves, charismatic warlord

I SPENT A LIFETIME HUNTING ANIMALS, FROM BEAR TO MARMOTS. NOW, I HUNT YOU.

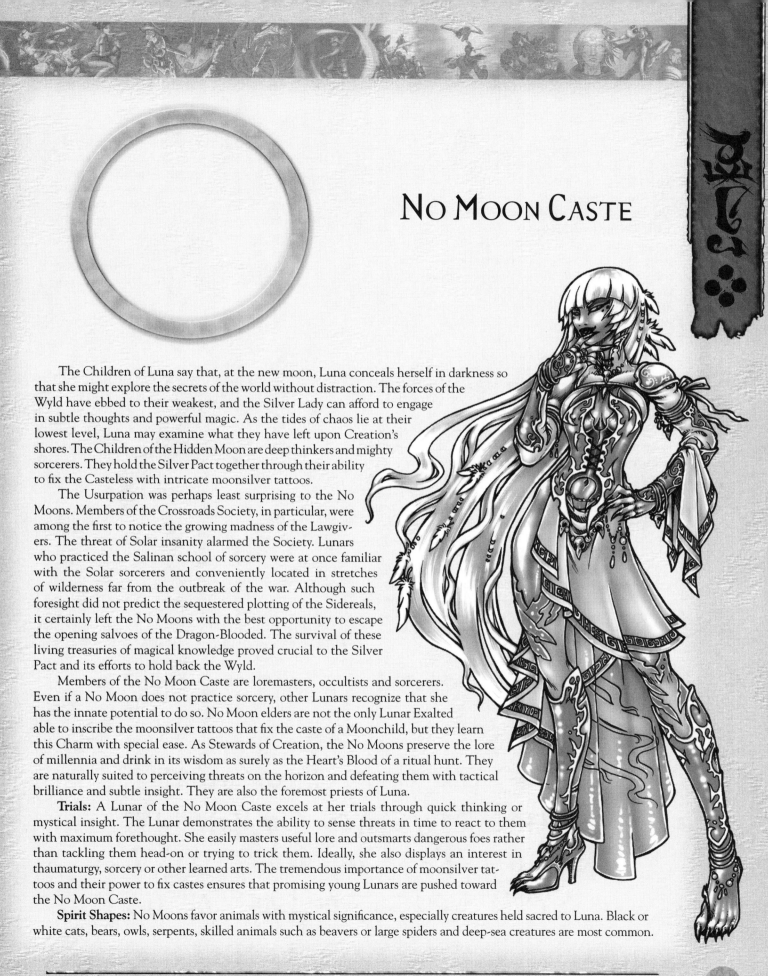

NO MOON CASTE

The Children of Luna say that, at the new moon, Luna conceals herself in darkness so that she might explore the secrets of the world without distraction. The forces of the Wyld have ebbed to their weakest, and the Silver Lady can afford to engage in subtle thoughts and powerful magic. As the tides of chaos lie at their lowest level, Luna may examine what they have left upon Creation's shores. The Children of the Hidden Moon are deep thinkers and mighty sorcerers. They hold the Silver Pact together through their ability to fix the Casteless with intricate moonsilver tattoos.

The Usurpation was perhaps least surprising to the No Moons. Members of the Crossroads Society, in particular, were among the first to notice the growing madness of the Lawgivers. The threat of Solar insanity alarmed the Society. Lunars who practiced the Salinan school of sorcery were at once familiar with the Solar sorcerers and conveniently located in stretches of wilderness far from the outbreak of the war. Although such foresight did not predict the sequestered plotting of the Sidereals, it certainly left the No Moons with the best opportunity to escape the opening salvoes of the Dragon-Blooded. The survival of these living treasuries of magical knowledge proved crucial to the Silver Pact and its efforts to hold back the Wyld.

Members of the No Moon Caste are loremasters, occultists and sorcerers. Even if a No Moon does not practice sorcery, other Lunars recognize that she has the innate potential to do so. No Moon elders are not the only Lunar Exalted able to inscribe the moonsilver tattoos that fix the caste of a Moonchild, but they learn this Charm with special ease. As Stewards of Creation, the No Moons preserve the lore of millennia and drink in its wisdom as surely as the Heart's Blood of a ritual hunt. They are naturally suited to perceiving threats on the horizon and defeating them with tactical brilliance and subtle insight. They are also the foremost priests of Luna.

Trials: A Lunar of the No Moon Caste excels at her trials through quick thinking or mystical insight. The Lunar demonstrates the ability to sense threats in time to react to them with maximum forethought. She easily masters useful lore and outsmarts dangerous foes rather than tackling them head-on or trying to trick them. Ideally, she also displays an interest in thaumaturgy, sorcery or other learned arts. The tremendous importance of moonsilver tattoos and their power to fix castes ensures that promising young Lunars are pushed toward the No Moon Caste.

Spirit Shapes: No Moons favor animals with mystical significance, especially creatures held sacred to Luna. Black or white cats, bears, owls, serpents, skilled animals such as beavers or large spiders and deep-sea creatures are most common.

Anima Banner: The anima of a No Moon is a dreamlike veil of dark blue and purple light, with a silver tint along the edges. Greater Essence expenditures darken the shadowy veil while the silver edge grows brighter. Once the No Moons' banners become iconic, the banners display abstract or realistic images of their spirit shapes.

Anima Effects: A No Moon Lunar may attune her Essence to that of the new moon. She must spend at least one mote of Essence, and may spend up to twice her permanent Essence in motes. In doing so, she gains a shadowy penumbra that causes attackers who cannot see through darkness to suffer a -1 external penalty. This aura amplifies the occult power of the Lunar for the remainder of the scene, allowing her to reduce the cost of all Charms that explicitly require an Occult roll by one per mote of Essence used to power her anima, though the cost of a Charm cannot be reduced by more than half. This aura also allows her to reduce the Essence cost of all spells cast for the rest of the scene by one per mote of Essence initially invested in her anima, but the cost of a spell cannot be reduced by more than half.

Whenever the Lunar has 11 or more motes of Peripheral Essence active, this anima effect activates automatically at full strength (or increases if originally activated at a lower power) without cost. The No Moon is just as obvious as any other flaring Lunar, but the light springs from the silver edge of her anima and the shadow within remains. She is treated as having spent twice her permanent Essence for purposes of Charm and spell cost reduction and retains the protection of the penumbra.

Caste Attributes: Members of the No Moon Caste excel in mental adeptness, memory, reasoning and occult skill. They possess a natural affinity for the Attributes of Perception, Intelligence and Wits.

Associations: The season of winter, the element of water, the color blue, the Maiden of Secrets

Sobriquets: Children of the Hidden Moon, the Silver Shadows, Luna's Chamberlains, Nightwitches, the Ogres (derogatory)

THE OGRES

So hideous were these twisted Anathema that they were forced to work their evil by the dark of the moon. Less potent than the Unclean, the Ogres were so desperate to prove their power that they forged pacts with demons so wicked they could only be called on the darkest of nights. The Dragon-Blooded razed the stygian groves of these Anathema and banished their hellish masters. Today, the wise itinerant monks of the Immaculate Order watch for signs of the vile Ogres among the heretics of the wilds.

Concepts: Tribal storyteller, spirit medium, Wyld shaman, master archer, keeper of forbidden lore, scavenger lord, clever silversmith

IF YOU DON'T KNOW WHAT YOU'RE DOING, YOU COULD HURT YOURSELF. FORTUNATELY, I KNOW ENOUGH FOR BOTH OF US.

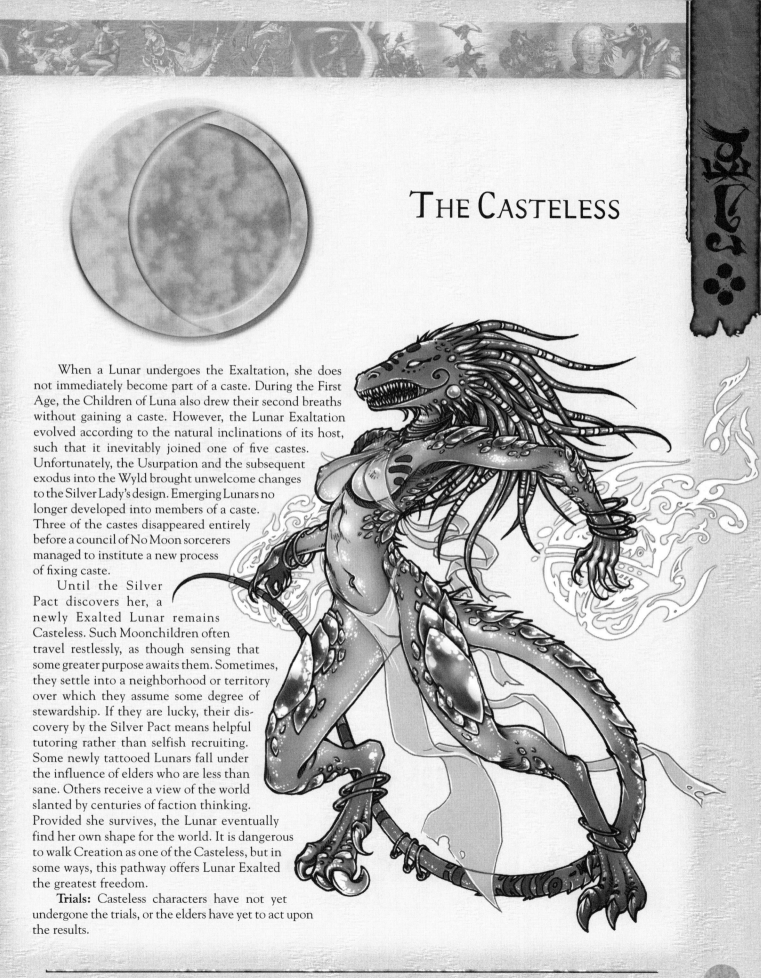

THE CASTELESS

When a Lunar undergoes the Exaltation, she does not immediately become part of a caste. During the First Age, the Children of Luna also drew their second breaths without gaining a caste. However, the Lunar Exaltation evolved according to the natural inclinations of its host, such that it inevitably joined one of five castes. Unfortunately, the Usurpation and the subsequent exodus into the Wyld brought unwelcome changes to the Silver Lady's design. Emerging Lunars no longer developed into members of a caste. Three of the castes disappeared entirely before a council of No Moon sorcerers managed to institute a new process of fixing caste.

Until the Silver Pact discovers her, a newly Exalted Lunar remains Casteless. Such Moonchildren often travel restlessly, as though sensing that some greater purpose awaits them. Sometimes, they settle into a neighborhood or territory over which they assume some degree of stewardship. If they are lucky, their discovery by the Silver Pact means helpful tutoring rather than selfish recruiting. Some newly tattooed Lunars fall under the influence of elders who are less than sane. Others receive a view of the world slanted by centuries of faction thinking. Provided she survives, the Lunar eventually find her own shape for the world. It is dangerous to walk Creation as one of the Casteless, but in some ways, this pathway offers Lunar Exalted the greatest freedom.

Trials: Casteless characters have not yet undergone the trials, or the elders have yet to act upon the results.

Spirit Shapes: Any. Casteless in the Time of Tumult are destined to join one of the castes, and their totemic animal might be anything suitable to a Full Moon, Changing Moon or No Moon.

Anima Banner: The anima of a Casteless Lunar is a chaotic swirl of purples, blues and silver. At lower levels, the anima is dull and muted, though greater Essence expenditures flare it to full color. Once their banners become iconic, the banner displays hazy or distorted images of their spirit shape.

Anima Effects: A Casteless Lunar uses the anima effect of the caste currently shown upon the moon's face. During the full moon, and the days immediately before and after, he has the Full Moon anima power. For the new moon, and the previous and subsequent days, he has the No Moon anima power. The remaining days of the month, he has the Changing Moon anima power. Arrogant No Moons, and their detractors, make much of the fact that during Calibration the Casteless take on a No Moon anima.

Caste Attributes: Without a fixed caste, the ever-shifting Lunar has no Caste Attributes. Instead he has two Favored Attributes. Usually these fit within the same category—Physical, Social or Mental—indicating the natural caste to which the young Lunar can aspire, but sometimes, the ways of the Fickle Lady are less clear, and the Lunar favors two unrelated Attributes. Elders often watch the trials of Moonchildren of mixed Favored Attributes with special interest.

Associations: Calibration, the Maiden of Journeys (being Casteless is seen as a temporary state)

Sobriquets: The Undiscovered, the Unblooded, Luna's Bastards, the Moon-Mad

Concepts: Guild assassin, mercenary, orphaned child, misshapen pariah

THE MOON-MAD

It can happen in any land, but especially among the poor and rustic who lack Immaculate piety: Morally weak people draw evil power from the moon and the Wyld to become shape-changing monsters. At first, they can still pass for human, but as time goes by, they become more and more bestial, more prone to rampage beneath the full moon's glow. They are the Moon-Mad: Lunar Anathema new to their wickedness.

LUNA GAVE US THE POWER TO DO ANYTHING. TO BE ANYTHING. WHY SHOULD WE LIMIT OURSELVES?

OTHER RULES

LUNAR ANIMA BANNERS

Similar to those of other Exalted, the anima banners of Lunar Exalted form temporary halos when excited by Peripheral Essence. When a Lunar anima flares, it doesn't just give away her identity through the brilliant display of Essence. The anima banner strips away the Lunar's disguises and displays her Tell. When the anima banner reaches the 8 to 10 mote level (or higher), the Lunar is forced into one of her true forms. Lunars whose anima banners lock them into their true forms may still shift between these shapes as normal. Although the Lunar loses access to any Knacks that do not explicitly provide a true form, a Lunar locked into her true forms can still use Charms that allow limited shapeshifting, such as growing armor, claws or tentacles. The duration of each level of anima banner display is the same as that experienced by Solars (see **Exalted**, p. 114).

LUNAR ANIMA BANNERS

Motes of Peripheral Essence	Effect
1-3	The character's caste mark glitters and is visible from certain angles, and her Tell becomes prominent. Make a (Perception + Awareness) roll at standard difficulty for anyone seeing the Exalted to notice her caste mark and Tell. If the character's tattoos or Tell is hidden by a Charm or Knack, they remain hidden, but her caste mark may still be spotted.
4-7	The character's caste mark and tattoos burn and shine through anything placed over them. The character's Tell becomes impossible to miss, and her nature is on display. The character is not yet locked into her true shapes, but Charms and Knacks that suppress her Tell or tattoos fail. Stealth Charms and other magics that mute impressions also fail. A character may use the Stealth Ability to hide in natural cover, but such attempts are at +2 difficulty.
8-10	The character radiates a coruscant, blue-silver aura bright enough to read by, and her caste mark becomes a shining silver brand on her forehead. Stealth is impossible. If the character is shapeshifted, she is forced to return to her true forms.
11-15	The character is locked in her true forms and engulfed in a brilliant bonfire of Essence, which burns from her feet to at least a foot above her head. Objects that come into contact with the aura may be left damp and warped, as if they had been exposed to the night air and elements for many days. The character is visible for miles. The brilliant, steady light illuminates the surroundings out to a spearcast's distance as if in moonlight, and is sufficient to read by within a dozen yards. The character's caste mark remains etched in the vision of anyone who sees it for minutes afterward.
16+	The character is surmounted by a coldly burning image totemic to her person—her spirit shape. A warrior might be surrounded by a great silver wolf, a No Moon sorcerer by a hooded snake, and so on. The character is, of course, locked into her true shapes.

THE GREAT CURSE

Just as all other Exalted, the Chosen of the Moon suffer from the Great Curse placed upon them by the slain Primordials. For the Lunars, the Curse arises from their connection to Luna and their shapeshifting powers. The dying Primordials cursed the Lunars to become the very beasts they emulated.

Lunar Exalted gain points of Limit in three fashions. As with Solars, any time the Lunar chooses to suppress her primary Virtue (the one associated with her Limit Flaw), she gains a point of Limit. Suppressing other Virtues does not add to the Exalt's Limit. In addition, any time a Child of the Moon resists an unnatural mental influence, she receives one point of Limit, up to once per scene. Finally, whenever the Lunar is first struck by the light of the full moon on a particular night, her player must roll a number of dice equal to her primary Virtue. Each success on this roll adds one point of Limit to her total, and rolling a 10 counts as two successes as usual. The Lunar can suffer this effect only once per full moon night, and only if she is touched by the moon's light. When a character's Limit reaches 10, she suffers Limit Break and immediately reduces her Limit to 0. For the duration of one scene, the character's behavior is ruled by her Virtue Flaw. She acts as it dictates and can only hope that the episode passes quickly.

Limit Break can be a extremely cathartic experience, and undergoing a Limit Break immediately gives the character temporary Willpower points equal to her rating in the Flaw's related Virtue, even if this raises her temporary Willpower above her permanent Willpower or above 10. The character gains this Willpower only if she does not attempt to control her behavior during the Limit Break, however. Characters may choose to partially control their actions during Limit Break, forgoing the Willpower bonus. The effects of doing so are listed under "Partial Control" in each Flaw's description.

SAMPLE LUNAR VIRTUE FLAWS

The following section presents examples of Flaws you may choose to match your Lunar's primary Virtue. These aren't the only Flaws that a Lunar might develop. Storytellers and players can work together to develop their own Flaws. Keep in mind that these Flaws are the result of an ancient and terrible curse, so they are never pleasant or useful. The slain Primordials intentionally set out to turn the Lunars into beasts, and any new Flaw should reflect this.

Choose one of the Flaws that match your character's primary Virtue. Each Flaw describes the behavior that overcomes the afflicted Lunar. Each Flaw also describes the constraints of partial control which a Lunar might manage. If a player refuses to act out the character's loss of control—even when the character struggles to maintain partial control, forfeiting the chance to gain Willpower from the experience—the Storyteller may take control of the character.

Compassion Flaws

The Curse of the Whipped Dog

The character is overcome with indecision and doubt. He capitulates in the face of adversity and cannot resist authority. The Whipped Dog refuses to take any sort of leadership responsibility, instead blindly following the suggestions of anyone around him. The character may defend himself if physically attacked, but he will try to remove himself from the confrontation as quickly as possible.

Partial Control: The character may choose to flee from a situation immediately rather than deal with the consequences of taking actions, even those proposed by others. He still feels a compulsion to obey, but balances it with concern for what others might think.

The Curse of the Mother Hen

The character is overcome with the desire to take care of those around her as though they were helpless baby birds. She hovers around them and eagerly tries to feed, clothe and bathe them, or insist that they rest quietly, regardless of cost to herself. The Mother Hen will not listen to refusals of her aid; she treats such attempts as though they were the confused cries of a child in need. If anyone tries to harm another person within

her presence, she first scolds everyone involved, but she will engage in non-lethal suppressive violence if necessary.

Partial Control: The character may restrict her instinctual mothering to people she knows personally. If no one she knows is present, then she must choose at least one individual per point of Compassion as her foster children (assuming sufficient targets exist) and protect them as above.

Conviction Flaws

The Curse of the Heartless Weasel

The character becomes a creature of pure selfishness. He ignores the needs, feelings or very survival of others, and does not consider how his actions may impact those around him. The Heartless Weasel has no mercy, and he will slaughter innocents who impede him as surely as his enemies. The character may not expend effort or take risk in order to help another. He may flee if threatened, though he will do nothing to help his comrades who are left behind.

Partial Control: The character spares the lives of his friends, even if they anger him. After all, they may be useful to him later. Nonetheless, he will happily fleece them for money and whatever else strikes his fancy.

The Curse of the Hungry Wolverine

The character is overcome with the boundless importance of the instant. He cannot ignore his vision of how things should be, no matter what the consequences. The Hungry Wolverine will cripple someone who tries to take his bowl of rice as surely as he will fight to preserve his own life. The character must always do what he thinks is right even if it means dying in the process. Storytellers should consider the character's own past history when judging what the character defines as "right."

Partial Control: The character may verbally bully an opponent into cooperating rather than resorting to violence. Of course, some foes may not cooperate in which case fighting may prove inevitable.

TEMPERANCE FLAWS

THE CURSE OF THE DRUNKEN MONKEY

The character becomes a creature of impulse and ignorance. He is a slave to his desires, unable to control himself long enough to resist temptation. The Drunken Monkey acts without thinking and does not consider the consequences of his actions. He gorges his appetites without restraint and ignores dangerous situations in the heat of the moment—but will drop any indulgence the moment some new temptation presents itself.

Partial Control: The character may give vague attention to the next day, provided it doesn't interfere with his pursuit of pleasure. He will still drink himself into a stupor, for example, but he might ask a close friend to watch out for him first.

THE CURSE OF THE HUMBLE SLOTH

The character becomes unconcerned with anything except for the bare essentials. He cares about nothing except eating and sleeping. The Humble Sloth cares not for the concerns of the rest of the world, for the true necessities of his daily life are all that matter. He will not take the slightest chance except to avoid a direct threat to his life. He will not study or work, or fight except in self-defense.

Partial Control: The character may be convinced that a brief chore is necessary to ensure his future needs are met. In addition, he may act to meet the immediate needs of his children or mate, provided they are essential to life.

VALOR FLAWS

THE CURSE OF THE RAGING BULL

The character becomes a fighting animal. He is dangerously quick-tempered, willing to fight anyone for any reason and unable to back down from any challenge to his dominance. While this Flaw is active, the character cannot fail Valor checks and can't spend Willpower points to ignore them. Just as an angry bull, he attempts to fight anything that inconveniences or startles him. He doesn't talk much, either, unless it is with his fists (or worse).

Partial Control: The character settles for bullying others into submission. Provided others answer him with abject cowardice, verbally abusing them is sufficient to satisfy his desire to fight. However, even the slightest hint of disrespect or backbone on the part of the abused party requires a physical attack.

THE CURSE OF THE LONE WOLF

The character needs no one. He feels no fear, and doesn't respect others. The Lone Wolf does not wait for help before wading into combat, and he doesn't share the glory for success. He feels nothing but contempt for "the pack" and will always proceed without waiting for others to catch up.

Partial Control: The character is without fear, but not without sense. He can flee if tactically advisable and needn't rush heedlessly into battle. However, if he chooses to join the fight, he will ignore efforts of his supposed allies and act as though he were the only one fighting on his side.

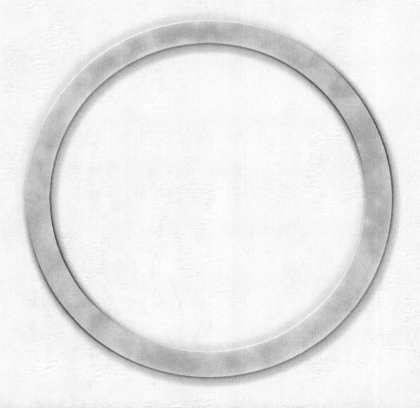

SO YOU'RE ANGRY, YES?

SKREEEE!

PAK! PAK!

I THINK I MADE... HOW YOU SAY... BAD FIRST IMPRESSION. NO?

NO MORE LIES, YOU SLIPPERY THIEF!

SKRANG!

YADE, YOU WOUND ME!

BUT IS OKAY. I WOUND YOU TOO.

DAMN IT!

CRASH!

CHAPTER FIVE
CHARMS AND SHAPESHIFTING

The Lunar Exalted have two separate magical skills granted them by Luna: their Charms, intuitive but powerful abilities, and an inherent ability to change their shapes, refined through Knacks. Both are integral to the lifestyle of a Child of Luna.

SHAPESHIFTING

As Luna shows many faces to Creation, so too do her Chosen, changing their shapes with skill and cleverness.

Changing from any form to any other takes a single miscellaneous action. Other than the time required, changing shape requires no concentration and only a little Essence. No dice roll is needed. Essence spent on changing form is not committed, and changing does not count as Charm use. As with other miscellaneous actions, the shapechange is effectively instantaneous—its Speed determines only when the character next gets to act.

During the change, observers see the character's features shift. Hair grows or scales form on his skin, the face acquires a beak or loses the porcine snout, and hands become hooves or talons turn to feet as he changes to or from an animal form. When in a given form, the Lunar is really that creature. His skin is its skin, his voice the animal's voice, his blood its blood. It does not register as a magical disguise to Essence sight. Only the character's mind and the core of his Essence remain his own.

Anything the character carries or wears disappears with the transformation. These tools usually fade into Elsewhere as the Lunar takes on a new form. When the new shape can use the equipment, it carries over instead. A character's clothing and knife go away when she changes from her human true form to her Spirit Shape, but remain when she changes into another person. Clothing and other fitted materials shift somewhat to make sure they fit. Lunars with Changing Plumage Mastery can shift their clothing even more.

When in a form other than her human form, the Lunar uses the Strength, Stamina and Appearance natural to the other form. A Lunar in animal form uses the *lowest* of her Dexterity or the animal's natural Dexterity—you just can't make a tortoise tap-dance or run like a racehorse… without the Internal Form Mastery Knack, anyway. (Human forms use the Lunar's own Dexterity.) Her other Attributes remain her own. Most characters in animal form suffer severe penalties trying to enter social combat with humans, if it is possible at all. The Lunar also gains any special attacks, such as trampling, and methods of movement, such as flight or speedy burrowing, available to the creature. Instincts that come with the animal form are under the Lunar's control, and they give the Exalt limited ability to communicate with animals of the same species.

No known physical or magical force can prevent one of Luna's Children from shifting shape. If a Steward chooses to wear a different form and it lies within her power, she can take the action to change, even when magic constrains her from taking any action at all. Only some force that prevents her from *choosing* to change shape, such as unnatural (or perhaps natural) mental influence or being unconscious. Some Charms may eliminate even that danger.

Although shapeshifting is not a Charm-based power, shapeshifting qualifies for the Obvious keyword. When observers see a Lunar transform, they know the character did something magical—no Essence display needed. On death, the Lunar always returns to the last worn of his true forms. Any Lunar's first true form is the shape he wore when he Exalted. The second is his spirit shape.

SPIRIT SHAPE

At the moment of Exaltation, a Lunar gains her first animal shape. This is the character's spirit shape, reflecting the character's nature and temperament. Exalted who are sly might discover the snake or raccoon, the mighty could find bulls or bears, the wise sometimes see raitons or the lone wolf. Of the last, for example, a character who speaks with wise deliberation found over many travels might take the wolf as spirit shape; the one who prefers to spend more time with the dead and speak in cryptic squawks chooses raiton.

From that moment on, the Lunar Exalt can take on the shape of her spirit animal. This is one of the Lunar's true forms, the first she receives after her natural human shape, and Luna's first gift to the Lunar. Changing to this true form or to the Lunar's true human form costs only one mote, no matter what shape the Lunar wears at the moment. As a true form, the Strength, Stamina and Appearance of the spirit shape are considered natural.

In her spirit shape, a Lunar displays her permanent moonsilver tattoos, which arrange themselves artfully along the natural contours of her animal body. Likewise, scars, losses of limb and other permanent damage suffered by one true form become visible in the other. Such markings benefit from the same magic as the Tell, becoming difficult to notice. It is the same for the war form.

Players may only choose creatures that are valid targets for the sacred hunt as a character's spirit shape. In order to create a character with a mouse or yeddim totem, the character must take the appropriate Knacks (see p. 131).

CHARM CONCEPT: NATURAL ATTRIBUTES

The Physical Attributes of Lunar Exalted are prone to change from time to time, as could only be expected of shapeshifters. Because the maximum number of dice Lunars can add through Charms is equal to the relevant Attribute, having different Attributes in different shapes makes the matter cloudy.

Shapes that reduce a character's Attributes do not decrease maximum dice added through Charms. Shapes that increase a character's Attributes do not increase that maximum, either. Increases in Attributes from a false shape count toward this dice maximum, but are not themselves limited by this value.

Example: Seven Devils Clever has a natural Strength of 3. When she changes into an omen dog (Strength 5), she can gain only one bonus die before she reaches her maximum increase from Charms and can no longer purchase bonus successes with the Second Excellency. If she changed into a large bear (Strength 7), she could not add any dice through Charms but would still benefit from having a Strength more than twice her natural value.

True forms break the rule. When a true form's Strength, Stamina or Appearance are greater than the human true form's, the Attributes do not count toward the maximum number of dice from Charms and are considered the character's "true" Attributes for the purposes of determining those limits. True forms that have fewer dots in an Attribute do not decrease a character's dice limits.

A Lunar can still only learn Charms when her *human* true form meets the Attribute minimums, and having a lower Attribute in a spirit shape does not disqualify her from using Charms that her animal Attributes suggest she cannot learn.

WAR FORM

Some of the Lunar Exalted also have a third true form, called the war form or the Deadly Beastman Transformation. In this form, the Lunar becomes a hybrid of man and beast, usually monstrous and several feet taller than the largest human and with great strength and resilience. Most Lunars prefer to enter combat using the war form, knowing that it affords them a tremendous advantage. Lunars who have a war form must spend five motes to don it.

Changing into the Deadly Beastman Transformation sends most mortal armors away into Elsewhere, and many weapons become too small to effectively use. Most artifact tools and weapons remain useable in this form, but only moonsilver armor is flexible enough to change with the Lunar into the war form. Moonsilver armor actually adopts a different shape ideal to the bestial man-beast form. Some characters have

smaller war forms, closer to a human size, in which they can use normal armors.

A Lunar can spend as much time as he wants in his war form, but wearing it makes an open statement to other Lunars (and other entities who can recognize it) that the Steward is ready for battle to break out at any moment—perhaps even eager for it. Few Lunar Exalted would visit the territory of a Lunar or god in the war form, knowing that they are likely to be met with force rather than warm greetings. On the other hand, the war form can be a calculated insult, suggesting that the offended entity cannot keep its territories safe to visitors or lacks the power to force the Lunar into a more socially acceptable shape.

Despite the frequency of war forms that are terrifyingly huge and intended to tear through enemies in battle, some war forms are simply person-sized or even of slighter builds. Not all warriors, after all, focus on sheer might.

MOON-FACED MAIL (ARTIFACT •)

Moon-faced mail is artifact armor that shifts to fit the Lunar's war form when desired. Any manner of mundane armor can be made into moon-faced mail, making it a desirable alternative to the rarer moonsilver armors.

OTHER SHAPES: THE SACRED HUNT

Were Lunars limited to a spirit shape and a war form, they would never have received the renown for their versatility and mastery of disguise they touted in the First Age. Lunar Exalted can wear the shape of anything and anyone living. But a Lunar must first earn the right.

To earn a new shape, the Lunar must hunt and dedicate the pursuit and kill to Luna. The hunt typically takes, at most, six hours: The Exalt must find a superlative example of the animal he wishes to hunt, chase the animal to the ground and slay it at the climax of the hunt. The Silver Pact calls this the sacred hunt, or the blood hunt.

Targeting a species with the blood hunt requires a simple (Wits + Survival) roll and a point of Willpower. Each success on the roll reduces the required time by one hour, to a minimum of one hour. If an animal is rare in an area, the ritual hunt may take longer and may have a higher difficulty. Animals that cannot be found in an area are not valid targets for the sacred hunt. Once the Lunar declares the hunt, he cannot rest or pursue any other goal until he completes it or he fails. Lunars instinctively know the ins and outs of the hunt.

Once the desired animal lies at his feet, bleeding its last, the Lunar tastes its heart's blood and gains mastery of the creature's form. From that point on, the Lunar can take on the shape of the precise animal it killed by spending three motes of Essence. The Steward becomes a perfect facsimile, including any scars or distinguishing marks.

A Lunar is not limited to just one example of an animal. He may have two or more, with different colorations to confuse pursuers or for different purposes. (Small lap dogs are good for sneaking around as a prefect's pet, while big hounds are more effective in battle.) Each additional form requires another day and another hunt. Just because the Lunar must find an ideal animal to hunt does not mean that he must always hunt the largest, strongest and fastest. If he wishes to find a small, skulking bear instead of a massive, mountain-shaking grizzly, he must simply find the most perfect example of an atypical animal. It is effectively the same process.

Shapes, once learned, do not age. No matter how long since the original victim's death, the shape the Lunar knows does not grow old or weak. The shape's hair and fingernails may grow, but only time spent in the form contribute to such growth. Skin may tan, but only when that shape is actually under the sun. In either case, any changes to the false shape disappear once the character re-dons that shape—letting a shape tan, then shifting to another form and back produces a shape as it appeared before it tanned. With Changing Plumage Mastery, Lunars may control these aspects of their shapes. While in another shape, the character's true forms age but do not otherwise suffer the passage of time—hair and nails do not grow, skin does not tan (but may eventually wrinkle), etc.

Not all creatures are valid victims of the sacred hunt. Beasts that have been tainted by the Wyld are too unnatural for the Stewards to master their shapes without the Luna's Hidden Face Knack. Also, some creatures are too small or large to hunt with the basic ritual: Any beast smaller than a housecat or larger than a moose is considered an invalid target without Humble Mouse Shape or Towering Beast Form, respectively. Attempts to hunt invalid targets with the blood hunt result in a rejection from Luna. The Lunar immediately knows that the attempt failed and does not spend the Willpower, though he does lose the 15 minutes or so necessary to begin the ritual.

There is a sacred hunt for human victims. Not all Lunar Exalted know it, unlike the rite for animals. Some Stewards consider it distasteful to take human forms. Most consider it too useful to quibble over the morality of it, however. With Prey's Skin Disguise, the Lunar learns to take on the shape of other humans (and humanoid creatures) and knows the ritual for claiming one. Just as for animals, the character takes on all the qualities of the human whose shape he takes—appearance, scent, voice. He gains the target's Strength and Stamina. Other Shifting Knacks allow Lunars to master other forms.

In no case does a Lunar gain anything other than the target creature's natural abilities when he dons its form. Some targets might have Essence-based powers. Constant or effortless powers usually function, but anything that requires Essence expenditure to activate does not. Lunar characters may begin with a collection of shapes by taking the Heart's Blood Background (see p. 109).

THE VALUE OF CHANGING SHAPE

Disguise is the simplest use of Lunar shapechanging. Want to look like that guard? Bite him. Need to be an inconspicuous horse? Hunt down a Marukani swift. In most cases, a Lunar disguising herself through shapechanging doesn't require a roll—as near perfect it is, nobody usually suspects anything. Only when the character must interact with people who know her victim well is there a chance. Perhaps the Lunar doesn't know that the guard always trades insults with his replacement at midnight or the doyenne who owns a noble steed has trained it to kneel for her when she whistles. Even then, people usually give the imposter the benefit of the doubt, because it has every blemish and feature of the original.

Beyond disguise, a Lunar might change shape for access to abilities that only another form can have. This is rarely the case for human shapes, but birds can fly, wolves have powerful noses, barracuda swim underwater and eight-tailed mole hounds can dig like the wind. A coral snake has poisoned fangs, while a gecko can climb anything. When a Lunar uses these innate abilities, it should manifest as automatic success or, when a roll is dramatically appropriate, bonus successes ranging from +1 to +3.

Lunars can also use their forms to gain bonuses in other respects. A Steward who becomes a monkey should receive a small bonus to Athletics due to increased flexibility. Taking the shape of anything small or nondescript, such as a mouse in a cellar or a cat in a city's alley, adds to a character's Stealth attempt to hide or blend in. Tiny creatures benefit significantly more from cover, gaining Defense Value bonuses from things as small as rocks or branches.

Having a broad library of creatures is like having scads of Charms the character doesn't have to buy. Use that to its greatest advantage.

WYLD TAINT AND TATTOOS

Leaving behind the devastation of the Usurpation, the flight of the Lunar Exalted brought them to the Wyld. They could evade the Sidereals and the Dragon-Blooded on Creation's rim, but the Lunars could not prevent the Wyld from warping their very nature. Today, the Lunar Exaltations that turn survivors into Moonchildren still carry that chaotic taint.

The moonsilver tattoos that most Lunars wear protect them from the effect of the Wyld taint… and from so much more. The tattoos protect Lunars from *any* influence that would change their shape other than their inherent abilities. Tattooed Lunar Exalted are completely immune to all such effects: A Lunar is as unaffected by a spirit's attack

that changes her bones to roots as she is by her own casting of Invulnerable Skin of Bronze. The tattoos themselves are equally proof against all attempts to affect them with magic, and all attempts to pry the moonsilver ink from Lunars' skins meet with failure.

Creating a moonsilver tattoo is an arduous process, and painful for the subject. An individual who wishes to master the tattooing procedure must learn the Charm called Form-Fixing Method and possess a large quantity of refined moonsilver. Although a character with sufficient expertise can gift anyone with the moonsilver tattoos, no one but a Steward has the Wyld inner core that binds the moonsilver to the body and provides the insuperable protection against external transformations. What benefit the characters may derive from the tattoos is up to the Storyteller and may make a good story.

Lunars' tattoos are always immediately evident on their true forms, though Hide of the Cunning Hunter can conceal them. Other shapes are not so revealing: They hide the moonsilver whorls beneath a bone-deep disguise. Not so with a Lunar's Tell, which is always present but rarely evident.

The Wyld taint has one additional benefit for the Lunar Exalted. It makes them forever just that little bit more slippery to Sidereal and mortal astrology. Any attempt to divine a Lunar's location or actions, or to levy an astrological blessing or curse on one, increases in difficulty by 1.

Tells

Just as all Lunars have a spirit shape, all Lunars also have a Tell. A Tell is a specific characteristic of the spirit shape that always manifests on the Lunar, no matter what form she wears. Similar to the spirit shape, the Tell usually reflects some special quality of the animal that the character displays. A deceitful Lunar might show the forked tongue of her snake-spirit, an unmannered boar might walk around with the natural, pungent musk of her totem animal and a talkative Lunar's voice might echo with the chattering of her squirrel totem. Tells can take any form as long as they are something that can be perceived with unenhanced senses. Visual Tells are often white or silver, or reflect moonlight supernaturally well.

Tells manifest however they can in any form the character wears. At the very least, the theme remains constant. A character whose Tell is a pair of hooves can take on shapes that do not actually display hooves—but his steps may click on the ground as a horse's would. A Lunar whose Tell is a barbed scorpion's tail might have strange markings on the fur of her wolf shape or a small barb hidden in the fur. The Tell of a Lunar may show up in his shadow if nowhere else. The Tell is usually thematic and only occasionally blatant. It must be noticeable, if not noticed. (No, you can't put a birthmark at a human shape's tailbone and then cover it with clothing.)

This does not mean that Tells are easy to detect. The Lunar Exalted could not wear others' skin with impunity if they were always recognizable by a specific tuft of fur or a wolf's fangs. Most of the time, the Tell goes unnoticed. The Lunar radiates a powerful and unnoticeable mental influence on people who perceive the Lunar in any form, commanding them to ignore the Tell. This counts as natural mental influence, despite its obviously magical nature. The Tell acts as an attack with 12 successes on the roll, automatically slipping into the blind spot (or the equivalent for other senses) of any target with a Dodge Mental Defense Value of 11 or less. The Tell is most important in false human and animal forms—in any true form, the Lunar is not concealing his identity.

Spotting the Tell

The Tell is not always equally effective. When the Lunar is wearing a false skin, that disguise becomes nearly perfect, and the Tell is most powerful. When a Child of Luna throws off the deceits and reveals his true glory as an Exalt of Luna, the Tell assails the senses to proclaim the character's allegiance. In a true form, the Lunar's Tell is only half as effective: Double observers' effective Mental Defense Values before any other modifications. Someone who has seen the Tell before more easily sees it again, increasing their Dodge Mental Defense Value by two. People on the lookout for shapeshifters increase their effective Mental Defense Value by one; those specifically looking for Lunar Exalted increase it by two. If the Lunar desires, he can consciously choose to make the Tell completely evident when in a true form. The Tell is, of course, completely irrelevant to a Lunar's hybrid war form: The animal characteristics are all openly displayed. However, someone who sees a Lunar's war form might then guess what to look for in his other forms.

For most purposes, the Tell is nearly inviolate. No mortal can see through the disguise at its best, and only the most clear-minded notice Tells even when faced with a Lunar in human true form. Gods and Exalted are more likely to notice the Tell, especially once Excellencies enter play. If a Tell fails to conceal itself with its magic, it draws attention to itself. Such is the nature of the Tell. The Tell becomes increasingly prominent as a Lunar Exalt expends Peripheral Essence, manifesting along with her caste mark and anima banner.

Modifiers to Spotting the Tell	
Observer is . . .	MDV gains . . .
Normal	+0
Observing a true form	x2*
Looking for shapeshifters	+1**
Looking for Lunars	+2**
Knows what the Lunar's Tell is	+2
* Apply this modifier first.	
** These modifiers do not stack with each other.	

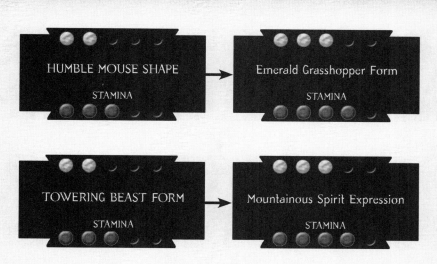

SHIFTING KNACKS

Not all Lunars are equal in the realm of shapeshifting. Some learn better how to control the mercurial nature of their bodies; others choose to master a wider range of shapes. Shifting Knacks cost 11 experience points to learn and sometimes have prerequisites. They take one week of training with a tutor, two without. Similar to the way Lunars use Charms, the Lunar Exalted can create custom Knacks unique to them, and Lunars of great experience often do so. Because Knacks are not Charms, Eclipse and Moonshadow Caste Exalted cannot learn Knacks, just as those generalists cannot learn the Lunars' natural shapeshifting.

FORM ACQUISITION KNACKS: ANIMAL

HUMBLE MOUSE SHAPE
Prerequisites: Essence 2, Stamina 3

This Knack teaches a character the proper ritual to begin a sacred hunt for smaller animals. Normally, a Lunar cannot master a shape smaller than a housecat. Now, creatures as small as a mouse become valid targets for the blood hunt. The hunt typically takes about half as long for creatures of this size. This Knack expands the range of possible spirit shapes for a starting character.

EMERALD GRASSHOPPER FORM
Prerequisites: Humble Mouse Shape, Essence 3, Stamina 4

A character with this Knack can become the literal fly on the wall. Creatures as small as the typical housefly become valid targets for the blood hunt (though some Lunars feel a bit silly spending six hours stalking an insect).

TOWERING BEAST FORM
Prerequisites: Essence 2, Stamina 3

Lunars without this Knack cannot master shapes any larger than something about the size of an adult moose. With it, even creatures as large as yeddim and tyrant lizards become valid targets of the sacred hunt. This Knack expands the range of possible spirit shapes for a starting character.

MOUNTAINOUS SPIRIT EXPRESSION
Prerequisites: Towering Beast Form, Essence 3, Stamina 4

Lunar Exalted who take this Knack increase the size of their spirit shape. The size increase requires no extra effort—the Lunar's animal true form doubles in size. Strength, Stamina and health levels may increase, if appropriate, as if the spirit form carried the *Large* mutation. Many Lunars never choose this Knack, especially those with small or subtle spirit shapes. Some Lunars choose to increase the size of their totem forms further, creating custom Knacks for the purpose.

FORM ACQUISITION KNACKS: HUMAN

PREY'S SKIN DISGUISE
Prerequisites: Essence 2, Appearance 3

This Knack enables the Lunar to take the form of another human (or basically human creature). She develops an instinctive understanding of the different sacred hunt necessary to make humans valid targets of the hunt. Taking on a false human shape costs a point of Willpower.

The base time of the hunt is half a day, during which time the character studies the person's habits and nature, absorbing them the same way she will steal the person's body. Some Lunars watch their victims covertly during the process; others hunt the target viciously, tormenting him and studying his reactions until the final blow. The latter method is faster but more difficult to perform in high-population areas. Either way, it's murder (unless the Lunar has Life of the Hummingbird and merely takes a person's shape temporarily). Taking a human's Heart's Blood triggers a Compassion roll in any character with Compassion 3 or greater, and each success adds one point of Limit to the Lunar's total, no matter what his dominant Virtue may be.

Lunars pursue human forms for many reasons: Having even a single human false form is useful when one's true form becomes dangerous and an animal shape is inappropriate. Some human forms are useful for their identities—becoming Great Forks' Minister of Lore is a significant advantage.

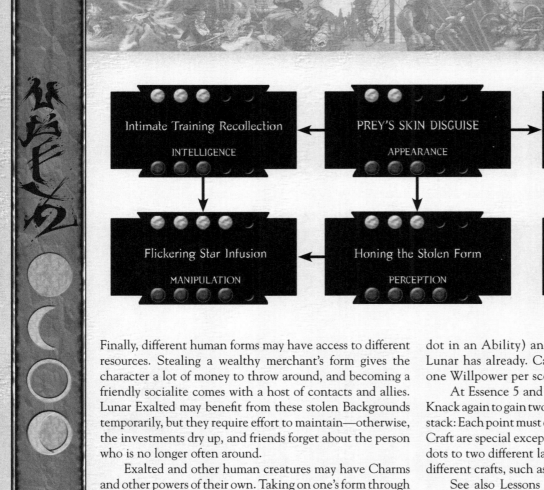

Intimate Training Recollection — INTELLIGENCE

PREY'S SKIN DISGUISE — APPEARANCE

Lunar Blood Shaping Technique — CHARISMA

Flickering Star Infusion — MANIPULATION

Honing the Stolen Form — PERCEPTION

Insidious Lunar Transformation — CHARISMA

Finally, different human forms may have access to different resources. Stealing a wealthy merchant's form gives the character a lot of money to throw around, and becoming a friendly socialite comes with a host of contacts and allies. Lunar Exalted may benefit from these stolen Backgrounds temporarily, but they require effort to maintain—otherwise, the investments dry up, and friends forget about the person who is no longer often around.

Exalted and other human creatures may have Charms and other powers of their own. Taking on one's form through the sacred hunt does not give the Lunar access to any of their Essence-based powers. Taking a Lunar's form in this way provides only the Lunar's human true form, not the spirit shape or any other form the victim might know. For that, a character needs Taste of Luna's Champions.

HONING THE STOLEN FORM

Prerequisites: Prey's Skin Disguise, Essence 3, Perception 4

Heart's Blood forms generally do not change with time. Just as they do not age, neither do they grow stronger, fatter or weathered from experience. This Knack allows a character to increase stolen human forms' physical Attributes just as she can increase her own. Increasing a stolen human form's Attributes costs the same amount of experience as to increase the character's own. The change is permanent.

INTIMATE TRAINING RECOLLECTION

Prerequisites: Prey's Skin Disguise, Essence 3, Intelligence 3

With practice, a Lunar can learn to consume a bit of a human's mind and soul along with his body. This Knack creates one "floating" Ability dot. Each scene, the Lunar can allocate this dot to an Ability held by a human whose form the Lunar took, but that he himself lacks. If a Lunar also has Life of the Hummingbird, he can access the Abilities of a person whose shape the Lunar has temporarily stolen. The "floating" Ability dot cannot be raised through training (though the character could train himself, using the stolen memories, to gain his first

dot in an Ability) and cannot be added to Abilities the Lunar has already. Calling up an Ability this way costs one Willpower per scene.

At Essence 5 and Intelligence 5, a Lunar can buy this Knack again to gain two "floating" Ability dots. These cannot stack: Each point must carry a different Ability. Linguistics or Craft are special exceptions: The character could assign the dots to two different languages or gain one dot each in two different crafts, such as Craft (Air) and Craft (Wood).

See also Lessons in the Blood (p. 189), which does something similar.

FLICKERING STAR INFUSION

Prerequisites: Honing the Stolen Form, Intimate Training Recollection, Essence 4, Manipulation 4

When one of the Lunar Exalts hunts a person and adds that body to the Lunar's library of forms, the victim's star flickers out and dies. Victims of the sacred hunt become invalid targets for astrology and other effects that target them by name or specific identity. Lunars occasionally find this weakness in their perfect disguises detrimental.

This Knack prevents that problem. When the Lunar takes a new human shape, she also consumes that person's destiny, though it remains subordinate to her own destiny and will. As long as the Lunar lives, so do the stars of every person whose heart's blood she took after learning this Knack. Effects that target those individuals specifically, such as Sidereal astrology and some spells, function against her (or to her benefit).

Ongoing effects, such as those from astrology, affect the Lunar whenever she assumes the targeted form. Instantaneous effects, such as an invocation of Infallible Messenger, target the Lunar no matter her current form. She may reflexively refuse any such an effect before it takes place; she does not know what the effect is without the use of Charms, and the effect's instigator realizes there is some unknown malfunction.

Forms that the Lunar possessed before she learned this Knack have already been stricken from Heaven's records; their stars do not return to the sky.

LUNAR BLOOD SHAPING TECHNIQUE

Prerequisites: Prey's Skin Disguise, Essence 3, Charisma 4

Lunars can learn more than to simply take human shapes—Lunars can give their shapes to other humans. A Lunar must feed her target a taste of the Lunar's blood. Then, if the target is willing, he takes the shape of one human or animal from the Lunar's library. True forms cannot be shared. The transformation lasts for one hour if the Lunar provides only a lick of blood, and lasts a full day if she provides one lethal health level's worth of blood.

Targets of this Knack have no control over the transformation outside the ability to refuse it at the start. After a target transforms, he remains in his new shape for the effect's duration. While the target wears the form given him by the Lunar, the character loses access to that shape.

INSIDIOUS LUNAR TRANSFORMATION

Prerequisites: Lunar Blood Shaping Technique, Essence 5, Charisma 5

This Knack enhances Lunar Blood Shaping Technique. Once the Lunar feeds an amount of his blood to a target unwilling to change, the Lunar and target's players make opposed (Willpower + Essence) rolls. If the Lunar wins, the target is forced into the chosen form for the normal duration, depending on how much blood she consumed. Otherwise, there is no effect.

FORM ACQUISITION KNACKS: SUPERNATURAL

GREEN SUN CHILD

Prerequisites: Essence 4, Intelligence 4

Creatures from outside Creation are beyond the powers of most Lunars. Some, however, strain to master the unnatural shapes of demonkind, to wear their skins. This was one of the most-used Knacks during the Primordial War, as Lunars strove to infiltrate their enemies. Green Sun Child makes demons valid targets for the sacred hunt, which takes the same default time as the hunt for a human. Demons who do not have blood are still valid targets; the Lunar simply has to consume some part of their vital ichors or insides. Characters do not get any of the demon's Essence-based powers.

HEART-THEFT OF THE BEHEMOTH

Prerequisites: Green Sun Child, Essence 5, Stamina 5

In the First Age, Luna's mightiest and most clever warriors learned how to hunt down the Primordials' greatest weapons and steal their shapes and power. This Knack makes even the strangest monster-beasts valid targets for the sacred hunt. Characters with this Knack may take on the shape of primordial creatures that are no larger than a tyrant lizard and rampage to their hearts' contents. An Essence 7 and Stamina 7 version of the Knack opens the blood hunt to all primordial behemoths.

HEARTH-AND-FLAME SHELL

STAMINA

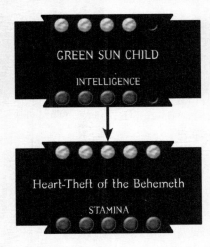

GREEN SUN CHILD

INTELLIGENCE

LUNA'S HIDDEN FACE

PERCEPTION

Heart-Theft of the Behemeth

STAMINA

HEARTH-AND-FLAME SHELL
Prerequisites: Essence 4, Stamina 4

Elementals are part of Creation—in a way, they comprise it. With this Knack, the character adds elementals to the list of the valid targets for the scared hunt. Hunting an elemental takes the same basic amount of time as hunting a human. Ending the hunt requires the Lunar to consume some vital part of the subject—for some elementals, this may cause the Lunar pain or harm. When the Lunar dons an elemental's shape, she acquires its elemental nature. She cannot use any of its Essence-fueled powers, but she may still benefit (or suffer) from being made of a certain element. A Lunar wearing a flaming skin may start fires or hurt others by touching them, and water may cause her harm, for example.

LUNA'S HIDDEN FACE
Prerequisites: Essence 3, Perception 4

Lunars have difficulty taking on a shape unnatural to Creation. This Knack makes creatures mutated by the Wyld, even to such an extent that they become unviable bloodlines in Creation, valid targets of the sacred hunt. A Lunar does not gain any of the creature's Essence-based powers.

FORM ACQUISITION KNACKS: MISCELLANEOUS

LAURELS-AND-IVY TECHNIQUE
Prerequisites: Essence 4, Perception 4

A few Lunars learn to assume the shapes of plants and other non-animal life. This Knack adds "plants" to the list of valid targets for the sacred hunt. Hunting a plant requires the character to meditate in the presence of many such plants for a base time of 12 hours. When the Lunar changes, he becomes a plant of approximately equal mass—many creepers of ivy or a small tree.

Lunar Exalted in the form of plants have only limited perception. They suffer a -2 internal penalty to all attempts to detect their surroundings. In plant form, a Lunar is constantly Inactive in any form of combat, but the character may change this at will by changing shape.

LIFE OF THE HUMMINGBIRD
Prerequisites: Essence 2, Wits 3

Sometimes, the Lunar Exalted don't have time to perform a full blood hunt, or need to take a shape without killing its owner. A Lunar can take on an animal's (or human's) shape without performing the sacred hunt so long as he gets a taste of its blood.

The new form does not last long. A simple taste of blood, even a minor trickle, gives the Lunar access to the shape for the next hour. More blood, which must be drawn by the character and accompanied by some sharp pain (inflicting at least one lethal health level), adds the shape to the character's library for one full day. The duration begins counting down the moment the blood leaves the body—a Lunar may not store blood for later use or lick up old, dried blood for the benefit. Any creature that is a valid target for the Lunar's sacred hunt can provide this benefit.

Without activating the blood hunt, a Lunar may take as little as a few minutes to find the blood of the right creature (for common, small animals) or a half-hour to an hour for larger or less common animals. At the Storyteller's discretion, this may take even longer, but it should never take more than half as long as the sacred hunt for the equivalent creature.

TASTE OF LUNA'S CHAMPIONS
Prerequisites: Life of the Hummingbird, Essence 3, Perception 4

The character with this Knack has the power to taste the blood of another Lunar Exalt, who must be willing, and learn a shape the other Lunar has mastered. The Knack requires a 15-minute ritual and costs a point of Willpower from the Lunar using this Knack, whose player rolls (Willpower + Essence). Each success increases the number of shapes he may learn by one (from a base of one) or doubles the period over which he can use each shape (base one hour). The

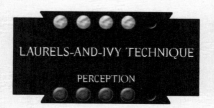

LAURELS-AND-IVY TECHNIQUE

PERCEPTION

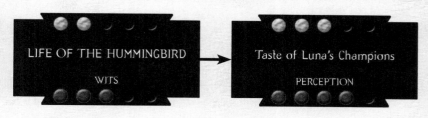

LIFE OF THE HUMMINGBIRD

WITS

→ Taste of Luna's Champions

PERCEPTION

character can instead master a shape forever by spending a point of experience per shape.

This Knack also gives the Lunar a rarely used ritual that targets another Lunar as the subject of the sacred hunt. In this case, the character must hunt down and fight the target Lunar. After killing the target, the Lunar drinks the target's heart's blood and gains every shape the other Lunar has mastered *and* the target's human and animal true forms (though they do not become new true forms). The war form is too unique to each Lunar's Essence to be duplicated in this way. (Note that cannibalizing a selection of heart's blood forms increases the character's Heart's Blood Background. Some Storytellers may rule that this costs experience points—see pp. 232-233.)

SHAPESHIFTING REFINEMENT KNACKS

HYBRID BODY REARRANGEMENT

Prerequisites: Essence 3, Wits 3

A dedicated Lunar can learn to change just *part* of his body to gain some special benefit or attack. This Knack is actually a "wild card": The player selects (Essence + 4) points of mutations the character can invoke at cost of one mote each, then make go away when she doesn't need them any more. Each mutation is based on changing part of the character's body—but not all—in a manner inspired by the Lunar's spirit shape or some other animal form from her Heart's Blood library. See **Exalted**, pages 288-290, for sample mutations, or Chapter Six: The Casteless and the Chimerae of this book. The character doesn't have to invoke every

mutation whenever she uses this Knack. A character can take this Knack more than once.

MONKEY ARM STYLE

Prerequisites: Hybrid Body Rearrangement, Essence 4, Dexterity 4

Some Lunars learn more than to simply change their shape and appearance. This technique allows the character to elongate her limbs and digits for the purpose of a single action. She multiplies the distance she may stretch an affected body part by the motes of Essence spent, and the character may not spend more than (Essence) motes. Because the increased flexibility sacrifices leverage and strength, attacking at extended range suffers a -2 penalty to accuracy and raw damage.

CHANGING PLUMAGE MASTERY

Prerequisites: Essence 2, Appearance 3

Shifting to another shape, the character develops greater control over superficial details. For any learned shape, she can control the creature's appearance to a degree. Fur or feathers can be any color appropriate to the creature, and such identifying marks as scars and birthmarks are under the character's control. Human shapes are more set, but the Lunar gains the ability to change the appearance of her clothes and hair length.

This power becomes inherent to shifting shape, not something the character can alter without also changing shape. She *can* change shape to a variation of the same creature, changing superficial features in the transition to a near-identical shape.

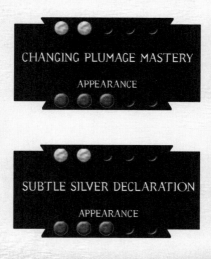

CHANGING PLUMAGE MASTERY

APPEARANCE

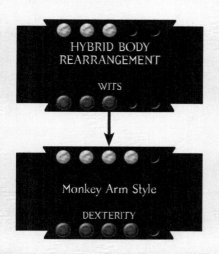

HYBRID BODY REARRANGEMENT

WITS

INTERNAL FORM MASTERY

WITS

SUBTLE SILVER DECLARATION

APPEARANCE

Monkey Arm Style

DEXTERITY

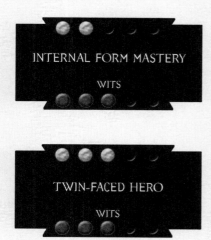

TWIN-FACED HERO

WITS

INTERNAL FORM MASTERY
Prerequisites: Essence 2, Wits 3

Lunars with this Knack learn how to master their false forms. When in other forms, human or otherwise, he may use the *higher* of his Dexterity or the form's Dexterity. He may still use the rating of a creature with less Dexterity, if he wishes—perhaps to conceal his Exalted nature.

SUBTLE SILVER DECLARATION
Prerequisites: Essence 2, Appearance 3

When the Lunar wears a shape that is not a true form, he may subdue his Tell so far that none can notice it. By spending one mote, the character ensures that his Tell's mental attack automatically succeeds for the rest of the scene as long as he is in a false shape. By spending one mote when in a true form, the character increases the base effectiveness of the Tell by two. This incidentally hides scars, birthmarks and other blemishes that could identify the character.

When Peripheral Essence expenditure forces the character into a true form and makes his anima flare, he may spend a mote to prevent the Essence from making his Tell immediately obvious. He must spend the mote of Essence with each Essence expenditure to maintain this benefit.

TWIN-FACED HERO
Prerequisites: Essence 3, Wits 3

Not all Lunar Exalted are bound to their gender. This Knack enables a character to transcend gender, becoming either a male or female rendition of any form she dons. This includes her true forms. Both genders are fully functional in all ways—she may sire or bear children, for example. The character makes the choice to shift gender as she changes shape, or she may spend the full Essence cost to change into a shape she already wears, just to shift gender. Some Lunars prefer a perfectly neuter shape, which this Knack also makes possible.

SHAPESHIFTING SPEED KNACKS

QUICKSILVER SECOND FACE
Prerequisites: Essence 2, Dexterity 4

By spending an extra mote, the character may change shape as a Speed 3 action instead of a normal miscellaneous action, which is Speed 5. He can change more quickly between any two forms for the extra cost.

LIGHTNING-CHANGE STYLE
Prerequisites: Quicksilver Second Face, Essence 3, Dexterity 5

Sometimes a Lunar simply must change shape *now*. Perhaps battle is imminent or someone is about to discover the character's true identity. This Knack enables a Lunar to shapeshift as a completely reflexive action by adding three motes to the cost. Used in attack resolution, the change takes place in Step 1 or 2 and can apply a difficulty to the attack roll (for tiny shapes), increased soak or other benefits.

CONSTANT QUICKSILVER REARRANGEMENT
Prerequisites: Lightning-Change Style, Essence 5, Wits 5

By committing four motes, the Lunar becomes able to change shape as a completely reflexive action. In combat time, the character may do so no more than once per tick. Lunar Exalted use this in combination with a wide range of forms to evade attacks through small size or soak them with great Stamina. Other uses include rapid evasion of pursuers (even other Lunars) or to bewilder enemies for purposes of confusion, interrogation, torture or other mind games.

WAR FORM KNACKS

DEADLY BEASTMAN TRANSFORMATION
Prerequisites: Essence 2, Stamina 3

This Knack forms the basis of many Lunar battle techniques. Once a character learns it, she can shift into the fearsome war form of the Lunar Exalted, a monstrous amalgam of her two other true forms. The Steward usually gains several feet in height and increases proportionally in mass. Muscles ripple across her form, which usually has fearsomely long and sharp teeth and/or claws. Even if the Lunar's spirit shape is something as harmless as a groundhog, the hybrid war form looks awesomely dangerous.

War forms are stronger, faster and more resilient than the character's normal forms. They have animal characteristics that give them an edge. Lunars in war form heal even faster than other Exalted, and war form allows them to make use of special aspects of certain Charms, called Gifts. Because Dexterity, animal qualities, healing and Gifts can all be useful outside of combat, some Lunars use war forms for purposes other than combat. At the very least, the war form is a tool of *purpose*—the Lunar dons this form to accomplish a goal. Design the war form as follows:

• **Bonus Attributes.** When a character takes Deadly Beastman Transformation, her player adds one dot each to

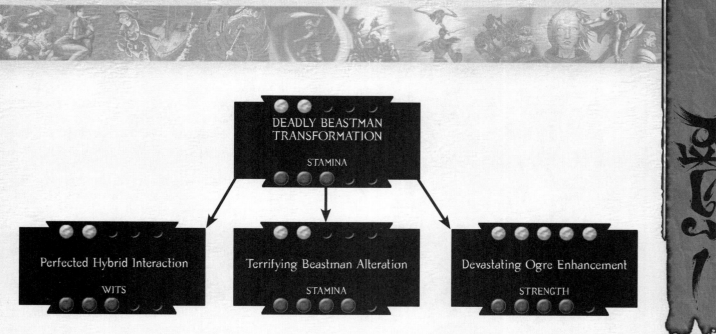

the character's Strength, Dexterity and Stamina. This increase can bring a character's physical Attributes above five and only affect the character when she is in war form. Any improved Attributes are considered natural when calculating the Lunar's dice maximums. (See the box on p. 128 for a description of natural Attributes.)

• **Wyld Mutations.** The character's player adds mutations to the form to represent animalistic features. She chooses from the list of Wyld mutations in **Exalted**, pages 288-290, or creates her own, then applies these to the war form. The player has (Essence + 4) special bonus points to spend on mutations, using the costs given on page 101. Increases in Essence later on allow the player to choose further mutations or "upgrade" existing mutations.

Ignore all negative aspects to these mutations beyond the obvious and frightening change in appearance. These are not actually Wyld mutations; they represent the admixture of human and animal of the hybrid form. Players can only choose or create mutations appropriate to the characters' spirit shapes. Characters cannot take negative mutations, such as deficiencies, and they cannot take single mutations multiple times.

Players cannot apply the *Large* mutation to the war form; war forms are already larger and stronger than a normal human form. Players may, however, apply the *Small* mutation, accepting its benefits and penalties. This is how some Lunars create their smaller, less monstrous-seeming war forms. Players and Storytellers must remember that not all mutations are appropriate as animal Traits. Those that are not may be altered, at the Storyteller's discretion, to represent an appropriate animal Trait.

Some mutations alter the character's health level track. Ignore these changes; Lunar Exalted remain hard to wound even when their war form is slight and fast, and the increased resilience of the Exalted is represented by their Ox-Body Technique.

Example: Travis creates a Lunar character whose spirit shape is a frog. At Essence 2, the character's war form has six points' worth of mutations. Looking through the list of mutations, Travis takes Wall Walking for the frog's sticky pads. With two points left, he wants to take horns, but his Storyteller suggests that another mutation may be more in theme. Instead, Travis takes Frog Tongue.

When the character's Essence increases, Travis may choose a beneficial pox for the war form or wait until his character's Essence increases again to pick an affliction. With those two points, he could also strengthen one of his Lunars' current afflictions to a blight-level mutation. Many mutations are not appropriate for upgrading, or do not yet have upgrades. There may not be any reasonable upgrade for Frog Tongue, but Travis could (with Storyteller approval) upgrade Wall Walking to make the character more capable in that activity.

While in the war form, Lunars also gain a supernatural resilience that helps them survive terrible wounds. The Lunar does not actually heal any faster (that requires Charms such as Bruise-Relief Method and Healing the Scarlet Flow). While in war form, however, a Lunar can completely regrow lost limbs or organs using such Charms. It takes at an hour to regenerate such an extreme wound.

When a Lunar in war form falls into her Dying health levels, her wounds do not worsen. She does not lose additional levels of damage until she dies; instead, she remains that wounded until either someone stabilizes her with surgery (returning her to Incapacitated) or she uses a Charm to heal a point of lethal damage, which accomplishes the same effect. (For this reason, the Lunars' Ox-Body Technique gives them two additional Dying health levels with each purchase.)

Taking Deadly Beastman Transformation also allows the character to make better use of Gift Charms. Legend says that Luna herself composed Gift Charms for her Exalted. When a character learns a Charm with the Gift keyword, she gains abilities that she can activate automatically when she dons her war form. See the individual Charms for more details.

PERFECTED HYBRID INTERACTION

Prerequisites: Deadly Beastman Transformation, Essence 2, Wits 3

When a Lunar isn't content to have a war form that represents the best of his animal and human natures, he may

take this Knack. It allows his player to reallocate the points for mutation ignoring Deadly Beastman Transformation's guidelines. The Lunar's shape in his war form no longer needs to reflect his true nature—just the deadly abilities he wishes to have. From this point on, this is the character's true war form.

Though the name would never reflect it, many Lunars consider this Knack a step along the road to chimerism and view its possessors with deep suspicion.

TERRIFYING BEASTMAN ALTERATION

Prerequisites: Deadly Beastman Transformation, Essence 4, Stamina 4

With a deeper understanding of one's true forms comes a truer merging between the two. Purchasing this Knack gives the Lunar's player (Essence) more points to play with when choosing mutations for the war form. The final formula becomes ([Essence x 2] + 4). When the character takes Terrifying Beastman Alteration, his player is free to redesign his war form from the ground up, following the same guidelines as normal. However, the Lunar's human form becomes more animalistic, and his Tell becomes more prominent, reducing the base MDV needed to see the Tell to 8.

DEVASTATING OGRE ENHANCEMENT

Prerequisites: Deadly Beastman Transformation, Essence 5, Strength 4

Taking this Knack increases the size and deadliness of the character's war form. The hybrid form becomes terrifying in size, dwarfing even the tallest human from at least 12 feet of height. The character also adds one additional dot to each physical Attribute when in the war form, on top of any bonus received from Deadly Beastman Transformation.

Lunars who possess Devastating Ogre Enhancement are widely respected and often feared, even by their peers, for their dedication to the ideal of warfare and their constant honing of their physical form. Most (Lunars, at least) consider them the foremost warriors of Creation.

CHARMS

Luna's power ebbs and flows over the course of the month, waxing to a crescendo of physical might at the full moon and waning into the mysteries of the moonless skies. Each cycle is a mere eyeblink to the ageless Incarnae and no more than a heartbeat to the long-lived Exalted. Appropriately, the fiercest Charms of the Lunar Exalted flare brightly and then die out. Short in duration, they have intense strength while they last.

NATURE OF THE BEAST

For the Lunar Exalted, Charms are not techniques learned through training but extensions of their natural capabilities. In short: Lunar Charms are based on Attributes instead of Abilities. Each Charm has a minimum

SORCERY AND MARTIAL ARTS

Both these arts are special institutions in **Exalted**. They have the qualities of being somewhat universal. A Solar Exalt and a Lunar may both learn Stormwind Rider or Foot-Trapping Counter (see p. 195). Even so, Lunars who learn sorcery often attempt to meet the Occult minimums as well. Most Lunars who study sorcery are smart enough to want to understand exactly what they're doing. The Crossroads Society will not teach sorcery to anyone who does not meet the art's normal Occult minimums.

Sorcery sometimes calls for certain dice rolls. Despite sorcery being Intelligence-based for Lunars, they roll the provided dice pools.

For a Lunar, Martial Arts Charms must be used with Martial Arts actions only. The exceptions to this rule are the Charms in Lunar Hero Style, which are Dexterity-based (for Lunars) and as flexible as other Dexterity Charms. To learn any other supernatural martial art, such as Snake Style (**Exalted**, p. 240), a Lunar must meet the Martial Arts minimums for each Charm, regardless of her Dexterity.

Once again, though, the differences between Lunar martial artists and Solar, Dragon-Blooded and other supernatural martial artists are more apparent than real. Expert martial artists develop *both* their Dexterity and Martial Arts.

Attribute requirement, and the Charm cascades are divided by Attribute. They still have prerequisite Charms as normal, but many Lunar Charm trees are shorter than those of the other Exalted.

Note that some Charms exist in more than one place in the chapter. Two Charms that have the same name and the same effects are the same Charm, and they function as prerequisites for any Charms that name them as prerequisites.

Just as Attributes are significantly broader and more expansive than Abilities, so are the Lunars Attribute-based Charms. This does not mean they are inherently more powerful (though some are quite effective), but it does mean that they come with fewer inherent boundaries. The Dexterity Excellency can be used with *any* Dexterity-based roll; and while other Dexterity Charms may not be so flexible, they are still less confining than Melee- or Martial Arts-based Charms. A Strength Charm that increases damage can apply to *any* attack, and a Dexterity Charm that decreases attack Speed works for Thrown, Archery and any other attack Ability.

LUNAR COMBOS

This makes the rules for Lunar Combos necessarily more flexible. They cannot be separated based on Ability, or even by Attribute. Instead, the Charms make it clear what kind of action they supplement or create. For the most part, Combos of Lunar Charms follow the same rules: no more than one extra action or simple Charm, as many supplemental and reflexive Charms as desired and so on. But there is no requirement that extra action, simple or supplemental Charms must come from the same Attribute to be Comboed with each other.

Example: Sharp-Beaked Octopus Barrage is an extra action Dexterity Charm. It may be included in a Combo with the simple Strength Charm Hibernation of the Dog, even though the two come from different Attributes and neither explicitly states that that is okay. But it is, because Sharp-Beaked Octopus Barrage provides extra actions that are all attacks, and Hibernation of the Dog is a single attack.

Some Charms can supplement more than one sort of action. When such a Charm is put in a Combo with a simple or extra action Charm, it often restricts the way the more flexible Charm can be used. By the Combo rules, a supplemental Charm Comboed with a simple Charm must be used to supplement the simple Charm—if alternative uses of the supplementing Charm do not work with the simple Charm, those uses cannot be activated as part of the Combo.

Example: The character instead Combos Sharp-Beaked Octopus Barrage with Tearing Claw Atemi, which supplements either an attack against an inanimate object or a feat of strength. Because the actions created by Sharp-Beaked Octopus Barrage must be attacks (feats of strength do not qualify), Tearing Claw Atemi cannot be used to supplement feats of strength when used inside the Combo. (For that matter, the extra attacks given by Sharp-Beaked Octopus Barrage cannot be used to attack animate objects because of Tearing Claw Atemi's restriction.)

Combos including Lunar Charms can get even more confusing when Eclipse or Moonshadow Caste Exalted learn them. For the most part, a Lunar Charm can Combo with any other Charm, so long as the Charms can function together according to Combo rules. Comboing Sharp-Beaked Octopus Barrage with Ox-Stunning Blow (see **Exalted**, p. 243) is fine—but requires that all the attacks be Martial Arts attacks. A Combo with Fire and Stones Strike (see **Exalted**, p. 190) is also possible, but all the extra attacks would have to be Melee-based.

Eclipses and Moonshadows may learn the Lunar Excellencies, but may not use them to add more than (Attribute) dice individually. Even while using Lunar Charms, characters may not exceed their normal maximum dice from Charms. A Solar using the First Dexterity and Melee Excellencies still cannot add more than (Attribute + Ability) dice to an action.

CHARM LIMITATIONS

Just as the Solar Exalted have a limit to their majesty, so do the Stewards. Since their Charms extend their natural potential rather than their training, a Lunar cannot increase his dice pools by more than (the relevant Attribute). No combination of Charms can increase a Lunar Exalt's dice pools by more than that amount. As is normal, Charms that add automatic successes or remove penalties do not count as increases to a dice pool unless otherwise noted.

Apply this limit to static values and increase them just as the Solars do. See **Exalted**, page 185, for more details.

CHARM CONFLICT

When the effects of two Charms conflict with each other, the players involved roll dice to determine whose Charm functions properly. The players *generally* roll the relevant (Attribute + Ability) or, if there is no clear Attribute, (Essence + Ability). Lunar Charms, based on Attributes as they are, go the other way round. A Lunar's player rolls (Attribute + Ability) or, if there is no clear *Ability*, (Attribute + Essence).

LUNAR KEYWORDS

Charms of the Lunar Exalted have some additional keywords that do not apply to the other Exalted.

Fury-OK: A Charm marked Fury-OK can activate automatically when the character uses Relentless Lunar Fury.

Gift: Gift Charms can activate automatically when the character wears the Deadly Beastman Transformation. Motes committed to the Gift Charms' activation cannot be uncommitted until the character leaves the war form.

Wyld: Charms with this keyword only function in at least the Bordermarches, or they have increased functionality within the Wyld.

GENERAL CHARMS

Where the other Exalted have Excellencies for each Ability, the Lunars' Charms are keyed to their Attributes. The three basic Excellencies exist for all the nine Attributes, and each character may purchase any or all of the Excellencies for each Attribute. Some Charms require Excellencies as prerequisites.

Lunar Exalted also have some general Charms that act as additional Excellencies or affect the Excellencies. These can only be purchased once per Attribute, as can other player- and Storyteller-created Charms of this sort.

FIRST (ATTRIBUTE) EXCELLENCY— ESSENCE OVERWHELMING

Cost: 1m per die; **Mins:** (Attribute) 1, Essence 1;
Type: Reflexive (Step 1 for attacker, Step 2 for defender)
Keywords: Combo-OK
Duration: Instant
Prerequisite Charms: None

Some Lunar Exalted excel at using their natural talents. The Exalt's player can invoke this Charm when making a roll based on the relevant Attribute. This Charm adds one die to that roll per mote spent. This Charm is the most common source of dice added to rolls; no combination of Charms can add more than (Attribute) dice to the roll.

This Charm can also enhance unrolled uses of the relevant Attribute. Common examples of this are increasing Defense Values with the Dexterity Excellency, climbing the Feat of Strength chart with the Strength Excellency or increasing alcohol Tolerance with the Stamina Excellency. When enhancing a static value, each success rolled with dice from this Excellency increases the effective relevant Attribute by two for an instant. Thus, one success increases Defense Value by one.

This Excellency, other Excellencies and other dice-adding Charms cannot "create" actions. They may supplement existing actions or increase static values that are already in use. Each Charm use also functions only for a single instant or task—the Charm supplements a single attack or defense but must be activated multiple times for multiple attacks or defenses, even on the same tick.

Essence Overwhelming may be Comboed with the Second Excellency, but can never be used on the same roll as the Third Excellency.

SECOND (ATTRIBUTE) EXCELLENCY— ESSENCE TRIUMPHANT

Cost: 2m per success; **Mins:** (Attribute) 1, Essence 1;
Type: Reflexive (Step 1 for attacker, Step 2 for defender)
Keywords: Combo-OK
Duration: Instant
Prerequisite Charms: None

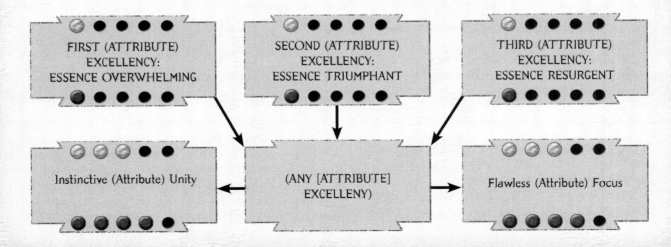

FIRST (ATTRIBUTE)
EXCELLENCY:
ESSENCE OVERWHELMING

SECOND (ATTRIBUTE)
EXCELLENCY:
ESSENCE TRIUMPHANT

THIRD (ATTRIBUTE)
EXCELLENCY:
ESSENCE RESURGENT

Instinctive (Attribute) Unity

(ANY [ATTRIBUTE]
EXCELLENY)

Flawless (Attribute) Focus

Lunars with this Charm consistently apply their base potential to solve problems. The character's player may invoke this Charm when making a roll based on the relevant Attribute. The character spends up to (Attribute) in motes, adding one success to the roll for every two motes. Each success purchased with this Charm is the equivalent of two dice purchased with the First Excellency or another dice-adding Charm. See **Exalted**, page 185, for examples on how this works.

This Charm can enhance unrolled uses of the relevant Attribute, just as the First Excellency. Each two motes spent increases the Attribute by two for an instant action or task, functioning just as a single rolled success with the First Excellency.

Essence Triumphant may be Comboed with the First Excellency, but it can never be used on the same roll as the Third Excellency.

THIRD (ATTRIBUTE) EXCELLENCY—

ESSENCE RESURGENT

Cost: 4m; **Mins:** (Attribute) 1, Essence 1;
Type: Reflexive (Step 4 for attacker, Step 6 for defender)
Keywords: Combo-OK
Duration: Instant
Prerequisite Charms: None

Lunars with this Charm obey their instincts, saving themselves from failure. A character's player may activate this Charm after making a roll based on the relevant Attribute. She then makes the roll again, using the new result if she prefers. The Lunar can use this Charm to enhance static values based on the relevant Attribute. Doing so doubles the character's Attribute for one instant or task, increasing applicable Defense Values by half the relevant Attribute.

INSTINCTIVE (ATTRIBUTE) UNITY

Cost: 2m+, 1wp; **Mins:** (Attribute) 4, Essence 3;
Type: Simple
Keywords: None
Duration: One scene
Prerequisite Charms: Any (Attribute) Excellency

Lunar Exalted find ways to become perfectly in touch with their natures. Every two motes spent when activating this Charm reduces the mote cost for the first three (Attribute) Excellencies by one, to a minimum of 0. A Lunar can spend up to (Essence x 2) motes on this Charm. The discount applies to the total expenditure on Excellencies relating to a given roll. In all other ways, Instinctive (Attribute) Unity works the same as the Solars' Infinite (Ability) Mastery (see **Exalted**, pp. 185-186).

FLAWLESS (ATTRIBUTE) FOCUS

Cost: —; **Mins:** (Attribute) 4, Essence 3; **Type:** Permanent
Keywords: None
Duration: Permanent
Prerequisite Charms: Any (Attribute) Excellency

Lunars are naturally instinctive creatures. This is part of why their Charms focus on Attributes, their natural potential, instead of the training represented by Abilities. Purchasing this Charm, the character becomes able to tap

CHARM CONCEPT: ATTRIBUTE EXCELLENCIES

The fact that Lunar Exalted get Attribute Excellencies has some important repercussions for their tactics.

Every Lunar character qualifies. Other Exalts need at least minimal training to gain Ability Excellencies, but every character has a rating of at least 1 in every Attribute.

Attribute Excellencies are powerful. Because they apply to Attributes and not to Abilities, Lunar Excellencies are incredibly broad. Possessing the Dexterity Excellency is far less limiting than having the Melee Excellency. You can use the Dexterity Excellency to aid an unarmed attack, catch the bow thrown to you, fire from that bow, dodge the attacks on you afterward and carve a stone knife that you can later throw with the Excellency as well. All the other Lunar Excellencies are equally broad in scope, though they are not all as purely useful in combat.

Attribute Excellencies can increase values that Ability Excellencies cannot. Excellencies can increase static values, such as Defense Values or a character's (Strength + Athletics) rating for lifting things. Lunar Excellencies can increase these values, but these Excellencies can also increase a character's Attributes directly. Using the Stamina Excellency to increase a character's Stamina lasts only for an instant, but that's long enough to apply the improved soak against an attack. Increasing Strength with the appropriate Excellency doesn't help a character *hit* the opponent (except in clinching), but having a greater Strength for just one instant also increases the attack's base damage. Increasing Appearance for an instant improves a character's Mental Defense Value against a single social attack, or it degrades a target's Mental Defense Value against the character's social attack.

Lunars cannot increase some values that others can. Some static values do not include an Attribute in their calculation. Most notable of these is the Dodge Mental Defense Value, which comes from (Willpower + Integrity + Essence). Although Solars may use the Integrity Excellency to increase this value, there are no Willpower Excellencies. This creates a weakness in Lunar mental defenses, because the Dodge Mental Defense Value is naturally the strongest. There are some cases when only the rating of an Ability matters. Lunar Exalted will never write the most eloquent letters, because they cannot increase their Linguistics as a static value.

into a more specific instinctive mastery over the relevant Attribute. She learns how to purchase Attribute specialties for the given Attribute. Purchase of this Charm provides one free Attribute specialty.

Attribute specialties cost the same as Ability specialties to learn: three experience points, one bonus point for a non-Favored Attribute or two-for-one for a Favored Attribute at character generation. A character can have no more than three specialties for a single Attribute. Since a character cannot have Attribute specialties without first buying this Charm, it is possible to lose half a bonus point when purchasing Attribute specialties at character generation.

Similar to Ability specialties, *Attribute specialties* add extra dice to specific uses of the Attribute. Because Attributes are broader than Abilities, their specialties should be correspondingly broad. Attribute specialties may be about as restrictive as a normal specialty but cross Abilities, such as "Forgeries" or "Long-Term Schemes," or they can include approximately one Ability, such as "Melee" or "Martial Arts" for Dexterity.

When channeling this deeper level of instinct, characters limit the amount of their training they can use. Attribute specialties are incompatible with normal specialties—a character must choose to use one or the other in any given instance.

(ATTRIBUTE) CHARM DESIGNATION

Although it could not be followed to the letter, the guiding principle when deciding under what Attribute to place a Charm is this: What rolls can the Charm cause, supplement or primarily affect? The strongest answer to the Charm is—usually—the Attribute under which the Charm goes. There are occasionally exceptions. What did you expect? The Fickle Lady doesn't care much about perfect, abstract systems.

STRENGTH

ATTACK ENHANCEMENT CHARMS

WIND-WINGS CARRY TECHNIQUE
Cost: 1m or 2m per; **Mins:** Strength 4, Essence 2;
Type: Supplemental
Keywords: Combo-OK
Duration: Instant
Prerequisite Charms: Any Strength Excellency

Little escapes the Stewards' reach. Every mote spent on this Charm increases the range of a single attack by a factor of (1 + motes spent). Melee and Martial Arts attacks cost two motes to do the same thing one mote accomplishes for naturally ranged weapons, and the Charm becomes Obvious as Essence does the work where the character cannot reach. As a rule, the range of a hand-to-hand attack is equal to one yard plus the length of the weapon.

AGITATION OF THE SWARM TECHNIQUE
Cost: 2m; **Mins:** Strength 4, Essence 2;
Type: Supplemental
Keywords: Combo-OK
Duration: Instant
Prerequisite Charms: Any Strength Excellency

Lunar Exalted know how to disrupt their opponents' calm and unbalance their foes' stances. Any attack supplemented by this Charm inflicts twice the normal onslaught penalty. Attacks supplemented by Agitation of the Swarm that successfully hit a target and inflict damage also cause great distraction: For each damaging blow supplemented by this attack, one point of onslaught penalty becomes a general Defense Value penalty until the target's Defense Value refreshes.

FEROCIOUS BITING TOOTH
Cost: 4m; **Mins:** Strength 4, Essence 2; **Type:** Supplemental
Keywords: Combo-OK
Duration: Instant
Prerequisite Charms: Any Strength Excellency

The Lunar imbues his blade or blow with such uncontestable strength that the blow or blade becomes incredibly hard to shift from its intended path. Halve the target's Parry Defense Value (round down) before applying it to the character's attack successes in Step 5 of attack resolution; players are aware that parrying becomes a less favorable option with this Charm and may choose to use their characters' Dodge Defense Values instead.

LIGHTNING STROKE ATTACK
Cost: 7m; **Mins:** Strength 5, Essence 4; **Type:** Supplemental
Keywords: Combo-OK, Obvious
Duration: Instant
Prerequisite Charms: Agitation of the Swarm Technique, Ferocious Biting Tooth

This charm is identical to the Dexterity Charm of the same name (see p. 154), but it focuses on the unstoppable nature of the attack due to the strength propelling it.

CRIPPLING CHARMS

FOE-MARKING STYLE
Cost: 2m; **Mins:** Strength 3, Essence 2; **Type:** Supplemental
Keywords: Combo-OK
Duration: Instant
Prerequisite Charms: Any Strength Excellency

In order to avoid killing or crippling each other to prove their points, Lunars of the Silver Pact use this Charm as a method of earning honor from one another. Foe-Marking Style supplements an attempt to inflict a scar on an opponent, either through a called shot or normal lethal damage. Wounds caused by this Charm do not heal normally for the Exalted, leaving scars instead of healing without a blemish. Although this is not a crippling effect, supernatural healing that can cure crippling effects can wipe clean these scars.

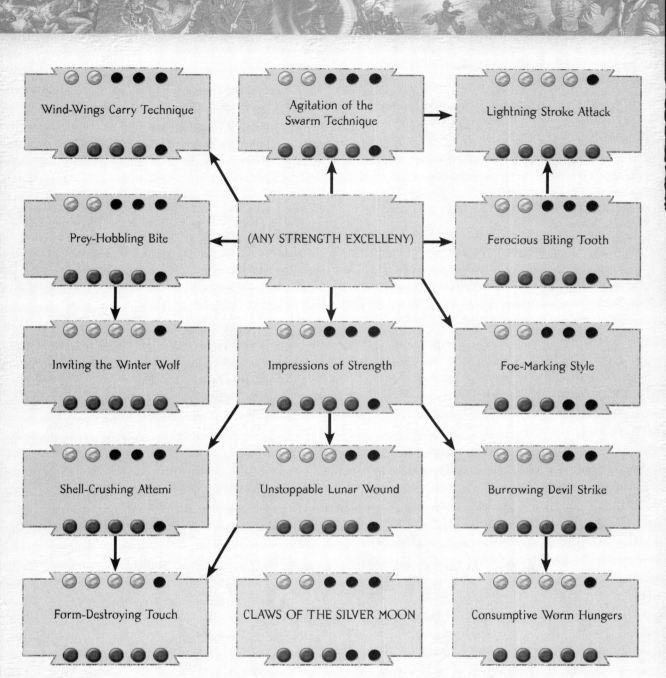

Wind-Wings Carry Technique

Agitation of the Swarm Technique

Lightning Stroke Attack

Prey-Hobbling Bite

(ANY STRENGTH EXCELLENY)

Ferocious Biting Tooth

Inviting the Winter Wolf

Impressions of Strength

Foe-Marking Style

Shell-Crushing Attemi

Unstoppable Lunar Wound

Burrowing Devil Strike

Form-Destroying Touch

CLAWS OF THE SILVER MOON

Consumptive Worm Hungers

PREY-HOBBLING BITE

Cost: 2m; **Mins:** Strength 4, Essence 2; **Type:** Supplemental
Keywords: Combo-OK, Crippling, Stackable
Duration: (Strength) actions
Prerequisite Charms: Any Strength Excellency

Through judicious placement of wounds, the Lunar ensures that his enemy cannot escape him. Each level of damage inflicted by an attack supplemented with this Charm reduces the target's Move and Dash actions by one yard and reduces the target's effective (Strength + Athletics) total by two for the purpose of jumping distance. The effect of this Charm stacks with normal wound penalties to movement, but wears off quickly.

INVITING THE WINTER WOLF

Cost: 3m; **Mins:** Strength 5, Essence 4; **Type:** Simple
Keywords: Combo-OK, Crippling, Obvious, Stackable
Duration: Instant
Prerequisite Charms: Prey-Hobbling Bite

Lunar Exalted find it useful to cast down their enemies and ensure that they cannot recover. In a single, Essence-driven blow, the character severs or breaks some part of his victim in a way that makes it unusable. As long as this attack inflicts even a single level of damage, the target suffers a crippling wound of some sort (see **Exalted**, p. 152).

The character may opt to spend an additional point of Willpower when activating this Charm. This infuses the crippling wound with the mercurial Essence of Luna, making it impossible

to heal the wound by mundane means. Surgical attempts to right the issue automatically fail, and even the Exalted do not heal the injury with its associated wounds. Only supernatural methods that heal *crippling* effects can right this injury.

DAMAGE ENHANCEMENT CHARMS

CLAWS OF THE SILVER MOON
Cost: 4m, 1wp; **Mins:** Strength 3, Essence 2;
Type: Simple (Speed 4)
Keywords: Combo-OK, Gift, Obvious
Duration: One scene
Prerequisite Charms: None

Channeling a nimbus of silver from her soul into her hands, the Lunar endows them with large, vicious silver claws. The claws improve the statistics of the character's basic natural attacks as follows: Speed +0, Accuracy +2, Damage +(Strength)L, Defense +0, Rate +0, and they may be used to parry lethal damage without magic or stunts. If the character possesses other natural attacks (in addition to kick or clinch, which are already affected), she may spend one extra mote to add the Charm's bonuses to those attack forms as well.

Once a character with this Charm reaches Essence 3, she may spend two additional motes to make the claws slimmer and more needlelike, providing Accuracy +(Dexterity). At Essence 4, she may spend *another* two motes to give the weapon Damage +(Strength + 2)L/(Essence + 1) and the Overwhelming tag. These extra options may be activated together or separately.

When the Lunar uses Deadly Beastman Transformation, she may commit one mote to add the basic bonuses to her natural attacks. By committing three motes, she gains the best bonuses she can access.

IMPRESSIONS OF STRENGTH
Cost: 2m; **Mins:** Strength 4, Essence 2; **Type:** Supplemental
Keywords: Combo-OK, Fury-OK, Knockback
Duration: Instant
Prerequisite Charms: Any Strength Excellency

The blows of the Lunar Exalted possess an unparalleled raw power. This Charm supplements an attack, to which the character applies one of the following edges.

Ogre's Loving Caress. Damage dice that show 10 count as two successes.

Rock-to-Pebbles Attitude. Increase pre-soak damage by three dice for each time this edge is activated.

Undeniable Might. Increase post-soak damage by one die for each time this edge is activated.

Birth of Flight. Add (Strength) to the difficulty of any knockdown or knockback check caused by the attack.

Mighty Ram Practice. Targets of this attack must check against knockback; this edge increases knockback distance (from a potential base of zero) by one yard for each activation.

The Charm provides one edge initially. Characters may acquire additional edges for one bonus point or two experience points each.

At Essence 4, a character may apply two edges at once (or the same edge twice) for four motes. An Essence 5 char-

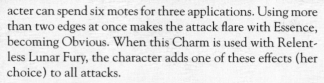

acter can spend six motes for three applications. Using more than two edges at once makes the attack flare with Essence, becoming Obvious. When this Charm is used with Relentless Lunar Fury, the character adds one of these effects (her choice) to all attacks.

SHELL-CRUSHING ATEMI

Cost: 2m; **Mins:** Strength 4, Essence 2; **Type:** Supplemental;
Keywords: Combo-OK, Fury-OK
Duration: Instant
Prerequisite Charms: Impressions of Strength

Stewards refuse to allow something as meager as magical armor or reinforced walls get in their ways. Using this Charm allows the character to ignore Hardness for a single attack.

UNSTOPPABLE LUNAR WOUND

Cost: 2m per die; **Mins:** Strength 4, Essence 3; **Type:** Reflexive (Step 10)
Keywords: Combo-OK
Duration: Instant
Prerequisite Charms: Impressions of Strength

The might of the Lunar Exalted may not be denied. The Lunar can use this Charm when he damages an opponent. Every two motes spent on this Charm turns a single die of damage into an automatic level of damage in Step 10 of attack resolution. The character may not affect more dice in this way than his Strength.

FORM-DESTROYING TOUCH

Cost: 10m, 1wp; **Mins:** Strength 5, Essence 4;
Type: Simple
Keywords: Combo-OK, Obvious, Sickness, Touch
Duration: Instant
Prerequisite Charms: Shell-Crushing Atemi, Unstoppable Lunar Wound

The Lunar Exalted carry within them a spark of the Wyld, and some Lunars learn how to channel it. This Charm is an action to touch a living target, which often requires a (Dexterity + Martial Arts) roll. If the Lunar successfully touches her target, she infects him with the Essence of the Wyld, which slowly tears him apart.

On a successful touch, the Lunar's player rolls (Strength + extra successes) at a difficulty of the target's Stamina. A failed roll inflicts one level of unsoakable aggravated damage as Wyld Essence surges through the target's body. The alternative is much, much worse for the victim.

Victims of this Charm's full extent suffer a *sickness* with no immediate effects. At least one full day after the attack, when the moon is high in the sky, the victim's player rolls (Willpower + [Integrity or Resistance] + Essence) at a difficulty of the Lunar's Essence. Failure inflicts the target with a pox and one level of aggravated damage. Each moonlit night thereafter, the victim suffers the same effect, and the player rolls again. Poxes occasionally increase in strength to become afflictions or even blights.

This Wyld disease cannot be cured without supernatural healing, and even such Essence-based methods suffer an external penalty equal to the Lunar's Essence. Without such efforts, the Wyld-sickness continues until a full lunar cycle passes, the victim succumbs or the victim becomes too severely mutated to exist within Creation (see **The Compass of Celestial Directions: The Wyld** for information about excessive Wyld mutation). Entering a Wyld zone counters the aggravated damage… but not the mutation.

BURROWING DEVIL STRIKE

Cost: 2m; **Mins:** Strength 4, Essence 3; **Type:** Supplemental
Keywords: Combo-OK, Fury-OK
Duration: Instant
Prerequisite Charms: Impressions of Strength

Deep within the Imperial Mountain, the small diamond beetle digs endlessly through even the hardest stone and white jade. Locals call the beetle the burrowing devil even as it leads them to rich veins for new mines. Lunar Exalted mimic this creature's capability by striking with such force that their attacks tear through armor to reach the soft flesh beneath. Treat this attack as piercing.

When activated as a part of Relentless Lunar Fury, the character's hand-to-hand attacks become piercing for the duration.

CONSUMPTIVE WORM HUNGERS

Cost: —; **Mins:** Strength 5; Essence 4; **Type:** Permanent
Keywords: None
Duration: Permanent
Prerequisite Charms: Burrowing Devil Strike

This Charm permanently enhances Burrowing Devil Strike. The Lunar temporarily becomes able to ignore a target's armor completely. When using Burrowing Devil Strike, the character must spend an additional point of Willpower to use this function.

FEATS OF STRENGTH CHARMS

TEARING CLAW ATEMI

Cost: 3m; **Mins:** Strength 3, Essence 2; **Type:** Supplemental
Keywords: Combo-OK
Duration: Instant
Prerequisite Charms: Any Strength Excellency

This Charm supplements a single attack or a feat of strength that targets or uses an inanimate object. The Charm doubles the attack's raw damage or doubles the character's Strength for the purposes of the feat. This applies equally to feats of strength for throwing or breaking objects, even though they normally work on different time scales.

MOLTED FEATHER-WEIGHT TECHNIQUE

Cost: 1m; **Mins:** Strength 3, Essence 2; **Type:** Supplemental
Keywords: Combo-OK
Duration: Instant
Prerequisite Charms: Tearing Claw Atemi

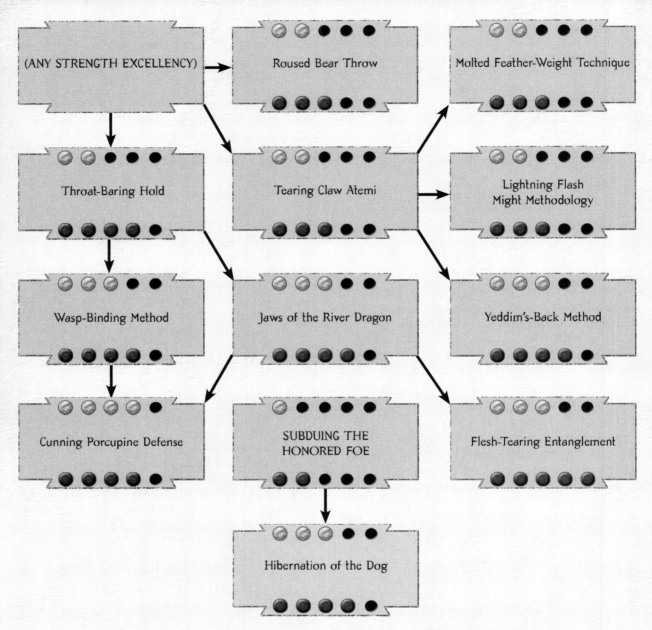

Using the power of her great Strength, the Lunar makes an object she attacks with light as a feather to her and just as maneuverable. This Charm negates the accuracy penalty of any weapon, improvised or otherwise, for a single attack.

LIGHTNING FLASH MIGHT METHODOLOGY
Cost: 2m; **Mins:** Strength 3, Essence 2; **Type:** Simple
Keywords: Combo-OK, Fury-OK
Duration: Instant
Prerequisite Charms: Tearing Claw Atemi

When a Steward is enraged, no mere object can stand in his way. Activating this Charm allows a character to break an object according to the feats of strength table (see **Exalted**, p. 127) as his action in combat, instead of as a dramatic action.

Using Lightning Flash Might Methodology with Relentless Lunar Fury allows the character to do so as a miscellaneous action while the Charm lasts.

YEDDIM'S-BACK METHOD
Cost: 4m; **Mins:** Strength 4, Essence 3; **Type:** Simple
Keywords: Combo-OK
Duration: Indefinite
Prerequisite Charms: Tearing Claw Atemi

Lunar Exalted have near endless might and endurance. Invoking this Charm allows the character to lift objects as though her effective (Strength + Athletics) rating were doubled. She maintains that superhuman strength as long as she commits the Essence. If she has Stamina 4 or higher, during that period she also accrues no fatigue from her extreme lifting.

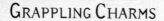

GRAPPLING CHARMS

ROUSED BEAR THROW
Cost: 3m; **Mins:** Strength 3, Essence 2;
Type: Reflexive (Step 10)
Keywords: Combo-OK, Knockback
Duration: Instant
Prerequisite Charms: Any Strength Excellency

Lunar Exalted are masters of close combat. When the character makes a successful clinch attack or manages to control a grapple, he may activate this Charm to throw his opponent up to (Strength x Essence) yards in any direction. This breaks the hold. Targets of this Charm as subtract an external penalty equal to the Lunar's Essence from their check against knockback.

THROAT-BARING HOLD
Cost: 4m; **Mins:** Strength 4, Essence 2;
Type: Reflexive (Step 10)
Keywords: None
Duration: Until next action
Prerequisite Charms: Any Strength Excellency

A Steward may place herself in danger to ensure her foe's defeat. This Charm gives the Lunar the option of automatically inflicting no damage with her crushing attack. Instead, she rolls (Strength + Martial Arts). Each success reduces her target's bashing and lethal soak by one until the Lunar's next action. Although the character does not get any opportunity to exploit this weakness, her packmates and allies do.

WASP-BINDING METHOD
Cost: 3m, 1wp; **Mins:** Strength 4, Essence 3;
Type: Supplemental
Keywords: Combo-OK, Obvious
Duration: (Strength x 2) actions
Prerequisite Charms: Throat-Baring Hold

This Charm supplements a clinch attack or an opposed grapple check, during which strands of Essence wrap around the Lunar's target at her direction. If the grapple check succeeds, the character leaves the grapple while her Essence solidifies around the target. The bindings appear to be constricting bands of silvery Essence, the papery cocoon of a wasp or some other strange containment. This leaves the Lunar free to perform other actions while her magic holds her opponent. On each of the Lunar's subsequent actions, her player rolls her opposed grapple check as normal, in addition to anything else the character does. If the Lunar desires, she may supplement this check with Excellencies but no other Charms.

JAWS OF THE RIVER DRAGON
Cost: 4m; **Mins:** Strength 4, Essence 3;
Type: Reflexive (Step 10)
Keywords: Combo-OK
Duration: Until next action
Prerequisite Charms: Throat-Baring Hold

None can escape a Steward's punishment. In addition to the normal crushing damage that a successful clinch or opposed grapple roll inflicts, the character's mighty arms also weaken her opponent. The victim of this Charm suffers an external penalty on the next opposed grapple check equal to the Lunar's Essence.

FLESH-TEARING ENTANGLEMENT
Cost: —; **Mins:** Strength 5; Essence 3; **Type:** Permanent
Keywords: Crippling, Stackable
Duration: Permanent
Prerequisite Charms: Jaws of the River Dragon

Lunars' mastery of their own bodies provides them superior knowledge of others'. This Charm permanently enhances Jaws of the River Dragon, allowing the character to also apply one of the following effects when she activates that Charm and inflicts at least one level of damage from the clinch:

- Reduce any one of the target's physical Attributes by one.
- Reduce the target's Appearance by one.
- Render a limb useless for the rest of the scene.

Exalted recover from diminished Attributes at a rate of one per day. Mortals recover only if given supernatural medical aid. All of these effects are considered *crippling*. Reducing an Attribute to zero renders the target unable to make any roll that requires that Attribute. Losing Strength disables one from inflicting any damage, although Charms that work on a mere touch can still take effect.

CUNNING PORCUPINE DEFENSE
Cost: 5m, 1wp; **Mins:** Strength 4, Essence 4;
Type: Reflexive
Keywords: Combo-OK, Obvious
Duration: Indefinite
Prerequisite Charms: Wasp-Binding Method, Jaws of the River Dragon

Stewards control their surroundings. A Lunar activates this Charm when he desires to keep people away from himself in close combat or inflict greater damage on them. This Charm applies a measure of the Lunar's shapeshifting talents to his anima, allowing it to manifest needles of deadly-looking silver light that emanate from the character and shift rapidly around him.

Any creature that attempts to engage the Lunar in unarmed combat automatically suffers (Lunar's Strength) dice of lethal damage per attack, and one that actually dares enter a grapple with him suffers (Strength + 5)L damage on each action that the grapple persists. Lunars can use this both to scare foes away from unarmed combat or to make them more deadly clinchers, as this damage is separate from any inflicted by the Lunar.

SUBDUAL CHARMS

SUBDUING THE HONORED FOE
Cost: 4m; **Mins:** Strength 2, Essence 1; **Type:** Supplemental
Keywords: Combo-OK, Fury-OK
Duration: Instant
Prerequisite Charms: None

Some opponents deserver better than death—it is a terrible thing to deprive the world of a skilled swordsman or a peerless archer. Activating this Charm guarantees that the Lunar will not kill her enemy and makes it easier to disable such a treasured opponent. She doubles the post-soak damage in Step 7 of attack resolution but automatically inflicts only bashing damage. Furthermore, the damage she inflicts cannot wrap over into lethal damage, no matter how many levels of bashing she actually inflicts.

Used as a part of the Relentless Lunar Fury, this Charm makes all damage the character inflicts bashing. This damage never wraps over into lethal.

HIBERNATION OF THE DOG
Cost: 6m; **Mins:** Strength 4, Essence 3; **Type:** Simple
Keywords: Combo-OK
Duration: Instant
Prerequisite Charms: Subduing the Honored Foe

At times, Lunar Exalted need to ensure that their enemies do not return to full capability too quickly. This Charm is a single attack. If it connects, the target ceases to be able to recover bashing damage from *any source* for the rest of the scene.

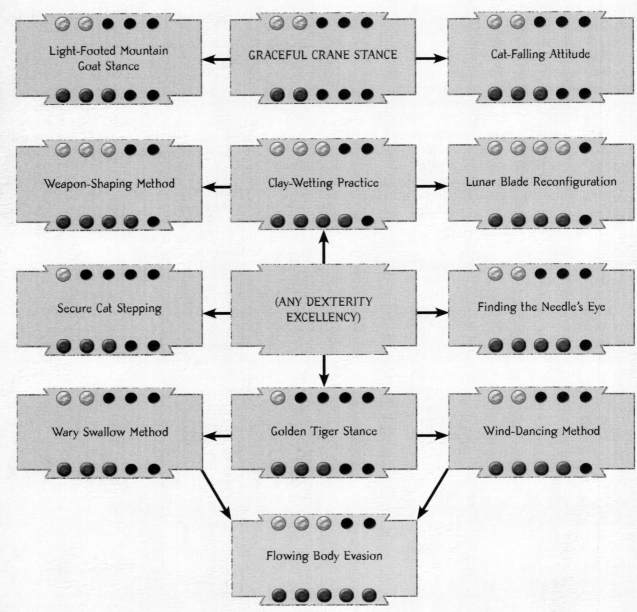

148

DEXTERITY

BALANCE AND GRACE CHARMS

GRACEFUL CRANE STANCE
Cost: 3m; **Mins:** Dexterity 2, Essence 2; **Type:** Reflexive
Keywords: Combo-OK
Duration: One scene
Prerequisite Charms: None

This Charm is identical to the Solar Charm of the same name, found in **Exalted** on pages 222-223.

LIGHT-FOOTED MOUNTAIN GOAT STANCE
Cost: 3m; **Mins:** Dexterity 3, Essence 2; **Type:** Reflexive
Keywords: Combo-OK
Duration: One scene
Prerequisite Charms: Graceful Crane Stance

Stewards do not fall and make slogging through the muck look elegant. The character is so light on her feet that she ignores environmental penalties to movement and actions. Add the character's Dexterity to her Athletics rating to determine whether her player must roll for the Lunar to keep her balance. Reduce the cost of this Charm to two motes if Graceful Crane Stance is already active.

CAT-FALLING ATTITUDE
Cost: 1m; **Mins:** Dexterity 3, Essence 2; **Type:** Reflexive
Keywords: None
Duration: Instant
Prerequisite Charms: Graceful Crane Stance

Height presents no danger to the Stewards. A Lunar may activate this Charm reflexively during or at the end of a fall. Divide the number of yards the character falls by two to determine appropriate damage from falling. The fall does not inflict lethal damage unless the fall covers a distance of at least 50 yards, and the Lunar always lands on her feet—never prone.

CRAFTING CHARMS

CLAY-WETTING PRACTICE
Cost: 5m; **Mins:** Dexterity 4, Essence 3; **Type:** Simple
Keywords: Combo-OK, Obvious, Touch
Duration: One scene
Prerequisite Charms: Any Dexterity Excellency

Just as a wasp digests paper to make its hive or certain creatures of the earth use their saliva to reinforce their burrows, the Lunar infuses an object with Wyld-bearing Essence to make it malleable. Invoking the Charm, the character chooses one discrete object of any mundane material. For the rest of the scene, the character may reshape the object with a brush of his hands. To everyone else, the object remains as hard as normal. Clay-Wetting Practice cannot affect the magical materials.

When a Lunar targets an object no larger than he can hold in one hand, he may reshape that object as a

miscellaneous action into any similar object of the same material and Resources value or less. Some Lunars use this Charm in combat so they always have the most appropriate weapon for the moment, although it doesn't work as well as Weapon-Shaping Method. Clay-Wetting Practice creates only average goods.

Clay-Wetting Practice also makes unworkable materials valid targets for Craft actions and eliminates any penalty for working without tools. In normal working conditions, this Charm reduces the target Resources value by one for determining the task's difficulty and time required, though long-term projects require many invocations of this Charm. Projects that normally involve dozens or hundreds of workers do not benefit from this Charm.

Characters may use this Charm to damage an object quickly. A Lunar ignores (Dexterity x 2) points of an object's soak after affecting it with this Charm.

WEAPON-SHAPING METHOD

Cost: 3m, 1wp; **Mins:** Dexterity 4, Essence 3;
Type: Simple
Keywords: Combo-OK, Obvious
Duration: One scene
Prerequisite Charms: Clay-Wetting Practice

Although nearly anything can be a weapon in a Lunar's hands, this Charm and the character's inconstant Essence make it literal. As long as no one else owns (see **Exalted**, p. 238) an object the character picks up, she may reflexively change it into an unremarkable, mundane weapon. An object can only become a weapon with about the same mass. Arrows are an exception—even the lightest materials can become arrows, though many objects may be too heavy.

Picking up an object to turn it into a weapon is an action equivalent to drawing a normal weapon of that sort: Picking up a stone as a sword is a miscellaneous action, while snapping off a twig to become an arrow is a reflexive part of launching that arrow. When the character lets go of an object-turned-weapon in this way, the object returns to its original form at the end of the tick. This provides enough time for thrown weapons and arrows shaped by this Charm to reach their targets before they revert.

Objects crafted of the magical materials cannot be affected by this Charm.

LUNAR BLADE RECONFIGURATION

Cost: 4m; **Mins:** Dexterity 4, Essence 4; **Type:** Simple
Keywords: Combo-OK, Obvious
Duration: One scene
Prerequisite Charms: Clay-Wetting Practice

Moonsilver is a gift from Luna, and this Charm enhances that gift. Once this Charm is active, an attuned moonsilver weapon can become nearly any weapon of the Exalted. On her action, the Lunar may reflexively change the target into any other weapon of equal or lesser Artifact rating. If she so chooses, she may also change the target into

any mundane weapon, which benefits from the moonsilver material bonus.

Any magical functions the weapon possesses (besides its basic weapon traits) function in all its forms unless they depend on the weapon's shape. For instance, a dire lance that increases damage even further when charging does not keep that bonus in the shape of a daiklave. At the end of the scene, the weapon returns to its original form.

When presented with an unworked nugget or deposit of moonsilver, this Charm allows a character to shape the material reflexively into any mundane weapon. Such weapons do not benefit from the moonsilver magical material bonus—they are not actually artifacts, and they are not attuned. At the end of the scene, the reconfigured moonsilver returns to its original shape.

DEFENSIVE CHARMS

SECURE CAT STEPPING

Cost: 1m; **Mins:** Dexterity 3, Essence 1; **Type:** Supplemental
Keywords: Combo-OK, Fury-OK
Duration: Instant
Prerequisite Charms: Any Dexterity Excellency

Stewards are cautious by nature. This Charm may supplement any action; actions so supplemented reduce the Defense Value penalty they apply to the character by one, to a minimum of zero.

Activated with Relentless Lunar Fury, this Charm reduces the Defense Value penalty of all *attack* actions by one for the duration.

FINDING THE NEEDLE'S EYE

Cost: 2m or 3m; **Mins:** Dexterity 4, Essence 2;
Type: Reflexive (Step 2)
Keywords: Combo-OK
Duration: Instant
Prerequisite Charms: Any Dexterity Excellency

The Lunar stops a ranged attack before it nears him. Invoked when the character is the target of a ranged attack, the Lunar forfeits his Defense Value to make an active attack in return to deflect or destroy the incoming attack. He might bat a chakram out of the air with his sword or fire one arrow to smash another. The player rolls (Dexterity + relevant Ability) at difficulty (attacker's Dexterity).

If the attack strikes the projectile, resolve damage. The damage may be enough to destroy the projectile outright—arrows are particularly fragile—completely negating the incoming attack. Assuming the projectile survives, each die of the Lunar's raw damage still reduces the incoming attack's damage by one die. The force of this defense can disrupt even projectiles that cannot be "destroyed," such as gouts of flame from firewands and blasts of Essence.

At Essence 3 or higher, a character may spend three motes on this Charm to defend another character against ranged attacks, if he himself has some way to attack at the proper range.

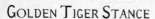

GOLDEN TIGER STANCE

Cost: 2m; **Mins:** Dexterity 3, Essence 1;
Type: Reflexive (Step 2)
Keywords: Combo-OK, Fury-OK
Duration: Instant
Prerequisite Charms: Any Dexterity Excellency

From the Lunar's flawless position, nothing can hinder his defenses. This Charm is used in response to an attack. The Charm eliminates up to (Dexterity) points of penalties that apply to the character's Dodge and Parry Defense Values. When activated with Relentless Lunar Fury, Golden Tiger Stance automatically eliminates up to (Dexterity ÷ 2) points of penalties to Dodge and Parry Defense Values at all times. This does not stack with invoked instances of Golden Tiger Stance.

WARY SWALLOW METHOD

Cost: 1m; **Mins:** Dexterity 3, Essence 2;
Type: Reflexive (Step 2)
Keywords: Combo-OK
Duration: Instant
Prerequisite Charms: Golden Tiger Stance

Wise Lunar Exalted are always prepared for an attack, sensing the reactions of animals, plants and sheer Essence around them to the offense. This Charm removes the unexpected quality from a single attack, allowing the character to use her appropriate Defense Values and defensive Charms against it. Attacks that are unblockable or undodgeable remain so.

WIND-DANCING METHOD

Cost: 3m; **Mins:** Dexterity 4, Essence 2;
Type: Reflexive (Step 9)
Keywords: Combo-OK, Counterattack
Duration: Instant
Prerequisite Charms: Golden Tiger Stance

Stewards are always where they need to be, nowhere else. The character may activate this Charm after using her Defense Value to defend against an attack, successful or not. In Step 9 of attack resolution, she skips lightly away from her aggressor. As part of a dodge, she may leap away; when parrying, the Lunar may let the attack she blocks propel her along. The character moves (Dexterity + Dodge) yards in any direction of her choice, so long as she moves generally away from her attacker.

Lunars use this Charm to get out of range of a close-combat flurry, forcing the flurry to end if the attacker does not have enough movement to keep up with her. Against ranged opponents, this Charm can help the character quickly find cover or make the attack more difficult due to range.

This Charm counts as a counterattack, so it reduces the character's Defense Value by one and cannot be used against a counterattack.

FLOWING BODY EVASION

Cost: 4m; **Mins:** Dexterity 5, Essence 3;
Type: Reflexive (Step 2)
Keywords: Combo-OK, Obvious
Duration: One action
Prerequisite Charms: Wary Swallow Method, Wind-Dancing Method

Lunar warriors move like the wind, impossible to grasp and futile to cut. A Lunar uses this Charm in response to all attacks of which she is aware. The character's flesh denies the assault, flowing around it or to one side. The character perfectly dodges the attack, even if it is undodgeable.

This Charm has one of the Four Flaws of Invulnerability (see **Exalted**, p. 194).

LUNAR HERO STYLE EXPANSION CHARMS

PREDATOR DISTRACTION METHOD

Cost: —; **Mins:** Dexterity 5, Essence 4; **Type:** Permanent
Keywords: Obvious
Duration: Instant
Prerequisite Charms: Running Through the Herd

This Charm permanently enhances Running Through the Herd. For the increased cost of two additional motes, the Lunar may apply that Charm in Step 2 of an attack resolution to which she is not party, so long as she is no further than

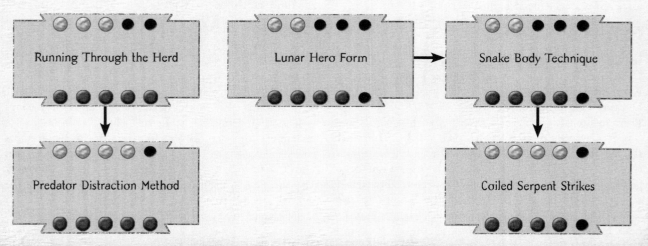

two move actions from the target of that attack. If Running Through the Herd fails to redirect the attack, the attacker affects his original target as intended.

SNAKE BODY TECHNIQUE
Cost: 3m, 1wp; **Mins:** Dexterity 4, Essence 2;
Type: Reflexive (Step 2)
Keywords: Combo-OK, Counterattack
Duration: Instant
Prerequisite Charms: Lunar Hero Form

To strike at a Steward brings swift retribution. Bending and moving with a snake's grace, the Lunar smoothly redirects an attack back toward its instigator. The attacker must be within the character's Melee or Martial Arts range. The Lunar may dodge into a blow and then shove the blade into her opponent or scamper through her foe's legs so he shoots himself in the foot—good stunts are the nature of this Charm.

Using this Charm allows the character to ignore all penalties to her defense against a single attack. As long as the character can successfully dodge or parry the attack, she counterattacks by forcing her enemy to suffer his own attack. Counterattack resolution begins in Step 7, as every success the attacker's player rolled is applied to his own soak. Any effects that would have taken place had the attack hit the Lunar affect the attacker. Also, the Lunar may use Charms or other supernatural powers to affect the damage as if she had started the attack (though they must be legally useable—either scene-long or in a Combo with Snake Body Technique).

COILED SERPENT STRIKES
Cost: —; **Mins:** Dexterity 4, Essence 4; **Type:** Permanent
Keywords: Obvious
Duration: Permanent
Prerequisite Charms: Snake Body Technique

No offender is safe from the Steward's retribution. This Charm permanently enhances Snake Body Technique, allowing the Lunar to spend two extra motes to apply the Charm no matter how far the attacker is from her. The Charm becomes obvious when used in this way, as the character swings arrows around in the air and hurls them back with their original force or reflects elemental bolts back at their source.

MOVEMENT CHARMS

GROUND-DENYING DEFENSE
Cost: 3m; **Mins:** Dexterity 3, Essence 2; **Type:** Reflexive
Keywords: Combo-OK, Obvious
Duration: Until next action
Prerequisite Charms: Any Dexterity Excellency

Stewards are masters of territory, and this Charm lets them command their ground in battle. By moving with grace, speed and forethought, the character limits the number of people who may attack him. Simply by spending three motes, he arranges positions on the battlefield such that one fewer people than normal can attack him in close combat. On open ground, this reduces the number from five to four; it

also protects him from suffering one unexpected attack due to restricted maneuvering. In closer quarters, this Charm reduces the maximum number of attackers to three.

INSTINCT-DRIVEN BEAST MOVEMENT
Cost: 4m+; **Mins:** Dexterity 3, Essence 2; **Type:** Simple
Keywords: Obvious
Duration: One scene
Prerequisite Charms: Any Dexterity Excellency

When pressed, Stewards can cover a great deal of ground without difficulty. Activating this Charm doubles the character's movement rate for every four motes spent. (Four motes doubles speed, eight motes triples speed, etc.) Every four motes spent also adds one automatic success to opposed speed rolls. This benefit stacks with those of Furious Hound Pursuit or Flight of the Sparrow. At the Storyteller's discretion, other speed-enhancing Charms might also benefit from this advantage.

FURIOUS HOUND PURSUIT
Cost: 4m; **Mins:** Dexterity 4, Essence 2; **Type:** Reflexive
Keywords: Combo-OK, Fury-OK, Obvious
Duration: One scene
Prerequisite Charms: Instinct-Driven Beast Movement

Once a Lunar Exalt chooses her prey, it cannot escape. The Lunar's player designates a single target, which the Lunar must have seen within the last hour. The character's Move and Dash actions both become one yard greater than those of her quarry, if that is greater than her current movement, and she automatically beats the target in contested rolls to determine relative speed by at least one success. In long-term movement, the character automatically moves one mile per day greater than her target. By spending a point of Willpower at activation, the Duration becomes Indefinite: As long as the character does not stop pursuing the target, the Charm persists.

If the target uses Charms to increase speed, the Lunar does not accelerate; his advanced movement is based on the target's natural values. At Essence 4, the Charm allows the Lunar to match her target's movement rates, including magic.

Activating this Charm in conjunction with Relentless Lunar Fury provides the Charm's benefit against any one target at a time, which she may reflexively re-designate each action.

FLIGHT OF THE SPARROW
Cost: 3m; **Mins:** Dexterity 4, Essence 2; **Type:** Reflexive
Keywords: Combo-OK
Duration: Indefinite
Prerequisite Charms: Instinct-Driven Beast Movement

Stewards know when they must retreat to survive and protect their lands in the future. This Charm doubles a character's Move and Dash actions so long as he attempts to escape pursuit or otherwise flee a scene, event or area. Outside of combat time, this doubles long-term movement rates and adds (Dexterity) successes to any roll to determine relative speed between the character and a pursuer.

Flight of the Sparrow ends when the character releases the Essence or is no longer fleeing.

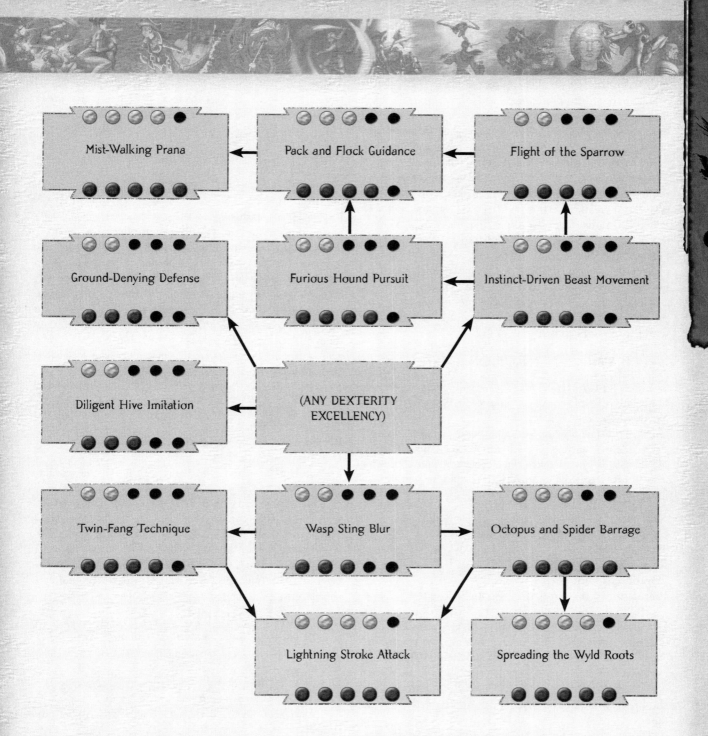

PACK AND FLOCK GUIDANCE

Cost: —; **Mins:** Dexterity 4, Essence 3; **Type:** Permanent
Keywords: None
Duration: Permanent
Prerequisite Charms: Furious Hound Pursuit, Flight of the Sparrow

This Charm permanently enhances Furious Hound Pursuit and Flight of the Sparrow, allowing the character to convey the Charm's benefit to an entire unit that he leads. This adds one Willpower to the cost and affects a unit of up to Magnitude (the character's Essence - 1). When leading a unit, a Lunar using Furious Hound Pursuit can only target another unit with that Charm's effects.

MIST-WALKING PRANA

Cost: 10m, 1wp; **Mins:** Dexterity 5, Essence 4;
Type: Simple (dramatic action)
Keywords: Combo-OK, Obvious, Wyld
Duration: Instant
Prerequisite Charms: Pack and Flock Guidance

There are holes in the Wyld, tunnels that connect two far places but that rarely exist for long. This Charm gives the character the preternatural speed to slip through these gaps in space before they disappear or move on.

The Lunar's player rolls (Dexterity + Occult) at a difficulty of 1 for Pure Chaos, 2 for the Deep Wyld, 3 for Middlemarches and 4 for the Bordermarches. Basic success allows the character

to exploit these distortions of the Wyld to travel one mile. Each threshold success allows him to add one zero to the distance or increase the Magnitude of people he leads on the path by one (from a base of zero, himself). Maximum distance is 1,000 miles; maximum Magnitude is (Essence - 1).

Traveling this way is a dramatic action that requires five minutes. Though the Lunar rarely stays in one place long enough for creatures of the Wyld to accost, taking any non-reflexive actions (to attack something, for example) breaks the character's concentration and disrupts the Charm. A Lunar who does not complete the trip as planned (i.e., the player fails a roll) usually ends up lost, sometimes far from his intended destination (by 1,000 miles or more distant, in the case of a botch). Assuming nothing goes wrong, the Lunar progresses the appropriate distance toward his destination with the Charm's conclusion.

SPEED AND EXTRA ACTION CHARMS

DILIGENT HIVE IMITATION
Cost: 3m; **Mins:** Dexterity 3, Essence 2; **Type:** Reflexive
Keywords: Combo-OK
Duration: Until next action
Prerequisite Charms: Any Dexterity Excellency

Stewards work quickly so they may return to the things they enjoy. Until the character's next action, he treats all miscellaneous actions as Speed 3.

WASP STING BLUR
Cost: 2m per tick; **Mins:** Dexterity 3, Essence 2;
Type: Reflexive
Keywords: Combo-OK, Fury-OK
Duration: Instant
Prerequisite Charms: Any Dexterity Excellency

With the blinding speed of a striking insect, the Lunar lashes out and almost immediately recovers. This Charm reduces the Speed of a Lunar's action by one for every two motes spent, after persistent effects, to a minimum of 3.

Used with Relentless Lunar Fury, this Charm reduces the Speed of all attacks by one (minimum three) for the duration.

TWIN-FANG TECHNIQUE
Cost: 5m; **Mins:** Dexterity 4, Essence 2; **Type:** Supplemental
Keywords: Combo-OK
Duration: Instant
Prerequisite Charms: Wasp Sting Blur

The Lunar Exalted are more dangerous than one expects. Invoking this Charm, the character lashes out with two weapons instead of just one. (Both weapons must be in hand.) The player and his single target go through attack resolution twice, skipping Steps 1, 3 and 4 the second time through—use the first attack roll both times. The target's defense suffers onslaught penalty the second time. When using ranged weapons that are constantly drawn (arrows for a

bow, daggers from a bandolier, etc.), the character may fire or throw two at once as long as he has sufficient ammunition.

OCTOPUS AND SPIDER BARRAGE
Cost: 6m, 1wp; **Mins:** Dexterity 5, Essence 3;
Type: Extra Action
Keywords: Combo-OK, Obvious
Duration: Instant
Prerequisite Charms: Wasp Sting Blur

Lunar Exalted are talented improvisers, using every method and advantage at hand to survive. This Charm gives a character one attack at her full dice pool for every combat-capable extremity she has. Each limb must actually be used for the attack—a character cannot use a weapon for each attack unless she can use it with each relevant limb. A Lunar in typical human form using this Charm receives four attacks when using this Charm, one for each arm and leg. In her war form, she may receive more attacks due to antlers, tusks or extra sets of limbs.

LIGHTNING STROKE ATTACK
Cost: 7m; **Mins:** Dexterity 5, Essence 4;
Type: Supplemental
Keywords: Combo-OK, Obvious
Duration: Instant
Prerequisite Charms: Twin-Fang Technique, Octopus and Spider Barrage

Endowing her attack with the speed of her natural grace or the blurring speed of brute force, the character's attack moves so quickly that both Parry and Dodge Defense Values become inapplicable. Onlookers may think the character and her weapon did not even move. Only a bright flash or blur (and often a falling opponent) indicate that anything happened at all.

SPREADING THE WYLD ROOTS
Cost: 10m, 1wp; **Mins:** Dexterity 5, Essence 4;
Type: Simple
Keywords: Combo-OK, Obvious, Wyld
Duration: Instant
Prerequisite Charms: Octopus and Spider Barrage

Within the Wyld, space is not always a matter of here and there. Sometimes, one location is in multiple places, or many points all fit into one small space. Though the Lunar Exalted are immune to such space-bending (to a degree), some learn how to exploit it. By perceiving and striking at one such multispatial point, or perhaps creating it with the Charm, the character attacks (Essence) points simultaneously with a single blow.

The character may target multiple individuals (who must all be within 30 yards), a single person or any mix thereof. Attacking one target with multiple strikes reduces that target's Defense Value by the total number of blows laid on the target, as if multiple people launched a coordinated attack.

Example: A Lunar with Essence 4 levies three blows against one target and one against another. The first target suffers a -3 DV penalty against the attack; the second target suffers no penalty.

By *attacking each target with two blows, the Lunar could give each a -2 DV penalty instead.*

The Lunar's player only rolls a single attack, which is applied against the Defense Values of all chosen targets simultaneously.

STAMINA

CONSUMPTION CHARMS

FERTILE BREATH INVERSION
Cost: 4m; **Mins:** Stamina 4, Essence 3; **Type:** Reflexive
Keywords: Combo-OK, Fury-OK, Gift
Duration: Indefinite
Prerequisite Charms: Any Stamina Excellency

By inverting a personal definition of what is breathable and what is not, the Lunar allows herself to breathe safely anything she currently allows into her lungs. While air still tastes sweet to her lungs, so does whatever she targets with the Charm.

Lunar Exalted used this Charm in the Primordial War to dive into Kimberry, the Sea That Marched Against the Flame, and do battle with her heart. Players should note that being able to breathe fire or a sandstorm without harm does not make it safe to be immersed in it. That requires other Charms.

When a character uses Deadly Beastman Transformation, she may activate this Charm by committing a single mote. Fertile Breath Inversion then allows her to breathe

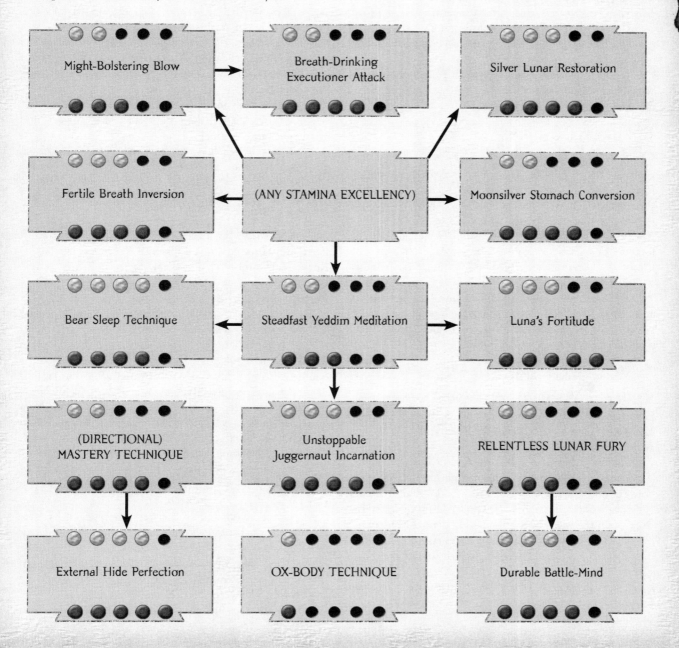

something appropriate to her hybrid form, such as water for a barracuda or sand for an eight-tailed mole hound. Activated with Relentless Lunar Fury, the character can safely breathe *everything* until the Charm ends.

MOONSILVER STOMACH CONVERSION
Cost: 3m; **Mins:** Stamina 4, Essence 2; **Type:** Reflexive
Keywords: Combo-OK, Gift
Duration: Indefinite
Prerequisite Charms: Any Stamina Excellency

In Creation, almost everything is edible to *something*. The Lunar Exalted mimic that capability by fortifying their gullets, digestive systems and, occasionally, teeth so they can safely consume nearly anything. Activating the Charm, a character becomes able to eat without harm whatever he puts into his mouth and obtain the same sustenance as from decent food.

Lunar Exalted use this Charm, among other things, to find all the food they need while surviving inhospitable regions of Creation.

When activating Deadly Beastman Transformation, the character may commit one mote to gain the ability to eat materials appropriate to the hybrid form.

ENDURANCE CHARMS

OX-BODY TECHNIQUE
Cost: —; **Mins:** Stamina 1, Essence 1; **Type:** Permanent
Keywords: Stackable
Prerequisite Charms: None

Lunar Exalted are able to take blows far better than weak things such as mortals or castles. As anyone who has fought Lunars knows, Luna's Chosen can suffer grievous injuries and keep on fighting. This Charm gives the Lunars additional health levels.

A player may purchase this Charm multiple times, but no more than once per dot of Stamina. Each purchase provides two additional Dying health levels (see **Exalted**, pp. 150-151) and the player's choice of the following:
- Two -1 health levels
- Four -2 health levels

STEADFAST YEDDIM MEDITATION
Cost: 2m+; **Mins:** Stamina 3, Essence 2; **Type:** Reflexive
Keywords: Combo-OK, Fury-OK, Stackable
Duration: One scene
Prerequisite Charms: Any Stamina Excellency

Lunar warriors are known for their ability to keep on going despite the pain. For each two motes spent, the character allows herself to ignore one point of internal penalties from wounds, fatigue or any manner of deprivation or pain. A Lunar may cancel up to (Stamina ÷ 2) points of penalties. The character need not have any penalties in order to use the Charm; she may preemptively render herself proof against these penalties. Penalties from wounds are always canceled first; other penalties are prioritized by the Lunar's player and may be reprioritized at will.

When this Charm is activated with Relentless Lunar Fury, the Lunar ignores wound penalties completely until her rage subsides.

BEAR SLEEP TECHNIQUE
Cost: 10m, 1wp; **Mins:** Stamina 4, Essence 4;
Type: Simple
Keywords: None
Duration: Indefinite
Prerequisite Charms: Steadfast Yeddim Meditation

Stewards save their power for when the land truly needs them. Some Moonchildren used this Charm to remain safely separate from a world that hated them until the present day. Most of those sleepers are now awakened… but who knows?

Activating this Charm, the Lunar settles down for a long hibernation, fueled by his will and Essence. The character's player declares up to (Essence) conditions that will awaken the Lunar. One of these conditions must be a maximum duration the character will sleep. Other conditions may be anything the character might perceive when asleep; the character's player makes relevant rolls as normal to determine if the sleeping Lunar detects the conditions. Suffering a wound always ends the hibernation.

While a Lunar hibernates, he does not age or need food, air or water. Lunars use Bear Sleep Technique to pass time they do not consider important to experience. They also use this Charm to stay alive in times of famine, drought or lack of breathable air.

UNSTOPPABLE JUGGERNAUT INCARNATION
Cost: 3m; **Mins:** Stamina 4, Essence 3; **Type:** Reflexive
Keywords: Combo-OK, Stackable
Duration: Indefinite
Prerequisite Charms: Steadfast Yeddim Meditation

This Charm allows a Lunar to remain upright even when everything demands that he be dead. A character uses Unstoppable Juggernaut Incarnation when he takes damage that would place a lethal wound in his Incapacitated health level. He does not suffer any damage beyond that Incapacitated level, and instead of taking *that damage*, he temporarily sets it aside and the player does not mark it wounded. He continues to operate as normal, but only as long as the three motes spent on the Charm remain committed.

Characters may activate this Charm multiple times in order to "delay" multiple killing blows. Each time the Lunar does so, another lethal wound enters his pool of waiting damage. Releasing one mote of Essence committed to this Charm releases them all. Having just one "delayed" Incapacitated wound level fills all the character's wound boxes when he releases it. Each additional delayed wound fills one of the character's Dying health levels with lethal damage.

This Charm is ineffective against aggravated damage.

LUNA'S FORTITUDE
Cost: 4m; **Mins:** Stamina 5, Essence 3; **Type:** Reflexive
Keywords: Combo-OK, Fury-OK
Duration: Until next action
Prerequisite Charms: Steadfast Yeddim Meditation

Sometimes, the Stewards do not know when they have already lost. Legend states that Lunars loyal to the Solar Deliberative sometimes fought on for days while holding the Dragon-Blooded hordes off from the Lunars' masters—the Lunars simply had not yet realized they were dead.

While this Charm is active, the character ignores the effects of falling unconscious or dying until her next action. At that time, she may activate Luna's Fortitude again in order to remain functioning. As long as she maintains enough Essence to continue using this Charm, she need not fall unconscious or die. Once the Lunar ceases to activate the Charm on her every action (or otherwise benefit from its effects), she suffers whatever fate she has avoided until then.

With Relentless Lunar Fury, this Charm provides the Charm's benefits until the rage ends. Usually, there is some opportunity for the Lunar then to activate this Charm or somehow remain functional.

ENVIRONMENTAL CHARMS

(DIRECTIONAL) MASTERY TECHNIQUE
Cost: 6m; **Mins:** Stamina 4, Essence 2; **Type:** Reflexive
Keywords: Combo-OK
Duration: Indefinite
Prerequisite Charms: None

Stewards may guard even the farthest, least-hospitable reaches of Creation without discomfort. (Directional) Mastery Technique is actually five Charms. Each Charm defines a category of environmental damage to which the Lunar is immune. The Charms are based upon the five directions:

• **Center:** The character is immune to environmental *crippling* effects. She takes no damage from avalanches or cave-ins, and being crushed by a ton of rubble is a mere inconvenience. A sandstorm tickles her skin.

• **East:** The character is unaffected by plant-based toxins. Irritating insects avoid her or cannot penetrate her skin, and she never develops annoying rashes. Other creatures that swarm ignore her. Insects that actually damage her subtract three from their dice pools and raw damage values.

• **North:** The character takes no damage from chill or extreme cold. She never catches a chill. Terrible ice storms provide a pleasant massage. She never feels uncomfortably cold, only pleasantly cool.

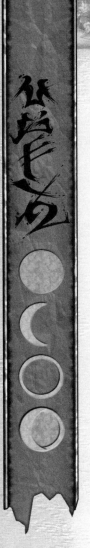

• **South:** The character may walk through natural and magical flames without pain. Fire does not burn her clothing. Extreme heat does not harm her. She never feels uncomfortably hot, only pleasantly warm. In sandstorms, particles do not even get stuck in her clothing.

• **West:** The character is comfortable and can breathe at all depths. Venoms of marine life do not affect her, and she takes no damage from schools of small, dangerous fish or other masses of underwater creatures.

These Charms are meant to be complete, protecting the character from all environmental dangers inherent to a given direction. Specific environmental threats not mentioned should fall under one of the five Charms. Some (such as sandstorms) may fall under more than one. When another character deliberately causes or uses environmental effects with intent to harm the Lunar, she is not immune.

EXTERNAL HIDE PERFECTION

Cost: —; **Mins:** Stamina 5, Essence 4; **Type:** Permanent
Keywords: None
Duration: Permanent
Prerequisite Charms: Any (Directional) Mastery Technique

Lunars become true masters of their territories. This Charm permanently enhances all (Directional) Mastery Technique Charms the character knows. It eliminates the exception made for other characters' deliberation and intention; the character never suffers damage or penalties from dangers covered by his (Directional) Mastery Technique Charms.

ESSENCE-REGAINING CHARMS

MIGHT-BOLSTERING BLOW

Cost: 2m; **Mins:** Stamina 3, Essence 2; **Type:** Supplemental
Keywords: Combo-OK, Fury-OK
Duration: Instant
Prerequisite Charms: Any Stamina Excellency

Lunar Exalted are creatures of great power, and they revel and grow strong in their might. When an attack supplemented by this attack hits its target, the character regains one mote for every extra success to a maximum of (Stamina). If the attack also inflicts damage, the character regains one mote for each level of damage to a maximum of (Stamina). This attack must be a display of the Lunar's prowess to provide any return in Essence. If there is no challenge in hitting a target, there is no return from striking it, and destroying a cushion in one blow is no mark of strength.

BREATH-DRINKING EXECUTIONER ATTACK

Cost: 2m; **Mins:** Stamina 4, Essence 2;
Type: Simple (Speed 4)
Keywords: Combo-OK, Fury-OK, Touch
Duration: Instant
Prerequisite Charms: Might-Bolstering Blow

With a person's death, the patterns of Essence that bind the decedent's higher and lower souls relax, releasing several motes into Creation. Activating this Charm, the Lunar's player rolls (his Essence + target's Essence) to prevent that Essence from going to waste. Any character who died within the last minute becomes a valid target for this Charm. Each success, to a maximum of the Lunar's Stamina, returns two motes to the Lunar's pools. This Charm cannot fill the character's Essence pool past its maximum.

Activating this Charm with Relentless Lunar Fury, the character regains one mote of Essence each time he kills a target.

SILVER LUNAR RESOLUTION

Cost: —; **Mins:** Stamina 4, Essence 3; **Type:** Permanent
Keywords: Obvious
Prerequisite Charms: Any Stamina Excellency

Lunars empower themselves through the successful strengthening and defense of others. The more effort a character puts into protecting a society or culture, the greater her power. With the purchase of this Charm, the Lunar may recover motes by working to protect any social or military unit from danger or dissolution. Each hour spent on such tasks recovers motes equal to the unit's Magnitude.

In addition, each purchase of this Charm adds 10 motes to the character's Peripheral Essence pool. This Essence cannot be committed to any artifact and can only be recovered through the method above or through Essence-recovery Charms. A character may not take this Charm more times than her permanent Essence.

FURY CHARMS

RELENTLESS LUNAR FURY

Cost: 1m, 1wp; **Mins:** Stamina 3, Essence 2;
Type: Reflexive (Step 1 or 2)
Keywords: None
Duration: (Essence x 2) actions
Prerequisite Charms: None

After activating this Charm, the character enters a devastating battle fury. She may slaughter her foes as dispassionately as the most cold-blooded assassin, show her rage with shouts and grimaces, or act any other way she desires. This short-lived Charm is the exemplar of Lunar—indeed, some say *Exalted*—combat. Shielded by their fury, the character becomes a truly frightening foe.

The Charm's initial benefits are modest. The character adds one automatic success to all combat actions, from attacking and resisting knockdown to keeping balance during the fight, but her Defense Values remain unaffected. She does not suffer wound penalties until they are worse than -1 and completely ignores fatigue for the duration. Finally, the maximum benefit the character may obtain from her physical Attribute Excellencies increases to (Attribute + Essence).

Relentless Lunar Fury's real power lies in other Charms. Certain Charms have the *Fury-OK* keyword. These Charms describe special (but related) effects that they have when activated simultaneously with the Relentless Lunar Fury. Any Fury Charm's special benefit may be activated as a part of Relentless Lunar Fury *without a Combo* by adding two motes to the cost of Relentless Lunar Fury. These Charms' fury effects always end with Relentless Lunar Fury. Characters may have the normal version of a Charm active at the same time the Fury-OK version of a Charm is active. A character may not activate more than (Essence) additional fury Charms at once.

Example: The Count's wax soldiers surround Kajeha Lef, a Dexterity 4, Essence 3 Lunar. Activating Relentless Lunar Fury as a preface to tearing them apart, Lef also activates the fury effects of Painless Warrior Meditation and Wasp Sting Blur, bringing the total cost of Relentless Lunar Fury up to five motes and one Willpower. She could add one more fury effect (since she has Essence 3) but not more than that until she gains Essence 4.

Normally, Kajeha Lef's player may use Dexterity Excellencies to purchase four dice or two successes. While channeling her character's rage, her player may purchase up to seven dice or three successes.

A Lunar's fury comes with one drawback: The Lunar becomes so very focused that she cannot perform non-combat actions. The Lunar must continue to hunt and kill enemies until the Charm ends. With a successful reflexive Willpower roll, the character can perform a non-combat action (at -2 dice) or come off the offensive for a single action. She can only stop the fury early by forcefully calming her anger and cooling her blood; to do so, her player rolls (Willpower) at a difficulty of the character's Valor.

When a character activates more than three additional Charms in tandem with Relentless Lunar Fury (which re-quires Essence 4 or higher), the Charm becomes Obvious. Silver and white light flows around the character's weapon and forms contrails to emphasize her prowess.

DURABLE BATTLE-MIND
Cost: —; **Mins:** Stamina 4, Essence 3; **Type:** Permanent
Keywords: None
Duration: Permanent
Prerequisite Charms: Relentless Lunar Fury

Durable Battle-Mind increases the duration of Relentless Lunar Fury by four actions.

HEALING CHARMS

BRUISE-RELIEF METHOD
Cost: 1m+; **Mins:** Stamina 2, Essence 2; **Type:** Reflexive
Keywords: Combo-OK, Gift
Duration: Instant
Prerequisite Charms: Any Stamina Excellency

Stewards heal quickly, the better to keep up with their duties. This Charm heals one level of bashing damage the character has suffered for each mote spent. She may recover no more than (Stamina) levels of bashing damage in a single action.

Characters may activate this Charm even when unconscious.

A Lunar may commit two motes when activating Deadly Beastman Transformation in order to regenerate one level of bashing damage reflexively each action; this does not stack with deliberate activations of this Charm for greater healing.

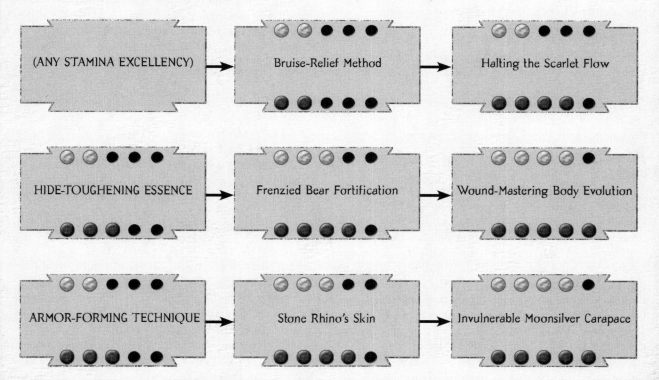

Halting the Scarlet Flow

Cost: 2m+; **Mins:** Stamina 4, Essence 2; **Type:** Reflexive
Keywords: Combo-OK, Obvious, Gift
Duration: Instant
Prerequisite Charms: Bruise-Relief Method

Silver light shines from the Lunar's wounds as lacerations close and bones knit instantly. When the light fades, all that is left are a few bruises. Each use of this Charm heals a single level of lethal damage. This miscellaneous action may be performed as part of a flurry.

Soak Enhancement Charms

Hide-Toughening Essence

Cost: 1m per 2 soak; **Mins:** Stamina 3, Essence 2;
Type: Reflexive (Step 7)
Keywords: Combo-OK
Duration: One scene
Prerequisite Charms: None

The Lunar Exalted know how to keep themselves alive. Stewards use this Charm to increase their soak.

Each mote spent on this Charm purchases two points of bashing and lethal soak for the rest of the scene. A character may spend up to (Essence) motes, and this added, innate soak stacks with armor.

Frenzied Bear Fortification

Cost: 3m; **Mins:** Stamina 4, Essence 3;
Type: Reflexive (Step 10)
Keywords: Combo-OK, Fury-OK
Duration: Until next action
Prerequisite Charms: Hide-Toughening Essence

Just as the raging bear, the Lunar shrugs off even the worst blows inflicted upon her. This Charm reduces any bashing or lethal damage the Lunar takes by one level per wound inflicted. At Essence 4 and higher, this Charm affects aggravated damage at all.

When activated with Relentless Lunar Fury, this Charm functions for the duration. The character may not invoke the Charm again for a double benefit.

Wound-Mastering Body Evolution

Cost: 12m, 1wp; **Mins:** Stamina 5, Essence 4;
Type: Simple
Keywords: Combo-OK, Obvious
Duration: One scene
Prerequisite Charms: Frenzied Bear Fortification

Powerful Lunars can teach their bodies to acclimatize to even the most dangerous things, rending the Lunars proof against what has already hurt them. After activating this Charm, any form of attack or event that causes the Lunar harm (i.e., at least a health level of damage or a dot of trait degradation) ceases to be a danger to him for the rest of the scene. Raw damage from any such sources automatically drops to zero in Step 7 of attack resolution. Other sources of damage still affect the character: A Lunar

can only use Wound-Mastering Body Evolution against one form of attack or damage at a time. Using this Charm a second time merely resets the Lunar's immunity; the effects do not stack.

Divide sources of damage in the same way that **Exalted** separates weapons. Edged weapons form one category, blunt weapons are another and so on. Artifact weapons have their own spread of the categories separate from the mundane weapons but are not separated by magical material. Fire, strangulation, crushing, acid and the like all have their own categories. Some unique effects may not fall into any category, and thus always harm the character at least once before he becomes temporarily immune.

Armor-Forming Technique

Cost: 1m per 3 soak; **Mins:** Stamina 3, Essence 2;
Type: Reflexive (Step 7)
Keywords: Combo-OK, Gift, Obvious
Duration: One scene
Prerequisite Charms: None

This Charm resembles Hide-Toughening Essence, but the character grows bony plates rather than directly strengthening his body. This adds three points of bashing and lethal soak and one point of aggravated soak for every mote spent; the Lunar may spend up to (Essence) motes. Soak from this Charm is Obvious and counts as armor for the purposes of Charms and piercing weapons. The bony armor renders other armor unwearable (the size and shape of the Lunar's body has changed), except for Moon-Faced Mail (see p. 128) and moonsilver armor.

When the Lunar shifts into war form, he may commit up to (Essence) motes in this Charm for as long as he keeps Deadly Beastman Transformation active. Other than the extended duration, it functions as normal.

Stone Rhino's Skin

Cost: 4m; **Mins:** Stamina 4, Essence 3; **Type:** Reflexive (Step 7)
Keywords: Combo-OK
Duration: Instant
Prerequisite Charms: Armor-Forming Technique

Even terrible wounds bounce from the flesh of the Lunar Exalted. After an attack hits the character, she may use this Charm to set her Hardness against that attack equal to her bashing and lethal soak values. Ignore soak from armor for determining the character's effective Hardness.

Invulnerable Moonsilver Carapace

Cost: 6m per action, 1wp; **Mins:** Stamina 5, Essence 4;
Type: Reflexive (Step 7)
Keywords: Combo-OK, Obvious
Duration: Until next action
Prerequisite Charms: Stone Rhino's Skin

Moonsilver flows from the pores of the character's skin to cover his body. This armor is so complete that observers can find no gaps or weaknesses. Even the head is completely covered, but the Lunar's perceptions are not in the least impeded. The character gains +15 aggravated/+15 lethal/+15 bashing soak and, until the Charm ends, considers all attacks against him to have a minimum damage of zero. This stacks with armor, if necessary, and does not count as armor. When this Charm would end, the Lunar may reflexively spend another six motes to maintain it for yet another action. This does not count as Charm use.

SUBSTANCE CHARMS

SCORPION AND TOAD ABSOLUTION
Cost: 2m; **Mins:** Stamina 3, Essence 2; **Type:** Reflexive
Keywords: Combo-OK
Duration: Instant
Prerequisite Charms: Any Stamina Excellency

Stewards are masters of their bodies and difficult to kill by treachery. Characters with this Charm may immunize their bodies against any poison or disease they experience. Activating Scorpion and Toad Assumption while suffering the effects, the character's player adds three automatic successes to all (Stamina + Resistance) rolls to endure the effects of that disease or poison.

SCORPION AND TOAD ASSUMPTION
Cost: 3m; **Mins:** Stamina 3, Essence 3;
Type: Simple (dramatic action)
Keywords: Combo-OK, Obvious
Duration: Instant
Prerequisite Charms: Scorpion and Toad Absolution

This Charm is a dramatic action to treat a target for poison or disease. The Lunar Exalt spends at least five minutes preparing the body, channeling the foreign substance within the target toward a specific place, where she then cuts the body and sucks out the tainted blood. This taste of the target's blood exposes the character to the disease or poison that plagues the target, which she then must deal with on her own.

SCORPION AND TOAD IMMUNITY
Cost: —; **Mins:** Stamina 4, Essence 3; **Type:** Permanent
Keywords: None
Duration: Permanent
Prerequisite Charms: Scorpion and Toad Assumption

Lunars do not fear what they have conquered. A character with this Charm becomes immune to any poison or disease that he has survived. Once the foreign substance has run its course, it can never harm that character again. Exalted may make exceptions at will: A Lunar does not *have* to lose the ability to enjoy alcohol, qat or other recreational drugs. Once a character becomes immune, however, she cannot go back.

SCORPION AND TOAD MASTERY
Cost: 1m+; **Mins:** Stamina 4, Essence 3; **Type:** Reflexive
Keywords: Combo-OK, Poison *or* Sickness
Duration: Instant
Prerequisite Charms: Scorpion and Toad Assumption

Creation holds thousands of unique poisons and drugs, enough to make a dedicated assassin or hedonist despair at ever having them all on hand. Some Stewards find another avenue, for which they were much-loved in

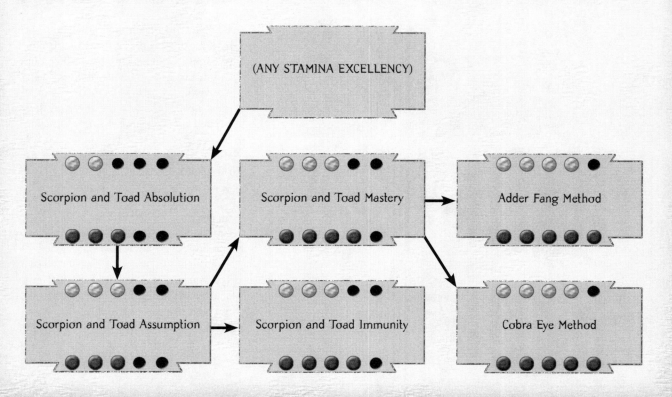

the First Age. Once a character has suffered the effects of a foreign substance on her body, she may reproduce it (assuming, of course, she survives).

The character may use a replicated drug, disease or poison in three ways:

• She may channel it directly into her system, feeling its effect immediately.

• She may excrete it onto a single weapon (natural or not), inflicting it upon the victim of her next successful attack. The usual method is to spit on a weapon. The character may activate Scorpion and Toad Mastery in Step 1 of attack resolution to invoke it with an attack.

• She can milk it from her flesh, much as poison-sellers harvest venom from snakes, creating a sample that may be used later.

Creating a poison or drug costs a number of motes equal to twice the substance's Resources value. The cost to generate a disease is equal to the disease's virulence.

ADDER FANG METHOD

Cost: —; **Mins:** Stamina 5, Essence 4; **Type:** Permanent
Keywords: Gift, Poison
Duration: Permanent
Prerequisite Charms: Scorpion and Toad Mastery

Lunars who can reproduce Creation's venoms sometimes invent their own. This charm adds a specific supernatural toxin to the list of those the character may create using Scorpion and Toad Mastery. (The attack must cause at least a level of damage to convey the poison, as normal.) This venom is known as Luna's Spite and has Damage (character's Essence x 2)/tick, Toxicity (character's Stamina + 1), Tolerance —/—, Penalty-(Essence). People who die of Luna's Spite grow very pale, and their eyes become silvery masks.

Luna's Spite is just one of many toxins the character can create. Here are other sample toxins. Each requires four experience points or two bonus points to learn.

Chosen's Bane: Damage 6L/tick, Toxicity (target's Essence), Tolerance —/—, Penalty -(target's Essence).

Closing Eye Toxin: Damage 5B/12 hours, Toxicity (character's Stamina-1), Tolerance (Stamina)/24 hours, Penalty -1.

Night's Lure: Damage 13B/tick, Toxicity (character's Stamina)L, Tolerance —/—, Penalty -0; poison does not take effect until the moon is in the sky.

Still Water Infusion: Damage 20B (4/tick), Toxicity (character's Stamina), Tolerance —/—, Penalty -1; actually inflicts 4 bashing each tick.

Adder Fang Method is a Gift Charm. By committing four motes, the character makes the toxin constantly available while she remains in her beastman form. This is not optional; if she uses Adder Fang Method in this way, it affects every one of her natural attacks while in war form. She cannot use more than one toxin in this way at a single time.

COBRA EYE METHOD

Cost: 3m; **Mins:** Stamina 5, Essence 4; **Type:** Simple
Keywords: Combo-OK, Obvious
Duration: Instant
Prerequisite Charms: Scorpion and Toad Mastery

In addition to injecting a venom with his attacks, the Lunar can also learn exude acid from his palms or spit it from his mouth. Cobra Eye Method adds acids and other damaging reagents to the list of natural substances he can, after experiencing them, create. This Charm is a single attack, either a natural attack or a launch from the character's mouth. The latter attack uses (Dexterity + [Athletics or Thrown]) at a -2 accuracy, with range 5.

The character may also invent his own supernatural acids, each of requires four experience points or two bonus points to purchase. Samples follow.

Burning Tar: This acid is gummy, sickly green and sticky. It inflicts eight lethal damage when first inflicted on a target and the same on each of the target's subsequent actions until someone removes the acid. Scraping off the acid is a miscellaneous action (-1 Defense Value) that does not require a roll.

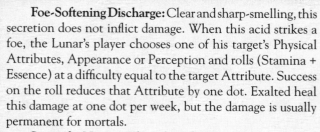

Foe-Softening Discharge: Clear and sharp-smelling, this secretion does not inflict damage. When this acid strikes a foe, the Lunar's player chooses one of his target's Physical Attributes, Appearance or Perception and rolls (Stamina + Essence) at a difficulty equal to the target Attribute. Success on the roll reduces that Attribute by one dot. Exalted heal this damage at one dot per week, but the damage is usually permanent for mortals.

Soporific Nectar: This white fluid gives off a powerful aroma that can set most creatures reeling. As long as the Nectar connects with its target, the Lunar's player rolls (Stamina + [Medicine or Survival]) at a difficulty of the target's Stamina. Success fills all the target's remaining health levels with bashing damage down to the -4 box; only Incapacitated remains empty.

Steel-Eater: This dull gray, watery acid inflicts only three lethal damage against creatures and quickly loses its potency. When used to target steel objects, such as many weapons or armors, this acid inflicts 10 lethal damage and ignores Hardness. Characters do not soak this. Instead, their weapons or armor soak with their own damage or soak ratings, respectively. Each die of damage left afterward automatically reduces the target object's damage or soak (or health levels, for items neither weapons nor armor) by one. Weapons reduced to +0 damage and armor reduced to no soak are considered destroyed. Some weapons or armors, especially family heirlooms, may be reparable at the Storyteller's discretion.

CHARISMA

ANIMAL AND TRAINING CHARMS

DOG-TONGUE METHOD
Cost: 1m, 1wp; **Mins:** Charisma or Perception 2, Essence 2;
Type: Simple
Keywords: Combo-OK
Duration: One scene
Prerequisite Charms: Any Charisma Excellency

Stewards may communicate with all things in their domain. Dog-Tongue Method gives a character the ability to speak the many tongues of animals. This Charm makes natural animals (or other creatures that potentially understand the same sounds and gestures) valid targets for *all* social attacks, because the Lunar can now communicate even the most complex ideas to them.

A character may choose to activate this Charm without the Willpower cost. This variation allows her to speak only to animals whose shape she currently takes.

When in animal form, a character using Dog-Tongue Method can also speak any human tongue she knows.

With Perception 2, the character also understands the speech of animals while this Charm is active. Lunars may purchase this Charm with Perception 2 instead of Charisma

2; the Charm is often then called "Dog-Ear Method" and functions only to understand animals until the character also has Charisma 2. Purchasing the Charm in this way requires a Perception Excellency instead of a Charisma Excellency.

PACK INSTINCT AFFIRMATION
Cost: 10m, 1wp, 1xp; **Mins:** Charisma 3, Essence 3;
Type: Simple (dramatic action)
Keywords: Combo-OK, Touch
Duration: Instant
Prerequisite Charms: Dog-Tongue Method

Stewards need faithful companions. The Lunar uses this Charm on a natural animal already loyal to her, and can only use it if she has no familiar. This is a dramatic action of several hours of personal interaction with the animal. Pack Instinct Affirmation functions identically to Spirit-Tied Pet (see **Exalted**, p. 209) except as further noted.

If the animal is the same creature as the character's spirit shape, the Charm increases the Familiar Background by two dots. Characters who have mastered the Shifting Knack Luna's Hidden Face can also use this Charm on animals mutated by the Wyld. Some such creatures require more than three dots of the Familiar Background before they become the character's familiar.

NATURE-REINFORCING ALLOCATION
Cost: 10m, 2wp; **Mins:** Charisma 4, Essence 3;
Type: Simple (dramatic action)
Keywords: Obvious, Touch, Training
Duration: One week
Prerequisite Charms: Dog-Tongue Method

Lunar Exalted infuse their animal companions with greater capabilities. The character spends a week training the target animal, in which time she must spend at least five hours per day on this effort. Each use of this Charm allows the character to endow the target animal with one of the following:

• One additional dot of Strength, Dexterity, Stamina, Wits or Perception; none may be increased more than once.

• One additional dot of Athletics, Awareness, Dodge, Integrity, Martial Arts, Presence, Resistance or Survival; none may be increased past the character's rating in the trait.

• One additional -1 health level; no more additional levels than the creature's Stamina.

• Intelligence equal to that of a six-year-old human; familiars become as intelligent as a full-grown human, acquiring Intelligence 2.

• One point of mutation; giving the creature mutations larger than poxes requires additional weeks of training before it has any effect. Mutations natural or reasonable to the animal have no overt effect on appearance—giving poison to a snake might increase the strength of the poison. Other mutations can make the animal or familiar look quite strange.

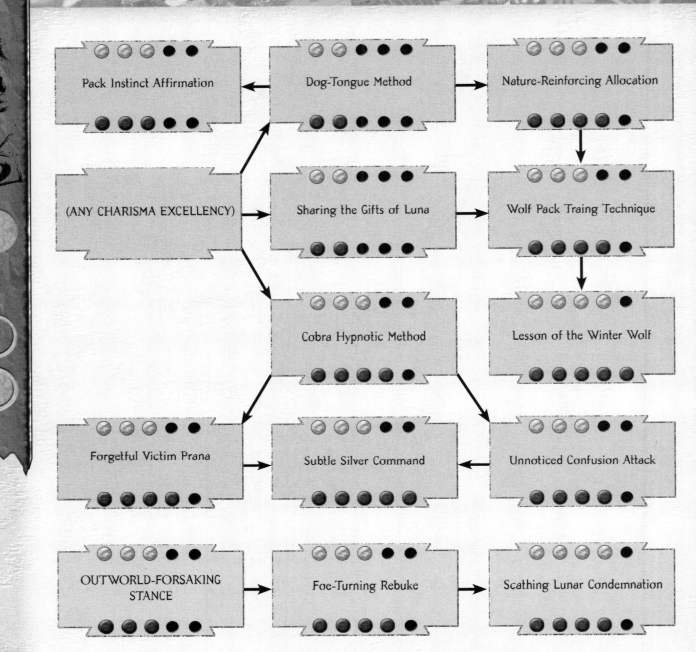

Sharing the Gifts of Luna

Cost: 10m, 1wp, 1lhl; **Mins:** Charisma 4, Essence 3;
Type: Simple
Keywords: Combo-OK, Obvious
Duration: Indefinite
Prerequisite Charms: Any Charisma Excellency

The Lunar Exalted may temporarily empower their follow-ers, servants and friends with their power. A character focuses some measure of her Essence into a bit of her flesh, which she tears away and rolls into a small, bloody ball. By eating this, the Lunar's companion gains a small measure of the Lunar's power. Subjects of this Charm immediately suffer the Enlightened Essence Wyld mutation (see **The Compass of Celestial Directions: The Wyld**, p. **XX**; grants motes equal to [Essence x 10]) and

gain an effective Essence of 2. The target's initial Essence pool is empty. Until the character releases the committed Essence, the target can learn Lunar Charms at normal training time for 12 experience points each. The target only has access to this increased Essence, pool and Charms when this Charm is active (i.e., until the Lunar releases the commitment of motes).

Lunar Exalted can use this Charm on their familiars.

Wolf Pack Training Technique

Cost: 10m, 2wp; **Mins:** Charisma 4, Essence 3;
Type: Simple (dramatic action)
Keywords: Mandate, Obvious, Touch, Training
Duration: One week
Prerequisite Charms: Nature-Reinforcing Allocation, Sharing the Gifts of Luna

Stewards inspire and teach the herd to defend itself—human as well as animal. This Charm trains a military unit and requires five or more hours of effort in any given work to be effective. This Charm increases the Drill of the unit by one for each week of training, to a maximum of four. The character also picks one Trait to improve: Strength, Stamina, Martial Arts, Melee, Stealth or Survival. The Charm increases that Trait for each member of the unit by one, to a maximum of four or the Lunar's rating in that Trait, whichever is lower. The Lunar can train herself (increasing her own Traits) and the unit at the same time.

This Charm can be used with the Mandate of Heaven system. The Charm adds the Lunar's Charisma to any roll to increase a target dominion's Military rating. Using it on the Lunar's dominion increases the dominion's Limit by one.

LESSON OF THE WINTER WOLF
Cost: —; **Mins:** Charisma 5, Essence 4; **Type:** Permanent
Keywords: None
Duration: Permanent
Prerequisite Charms: Wolf Pack Training Technique

This Charm permanently enhances Wolf Pack Training Technique. The Lunar trainer becomes able to train an individual or unit to proof them against fear. This requires one invocation of Wolf Pack Training Technique per dot of the target's Conviction before it becomes effective and complete. The process may work many ways, but always involves a brutal separation of the targets from their fear. Warriors who have completed this lesson never make or fail Valor checks while in the Lunar's service. Exalted cannot be targeted by this Charm.

HOLY CHARMS

OUTWORLD-FORSAKING STANCE
Cost: 3m; **Mins:** Charisma 3, Essence 3;
Type: Reflexive (Step 2)
Keywords: Combo-OK, Holy, Obvious, Social
Duration: Instant
Prerequisite Charms: None

Stewards stand strong against the blandishments of Creation's enemies. The character makes an argument that shapes his belief, protecting him from untoward influences. When activated in response to a social attack from a creature of darkness, this Charm acts as a perfect mental parry that defends even against unblockable social attacks. Outworld-Forsaking Stance may also be activated as a part of a physical parry or dodge, adding (Charisma) to the chosen Defense Value—but only against an attack from a creature of darkness.

FOE-TURNING REBUKE
Cost: 4m; **Mins:** Charisma 4, Essence 3; **Type:** Simple
Keywords: Combo-OK, Compulsion, Holy, Obvious, Social
Duration: (Essence x 2) actions
Prerequisite Charms: Outworld-Forsaking Stance

With a single word, the Lunar shames the enemies that he and Creation share, forcing them to leave him and his alone. The player rolls (Charisma + Presence) at a difficulty of the target's Mental Defense Value. If the roll succeeds, targeted creatures of darkness must cease approaching him and any people who are obviously under his protection. Shaking off this compulsion costs three points of Willpower. By spending a point of Willpower when activating this Charm, the Lunar may use this Charm with his Performance ability and target all creatures of darkness within range instead of just one.

SCATHING LUNAR CONDEMNATION
Cost: 8m, 1wp; **Mins:** Charisma 4, Essence 4;
Type: Simple
Keywords: Combo-OK, Compulsion, Holy, Obvious, Social
Duration: Instant
Prerequisite Charms: Foe-Turning Rebuke

Powerful Stewards can banish creatures of darkness completely from the Lunars' territories, sending the foul monsters away for a long time. Invoking this Charm, the player rolls (Charisma + Presence) against a single target or (Charisma + Performance) against a group; against creatures of darkness, double the successes before subtracting the target's Mental Defense Value as an external penalty. If the roll succeeds, the target creature must travel as far from the Lunar's presence as it can manage within the scene or spend two points of Willpower to resist. Creatures of darkness are more susceptible—they must spend *four* points of Willpower or travel away from the Lunar for the rest of the *story*. A character may only use this Charm on a single target or target group once per story.

Scathing Lunar Condemnation is perfect for use with a Performance roll to clear out enemy creatures of darkness. This Charm is most effective at eliminating lower-level enemies, because powerful creatures of darkness usually have the Willpower reserves to combat its effects.

FASCINATION CHARMS

COBRA HYPNOTIC METHOD
Cost: 7m; **Mins:** Charisma 4, Essence 3; **Type:** Simple
Keywords: Combo-OK, Obvious, Social
Duration: (Essence) actions
Prerequisite Charms: Any Charisma Excellency

Manifesting the hypnotic swaying that many creatures evince, the Lunar can slow or stop her enemies in their tracks. She may use this Charm in physical or social combat; in social combat, its Speed is six long ticks. The Lunar's player rolls (Charisma + [Presence for single targets, or Performance for groups]). Any person whose Mental Defense Value is less than the rolled successes stops. That person immediately becomes Inactive for a number of actions equal to the Lunar's Essence. This unnatural mental influence can be overcome by spending two points of Willpower.

Lunars use this technique in order to attack their victims without resistance, to escape from crowds and for many other purposes.

FORGETFUL VICTIM PRANA

Cost: 5m; **Mins:** Charisma 4, Essence 3; **Type:** Simple
Keywords: Combo-OK, Social
Duration: (Essence) actions
Prerequisite Charms: Cobra Hypnotic Method

Lunars use this Charm to work in peace, and without leaving an incriminating trail. Forgetful Victim Prana causes unnatural mental influence on up to (Essence) targets, or up to a unit of (Essence) Magnitude if the Lunar spends an additional point of Willpower. Used in social combat, the Charm's Speed is six long ticks. The Lunar's player rolls (Charisma + [Presence for individuals or Performance for social units]) against the highest Mental Defense Value of all her targets.

If the roll succeeds, all targets will forget everything they experience for the next (Essence) actions, once the Charm ends. Until the Charm ends, affected targets act and react normally to whatever they experience, but they forget it all, including the activation of the Charm. Once the Charm is over, victims may spend one point of Willpower to remember what occurred for a scene or three points all at once to remember forever—if they ever have reason to try remembering.

The Charm affects memories, not physical evidence, and some changes are jarring. Wounds inflicted, objects broken and great distances moved become sources of remarkable confusion. A guardswoman who suddenly finds herself holding her sword may believe she drew it out for polishing or out of boredom, but not if there's blood on it. In social events, this Charm is often more subtle. Movement at a party is easy to rationalize, as is picking up or leaving behind a drink or courtesan. Compulsions or Intimacies gained from forgotten social attacks remain, but often feel like the target's own inspiration.

UNNOTICED CONFUSION ATTACK

Cost: 4m; **Mins:** Charisma 4, Essence 3; **Type:** Supplemental
Keywords: Combo-OK, Social
Duration: Instant
Prerequisite Charms: Cobra Hypnotic Method

This Charm may supplement any social attack, allowing the Exalt's player to roll (Charisma + relevant Ability) reflexively, and makes anyone whose Mental Defense Value is less than the successes on that roll forget the supplemented social attack. This unnatural influence may still be countered by spending two points of Willpower.

SUBTLE SILVER COMMAND

Cost: 8m; **Mins:** Charisma 5, Essence 3; **Type:** Simple
Keywords: Combo-OK, Compulsion, Social
Duration: Lunar's Presence in days
Prerequisite Charms: Forgetful Victim Prana, Unnoticed Confusion Attack

With the great force of her personality, a Steward shares the power of her will and beliefs with another. This Charm is an unnatural mental influence that the character may exert even on targets that normally are not valid targets for social attacks, such as sleeping people. Such targets may only defend with their Dodge Mental Defense Values and suffer a -2 penalty to that.

The Lunar's player rolls (Charisma + Presence) against the target's Mental Defense Value. Success levies a Compulsion effect on the target to act as though she shares one of the Lunar's powerful beliefs. The target acts as though she has the character's Motivation, one of the character's Intimacies or one Virtue equal to the Lunar's (which must be rated at three dots or higher). This compulsion becomes the greatest thing in the target's life, overwhelming other Intimacies and the target's natural Motivation for the duration.

Targets of this Charm may spend a point of Willpower to resist the compulsion for a full day or three points to cancel it entirely. People targeted when they were unaware of the Charm never know they had anything other than a sudden epiphany. Other targets know the Lunar somehow inspired them to a different belief.

INTERACTION CHARMS

RAPID-SPEECH TECHNIQUE

Cost: 1m per penalty; **Mins:** Charisma 3, Essence 2;
Type: Supplemental
Keywords: Combo-OK, Social
Duration: Instant
Prerequisite Charms: Any Charisma Excellency

Lunar Exalted learn how to get their points across—all of them—without sacrificing effectiveness. Each mote spent on this Charm reduces the multiple action penalties on a single social attack by one, to a minimum of -1.

SECRET SPEECH METHOD

Cost: 5m; **Mins:** Charisma 4, Essence 2;
Type: Supplemental
Keywords: Combo-OK, Illusion, Social
Duration: Instant
Prerequisite Charms: Rapid-Speech Technique

Stewards work in the night to protect what they govern during the day. At times, it would hurt their plans more to be heard by unknown ears than to be ignored. Any social attack supplemented by this Charm can be detected only by individuals selected by the Lunar, up to (Essence x 2) people at a single time. Stewards use Secret Speech Method for secrecy when they suspect the presence of spies or to limit the targets of a broadcast Performance-based attack. The Lunar's player must roll (Charisma + Performance), however. Any non-targeted person whose Dodge Mental Defense Value is less than the rolled successes suffers an *illusion* effect: Instead of the Lunar's message, the person hears ordinary chit-chat, a bloviating speech or some other content-free communication that suits the circumstances.

INSTINCT MEMORY INSERTION

Cost: 3m; **Mins:** Charisma 3, Essence 2; **Type:** Supplemental
Keywords: Combo-OK, Social
Duration: Instant
Prerequisite Charms: Any Charisma Excellency

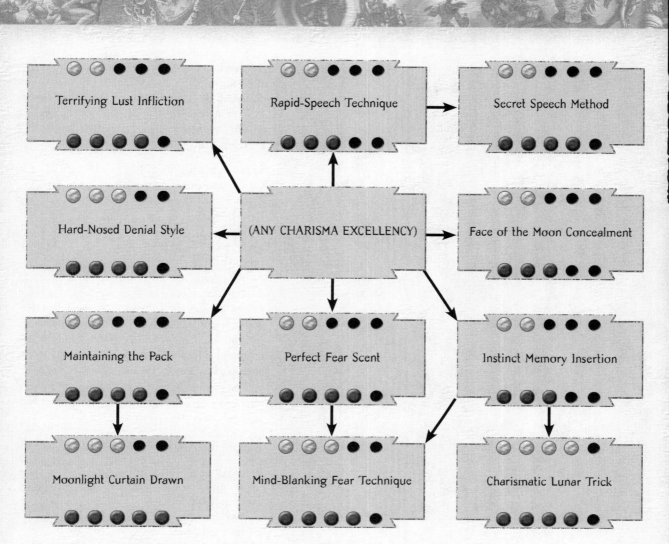

Lunar Exalted tell memorable tales. This Charm supplements a Charisma-based action to relate information to another person, whether it is a long-winded story, a series of brief but complex instructions or boring genealogy of an important family. The information becomes supernaturally memorable to the target or targets, giving them the storyteller's (Charisma) in bonus dice to any attempt to remember the information, details and all, at any point in the future. Lunars use this to pass on their oral history while losing as few details as possible… not that they don't occasionally embellish or leave out embarrassing bits.

CHARISMATIC LUNAR TRICK

Cost: 6m; **Mins:** Charisma 4, Essence 4; **Type:** Supplemental
Keywords: Combo-OK, Social
Duration: Instant
Prerequisite Charms: Instinct Memory Insertion

Lunars can become extraordinarily persuasive, to the point where their influence becomes difficult to shake off. This Charm infuses Essence into any form of natural mental influence the character attempts, forcing people to consider its validity and turning it into unnatural mental influence. It may be resisted with one point of Willpower, as normal.

PERFECT FEAR SCENT

Cost: 5m; **Mins:** Charisma 4, Essence 2; **Type:** Supplemental
Keywords: Combo-OK, Emotion, Social
Duration: One scene
Prerequisite Charms: Any Charisma Excellency

Lunars drive people's fears into the open. This Charm supplements a Social roll to rouse the emotion of fear in one or many targets (using Presence or Performance). The roll takes an internal penalty equal to the group's Magnitude. The Charm exerts unnatural mental influence on any target whose Mental Defense Value is less than the character's successes. The Lunar may inflict a general fear, usually causing panic, or name a specific "fear of X," which everyone then feels. Spending two Willpower allows a character to resist this influence for the scene.

MIND-BLANKING FEAR TECHNIQUE

Cost: 6m, 1wp; **Mins:** Charisma 4, Essence 3;
Type: Simple (5 long ticks)
Keywords: Combo-OK, Illusion, Social
Duration: Instant
Prerequisite Charms: Instinct Memory Insertion, Perfect Fear Scent

CHRIS "SATYR" READY

The Stewards may inflict enough fear to wipe their foes' minds clear. The player rolls (Charisma + Presence + Essence) against a single target's Mental Defense Value. If the roll is successful, the character makes that person believe one memory to be false, a dream or otherwise not real. In effect, the character gets to *remove* one memory from the target's mind. This Charm also creates an instant Intimacy to the belief that the memory is not real. It requires one Willpower per scene to pierce the illusion, and the effect remains until the target breaks the Intimacy completely.

TERRIFYING LUST INFLICTION
Cost: 5m; **Mins:** Charisma 4, Essence 2; **Type:** Supplemental
Keywords: Combo-OK, Emotion, Social
Duration: One scene
Prerequisite Charms: Any Charisma Excellency

Lunars bring out people's desires. This Charm supplements a Social roll to rouse the emotions of hunger, lust or some other physical craving in one or many targets (using either Presence or Performance). The roll takes an internal penalty equal to the group's Magnitude. The Charm exerts unnatural mental influence on any target whose Mental Defense Value is less than the character's successes. The Lunar may inflict general hunger or lust, allowing affected

targets to express the emotion in their preferred manners, or name a specific "lust for X," which everyone then feels. A Lunar can instill any desire whose gratification brings physical pleasure, from alcohol to comfy chairs. Spending two Willpower allows a character to resist this influence for the scene.

HARD-NOSED DENIAL STYLE
Cost: 4m; **Mins:** Charisma 4, Essence 3;
Type: Reflexive (Step 2)
Keywords: Combo-OK, Social
Duration: One scene
Prerequisite Charms: Any Charisma Excellency

Stewards are not easily convinced when they do not wish to be. The character responds to any natural mental influence with a perfect verbal rejoinder, completely defusing the attempt to convince him of something. This Charm functions as a perfect social parry, even against attacks that may not be socially parried, and levies a -2 external penalty on all subsequent natural attempts to make the same, similar or supporting arguments for the rest of the scene.

MILITARY UNIT CHARMS
FACE OF THE MOON CONCEALMENT
Cost: 2m; **Mins:** Charisma 3, Essence 2;
Type: Supplemental
Keywords: Combo-OK, Social, War
Duration: Instant
Prerequisite Charms: Any Charisma Excellency

The Lunar Exalted are masterful guerilla warriors who can lead a unit through thick brush without a trace. This Charm supplements an attempt to conceal a unit for ambush or to disguise a social unit's intentions until the last moment. Subtract the Lunar's Essence from the unit's Magnitude when determining the dice pool for concealment.

MAINTAINING THE PACK
Cost: 4m, 1wp; **Mins:** Charisma 4, Essence 2;
Type: Reflexive (Step 10)
Keywords: Combo-OK, Social, War
Duration: Instant
Prerequisite Charms: Any Charisma Excellency

Lunars have their own personal brand of heroism, and Lunar generals keep their forces intact almost through force of will alone. A character invokes this Charm when the unit he leads suffers damage that would cause it to lose a dot of Magnitude. Instead, the unit remains one health level above Incapacitated and maintains its Magnitude as wounded soldiers refuse to flee the battlefield or confused supporters struggle against disillusionment.

MOONLIGHT CURTAIN DRAWN

Cost: 3m, 1wp; **Mins:** Charisma 5, Essence 3;
Type: Simple (Speed 5 in long ticks)
Keywords: Combo-OK, Obvious, Social, War
Duration: One scene
Prerequisite Charms: Any Charisma Excellency

Stewards can display their might in an effort to protect their peoples. A great moonlit sheen spreads outward from the Lunar's anima, enfolding everyone around him. People in a Lunar's social or war unit redouble their efforts on his behalf, resisting adversity with all their might. Double the effective Magnitude of a unit the Lunar commands for the purposes of defense, to a maximum of (Lunar's Essence x 2).

SOCIAL UNIT CHARMS

HERD REINFORCEMENT STANCE

Cost: 4m, 1wp; **Mins:** Charisma 4, Essence 2;
Type: Simple (Speed 5 in long ticks)
Keywords: Combo-OK, Mandate, Social
Duration: Instant
Prerequisite Charms: Any Charisma Excellency

Stewards help shape societies, strengthening them as appropriate. This Charm targets one person or one social unit, immediately creating a fully fledged Intimacy in the target. The Intimacy is either to the target's native culture or society or to the culture and society to which the target is currently exposed. If the new Intimacy is mutually exclusive with the target's Motivation, the Intimacy fails; if it cannot coexist with an existing Intimacy, the Lunar's player rolls

(Charisma + Essence) at a difficulty of the target's (Conviction + Magnitude) to override the conflicting Intimacy. (Individuals have Magnitude 0.)

When this Charm makes the target have too many Intimacies, one older and weaker Intimacy drops out at the end of the story unless the target makes an effort to retain it. Regardless, Herd Reinforcing Stance also functions as an automatic mental dodge against any attempts to undermine this new Intimacy for the rest of the scene.

Though there is no roll, this Charm uses unnatural mental influence. It may be countered any time within 24 hours of its Charm use by spending two points of Willpower (or four points of Loyalty for a group). After that time, the Charm-created Intimacy becomes natural to the target.

This Charm functions in Mandate of Heaven to add the Lunar's Charisma to a roll in defense against a conquest or diplomatic action that would obviously harm the dominion.

FORSAKING THE BLOOD POSTURE

Cost: 4m, 1wp; **Mins:** Charisma 4, Essence 2;
Type: Simple (Speed 5 in long ticks)
Keywords: Combo-OK, Mandate, Social
Duration: Instant
Prerequisite Charms: Herd Reinforcement Stance

This Charm is the reverse of Herd Reinforcement Stance. Instead of instantly creating an Intimacy for the target's native or current culture, the Lunar creates an Intimacy *against* either of those societies. Assuming the Intimacy remains undisturbed, the target becomes a steadfast antagonist to the relevant culture, rationalizing the hate any way he likes.

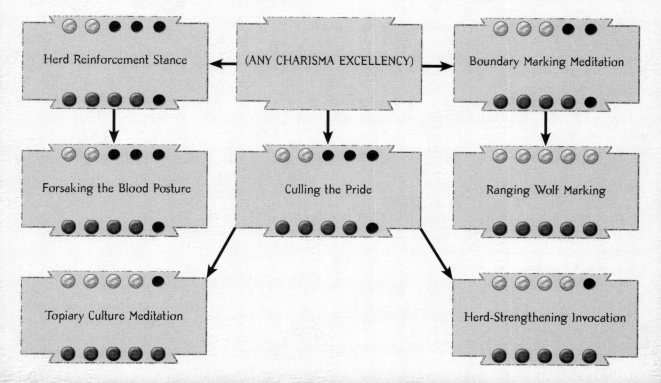

CULLING THE PRIDE

Cost: 6m; **Mins:** Charisma 4, Essence 2; **Type:** Supplemental
Keywords: Combo-OK, Social
Duration: Instant
Prerequisite Charms: Any Charisma Excellency

Lunars excel at tearing the followers and believers away from their foes, leaving a lonely individual with no one to command. This Charm supplements any social attack against a unit and sets the points of Loyalty to resist the attack's compulsion equal to half the Lunar's Charisma.

TOPIARY CULTURE MEDITATION

Cost: 6m, 1wp; **Mins:** Charisma 5, Essence 4;
Type: Simple (6 long ticks)
Keywords: Combo-OK, Mandate, Social, Compulsion
Duration: Instant
Prerequisite Charms: Culling the Pride

Stewards shape cultures by removing weaknesses—or by dictating weaknesses. This Charm's social attack targets a group. The Lunar's player rolls (Charisma + [Performance or Socialize]) with an external penalty equal to the unit leader's Dodge Mental Defense Value plus half the unit's Magnitude. On a success, the Lunar's player names one Intimacy that is part of the target unit's Policy; that Intimacy becomes less valued and harder to defend. The unit must spend two Loyalty points for the group to resist any compulsion that opposes or is opposed by the targeted Intimacy.

The leader can completely remove this unnatural mental influence by spending eight points of Loyalty. Acting against the compulsion for a scene costs one point of Loyalty. Units that break off from a parent unit affected by this Charm must also spend eight points of Loyalty to free themselves of this Charm. Topiary Culture Meditation has no effect on individuals.

In the long term, this Charm makes targeted Intimacies less valuable to the unit. Groups are likely to forsake Intimacies that become too difficult to maintain or otherwise represent a weakness.

Topiary Culture Meditation increases the difficulty of the targeted dominion to resist the Lunar's dominion's conquest or diplomacy actions by two, provided the Lunar can find an appropriate Intimacy held by the target dominion's populace to target.

HERD-STRENGTHENING INVOCATION

Cost: 8m, 1wp; **Mins:** Charisma 5, Essence 4;
Type: Simple (6 long ticks)
Keywords: Combo-OK, Social, Mandate
Duration: Instant
Prerequisite Charms: Culling the Pride

Over the millennia, the Stewards have shaped societies into forms they desired. Lunars use this Charm to keep positive traits in a society while letting others fall to the wayside. Invoking this Charm on a target social unit, the player names a single Virtue (three dots or more) or Intimacy contained within that group's Policy. The unit gains (Lunar's Charisma) phantom points of Loyalty. The unit's leader may spend this in place of normal Loyalty to resist compulsions that oppose the named Virtue or Intimacy.

The phantom Loyalty applies to the entire unit and to subsections of the unit. This pool does not replenish and is gone forever once depleted. Using this Charm twice on the same culture for the same purpose only resets or refills the pool, unless the player names a completely different part of the unit's Policy. In the long term, this Charm can keep certain aspects of a culture constant while others change.

When used with the Mandate of Heaven system, this Charm adds (Lunar's Essence) to the target dominion's Culture rating for any purpose (influencing or resisting influence) involving that Policy.

TERRITORY CHARMS

BOUNDARY-MARKING MEDITATION

Cost: 12m, 1wp; **Mins:** Charisma 4, Essence 3;
Type: Simple (Speed 7 in long ticks)
Keywords: Combo-OK, Mandate, Obvious
Duration: Instant
Prerequisite Charms: Any Charisma Excellency

The land knows its Steward. This Charm claims a territory for the Lunar. The target region must not be owned (see **Exalted**, p. 238) by another Essence channeler, and this Charm makes the character own the territory instantly. Boundary-Marking Meditation cannot target a region larger than (Essence x 10) square miles.

All the little gods within the territory accept the Lunar's primacy; if any did not, the Charm would not have functioned. Within the territory, anyone who is not the Lunar or a native little god suffers a -1 external penalty to all actions. The Lunar may exempt individuals from this penalty by announcing this in the presence of the affected person or revoke this exemption the same way.

Characters who survey the land's geomancy or view it with any form of Essence sight can see the boundaries of the Lunar's territory. Thaumaturges' instruments decipher the boundary as a mystic warning away, as if the land is owned by a being of great power. To Essence sight, the edges of the territory simply glow with a pale moonlight.

In the Mandate of Heaven, this Charm makes the character a savant in the region regardless of Background dots.

RANGING WOLF MARKING

Cost: —; **Mins:** Charisma 5, Essence 5; **Type:** Permanent
Keywords: None
Duration: Permanent
Prerequisite Charms: Boundary-Marking Meditation

This Charm permanently enhances Boundary-Marking Meditation. It increases the maximum area of that Charm's targeted region to (Essence x 100) square miles. Purchasing Ranging Wolf Marking does not automatically expand existing uses of Boundary-Marking Meditation.

Manipulation

Belief Charms

False Burrow Pursuit

Cost: 4m; **Mins:** Manipulation 3, Essence 2; **Type:** Simple
Keywords: Combo-OK, Illusion, Social
Duration: One scene
Prerequisite Charms: Any Manipulation Excellency

The Lunar's magic brings a specific point or detail to the forefront of his target's mind and makes it seem important. The player rolls (Manipulation + Presence) at a difficulty of (the target's highest of Perception or relevant Ability). The relevant Ability depends on what the Lunar gives significance: Awareness for a visual detail or a scent, Socialize or Bureaucracy for particular wordings and Melee to notice something about a person's blade katas, for a few examples. If the roll succeeds, the target notices whatever detail—be it a bent blade of grass in the field, a particular wording at a dinner party or part of a blueprint—and *knows* that it is important. Three points of Willpower throw off this effect.

Mirror Sight Dismay

Cost: 5m; **Mins:** Manipulation 4, Essence 2;
Type: Simple (4 long ticks)
Keywords: Combo-OK, Illusion, Social
Duration: One scene
Prerequisite Charms: Any Manipulation Excellency

Lunar Exalted can be manipulative bastards. With just a word or a well-timed phrase, the character convinces a person or people that one thing they believe is factually incorrect. The Charm won't affect general, emotional attitudes (such as an Intimacy for Lookshy) but can counter specific beliefs (such as thinking Lookshy's alliance with Marukan is a good thing).

The Lunar's player rolls (Manipulation + [Presence or Performance]). Any targets of this Charm whose Mental Defense Values are less than the number of successes on the roll maintain this belief for the rest of the scene. Shaking off this unnatural mental influence costs two points of Willpower. The Lunar's player selects the belief to invert. When using this Charm on many targets at once, it does not affect anyone who does not hold the targeted belief in the first place. The Lunar cannot affect a group whose Magnitude exceeds (his Essence - 1).

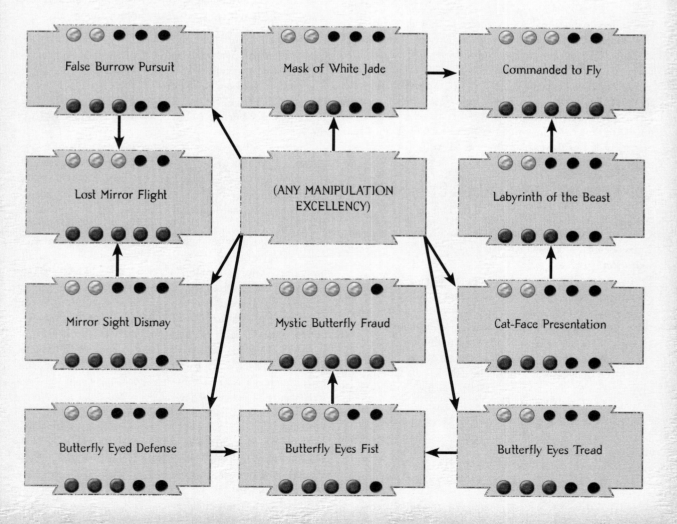

LOST MIRROR FLIGHT

Cost: 4m; **Mins:** Manipulation 5, Essence 3; **Type:** Simple
Keywords: Combo-OK, Obvious, Social
Duration: Instant
Prerequisite Charms: False Burrow Pursuit, Mirror Sight Dismay

The Lunars' experience with the Wyld makes most of them unhappily familiar with madness. Weaving a scene with his words, gestures and convenient props, the character introduces his target to one of the many insanities found in the Wyld. With the end of the speech, the character inflicts that insanity upon the target. The player rolls (Manipulation + Presence) in a social attack that cannot be parried. Success allows the player to name one abnormality of the mind—a strong obsession, phobia or similar malady—that now afflicts the target, at the strength of a debility. At Essence 5, the inflicted derangement can have the strength of a deformity.

Targets of Lost Mirror Flight must spend one point of Willpower to ignore the effects of the madness for a single scene. After subduing the insanity a number of times equal to (Lunar's Essence x 2), the effect ends.

By adding a point of Willpower to the Charm's cost, the Lunar may instead make a (Manipulation + Performance) roll, affecting a group with a Magnitude no greater than his (Essence - 1). Against groups, only lesser insanities apply (the strength of a deficiency).

Storytellers can use the Wyld derangements found in **Exalted** (see pp. 288-289), **The Compass of Celestial Directions: The Wyld,** or this book, pages 209-210, as guidelines for this Charm. They do not derive from Wyld energy, so Charms such as Order-Affirming Blow cannot right them.

DEFENSE AND DISSEMBLING CHARMS

MASK OF WHITE JADE

Cost: 2m; **Mins:** Manipulation 3, Essence 2; **Type:** Reflexive
Keywords: Combo-OK
Duration: Instant
Prerequisite Charms: Any Manipulation Excellency

Lunar Exalted are master dissemblers. When someone takes an action opposed by a difficulty or a roll based on the character's Manipulation, such as trying to read the character's intentions or motivations, the character may activate this Charm to make that action automatically fail. When the opponent's action is supported by a Charm, the character must spend an additional point of Willpower to activate Mask of White Jade.

Multiple characters might use (Perception + Investigation) to detect a lie or deception from the Lunar. When that happens, the Lunar need not activate this Charm multiple times; one activation suffices to make the character unreadable to all observers for a single lie or deception.

CAT-FACE PRESENTATION

Cost: 2m; **Mins:** Manipulation 3, Essence 2;
Type: Supplemental
Keywords: Combo-OK, Social
Duration: Instant
Prerequisite Charms: Any Manipulation Excellency

Lunars' intentions surprise their foes. This Charm supplements a (Manipulation + Socialize) roll to conceal the intention to make a social attack, making it an unexpected social attack. Only supernatural perceptions see through this deception.

LABYRINTH OF THE BEAST

Cost: 2m; **Mins:** Manipulation 3, Essence 2;
Type: Reflexive (Step 2)
Keywords: Combo-OK, Social
Duration: Instant
Prerequisite Charms: Cat-Face Presentation

This Charm briefly renders the Lunar's own mind no more complicated than that of a simple, unenhanced animal, though always a predator. Losing all capacity for language and higher cognition temporarily protects the character perfectly against all forms of natural mental influence. Once the character's intelligence returns, she remembers what was said, but the argument has already become impotent.

COMMANDED TO FLY

Cost: 6m; **Mins:** Manipulation 5, Essence 3;
Type: Reflexive (Step 9)
Keywords: Combo-OK, Counterattack, Social
Duration: Varies
Prerequisite Charms: Mask of White Jade, Labyrinth of the Beast

Lunar Exalted use whatever means necessary to escape unwanted mental influence. This Charm exerts unnatural mental influence on *the Lunar*. The character invokes the Charm as a counterattack, then makes an attack on herself. Her player rolls (Manipulation + Presence) against the Lunar's own Dodge Mental Defense Value (-1 for the counterattack). She may not "throw" the defense—her mental argument must truly convince herself. If it succeeds, the character successfully amends the foreign unnatural influence with additional commands that are impossible for her. Usually, these riders are as outlandishly impossible as the Lunar can make them.

Example: A Solar uses the Hypnotic Tongue Technique to compel Seven Devils Clever to climb a building and report on what she sees there. Successfully using Commanded to Fly, the Lunar amends the command to become "climb a building using only your teeth and report." It may not be truly impossible, but it is implausible enough for Seven Devils Clever now to ignore the unnatural mental influence without spending Willpower.

This resistance lasts only as long as the character leaves the Essence committed. Should she release the Essence while the unnatural influence the Charm amends remains active, she becomes subject again to the compulsion or the need to spend Willpower.

FEINT CHARMS

BUTTERFLY EYES DEFENSE

Cost: 3m; **Mins:** Manipulation 3, Essence 2; **Type:** Reflexive
Keywords: Combo-OK, Illusion
Duration: Until next action
Prerequisite Charms: Any Manipulation Excellency

When the Lunars cannot surpass their foes, at least they can fake it. Whether the Moonchild fights with a grand goremaul or tooth and claw, he seems to move with impossible grace to block or evade any possible attack. Butterfly Eyes Defense does not actually do a thing for the character's Defense Values; the Charm merely makes a foe believe she faces a perfect defense, unless her player succeeds at a reflexive (Perception + Awareness) roll at a difficulty of (Lunar's Manipulation). The target may also spend a Willpower to ignore this unnatural mental influence.

BUTTERFLY EYES TREAD

Cost: 2m; **Mins:** Manipulation 3, Essence 2; **Type:** Reflexive
Keywords: Combo-OK
Duration: Until next action
Prerequisite Charms: Any Manipulation Excellency

Ground that Lunars walk safely may betray others. The Lunar draws her opponent's attention upward, distracting the opponent from the ground. This triggers a reflexive (Perception + Awareness) roll in her target at a difficulty of (Lunar's Manipulation). If the target fails, she fails to notice the treacherous ground. The target may spend a point of Willpower to ignore this unnatural mental influence. When someone affected by this Charm must make any roll to keep her balance or suffers penalties because of the terrain, the difficulty of that roll or the penalties imposed increase by one. Lunars use this to lead people into traps, or just to make their foes more likely to fall.

BUTTERFLY EYES FIST

Cost: 5m; **Mins:** Manipulation 4, Essence 3; **Type:** Simple
Keywords: Combo-OK, Compulsion
Duration: One action
Prerequisite Charms: Butterfly Eyes Defense, Butterfly Eyes Tread

Lunar Exalted distract and confuse their foes to gain advantage. Butterfly Eyes Fist is an action calculated to evoke a specific reaction in the target—it might be a threatening feint or a single, startling word. The Lunar's player rolls (Manipulation + Presence) against a target within (Essence x 10) yards. If the roll achieves more successes than the target's Dodge Mental Defense Value, the Lunar bewilders the target and gets to dictate what combat action the target takes when the target is next able to act. The target may spend two points of Willpower to ignore this unnatural mental influence.

MYSTIC BUTTERFLY FRAUD

Cost: 5m; **Mins:** Manipulation 5, Essence 4;
Type: Supplemental
Keywords: Combo-OK, Illusion
Duration: Instant
Prerequisite Charms: Butterfly Eyes Fist

Luna's tricksters know that the illusion of power is often as useful as power itself. This Charm enables a Lunar to convince onlookers that some ordinary object has magical powers. People actually see the sword blaze with deadly power, the potion purge disease or the jewel glow with channeled Essence.

The Lunar's player rolls (Manipulation + [relevant Ability] + Essence). The Ability may be Melee for an ersatz artifact weapon, Medicine for a phony potion, Lore for a fake hearthstone, or whatever seems appropriate. Any target with a Dodge Mental Defense Value less than the resulting successes sees the supposed magical item perform whatever magic the Lunar suggests. Magical effects of great power, however, can impose external penalties: It's easier to convince people of a false hearthstone than that a false Essence cannon just blew up a fortress. Anyone who spends a point of Willpower sees through the illusion; and the illusion fails as soon as anyone puts the supposed artifact or its effects to the test. For instance, a person might think a "magical" purse turns common pebbles to jade—but when he tries to sell the jade, the buyer sees only pebbles, points this out, and the illusion is revealed.

INTERACTION CHARMS

CHATTERING MAGPIE INFLECTION

Cost: 3m per; **Mins:** Manipulation 3, Essence 1;
Type: Reflexive (Step 1)
Keywords: Combo-OK, Social
Duration: One tick
Prerequisite Charms: Any Manipulation Excellency

The Lunar Exalted are inherently flexible, not just in their form but in their attention. Chattering Magpie Inflection enables a character to make many more social attacks in a single flurry than normal, increasing the rate of all social "weapons" by one for every three motes spent. This Charm can no more than double a social attack's rate.

FALLING LEAF DISTRACTION

Cost: 3m; **Mins:** Manipulation 3, Essence 2;
Type: Supplemental
Keywords: Combo-OK, Social
Duration: Instant
Prerequisite Charms: Any Manipulation Excellency

Lunars are skilled at misdirection, and they are subtle socialites. This Charm supplements any social attack and makes it difficult to notice. Characters using this Charm say something unthreatening and unrelated to relevant topics in such a way that it elicits the proper response to the intended attack. Players of characters targeted by Falling Leaf Distraction Technique may make (Perception + Investigation) rolls at a difficulty equal to the Lunar's ([Manipulation + Socialize] ÷ 2) for their characters to notice the attack's source. Characters recognize they are being convinced of something but generally chalk it up to changing their own minds if they cannot find another cause.

Lunar Exalted use this Charm to conceal social attacks in innocent conversation, oration or even musical performances.

THIRD-VEIL SUGGESTION

Cost: 3m, 1wp; **Mins:** Manipulation 3, Essence 4;
Type: Simple (Speed 3, long ticks)
Keywords: Combo-OK, Social
Duration: One scene
Prerequisite Charms: Falling Leaf Distraction

Lunar Exalted are not limited to one conversation at a time. Shaping words with his Essence, the character can speak to one individual while simultaneously carrying on a separate conversation or oration. Only the target of the Lunar's second speech can hear those words. The character need not speak to the public to conceal his secret words; any significant ambient noise will suffice.

Effectively, the character makes social attacks that only one person notices. The character may change this target within the scene. Talking to conceal the speech does not consume any action. Attacks made in the secret speech benefit from two automatic successes, but remain natural mental influence.

PERFECTION OF THE MOCKINGBIRD

Cost: 4m; **Mins:** Manipulation 3, Essence 2;
Type: Supplemental
Keywords: Combo-OK, Illusion
Duration: Instant
Prerequisite Charms: Any Manipulation Excellency

Even without a person's heart's blood, a Lunar can fool most people about her identity. When making an action to imitate another person's voice, habit or appearance—or just trying not to be recognized as herself—the character may use this Charm to make the imitation supernaturally deceptive. The imitation sounds or looks perfect; no mundane sense can detect a flaw. Supernaturally perceptive creatures may see through the trick.

MILITARY UNIT CHARMS

SCHOOL BECOMES SHARK FORMATION

Cost: 3m; **Mins:** Manipulation 3, Essence 2;
Type: Simple (5 long ticks)
Keywords: Combo-OK, Social, War
Duration: (Essence) actions
Prerequisite Charms: Any Manipulation Excellency

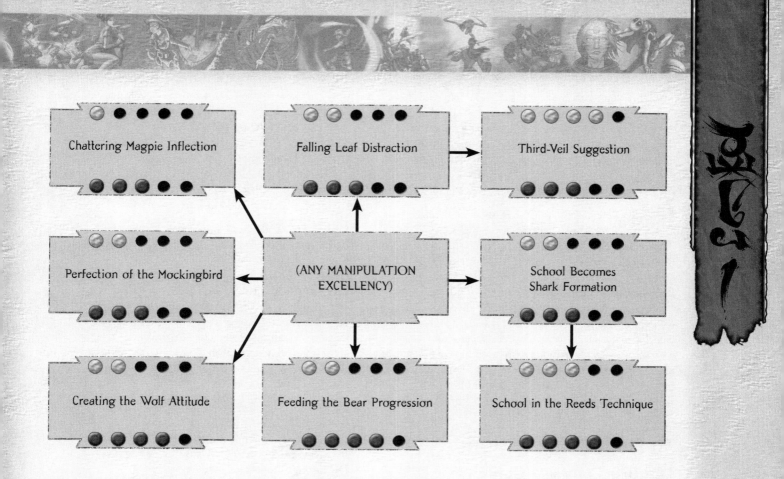

Stewards make the most of limited resources, including people. When leading a unit, the Lunar can invoke this Charm to make her soldiers or followers appear more numerous than they really are. Each soldier may bear two torches or paint figures on his shield; socialites can talk loudly or dance to seem twice as numerous. This Charm targets another unit and calls for a (Manipulation + [War or Socialize]) roll at a difficulty equal to the Perception of the target unit's leader. If the roll is successful, the targeted unit treats the Lunar's unit as double its Magnitude for all purposes until the Charm ends.

SCHOOL IN THE REEDS TECHNIQUE
Cost: 4m; **Mins:** Manipulation 4, Essence 3;
Type: Simple (5 long ticks)
Keywords: Combo-OK, Social, War
Duration: Instant
Prerequisite Charms: School Becomes Shark Method

Through the Lunar's powerful raw personality, she commands the organized dispersal and concealment of her unit—in this way, her unit falls from the eyes of its enemies. This Charm is an action to reestablish surprise in mass combat or social mass combat. The player rolls (Manipulation + Socialize), at a difficulty of the unit's Magnitude. If the roll succeeds, the unit is hidden, imposing an external penalty equal to the Lunar's Essence on Perception rolls to find it until the unit declares itself by taking a new action.

SOCIAL UNIT CHARMS
CREATING THE WOLF ATTITUDE
Cost: 5m, 1wp; **Mins:** Manipulation 4, Essence 2;
Type: Simple (6 long ticks)
Keywords: Combo-OK, Emotion, Mandate
Duration: Instant
Prerequisite Charms: Any Manipulation Excellency

Stewards tell their people what to feel. This Charm is a Manipulation-based social attack to induce the emotion of *fear* in a social group with Magnitude 1+. The character must have spent several hours within the past year encouraging the desired belief within this group before using this Charm, and this Charm must be invoked within the presence of at least one member of that group. The Lunar's player rolls (Manipulation + Socialize), subtracting an external penalty equal to the group leader's Mental Defense Value plus half the group's Magnitude. If the character succeeds, the group feels the emotion.

Creating the Wolf Attitude generates unnatural mental influence. The target group and any group of Magnitude 1+ that breaks off from the target group must spend six points of Loyalty to break free of the influence forever, or one point to ignore the emotion for a scene.

The Lunar may loose pure fear, generally inciting panic. More creatively, the character may bestow fear of *something* within the target populace. The character might invoke fear of an enemy to smooth political efforts. The nature of the fear is up to the Lunar. This Charm has no effect on individuals.

A character may use this Charm as a dominion action, the player rolling (Manipulation + Socialize) instead of a dominion dice pool for appropriate actions. The character must pay the cost for this Charm and any other Charms Comboed with it at the beginning of her next played out scene.

FEEDING THE BEAR PROGRESSION

Cost: 5m, 1wp; **Mins:** Manipulation 4, Essence 2;
Type: Simple (6 long ticks)
Keywords: Combo-OK, Emotion, Mandate
Duration: Instant
Prerequisite Charms: Any Manipulation Excellency

Lunar Exalted encourage lust for life. This Charm is identical to Creating the Wolf Attitude save that this Charm triggers an emotion of *craving*. This can be a general emotion, causing the social group affected to indulge whatever lusts or hungers occur to it. More commonly, the Lunar triggers a craving for a specific indulgence, be it food, love, conquest or Haslanti tapestries.

In the Mandate of Heaven, this Charm uses the same rules as Creating the Wolf Attitude.

APPEARANCE

DISGUISE CHARMS

HIDE OF THE CUNNING HUNTER

Cost: 2m; **Mins:** Appearance 2, Essence 1; **Type:** Reflexive
Keywords: Combo-OK
Duration: Indefinite
Prerequisite Charms: None

This very basic Charm allows the Lunar Exalted to conceal any distinctive marks they might have, including their protective moonsilver tattoos. With just a second of concentration, any of the tattoos, scars or blemishes the character desires fade completely into the Lunar's body, where they cannot be detected by sight or touch. (Supernatural senses still reveal them.) They remain hidden as long as the character commits the necessary Essence.

PERFECT SYMMETRY

Cost: 4m; **Mins:** Appearance 3, Essence 2; **Type:** Simple
Keywords: Combo-OK
Duration: One scene
Prerequisite Charms: Any Appearance Excellency

In nature, creatures that appear more symmetrical are considered more fit to survive, better mates and therefore more attractive. Calling on her Essence, the Lunar gives herself an air of impossible perfection, doubling the maximum Mental Defense Value bonus or penalty she can inflict or benefit from based on difference in Appearance. At Essence 6, the Exalt does away with the limit altogether.

ONE OF THE HERD

Cost: 3m; **Mins:** Appearance 2, Essence 2; **Type:** Reflexive
Keywords: Combo-OK, Illusion
Duration: One scene
Prerequisite Charms: Any Appearance Excellency

Although one water buffalo can tell itself apart from another, a watching predator cannot do so. They see only differences in function—which is the most dangerous, and which are old or sick. Activating this Charm, the character's face looks like everyone around her. Perception rolls to pick the character out

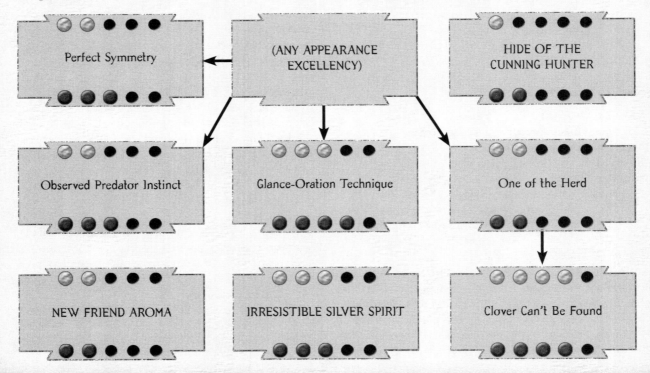

Perfect Symmetry

(ANY APPEARANCE EXCELLENCY)

HIDE OF THE CUNNING HUNTER

Observed Predator Instinct

Glance-Oration Technique

One of the Herd

NEW FRIEND AROMA

IRRESISTIBLE SILVER SPIRIT

Clover Can't Be Found

of a crowd take an internal penalty of the character's Essence. Even if the character is alone, her appearance is so bland that no one can remember it. An observer must spend a point of Willpower to overcome this illusion of anonymity.

CLOVER CAN'T BE FOUND

Cost: 6m, 1wp; **Mins:** Appearance 4, Essence 4;
Type: Instant
Keywords: Combo-OK, Illusion
Duration: One scene
Prerequisite Charms: One of the Herd

Sometimes, it doesn't pay to hide from the world—just the people who are looking for you. After activating this Charm, the character becomes entirely unnoticeable to *all* trying to find her. Not only can they not see her, they cannot discern her presence from the world's reactions. They cannot notice people talking to her or moving around her, or the ripples she makes swimming in a river. Everyone else may notice and interact with the character as normal. Spending two Willpower lets a character perceive the nature of this Charm for a moment; finding a way to stop seeking the character requires only extraordinary mundane self control.

INTERACTION CHARMS

NEW FRIEND AROMA

Cost: 3m; **Mins:** Appearance 2, Essence 2; **Type:** Simple
Keywords: Combo-OK, Social
Duration: One scene
Prerequisite Charms: None

Animals know one another as friend or foe. Lunar Exalted sometimes share this instinctive understanding. A character may invoke this Charm at her first meeting with an individual to convince the target that the Lunar is her friend or foe. The Lunar's player rolls (Charisma + Presence) against the target's Mental Defense Value for this unnatural mental influence. Success creates an Intimacy in the target toward the character as a friend or foe, as desired. Recognizing and rejecting this influence costs one point of Willpower. Only natural mental influence or stronger Charms can make the Intimacy permanent.

OBSERVED PREDATOR INSTINCT

Cost: 4m; **Mins:** Appearance 3, Essence 2; **Type:** Simple
Keywords: Combo-OK, Illusion
Duration: One scene
Prerequisite Charms: Any Appearance Excellency

When a Lunar believes she is being watched, she may activate this Charm to confuse or upset those who spy upon her. Observed Predator Instinct can end their observation or cause them to make mistakes. The character's player rolls (Appearance + [Presence or Performance] + Essence) against the target's Mental Defense Value. People who succumb receive the unmistakable impression that the Lunar knows they are watching her, is watching them

with equal care and is comfortable—if not pleased—with the arrangement.

GLANCE-ORATION TECHNIQUE

Cost: 5m, 1wp; **Mins:** Appearance 4, Essence 3;
Type: Simple
Keywords: Combo-OK, Obvious
Duration: One scene
Prerequisite Charms: Any Appearance Excellency

The Lunar's body language becomes incredibly graceful, eloquent and *effective*. With a single sultry glance, a subtle turn of the head, the lightest caress or many other aspects of body language, the character can communicate as effectively and completely in a silent instant as he can with a lengthy speech. He can use Performance, Presence, Socialize and other Abilities potentially hindered by a lack of speech, and he reduces the Speed of all social combat actions by one while the Charm lasts. Outside of social combat, the character may communicate significant messages instantly.

Furthermore, the character can speak to anyone or anything, regardless of native tongue, though he may not always understand the answer. Many things are unable to comprehend the Lunar's message or respond, such as rocks, but he can still communicate with them easily with only his appearance and body language. This is especially useful when a Lunar finds human form imprudent, but wants to tell someone that a Realm legion approaches or her child is trapped in a collapsed mineshaft.

IRRESISTIBLE SILVER SPIRIT

Cost: 5m, 1wp; **Mins:** Appearance 3, Essence 3;
Type: Reflexive (Step 1)
Keywords: Combo-OK
Duration: (Essence x 2) long ticks
Prerequisite Charms: None

When the Stewards focus their efforts, they can nearly match the Lawgivers in their skill at handling people and cultures. Activating this Charm, the character's personality becomes attractive to those around her. People want to help her, the things she says make sense and she seems very convincing. She could act outgoing and positive or distantly alluring.

Irresistible Silver Spirit adds one automatic success to all social actions (but not her Mental Defense Values). The character ignores fatigue penalties and increases the maximum number of dice she may add from her Social Attribute Excellencies to (Attribute + Essence).

After activating the Charm, the Lunar's player names an objective she wishes to achieve through social combat. Each action, she must make a social attack in an effort to reach that goal. It requires a (Willpower) roll to take any other action (even another social attack), and that suffers a -2 internal penalty. Her player must roll (Willpower) at a difficulty of her Essence in order to end the Charm prematurely.

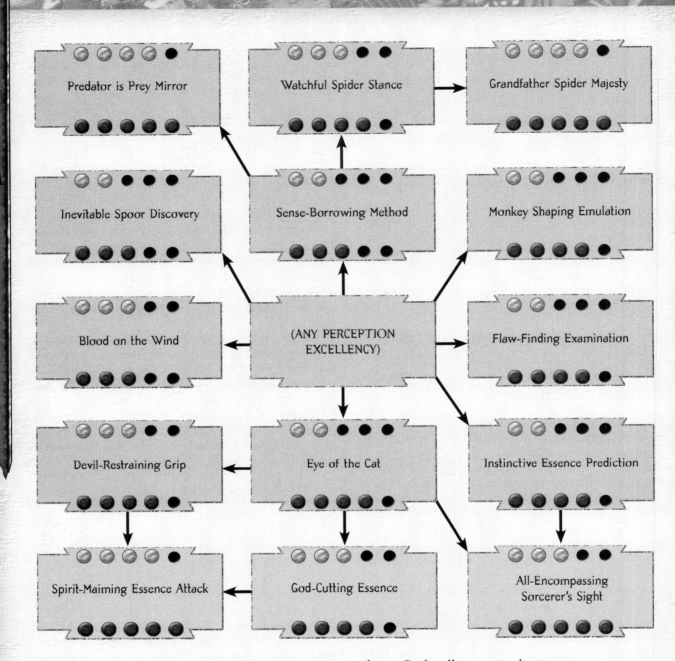

PERCEPTION

CRAFT CHARMS

FLAW-FINDING EXAMINATION

Cost: 8m; **Mins:** Perception 4, Essence 2;
Type: Supplemental
Keywords: Combo-OK
Duration: Instant
Prerequisite Charms: Any Perception Excellency

So-named out of respect for Pasiap's Children's skill with a similar Charm, this Charm allows Stewards to see the flaws in their constructions and correct them—or destroy them. Flaw-Finding Examination supplements either a Craft roll to repair the item or an attempt to destroy it. The player reflexively rolls (Perception + relevant Craft skill). Each success on that roll reduces the time necessary to repair the object by one hour, to a minimum of one hour. If the character attempts to destroy the target, each success adds two dice to damage after the character hits it or one to the character's rating on the feats of strength chart.

MONKEY SHAPING EMULATION

Cost: 5m; **Mins:** Perception 4, Essence 2;
Type: Supplemental
Keywords: Combo-OK
Duration: Instant
Prerequisite Charms: Any Perception Excellency

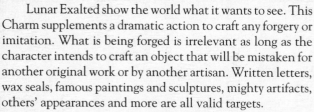

Lunar Exalted show the world what it wants to see. This Charm supplements a dramatic action to craft any forgery or imitation. What is being forged is irrelevant as long as the character intends to craft an object that will be mistaken for another original work or by another artisan. Written letters, wax seals, famous paintings and sculptures, mighty artifacts, others' appearances and more are all valid targets.

The action to create the object takes the normal length of time, but each roll takes no penalty from the attempt at forgery. A Lunar with this Charm has no special advantage in crafting, say, a daiklave that actually functions… but if he can craft it at all, he can just as easily make an exact copy of Tepet Arada's daiklave Restless Wind… or if the Lunar can only forge mundane blades, he can craft an ordinary sword that *looks* just like the famous Tepet heirloom—assuming he knows what it looks like in the first place.

ESSENCE CHARMS

EYE OF THE CAT

Cost: 6m; **Mins:** Perception 4, Essence 2; **Type:** Simple
Keywords: Combo-OK, Fury-OK
Duration: One scene
Prerequisite Charms: Any Perception Excellency

Stewards can see the impossible. The character automatically notices anything within eyeshot, earshot or scent range that is not currently a valid target for a Perception roll based on one of those senses. If it denies the Lunar's player any roll whatsoever to notice or detect something, the Lunar sees it perfectly. This includes immaterial beings such as gods and demons. It also covers targets so perfectly invisible, scentless or silent that there is no chance for a Perception roll. Against targets that the character *could* notice, even if the possibility is slight, this Charm provides no benefit. Add the Lunar's (Essence) in automatic successes when another Charm contests this effect.

Activating this Charm in conjunction with Relentless Lunar Fury provides its benefits for the duration.

DEVIL-RESTRAINING GRIP

Cost: 5m, 1wp; **Mins:** Perception 4, Essence 3;
Type: Simple
Keywords: Combo-OK, Obvious
Duration: One scene
Prerequisite Charms: Eye of the Cat

What the Stewards see, they can command. This Charm targets a single spirit that the Lunar can perceive. The player rolls (Perception + Occult) at a difficulty of the target's Essence as she binds the spirit to her awareness. If the roll succeeds, the spirit cannot stray farther than (spirit's Essence x 4) yards from the Lunar. It may not dematerialize unless the Lunar allows it, and it must materialize if the Lunar wishes. If the spirit lacks enough Essence to pay for the Materialize Charm when the Lunar demands it, the Lunar must pay the balance. If they cannot afford it in a sum, the spirit does not materialize. No Essence is wasted.

GOD-CUTTING ESSENCE

Cost: 1m; **Mins:** Perception 4, Essence 3;
Type: Supplemental
Keywords: Combo-OK, Obvious
Duration: Instant
Prerequisite Charms: Eye of the Cat

Luna imbued her Chosen to overthrow the oppressors of Creation. With her supernal perceptive abilities, the Steward knows exactly where to channel her Essence in order to disrupt even an immaterial spirit. This Charm supplements any attack, allowing it to harm immaterial spirits and inflict aggravated damage against them.

SPIRIT-MAIMING ESSENCE ATTACK

Cost: 3m; **Mins:** Perception 5, Essence 4;
Type: Reflexive (Step 8)
Keywords: Combo-OK, Obvious
Duration: Instant
Prerequisite Charms: Devil-Restraining Grip, God-Cutting Essence

The Stewards have the ability to destroy gods and demons. The character invokes this Charm when he inflicts damage upon a spirit. He adds (Essence) to his *post*-soak damage, and a spirit "killed" by this attack is destroyed permanently.

INSTINCTIVE ESSENCE PREDICTION

Cost: 4m; **Mins:** Perception 4, Essence 2; **Type:** Simple
Keywords: Combo-OK, Fury-OK
Duration: One scene
Prerequisite Charms: Any Perception Excellency

Attuning herself to her sense of burgeoning Essence, the character gains an instinctive sense for how to counter its applications. When anyone the Lunar can perceive activates a Charm or magical effect, the Lunar's player attempts a reflexive (Perception + Essence) roll at a difficulty equal to the Charm's minimum Essence requirement. (Effects without such a minimum are difficulty 1.) Success indicates that the Lunar knows roughly what the Charm does. (Use the labels for Lunar Charm Trees as a guideline for the degree of information the character gains, such as a Strength-based Crippling Charm from a fellow Lunar, or a Performance-based mind control charm from a Solar.) The player adds any threshold successes to contested rolls if the Lunar attempts to resist the target's Charm with another.

ALL-ENCOMPASSING SORCERER'S SIGHT

Cost: 6m; **Mins:** Perception 5, Essence 3;
Type: Reflexive (Step 1)
Keywords: None
Duration: One scene
Prerequisite Charms: Eye of the Cat, Instinctive Essence Prediction

This Charm functions identically to the Solar Charm of the same name. See **Exalted**, page 222.

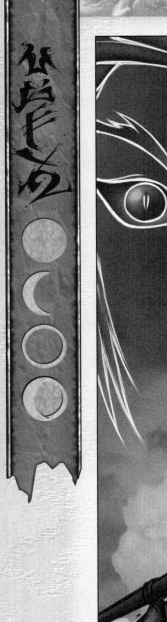

Extended Sense Charms

Sense-Borrowing Method

Cost: 5m; **Mins:** Perception 3, Essence 2; **Type:** Simple
Keywords: Combo-OK, Touch
Duration: Indefinite
Prerequisite Charms: Any Perception Excellency

The Lunar Exalted can tap other creatures for their senses. This Charm requires the character to touch his target. Against animals with ordinary, animal intelligence and Essence 1, the Charm succeeds automatically. Against other targets, the character's player rolls (Perception + Occult + Essence) at a difficulty of (the target's Intelligence + Essence). On a success, the Lunar acquires access to all of his target's perceptions.

Attunement to or relinquishment of the target's sense requires a dramatic action of one minute. While tapping the target's senses, the character shares his target's every sensation: sight, hearing, touch, taste and smell. He depends on his target's Awareness or Perception actions for the volume of information—that is, the target's player rolls to determine what scents or sounds she picks up—but effects that provide automatic successes add to the target's roll to determine what the Lunar notices.

The character remains slightly aware of his own perceptions while experiencing those of his target. The Lunar may take actions at a -3 external penalty. Strong interruptions, such as violent shaking or taking any amount of damage, shock the Lunar directly back to his body, where he suffers a -1 external penalty to all actions for the next five actions.

As long as the Essence for this Charm remains committed, the character may borrow the target's perceptions at any time. The character can affect multiple targets simultaneously as long as he commits the Essence for each of them. Subjects of this Charm usually do not know they are "ridden" in this way, and detecting this Charm is a difficulty 3 (Perception + Awareness) roll even for characters who can see Essence flows.

Sense-Borrowing Method does not allow a character to control his targets' actions or where they focus their senses. The Lunar must use other Charms for such effects.

Predator Is Prey Mirror

Cost: 4m, 1wp; **Mins:** Perception 5, Essence 4;
Type: Simple
Keywords: Combo-OK, Obvious
Duration: One scene
Prerequisite Charms: Sense-Borrowing Method

Enemies of the Lunars fear them terribly, and the reputation is warranted. To really invoke terror and disorient her prey, the character shows the target the hunt from the hunter's perspective. The character may only affect targets within speaking distance. Both the character's and the target's eyes shine silver for a moment, and the Lunar's player rolls (Perception + Survival) at a difficulty of the target's Perception.

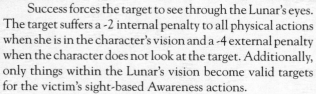

Success forces the target to see through the Lunar's eyes. The target suffers a -2 internal penalty to all physical actions when she is in the character's vision and a -4 external penalty when the character does not look at the target. Additionally, only things within the Lunar's vision become valid targets for the victim's sight-based Awareness actions.

In some cases, a Lunar may use this Charm on an ally in order to share sight. Willing victims make the Charm automatically successful.

Players of characters targeted by this Charm must also roll Valor at difficulty two. Failure indicates that the target's fear overwhelms her. Her Defense Values drop by two.

WATCHFUL SPIDER STANCE

Cost: 6m, 1wp; **Mins:** Perception 4, Essence 3;
Type: Simple
Keywords: Combo-OK
Duration: Indefinite
Prerequisite Charms: Sense-Borrowing Method

Stewards are as aware of their territory as the spider is aware of its web. The character using this Charm becomes completely aware of the region known as her territory. She must own the territory as a person owns an object (see **Exalted**, p. 238); she may target an area no greater than (Essence x 10) square miles at a single time; and she must be within the targeted territory for the Charm to function.

Once the Charm activates, the character may use Perception with any appropriate Abilities to notice or seek out things within the affected territory. Anything that normally would be a valid target for such a roll in her presence becomes a valid target if it lies within her territory. The character may enhance her perceptive abilities with any Charms at her disposal. This awareness of her territory does not conflict with her awareness of her surroundings, and unusual events within her territory merit reflexive (Perception + Awareness) rolls.

Elder Lunars, especially paranoid ones, keep this Charm active at all times.

GRANDFATHER SPIDER MAJESTY

Cost: —; **Mins:** Perception 5, Essence 4; **Type:** Permanent
Keywords: None
Duration: Permanent
Prerequisite Charms: Watchful Spider Stance

This Charm permanently enhances Watchful Spider Stance, and allows the Lunar's player to declare conditions that allow the character to activate Watchful Spider Stance reflexively and immediately observe the phenomenon. Examples include the following:

• When a person or party the Lunar does not know enters the territory.

• Various odd effects, such as unusual weather patterns, cultural migrations or encroachment of the Wyld.

• When a specifically named person enters the territory, subtract successes on any Stealth or Survival roll made

to conceal that person from the Lunar's Perception. If this number is greater than zero, the character may choose to reflexively activate Watchful Spider Stance.

• When a Charm or Essence power is activated within the character's territory, add the power's minimum Essence requirement (if it has one) to the Lunar's Perception. If that number is greater than six, the character may choose to reflexively activate Watchful Spider Stance. Treat powers without a minimum Essence requirement as minimum Essence zero for this purpose.

Players should come up with conditions relevant to their characters. A character may not set more conditions than her Essence.

BLOOD ON THE WIND

Cost: 4m, 1wp; **Mins:** Perception 3, Essence 3;
Type: Supplemental
Keywords: Combo-OK
Duration: Indefinite
Prerequisite Charms: Any Perception Excellency

Once a true predator catches a scent, she never lets it go. This Charm supplements a roll to track someone. Once the character has her quarry's scent, she cannot fail to track that target as long as the Charm remains active. Across hard stone, white-water rapids and through the most overpowering opium dens or raging firestorms, the Lunar does not lose the trail. She automatically gains one success more than the person she tracks in a tracking contest; this does not necessarily imply the ability to catch up.

When competing with opposing Charms, add (Essence) successes to the contested roll to determine which wins out. If the Lunar has tasted her quarry's blood, the Lunar retains a benefit even if the rest of this Charm fails: Even when the Lunar is unable to close distance with her prey due to enemy Charms, the quarry also never accumulates enough successes in the tracking contest to lose her.

INEVITABLE SPOOR DISCOVERY

Cost: 4m; **Mins:** Perception 3, Essence 2; **Type:** Simple
Keywords: Combo-OK
Duration: Instant
Prerequisite Charms: Any Perception Excellency

Stewards know their territory better that most people know their bedrooms. The player makes a (Perception + Investigation) roll to detect the scents or Essence residue left behind by everyone who has passed through an area recently. The number of successes on the roll dictates how far back the character detects. One success provides traces from the last 24 hours, and each additional success doubles that number. The vast catalog of information available on a roll with many successes does not overwhelm the Lunar, and the character knows how recently (or within which time-category) each scent visited.

These scents lack connection to names or faces unless the Lunar is already familiar with a person. Otherwise, the player receives a reflexive (Perception + Awareness) roll to notice the scent of a person identified by this Charm when that person comes nearby. The player makes no more than one such roll per person in a single scene.

Characters may target weapons, concubines or other tools to lift the scents of people who have touched them.

MILITARY UNIT CHARMS

DIVING HAWK INSPIRATION

Cost: 3m; **Mins:** Perception 3, Essence 2;
Type: Supplemental
Keywords: Combo-OK, War
Duration: Until next action
Prerequisite Charms: Any Perception Excellency

The Lunar's example forces others to rise to her challenge. By firing a perfect shot, the character guides all other archers in her unit (whether she commands it or not) in their efforts. Until the Lunar's next action, all ranged attacks by the unit ignore any bonuses its targets gain against ranged attacks due to formation.

BIRD FALLS FROM FLOCK TARGETING

Cost: 3m; **Mins:** Perception 4, Essence 3;
Type: Supplemental
Keywords: Combo-OK, War
Duration: Instant
Prerequisite Charms: Diving Hawk Inspiration

A hawk can dive through a cloud of thrushes and kill only one. Borrowing that perspective, the Lunar uses this

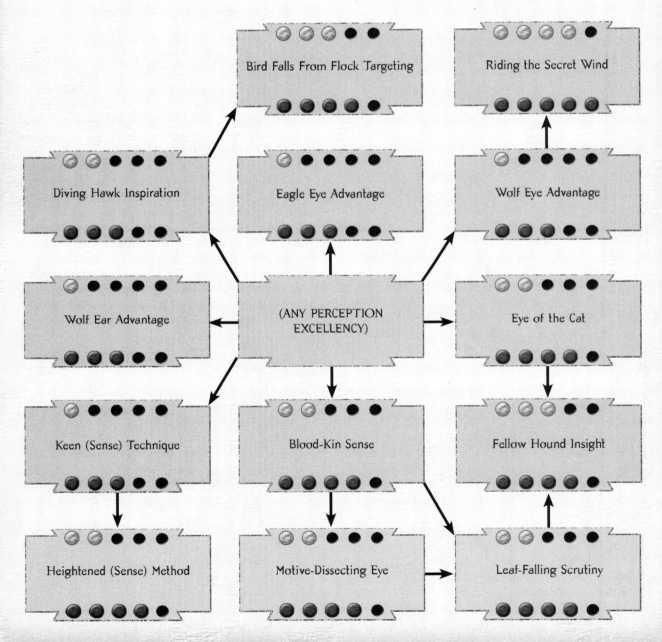

Charm to ignore all external penalties based upon Drill or Magnitude for specifically targeting a commander or special character within an enemy unit. In addition, if the Lunar is a solo unit, he does not need to rely on ranged attacks; he can wade into the enemy unit to attack a special character directly, if he desires.

PERCEPTION ADVANTAGE CHARMS

EAGLE EYE ADVANTAGE

Cost: 2m; **Mins:** Perception 3, Essence 1; **Type:** Simple
Keywords: Combo-Basic
Duration: Until next action
Prerequisite Charms: Any Perception Excellency

By increasing her ability to process what she sees and hears, the Lunar benefits more from the aim action than others do. This Charm is identical to the aim action (see **Exalted**, p. 142) with these exceptions: It is Speed 6, and it may add no more than *six* bonus dice. These dice accrue at the normal rate of one per tick of aiming, and the character can still abort the action at any time to attack her chosen target. If the Lunar chooses, she may continue to take normal aim actions after the Charm ends without losing any extra dice. Dice from this special aiming action do not count as dice from Charms.

Example: Magnificent Jaguar activates Eagle Eye Advantage and begins aiming at a target. For each tick he aims, his player adds one die to the attack he eventually makes on that target. After six ticks (the full action), Magnificent Jaguar's player has six dice to add to that attack. The Lunar chooses to wait, taking normal aim actions until the time is right. Even after several normal aim actions, Magnificent Jaguar still has six dice "banked" for the attack.

WOLF EYE ADVANTAGE

Cost: 1m; **Mins:** Perception 3, Essence 1;
Type: Supplemental
Keywords: Combo-OK
Duration: Instant
Prerequisite Charms: Any Perception Excellency

The Stewards do their work with unclouded eyes. This Charm supplements any action. For that single action, the character ignores all penalties that arise from obscured vision or dulled senses.

RIDING THE SECRET WIND

Cost: 4m; **Mins:** Perception 5, Essence 4;
Type: Supplemental
Keywords: Combo-OK
Duration: Instant
Prerequisite Charms: Wolf Eye Advantage

No obstacle keeps one of the Lunar Exalted from striking his target. This Charm supplements any attack, making any target within range a valid target regardless of walls, hard cover or anything else that might make them an invalid target, so long as the character is aware of them.

He sights down a pathway that does not exist and sends his attack along it to his target, regardless of any mundane barriers in between them.

WOLF EAR ADVANTAGE

Cost: 2m; **Mins:** Perception 3, Essence 1; **Type:** Simple
Keywords: Combo-Basic
Duration: Until next action
Prerequisite Charms: Any Perception Excellency

This Charm functions identically to Eagle Eye Advantage (see pp. 182-183) except it is a modified monologue/study action (see **Exalted**, p. 171).

KEEN (SENSE) TECHNIQUE

Cost: 3m; **Mins:** Perception 3, Essence 1; **Type:** Reflexive
Keywords: Combo-OK
Duration: One scene
Prerequisite Charms: Any Perception Excellency

Keen (Sense) Technique is actually three Charms, functionally identical to the Solar Charm of the same name (see **Exalted**, pp. 225-226).

HEIGHTENED (SENSE) METHOD

Cost: 2m; **Mins:** Perception 4, Essence 2; **Type:** Reflexive
Keywords: Combo-OK
Duration: One scene
Prerequisite Charms: Appropriate Keen (Sense) Technique

The Lunar Exalted are nearly impossible to fool. Heightened (Sense) Method is actually three Charms, covering the same three sets of senses as Keen (Sense) Technique. Activating this Charm doubles any successes the Lunar earns on appropriate Perception rolls before applying external penalties, to a maximum of (Perception) additional successes. Characters in the form of an animal renowned for one of its senses (a bloodhound for scent, an eagle for vision, etc.) double the successes without limit for that sense.

PERSON EXAMINATION CHARMS

BLOOD-KIN SENSE

Cost: 1m, 2m or 4m; **Mins:** Perception 4, Essence 2;
Type: Simple
Keywords: Combo-OK
Duration: Instant
Prerequisite Charms: Any Perception Excellency

Everyone carries traces from the people they care about, and the Lunars can detect them. Blood-Kin Sense allows the character to detect the most important social tie the target has to another person. This is from the target's perspective, which may change with time, or even with mood. The Lunar's player rolls (Perception + Investigation) with a difficulty of the target's (higher of Manipulation or Socialize). Success on this roll reveals the information.

Blood-Kin Sense costs one mote if the social tie is to a blood relative or spouse, two motes for a longtime friend or lover and four motes for a recent friend or a business associate, priest, commanding officer or other important person in the target's life. People almost certainly have Intimacies toward the individuals they consider their most important social connections. If the object of this connection is present, the Lunar knows who it is in addition to the connection's meaning to the target. Otherwise, the character only learns about the connection and not to whom it points—this Charm does not reveal names or appearances.

By spending four motes instead, the Lunar may simply declare an individual (whom the character must have met). Then, the Charm serves to determine the target's relationship with the named individual and the importance thereof to the target. Tasting the target's blood, at most a day before using this Charm, adds one success to the roll.

Lunars can use this Charm with an automatic success on any form they can take with their natural shapeshifting powers.

MOTIVE-DISSECTING EYE

Cost: 3m; **Mins:** Perception 4, Essence 2; **Type:** Simple
Keywords: Combo-OK, Fury-OK
Duration: Instant
Prerequisite Charms: Blood-Kin Sense

Lunar Exalted have incredible insight into the souls of others. This Charm allows the character's player to roll ([Perception or Intelligence] + Investigation) at difficulty 1. Subtract an external penalty of ([the target's Manipulation + Socialize] ÷ 2). On a success, the character learns one of the following about the target (player's choice):

• Motivation
• Primary Virtue
• A chosen Virtue's value
• A previously unknown Intimacy
• A current intention, desire or emotion, including intent to attack someone

A character may attempt to learn many of these things simply by reading other people (see **Exalted**, p. 131), but this Charm provides that information more quickly, and often without any evidence on the target's part. When this Charm is activated as a part of Relentless Lunar Fury, the character's heightened awareness makes him aware of all attacks upon him.

LEAF-FALLING SCRUTINY

Cost: 2m; **Mins:** Perception 4, Essence 2; **Type:** Reflexive
Keywords: Combo-OK
Duration: Instant
Prerequisite Charms: Blood-Kin Sense

Stewards know who resides within their territories and what they can do. Lunars read people well, finding the smallest tells of familiarity and habit to determine a person's training. They use this Charm in the following three ways:

• The Lunar may target specific individuals and determine if the target has a faculty with one named Ability. In general, this tells the player the target's rating in the named Ability.

• A character may also examine someone and determine that person's highest-rated Ability. In the case of a tie, the character learns one and knows that there are others; further invocations of Leaf-Falling Scrutiny reveal skills not yet perceived by the Lunar.

• The player can name an Ability, and the character judges everyone within her sight. The character detects people who possess the Ability at three dots or higher. People the character does not see (because they use Stealth or other means to remain unnoticed) are not judged. The group's Magnitude may not exceed the Lunar's permanent Essence.

This Charm allows a reflexive (Perception + [the named Ability] roll at standard difficulty. When targets want to conceal their skills or natures, the difficulty becomes the target's (higher of Manipulation or Socialize).

Lunars use the mass version of this Charm to quickly find people suited for a particular task: sailors to man a boat or warriors for a raid, for example.

FELLOW HOUND INSIGHT

Cost: 2m; **Mins:** Perception 4, Essence 3; **Type:** Reflexive
Keywords: Combo-OK
Duration: Instant
Prerequisite Charms: Eye of the Cat, Leaf-Falling Scrutiny

The Lunar Exalted recognize their own and can sniff out other supernatural creatures. When a character activates

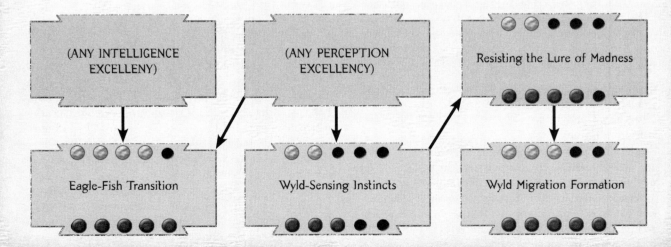

this Charm, his player names a type of supernatural creature. A single sniff or glance informs the character whether any being of that type is within (Essence x 5) yards, if the player succeeds at a (Perception + Essence) roll with a difficulty of the highest permanent Essence of any creature in the area, whether it's the named type or not (but not counting the Lunar himself). The Lunar also knows who falls into that category out of those people he can detect.

Although there is a little or least god for nearly every thing in Creation, only self-aware and active gods trigger Fellow Hound Insight. Otherwise, activating it to detect gods in Creation would be a near-pointless endeavor.

WYLD PERCEPTION CHARMS

WYLD-SENSING INSTINCTS

Cost: 3m, 1wp; **Mins:** Perception 3, Essence 2;
Type: Simple
Keyword: Combo-OK, Wyld
Duration: Indefinite
Prerequisite Charms: Any Perception Excellency

By honing her senses, the Lunar attunes herself to the ebbs of the Wyld around her. So long as the character keeps this Charm active, the character's player may roll (Perception + Awareness) to detect where the Wyld is nearest, where it is strongest and how dangerous it may be to her or her companions. After a simple roll, she may determine these things within a number of miles equal to her rolled successes.

Outside of Creation, each level of the Wyld (Bordermarches, Middlemarches, Deep Wyld) doubles this range. (The Charm is useless in Pure Chaos, where distance is meaningless and everything is equally dangerous.)

Wyld-Sensing Instincts guarantees that any travel the character leads through the Wyld can avoid its worst perils. Only if her awareness fails her or a malicious intent conspires against her does she risk dangerous winds of Chaos. Even then, the player may make a reflexive (Perception + Awareness) roll to detect the incoming danger, which should provide an advantage in the difficult times ahead. Wyld-Sensing Instincts never tells the character what *sort* of danger the Wyld presents. The Lunar may lead a group of no more than Magnitude 1 through the Wyld safely using this Charm.

A character using this Charm adds (Essence) successes to any Perception-based rolls to examine or find Wyld influence. Rolling (Perception + Investigation) to reconstruct past events, (Perception + Medicine) to determine a creature's cause of death or (Perception + Occult) to examine the Essence resonance would all qualify, so long as the Wyld is involved. The character need not be aware that Wyld is involved ahead of time to gain the bonus, so long as the Charm is active.

RESISTING THE LURE OF MADNESS

Cost: 5m; **Mins:** Perception 4, Essence 2; **Type:** Simple
Keyword: Combo-OK, Wyld
Duration: Indefinite
Prerequisite Charms: Wyld-Sensing Instincts

Even Lunars, with their powerful moonsilver tattoos, can be driven mad or enthralled by the Wyld. This Charm alters the character's perceptions, filtering the true experience of the capering joys and murmuring deaths to prevent madness. The character becomes immune to derangements due to Wyld exposure and Wyld addiction.

When invoking this Charm, the character may also target his companions for similar protection, but no more than make up Magnitude 1. Companions who wander farther than (Lunar's Essence x 10) yards from the character are no longer protected, giving Lunars cause to keep track of their associates.

WYLD MIGRATION FORMATION
Cost: —; **Mins:** Perception 5, Essence 3; **Type:** Permanent
Keyword: None
Duration: Permanent
Prerequisite Charms: Resisting the Lure of Madness

This Charm permanently enhances Wyld-Sensing Instincts and Resisting the Lure of Madness. The maximum Magnitude the character may lead safely or affect with those Charms rises to (the character's Essence - 1).

EAGLE-FISH TRANSITION PROPHECY
Cost: 12m, 2wp; **Mins:** Perception 5, Essence 4;
Type: Simple (dramatic action)
Keywords: Combo-OK, Obvious, Wyld
Duration: Instant
Prerequisite Charms: Any Perception Excellency, Any Intelligence Excellency

Stewards use any means necessary to protect their chosen wards—including the Wyld. Some Lunars learn to read its tides of chaos and narrative nature, as a way to predict future events. Lunars use this to reduce the uncertainty of thaumaturgic astrology.

Eagle-Fish Transition Prophecy is a dramatic action that requires one scene. It resembles vision-questing in the Wyld, wandering through the chaos to find a relevant scene, but this Charm aids the Lunar's perceptions and draws the proper clues to him. The player poses a specific question about the future, such as "Will Lookshy fall if I attack it?" or "How can I find the Sidereal Vlan Mors before he finds my lover?"

Questions that are more specific pose higher difficulties to the (Intelligence + Occult) roll the player makes, as do questions with answers that are more complicated. The simplest yes/no questions are difficulty 1, while very specific questions with potentially lengthy answers are as high as difficulty 5 or 6. Some examples follow:

Difficulty 1—"Will my chosen culture flourish?" "Do the Arczeckhi attack Nexus before I can gather my pack?"

Difficulty 3—"Where do I find the secret to the Empress' defeat?" "Does civil war break out in the current Realm before the 15th day of Ascending Wood of next year?"

Difficulty 5+—"How can I recover the lost Lunar Castes?" "Where am I in exactly 236 days?"

Results play out in a scene that the Lunar observes or experiences. Straightforward answers usually receive straightforward answers: an image of the culture flourishing or the city untouched by war is enough to communicate clearly. Questions that are more difficult reveal scenes that are more complicated, which the character must interact with to find his answer. Some questions have no "simple" solutions, and the scenes they reveal may be improbable, incomprehensible or far from immediately clear or useful.

This Charm has some consequences. Failing to meet the difficulty by two successes or more produces a flawed scene that the character does not realize is incorrect. Botching the roll gives the character a vision of whatever answer he most fears.

INTELLIGENCE

CRAFTING CHARMS

LUNA'S BLESSED HANDS
Cost: —; **Mins:** Intelligence 5, Essence 5; **Type:** Permanent
Keywords: None
Duration: Permanent
Prerequisite Charms: Instinctive Intelligence Unity, Lunar Blade Reconfiguration

Lunar Exalted are unparalleled at crafting their native magical material. This Charm permanently enhances a Lunar's capabilities, reducing by one the minimum Craft, Lore and Occult requirements required for the character to craft artifacts that are completely or mostly forged from moonsilver.

FORM-FIXING METHOD
Cost: 5m, 1wp, 3xp; **Mins:** Intelligence 4, Essence 3;
Type: Simple (dramatic action)
Keywords: Shaping
Duration: Instant
Prerequisite Charms: Any Intelligence Excellency

The single most important Charm known to Lunars creates the magical tattoos that protect them from the Wyld and fix their castes. The entire process of tattooing can take days—as long as the character thinks is necessary to get a feel for the novice Lunar's aptitudes and life story. The user of this Charm also needs mundane tools and certain Abilities to prepare and use the moonsilver ink: Lore 3 to create the ink and Craft (Air or Wood) 1 to perform the tattooing. Alternatively, the character can do the work entirely by magic using Lunar Blade Reconfiguration. (This is not a Combo; the Charms may be used together by special dispensation.) The experience points spent are gone forever.

Note that this Charm also presumes the character himself is a tattooed Lunar: the Charm draws upon the stabilizing magic in the character's own body to impart the enchanted tattoos to another Lunar. Recreating the moonsilver tattoos from *scratch* would involve crafting a four-dot artifact. Even with the help of Luna's Blessed Hands, the intrepid character would need multiple Attributes and Abilities rated 5 or higher.

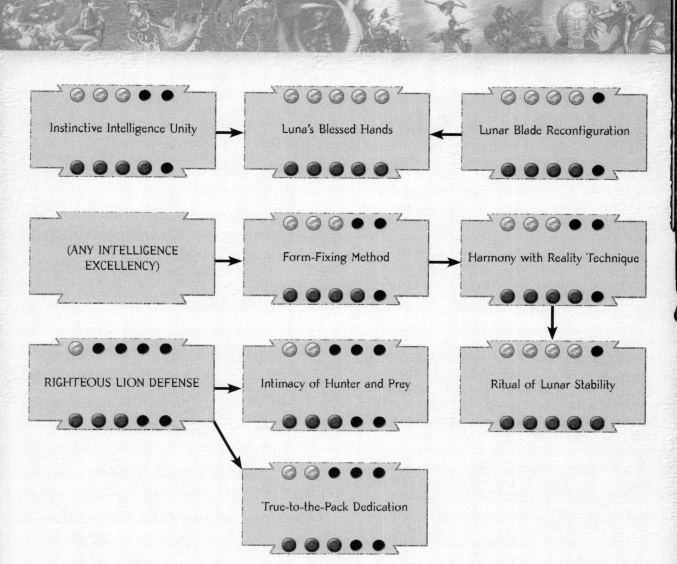

Instinctive Intelligence Unity → Luna's Blessed Hands ← Lunar Blade Reconfiguration

(ANY INTELLIGENCE EXCELLENCY) → Form-Fixing Method → Harmony with Reality Technique

RIGHTEOUS LION DEFENSE → Intimacy of Hunter and Prey   Ritual of Lunar Stability

True-to-the-Pack Dedication

HARMONY WITH REALITY TECHNIQUE

Cost: 10m or 20m, 1wp; **Mins:** Intelligence 4, Essence 3;
Type: Simple
Keywords: Combo-OK, Obvious, Shaping, Touch, Wyld
Duration: Instant
Prerequisite Charms: Form-Fixing Method

Stewards' dedication can pull wonders from the dreamland of the Wyld. This Charm uses the connection between Wyld and Creation inherent in every Lunar to make the target, one creature or object of any size, natural to and safe within Creation. To work this Charm, the Lunar must alter a target object in some way, such as drawing her personal symbol upon it; a living creature must hold or wear something the Lunar made with her own hands.

Portable objects affected by this Charm may be brought out of the Wyld without fear that they will evaporate into figment, while living things may leave the Chaos and live out their days in Creation without degenerating under the weight of its stasis. Objects too large to move do not fade quickly in the Wyld, though they become susceptible to its mutative energies just like any structure built out of Creation-based materials. Lunars sometimes use this Charm to stabilize buildings, caves or other small places created by the

Wyld to use them for bases of operation. A Lunar may also want to preserve some oddity of the Wyld for study. Used at the edge of Creation, Lunars can slowly push back the Wyld's boundaries a little patch of ground at a time. Using this Charm on objects too large to be moved costs 20 motes; all other uses cost 10 motes.

Things maintained by this Charm do not have their own reality. They share the Steward's reality and that of Luna and Gaia. Unless someone in Heaven undertakes to connect the person or object to the Loom of Fate, the object remains only partially real. If an object tied to Creation by this Charm does not interact meaningfully with things naturally of Creation during a story, roll the Lunar's Essence at difficulty 1, difficulty 2 if it does not interact with real things *at all*. Three cumulative failures on this roll indicate that the object's reality is lost, and it fades away.

Creatures who were once part of Creation but are now too mutated to survive within it suffer a level of unsoakable bashing damage when the Essence roll fails. This damage cannot heal naturally unless the creature recuperates in the Wyld. After six cumulative failures on the roll, Creation becomes inhospitable to the creature as normal, generally forcing it to return to the Wyld.

RITUAL OF LUNAR STABILITY
Cost: 10m, 1wp; **Mins:** Intelligence 5, Essence 4;
Type: Simple (Dramatic Action)
Keywords: Combo-OK, Obvious, Shaping, Wyld
Duration: One lunar month
Prerequisite Charms: Harmony with Reality Technique

Stewards must be able to protect their lands from the dangers of the Wyld. Activating this Charm is a dramatic action that requires the Lunar to pace the boundaries of her territory and mark it with Essence. This Charm affects a maximum area of one waypoint, the basic geographical unit of the Wyld—about 30 miles across. The Charm fails if anyone interrupts the Lunar before its completion.

Once the character has invoked the Charm, the Wyld energies in the region become quiescent. While the local abnormal physical (and metaphysical) laws remain the same, they do not change as long as the Charm remains effective. This Charm cannot affect territory owned (see **Exalted**, p. 283) by another Essence user, which are more common in the Wyld than in Creation. While the Charm is active, Fair Folk (and other Wyld denizens) with Essence less than the Lunar's cannot affect the region with shaping actions or effects.

A Lunar cannot always stay to protect the territory she claims in the Wyld. By sacrificing one dot of *permanent* Willpower (which the character may regain through experience points), the character no longer needs to spend further Willpower to maintain the Ritual of Lunar Stability and can give the Charm its monthly 10 motes no matter where she is. The perpetuated Charm is tied to a small object of the Lunar's choice; destroying the object instantly destroys the Charm.

Lunars use this Charm to solidify their personal redoubts or make their lands safer against the Wyld. In the First Age, the Ritual of Lunar Stability often accompanied an invocation of Wyld-Shaping Technique in the Deep Wyld to protect the new annexation from being reabsorbed by chaos.

DEFENSIVE CHARMS

RIGHTEOUS LION DEFENSE
Cost: —; **Mins:** Intelligence 3, Essence 1; **Type:** Permanent
Keywords: None
Duration: Permanent
Prerequisite Charms: None

This Charm is identical to the Solar Charm of the same name (see **Exalted**, p. 199) with the following change. Rather than making inviolate an Intimacy to any ideal, the Lunar must choose an Intimacy dedicated to the protection of something, be it a way of life, a place, a society or a specific individual.

INTIMACY OF THE HUNTER AND THE PREY
Cost: 6m, 1wp; **Mins:** Intelligence 3, Essence 2;
Type: Reflexive
Keywords: Combo-OK
Duration: Instant
Prerequisite Charms: Righteous Lion Defense

Lunars make it their duties and their lives to catch their prey. This Charm prevents a Lunar from betraying the hunt. The player declares a target the character currently attempts to capture or kill. Intimacy of the Hunter and the Prey forms an immediate connection between the Lunar and her target, creating a magically backed Intimacy towards that hunt. She treats mental influence to betray or forsake that hunt as an unacceptable order.

When the hunt ends, the Intimacy fades away. A character may have no more than (Essence) Intimacies empowered by this Charm at one time.

TRUE-TO-THE-PACK DEDICATION
Cost: 5m, 2wp; **Mins:** Intelligence 3, Essence 2;
Type: Reflexive
Keywords: Combo-OK, Fury-OK
Duration: Instant
Prerequisite Charms: Righteous Lion Defense

Lunar Exalted often feel unbreakable bonds to their packmates. Activating this Charm instantly shatters any mental influences on the Lunar that turn him against his pack, his Solar mate, other Lunar Exalted or Luna. The character may activate True-to-the-Pack Dedication as a perfect defense against such mental attacks.

Knowing this Charm also allows the character to designate whom he considers "his pack" by touching a person and spending a mote. He may mark no more than (Compassion x 2) individuals.

Activating this Charm with Relentless Lunar Fury perfectly protects the character against any mental influence that costs two Willpower points or less to overcome. This protection lasts as long as the fury itself.

INSIGHT CHARMS

COUNTING THE ELEPHANT'S WRINKLES
Cost: 1m; **Mins:** Intelligence 3, Essence 1; **Type:** Reflexive
Keywords: Combo-OK
Duration: Instant
Prerequisite Charms: None

Stewards have excellent memories for the past. This Charm allows the character to recall anything he has learned or observed with perfect clarity. Using the Charm calls for a (Intelligence + Lore) roll, although another Ability might be appropriate for certain subject matters. Even a single success calls back the memory in question in flawless and true detail. When the Charm is used to remember something originally conveyed with Instinct Memory Insertion (see pp. 166-167), success is automatic.

INEVITABLE GENIUS INSIGHT
Cost: 5m, 1wp; **Mins:** Intelligence 3, Essence 2;
Type: Simple
Keywords: None
Duration: One project
Prerequisite Charms: Any two Intelligence Excellencies

Lunar Exalted are brilliant, if erratic. Focusing her Essence, the character expands her mind and senses to encompass greater things. She becomes an unstoppable mental juggernaut, nearly immune to distraction and capable of reaching heights previously beyond her. Lunars used this Charm after the Usurpation to develop the moonsilver tattoos that protect them.

When the character activates this Charm, the player declares a single project or research target for the Charm. While this Charm is active, the character adds one success to all rolls related to her chosen research. Increase the maximum number of dice she may add to any rolls based on mental Attributes by her Essence. She ignores all fatigue penalties.

Until the project's completion, the player must make a successful (Willpower) roll in order to take actions unrelated to her declared focus for a scene. Those suffer a -2 penalty. To end the Charm before concluding the project, the player must roll (Willpower) at a difficulty of (Temperance), something she may only attempt once per scene.

LESSONS IN THE BLOOD

Cost: 1m, 1wp; **Mins:** Intelligence 4, Essence 4;
Type: Simple
Keywords: None
Duration: One scene
Prerequisites: Any Intelligence Excellency

By spending a point of Willpower and a mote of Essence while tasting another person's blood, the Lunar may temporarily use that person's Abilities and memories. The Lunar does not have to take the person's shape (though this Charm can be used with Prey's Skin Disguise and Life of the Hummingbird). He may also call on the Abilities of a sentient creature whose shape he previously took using Prey's Skin Disguise or other Knacks. For the next scene, the character can use either his own Ability or the other person's, whichever rating is greater. Once the Charm's duration ends, the memories and Abilities vanish forever. This Charm can only be used once per person, ever. Lunar Exalted usually reserve this Charm for important short-term impersonations and emergency skill uses.

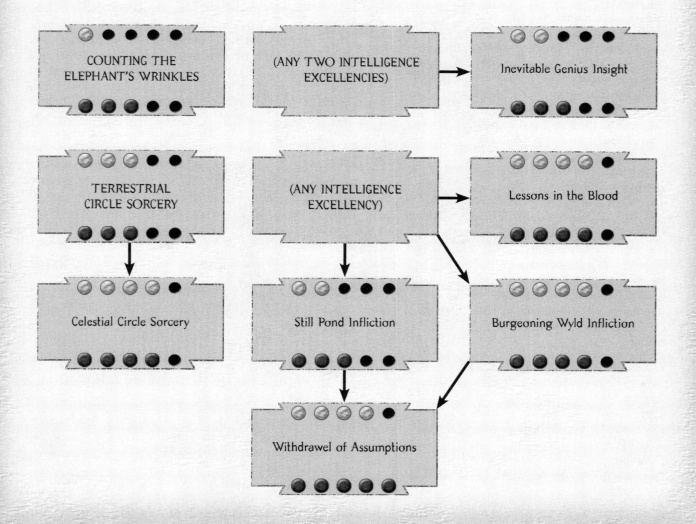

SORCERY CHARMS

TERRESTRIAL CIRCLE SORCERY

Cost: —; **Mins:** Intelligence 3, Essence 3; **Type:** Permanent
Keywords: None
Duration: Instant
Prerequisite Charms: None

This Charm allows the character to take Terrestrial Circle Sorcery actions. See **Exalted**, page 220 and page 252.

CELESTIAL CIRCLE SORCERY

Cost: —; **Mins:** Intelligence 4; Essence 4; **Type:** Permanent
Keywords: None
Duration: Instant
Prerequisite Charms: Terrestrial Circle Sorcery

This Charm allows the character to take Celestial Circle Sorcery actions. See **Exalted**, pages 220-221 and page 252.

WYLD CHARMS

STILL POND INFLICTION

Cost: 4m; **Mins:** Intelligence 3, Essence 2; **Type:** Simple
Keywords: Combo-OK, Touch
Duration: Instant
Prerequisite Charms: Any Intelligence Excellency

When Fair Folk threaten Creation, the Stewards deny them ground—and sustenance. With a mere touch, the Lunar dims all sense of a single target's emotions, desires and Virtues. For (Lunar's Essence) days, a mortal target benefits from +1 Mental Defense Value, the difficulty to read the target's mental state increases by one and the target becomes proof against any attempt to consume his Virtues for sustenance, as the Fair Folk do. This Charm only works on mortals; the Stewards can look out for themselves.

BURGEONING WYLD INFLICTION

Cost: 5m, 1wp; **Mins:** Intelligence 4, Essence 4;
Type: Simple
Keywords: Combo-OK, Obvious, Shaping, Stackable, Touch
Duration: (Lunar's Essence) days
Prerequisite Charms: Any Intelligence Excellency

Stewards aid their charges in indirect ways. Applying Wyld Essence with a caress or well-placed strike, the Lunar triggers a sudden mutation in her target. Against unwilling targets, the character can communicate this effect with a normal attack that inflicts no damage.

The Lunar's player rolls (Intelligence + Essence) at a difficulty of the target's Essence. Targets may submit willingly, adding one automatic success to the roll. Each success in the roll's threshold becomes one point of mutation the character may dictate in the target. Mutations develop over the next five minutes, often painfully.

The Lunar has no power to make these changes permanent. The recipient does, if he has sufficient experience points to spend (see p. 101).

WITHDRAWAL OF ASSUMPTIONS

Cost: 3m, 1wp; **Mins:** Intelligence 5, Essence 4; **Type:** Simple
Keywords: Combo-OK, Holy, Obvious, Stackable, Touch
Duration: Instant
Prerequisite Charms: Still Pond Infliction, Burgeoning Wyld Infliction

Things from beyond Creation are the enemies of all Luna's Chosen. Surrounding herself with a halo of silver-gold light, the Lunar strikes out at a creature of darkness and weakens it greatly. Touching the target, which usually requires a Martial Arts attack that may inflict damage, causes the creature of darkness to lose (attacker's Essence x 3) motes in a brilliant display of Essence. If the target's player fails a Willpower roll at a difficulty equal to the Lunar's Essence, the attack also reduces the target's effective Essence by one dot for all purposes.

Creatures reduced to zero effective Essence by this Charm are destroyed, though some may have the ability to reform or be reformed by another entity. Reduced permanent Essence returns at a rate of one per day; Essence pools refill normally.

WITS

CONCEALMENT CHARMS

THE SPIDER'S TRAP DOOR

Cost: 4m; **Mins:** Wits 4, Essence 2; **Type:** Supplemental
Keywords: Combo-OK, Illusion
Duration: Instant
Prerequisite Charms: Any Wits Excellency

Lunar Exalted are masters at concealing the truth. This Charm supplements any action (usually dramatic) to conceal something, whether it is a (Wits + Survival) action to hide from animals, (Wits + Stealth) to set up an ambush, (Wits + Investigation) to hide evidence or others. The concealed object becomes undetectable by any Awareness rolls using mortal senses.

By committing the Essence spent on this Charm, the character may attach an *illusion* effect. Any person who comes near suffers an unnatural mental attack with a number of successes equal to those rolled for concealment plus the Lunar's Essence. Those whose Mental Defense Values are less than this value see the area as completely undisturbed and empty, even if they look exactly where the object rests. People who break through this mental influence must still find the object in order to see it.

THIEVING MAGPIE PRANA

Cost: 3m; **Mins:** Wits 4, Essence 2; **Type:** Simple
Keywords: Combo-OK
Duration: Instant
Prerequisite Charms: The Spider's Trap Door

When necessary, the Lunar can make something disappear in an instant. This Charm is a Wits-based action to conceal something, making it possible to do so in scant seconds instead of the several minutes such an action usually requires.

MANY-POCKETS MEDITATION

Cost: 2m; **Mins:** Wits 3, Essence 3; **Type:** Simple (Speed 5)
Keywords: Combo-OK, Touch
Duration: Indefinite
Prerequisite Charms: Thieving Magpie Prana

Occasionally, a Lunar must hide something where no one else can find it. Holding any object the character can lift with one hand, he invokes this Charm, and the object disappears into Elsewhere. For smaller objects, Lunars tuck them inside cloaks or pockets to conceal use of this Charm. Because the object is not actually on his person, it cannot be found by any natural means. Withdrawing the item is a miscellaneous action.

A character can "pocket" no more items in this way than his Essence. Should the character release the Essence committed to an item (or items) hidden in this way, the item falls to the ground at his side.

SECURE DEN PRANA

Cost: 4m, 1wp; **Mins:** Wits 4, Essence 4;
Type: Simple (Speed 7, -3 Defense Value)
Keywords: Combo-OK
Duration: Indefinite
Prerequisite Charms: Many-Pockets Meditation

Every animal cares about safety, and often, the Lunar Exalted also desire a touch of security. Activating this Charm, a character steps through an invisible door into a small area of Elsewhere just big enough for her to rest comfortably. The door closes instantly behind her, leaving her safe and sound within her small hole. Inside, the den looks just as the real place the Lunar feels most safe; over a significant number of uses of this Charm, the den may grow colorless and indistinct as Elsewhere becomes her safest location. The Steward may rest there until she ends the Charm, at which point she steps back to the point she left behind. The Elsewhere refuge does not offer a view outside, so the character can only guess when it's safe to leave.

For four additional motes per person, the Lunar may bring up to (Essence) companions into her Elsewhere den. The den grows to accommodate them all comfortably. The door cannot be seen by any mundane means, so the character often needs to direct companions through it. The Lunar steps through last, but always on the same tick as when she opened the door. This means that everyone who enters must be within one move action of the Lunar.

When the Lunar does not enter alone, uninvited guests may attempt to dash through the door. All characters roll (Dexterity + Athletics) to determine who gets inside in what order. Characters with the lowest results get shut out. Ending Secure Den Prana is equal to the Lunar leaving the den: All inhabitants then leave, and no one may leave until that time.

INVISIBLE WARREN CREATION

Cost: —; **Mins:** Wits 5, Essence 5;
Type: Permanent
Keywords: Social, War
Duration: Permanent
Prerequisite Charms: Secure Den Prana

This Charm permanently enhances Secure Den Prana. A character may choose to increase the cost to 20 motes and 1 Willpower in order to carve a significantly larger refuge out of Elsewhere. The Charm's Speed lengthens to long ticks. She may fit in a unit of Magnitude up to (Essence - 2).

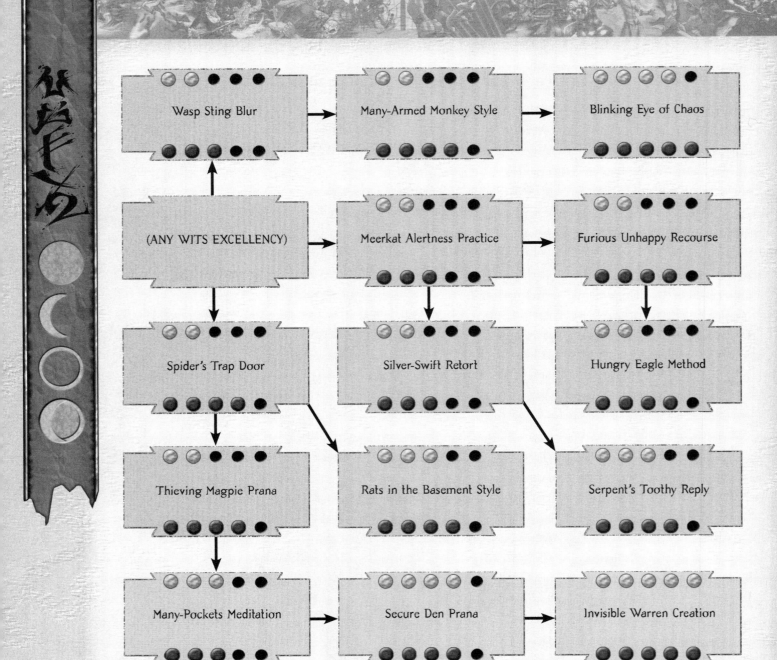

RATS IN THE BASEMENT STYLE

Cost: 5m; **Mins:** Wits 4, Essence 3;
Type: Simple (dramatic action)
Keywords: Combo-OK
Duration: Indefinite
Prerequisite Charms: The Spider's Trap Door

This Charm mimics the effects of its prerequisite Charm, but is a dramatic action (half an hour) that allows the character to conceal a unit from detection. This can be a group of barbarians in the jungles of the Southeast, a street gang in Nexus or awkward socialites at a large party.

The player rolls a Wits-based dice pool (usually combining it with Survival or Stealth) and conceals a unit with no greater a Magnitude that his Essence. The unit must be cooperative, and it receives the same protections from detection as the Spider's Trap Door.

If the unit moves appreciably from its position or deviates from the character's instructions to remain concealed, the deception is ruined. Individuals who peel off from the unit cease to be concealed but do not ruin it for the entire unit unless the departure reduces the unit's Magnitude.

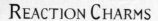

REACTION CHARMS

MEERKAT ALERTNESS PRACTICE

Cost: 2m; **Mins:** Wits 3, Essence 2; **Type:** Supplemental
Keywords: Combo-OK
Duration: Instant
Prerequisite Charms: Any Wits Excellency

Lunars are alert at all times. This Charm supplements a Join Battle, Join War or Join Debate action by adding (Essence) successes.

FURIOUS UNHAPPY RECOURSE

Cost: 6m; **Mins:** Wits 4, Essence 2; **Type:** Reflexive (Step 9)
Keywords: Combo-OK, Counterattack
Duration: Instant
Prerequisite Charms: Meerkat Alertness Practice

Lunars under assault burst out from under their foes' many blows. This Charm provides a counterattack at the character's full dice pool, to which the character adds a number of successes equal to whatever onslaught penalty she suffered in this round of attack resolution. If the attack hits, the target's player rolls (Stamina + Resistance) at a difficulty of the Lunar's Essence. Failure indicates that the attacker's flurry has been disrupted and immediately ends.

HUNGRY EAGLE METHOD

Cost: 5m; **Mins:** Wits 4, Essence 2; **Type:** Reflexive (Step 9)
Keywords: Combo-Basic, Counterattack
Duration: Until next action
Prerequisite Charms: Furious Unhappy Recourse

The overprotective bird pecks anything that comes near her nest or her food. Activating this Charm allows a character to make a counterattack against any person who makes a Melee or Martial Arts attack against her until her next action.

SILVER-SWIFT RETORT

Cost: 2m per; **Mins:** Wits 3, Essence 2;
Type: Supplemental
Keywords: Combo-OK, Social
Duration: Instant
Prerequisite Charms: Meerkat Alertness Practice

Stewards save their arguments for the right time. This Charm supplements a social attack, allowing the Lunar to recover more quickly after making her point. Each two motes spent on Silver-Swift Retort reduce the attack's Speed by 1, to a minimum of 3.

SERPENT'S TOOTH REPLY

Cost: 5m; **Mins:** Wits 4, Essence 3; **Type:** Reflexive (Step 2)
Keywords: Combo-OK, Social
Duration: Instant
Prerequisite Charms: Silver-Swift Retort

In response to a social attack that may be blocked, the character makes a statement that both refutes her opponent's argument and drives her own home. The player rolls her appropriate (Attribute + Ability) pair for the sort of social attack she wishes to make and applies those successes as an external penalty after the character's normal Parry Mental Defense Value. If any successes are left over (that were unnecessary to defeat the incoming attack), these plus her Essence become the successes on her social counterattack.

SPEED AND EXTRA ACTION CHARMS

WASP STING BLUR

Cost: 2m per tick; **Mins:** Wits 3, Essence 2; **Type:** Reflexive
Keywords: Combo-OK, Fury-OK
Duration: Instant
Prerequisite Charms: Any Wits Excellency

This Charm is identical to the Dexterity Charm of the same name, on page 154.

MANY-ARMED MONKEY STYLE

Cost: 3m per action; **Mins:** Wits 4, Essence 2;
Type: Extra Action
Keywords: Combo-OK, Obvious
Duration: Instant
Prerequisite Charms: Wasp Sting Blur

Lunars act with furious, unrelenting speed. This Charm is a magical flurry of two or more actions of any sort. Each action costs three motes, including the first, and the character can buy up to (her Wits) actions. These actions can be used for any purpose.

BLINKING EYE OF CHAOS

Cost: 10m, 1wp; **Mins:** Wits 5, Essence 4;
Type: Extra Action
Keywords: Obvious, Wyld
Duration: Instant
Prerequisite Charms: Many-Armed Monkey Style

With mastery of the Wyld comes a deeper understanding of its tides. Sometimes, the Wyld bends time, accelerating or slowing this aspect of Creation. In the Deep Wyld and Pure Chaos, eddies of bent time can flow right past each other. Luna's Chosen are immune to such effects, but by predicting and perhaps calling for such an eddy, they can force it over their enemies and gain a temporary edge.

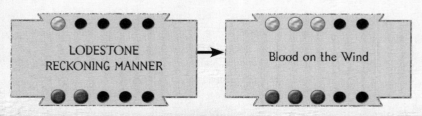

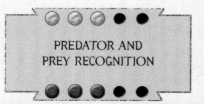

The character directs the fight into an eddy of slow time—or perhaps creates one; cause and effect can be hard to discern in the Wyld. Everyone else involved in the scene (apart from other Lunars) slows down. In effect, the character acts once, then gets to act again in the same tick as though she had waited for her next action. To everyone else, she appears to move and bend impossibly as time blurs their perceptions. For the Lunar, each action is fully independent: She may flurry in each, and use Charms or Combos in each without conflicting with the use of this Charm or Charms or Combos used in the other action.

SURVIVAL CHARMS

LODESTONE RECKONING MANNER
Cost: 2m; **Mins:** Wits 2, Essence 1; **Type:** Reflexive
Keywords: Combo-OK
Duration: Indefinite
Prerequisite Charms: None

Similar to a swallow flying south, the Lunar knows his way. With this Charm active, the character can never become lost. He has an absolute direction sense, and he can perfectly retrace the path he trod in the last 24 hours. For this Charm to function, the Lunar must have checked his position against the moon sometime within the last 24 hours. Otherwise, the Charm cannot be activated or ends.

BLOOD ON THE WIND
Cost: 4m, 1wp; **Mins:** Wits 3, Essence 3;
Type: Supplemental
Keywords: Combo-OK
Duration: Indefinite
Prerequisite Charms: Lodestone Reckoning Manner

This Charm is identical to the Perception Charm on page 181.

PREDATOR AND PREY RECOGNITION
Cost: 1m; **Mins:** Wits 3, Essence 3; **Type:** Simple
Keywords: Combo-OK
Duration: Instant
Prerequisite Charms: None

The Lunar sniffs at the local game trails and looks at her surroundings, then she is master of her domain. On a successful (Wits + Survival) roll, she knows the species that are common in the area, which are good food and which are dangerous, for a region (successes x 10) miles in diameter. Being in Wyld areas, or in areas where foreign animals have been imported, can levy a one- to four-die penalty to the roll.

LUNAR HERO STYLE

This supernatural martial art comes naturally to the Lunar Exalted. Although it is a complete style, Lunars (and their players) may design custom Charms that bridge off of this style. (See the expansion Charms on pp. 151-152 for examples.) Other Exalted may not.

Lunar Hero Style is best practiced only with natural weapons. Lunar Exalted often use the claws, teeth, hooves or horns of the Deadly Beastman Transformations with it, but other Exalted rarely have that capability. Practitioners may emulate this with tiger claws, even to the point of being usable with Charms. Because they are not truly part of the warrior, tiger claws (and razor claws) lose their accuracy bonus when used with this style.

Practitioners other than Lunars substitute their Martial Arts rating for the Dexterity requirements for this style. This does not extend to *any* Lunar Charms outside this style: Eclipse and Moonshadow Caste Exalted must still possess the minimum Dexterity requirement to learn Lunar Charms that branch off from this basic tree.

FOOT-TRAPPING COUNTER
Cost: 2m; **Mins:** Dexterity 3, Essence 1; **Type:** Reflexive
Keywords: Combo-OK
Duration: Instant
Prerequisite Charms: None

Combat does not end until the Lunar allows it. Against an opponent within hand-to-hand range, the Lunar's skilled footwork prevents the opponent from moving away from the character. The target's player rolls (Dexterity + Athletics) at a difficulty of the Lunar's Dexterity. Failure indicates that he cannot move away from the Lunar until his next action. Foot-Trapping Counter does not function against other Charms that allow a character to reflexively retreat.

RABID BEAST ATTITUDE
Cost: 1m; **Mins:** Dexterity 3, Essence 2; **Type:** Reflexive
Keywords: Combo-OK
Duration: (Essence) actions
Prerequisite Charms: Foot-Trapping Counter

The grace and speed of the Stewards is such that wounds cannot hinder them. Reduce all the character's wound penalties by one point for this Charm's duration.

THOUSAND CLAW INFLICTION
Cost: 1m; **Mins:** Dexterity 3, Essence 2; **Type:** Reflexive
Keywords: Combo-OK
Duration: Instant
Prerequisite Charms: Foot-Trapping Counter

Only the Lunar's skill limits him, not the restrictions of capability. The character's attacks each use his last attack position, defeating normal limits on the weapon. Activating this Charm allows the character to treat all Rate values as infinite until his next action.

LUNAR HERO FORM
Cost: 6m; **Mins:** Dexterity 4, Essence 2;
Type: Simple (Speed 5)
Keywords: Form-type, Obvious
Duration: One scene
Prerequisite Charms: Rabid Beast Attitude, Thousand Claw Infliction

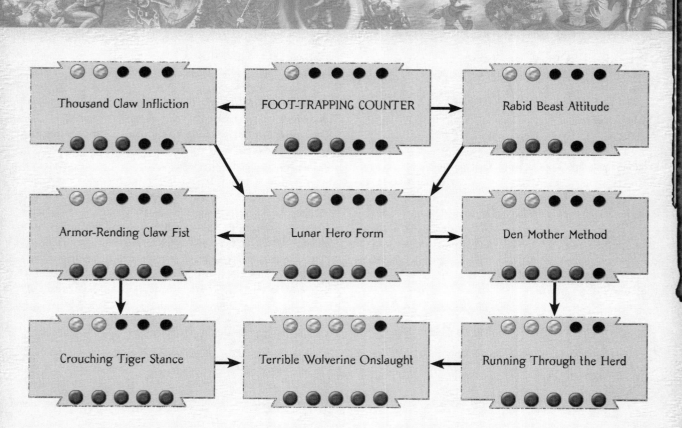

Drawing the Essence of Luna into her, the Exalt becomes an endlessly fluid warrior, seamlessly flowing from one movement to the next and capable of surprising her targets with every blow. The character reduces Defense Value penalties from onslaught by 1 and from coordinated attacks by 2. Her attacks often catch people from behind while she stands in front or strike at her enemies through innocuous objects and scenery. Double the dice bonus (but not Essence reward) for stunts of this nature.

ARMOR-RENDING CLAW FIST
Cost: 4m; **Mins:** Dexterity 4, Essence 2;
Type: Simple (Speed 5)
Keywords: Combo-OK
Duration: Instant
Prerequisite Charms: Lunar Hero Form

With either a single swipe or a flurry of blows, the Lunar's attack moves so quickly that it tears through even steel armor as though it were paper. This attack target's a foe's armor, rather than the person wearing it. Only soak from armor reduces the attack's raw damage, and (unlike normal attacks) this can reduce the attack's dice to zero. Then, roll unsoaked damage normally. Each level of damage remaining in Step 10 of attack resolution reduces the armor's soak (bashing and lethal). Mundane armor remains damaged until repaired; armor constructed from the magical materials recovers its full soak value at the end of the scene.

When a target's soak from armor drops to zero, the Lunar may rend the target's natural soak. The Lunar looses blows so rapid they weaken the victim's body through and through; each success rolled on damage reduces the target's effective Stamina by one. This only affects the target's soak values, not any other aspect of health.

CROUCHING TIGER STANCE
Cost: 4m; **Mins:** Dexterity 5, Essence 2;
Type: Reflexive (Step 2)
Keywords: Combo-OK, Counterattack
Duration: Until next action
Prerequisite Charms: Armor-Rending Claw Fist

To strike a Lunar is to taunt a tiger. Dropping into a low, threatening stance, the character becomes more difficult to strike. All attacks upon him lose two dice. In addition, when the Lunar successfully parries any close combat attack, he may launch a counterattack against the attacker.

DEN MOTHER METHOD
Cost: 2m; **Mins:** Dexterity 4, Essence 2;
Type: Reflexive (Step 6)
Keywords: Combo-OK, Counterattack
Duration: Instant
Prerequisite Charms: Lunar Hero Form

When a companion of the Lunar is in danger, he runs to his friend's aid. A character may invoke this Charm when an attack within range reaches Step 6 of combat resolution. So long as the character is no farther than two move actions from the target and can physically get to her, the Lunar dashes to close the distance. He adds half his Dexterity to the target's Defense Value against the incoming attack.

RUNNING THROUGH THE HERD

Cost: 4m, 1wp; **Mins:** Dexterity 5, Essence 3;
Type: Reflexive (Step 2)
Keywords: Combo-OK, Counterattack
Duration: Instant
Prerequisite Charms: Den Mother Method

In a combination of leading the attack, fooling her attacker and quickly dodging out of the way, the Lunar redirects an attack on her person toward someone else. The Lunar must be aware of the attack, which must have another valid target within (Dexterity) yards of the attack. The Lunar's player rolls (Dexterity + Athletics) at a difficulty of the attacker's Perception. Success indicates that she redirects that attack, with all of its successes and effects, at another valid target of her choice. That attack then plays out as normal.

TERRIBLE WOLVERINE ONSLAUGHT

Cost: 5m, 1wp, 1+lhl; **Mins:** Dexterity 5, Essence 4;
Type: Reflexive
Keywords: Obvious
Duration: Until released
Prerequisite Charms: Crouching Tiger Stance, Running Through the Herd

After activating this Charm, the character becomes a ravenous, unstoppable beast. The character's move and dash actions triple in distance, and the player adds one automatic success to all Dexterity actions. Each action, the character suffers one level of lethal damage and must attempt three Martial Arts attacks or one attack and one non-attack flurry. Players of characters under the effects of this Charm must roll (Willpower) at difficulty of the character's Valor in order to take any non-attack action without ending the Charm.

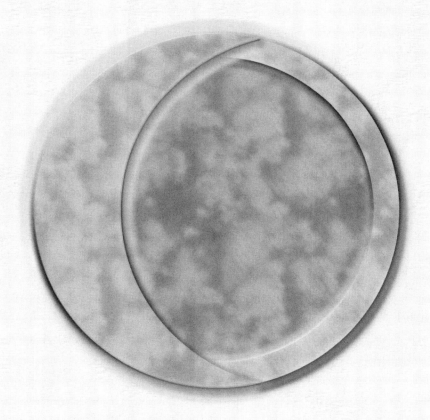

CHAPTER SIX
THE CASTELESS AND THE CHIMERAE

While most Lunars gratefully accept the blessing of moonsilver tattoos, not all do. Most likely, the young Lunar just never received the offer. Creation is vast, the Lunars few and the horoscopes of their astrologers are less than perfect. By the time the Silver Pact finds a novice Lunar, she might have her own ideas about castes and casteless-ness. A Lunar might reject the tattoos because she suspects the Silver Pact elder has some nefarious secret agenda. Other Casteless argue that their shifting nature is part of Luna's plan. Still others see advantages in a shifting caste. Whatever their reasons, these Moonchildren think they can live without a fixed caste.

The Silver Pact holds no consensus about such Casteless Lunars. A narrow majority says the Pact should leave Luna's Bastards to find their own way. Forcing a caste upon them would only mean resentful Lunars, which wouldn't help the Pact. If the Casteless know the dangers of their state, they can make their own choices and live with the consequences.

Other Pact members say that all Unblooded should be tattooed whether they want it or not, to save them from becoming chimerae. Not many Pact members take action, though. The caste-fixing process requires the young Lunar's cooperation in the trials and declarations of achievement, so imposing a caste by force is rarely feasible. A very few Lunars, however, try to kill these "arrogant pups" before the Wyld has a chance to taint them and hope the Pact can get them in their next incarnation.

And then, there are the chimerae. The Silver Pact never offers them tattoos. It is far too late for such preventative measures. Each chimera, twisted and maddened by the Wyld, began as a Casteless Lunar who ignored the warning signs and plunged headlong into Wyld mutation. Silver Pact members consider it their duty to put down such creatures… if possible. Many of these beasts have lived for centuries, though, growing in power all the while. Often, only an entire pack of Lunars has any chance of killing a chimera.

THE CASTELESS

The Silver Pact recognizes two classes of Casteless Lunars. The most common Casteless are the Unblooded, newly Exalted Lunars who have only just begun to understand what they have become. Unblooded Lunars do not yet know how to drink the heart's blood of animals or people and so are limited to their true forms. They might not have learned any Charms or Knacks. The Silver Pact regularly sends retrieval packs to rescue Unblooded when such missions seem likely to succeed. Virtually all Unblooded accept being marked with "the blood of Luna." Indeed, after listening to horror stories about chimerae from their rescuers, most Unblooded don't even consider the option of remaining Casteless.

Other Casteless Lunars Exalt far from Lunar territories but find a way to survive and learn on their own. Whether by instinct, trial and error or by vague recollections of previous lives, these young Exalts figure out how to drink heart's blood and master a number of Charms and Knacks. Most of these more experienced novice Stewards accept tattoos once they reach Lunar territory and a Silver Pact member explains the advantages of membership and the dangers of remaining Casteless. Despite the pressure to conform, however, some of these young Lunars have grown enamored of shifting caste marks and elect to remain Casteless.

Of course, this assumes that tattooing is presented as an offer instead of a demand. Some Silver Pact Lunars are so paranoid about chimerism that they try to force tattoos on all Casteless, regardless of the other Lunars' desires. This requires browbeating, threats or use of Charms to force compliance, and typically results in a very angry Lunar.

Thus, when the Silver Pact uses the term "Casteless," the word most commonly refers to Lunars who have actively rejected the opportunity to receive moonsilver tattoos and become "blooded." The Casteless are a very small subculture within Lunar society; estimates of their number range from five to a dozen or two. Given the substantial difficulties such a decision imposes on a Lunar's life, the existence of even that many Casteless surprises many other Lunars.

DISADVANTAGES OF CASTELESSNESS

From the perspective of the Silver Pact, lack of caste makes life so difficult and fraught with danger that deliberately choosing such a state is sheer madness. Indeed, one disadvantage to Castelessness is the lack of respect the Casteless receive from Silver Pact Lunars. Almost every Silver Pact Lunar accepts as an article of faith that by remaining Casteless, a Lunar places herself in constant risk of chimerism. As such, even the most open-minded Silver Pact members distrust the Casteless and constantly watch them for new Wyld mutations. Only the most trusting Lunar would not

put down a Casteless who acquired a noticeable number of such mutations within a short period.

The Silver Pact has good reason for such fears. A Casteless *is* likely to devolve into a chimera if he does not take extraordinary care. As noted below, whenever a Casteless Lunar changes form, the Wyld spark within him tries to twist the change and create a permanent mutation. Being in the Wyld itself makes the Lunar more susceptible to these warpings of mind and body.

PERILS OF SHAPESHIFTING

The most insidious danger to Casteless Lunars may come from their own shapeshifting. Whenever a Casteless Lunar changes shape, the Wyld spark within his Exaltation tries to force permanent transformation upon him—maybe something related to his previous form or the form he assumes, or maybe something utterly random. Maybe the change is all in his mind. The more times a Casteless shapeshifts within a short period, the stronger this Wyld spark grows. Shapeshifting in the Wyld itself makes the spark even stronger.

WYLD TAINT DICE POOL

In rules terms, each time a Casteless Lunar takes a different shape, her player rolls a dice pool and compares the result to the character's Dodge Mental Defense Value. (As usual, a 10 counts as two successes.) If the result exceeds the character's Dodge Mental Defense Value, the character gains a Wyld mutation. The greater the roll's threshold, the more severe the mutation will be.

The dice pool starts at one die, for the first time a Lunar changes between true forms. Each subsequent shapeshift adds one die to the pool. Taking any other shape from character's library of heart's blood forms increases the dice pool by two. These accumulate.

Example: John's Casteless character, the mercenary Captain Faron, takes his spirit form—a mospid—to sneak into a fortress and open the gates. John rolls a pool of one die. Once inside, Faron takes the shape of a coral snake, one of his heart's blood forms. This adds two dice to the pool, so John rolls three dice. Since Faron has a Dodge Mental Defense Value of 5, though, the roll has little chance to succeed (and does not). After Faron-the-snake slithers into the guardhouse and bites two guards, the others run. Faron resumes human form to open the gates, and John rolls a pool of four dice... three successes, still safe. The heavy gates jam, however, so Faron shapeshifts into a bear to force them open: John rolls six dice this time, but rolls only two successes. Finally, Faron takes his human form before his troops charge inside. The dice pool rises to seven dice, and John rolls five successes—not quite enough, but Faron can feel he's pushing his luck. Faron decides not to shapeshift for a while.

A character can reduce the chance of Wyld mutation in various ways.

She can wait. Each day that passes in which the character does not shapeshift at all reduces the accumulated pool by one die, though the pool will not drop below the starting one die.

The character can spend Willpower. Instead of adding an automatic success, the Willpower cancels one success. Even though the Wyld taint pits itself against the character's Dodge Mental Defense Value, this does not count as resisting unnatural mental influence, *unless the character is in the Wyld itself.*

The character can channel a Willpower through a Virtue. In this case, the character subtracts dice from the pool equal to the Virtue's rating. However, this does not reduce the pool itself, whose cumulative total still increases. During such moments of heroism, however, a Casteless Lunar can shift the odds.

The character may observe taboos that help stabilize her mind and body against the Wyld within her. See "Taboo," page 111, for this Background.

Finally, suffering a mutation resets the dice pool back to one die for the next time the Casteless shapeshifts.

MUTATION POINTS

If the player *does* roll more successes than the character's Dodge Mental Defense Value, count the number of extra successes. These are the *mutation points* that determine how severe a Wyld mutation the character suffers.

Each class of mutations has a point value: 1 for poxes and deficiencies, 2 for afflictions and debilities, 4 for blights and deformities and 6 for abominations. (These equal the bonus point costs of the mutations—see p. 101.) The character suffers a mutation of the highest point value the player can buy with the rolled number of mutation points. The character has no control over which mutation he suffers, though; the Storyteller decides. Any mutation points that exceed the most costly single mutation the character can buy go toward a second mutation that is always completely harmful (a deficiency or, in extraordinary cases, a deformity).

This Wyld attack occurs every time the Casteless changes shape, and any Wyld mutations gained become a part of the Lunar's true forms. If the successful attack took place after the Lunar shifted into a human form, including his own human true form, the Lunar instead gains a Wyld-based mental derangement.

SHAPESHIFTING IN THE WYLD

Shapeshifting in the Wyld adds a further, but non-cumulative bonus to the mutation roll. Shapeshifting in the Bordermarches adds one die, the Middlemarches add two dice, the Deep Wyld adds four dice and Pure Chaos adds six dice.

Even worse, a Casteless Lunar in the Bordermarches must go a full week without changing shape to reduce the mutation pool by just one die, while a Lunar in the Middlemarches must go a full month. A Casteless Lunar in the Deep Wyld or in Pure Chaos can never reduce her Wyld attack dice pool

while she remains there, assuming she doesn't fall to chimerism almost instantly upon entering such a mad place.

FROM LUNAR TO CHIMERA: PERMANENT LIMIT

A Casteless Lunar who insists on staying in the Wyld for any length of time almost certainly gains a wide variety of disturbing physical and mental characteristics. While in the Wyld, a Casteless Lunar suffers two final disabilities. First, when a Lunar in the Wyld spends Willpower in hopes of resisting his inner Wyld taint, he gains a point of Limit, as if resisting unnatural mental influence. Second, every time a Casteless Lunar's Limit breaks *while in the Wyld*, he gains a point of *permanent* Limit.

When a Casteless gains a dot of permanent Limit, the player should note the development by permanently filling in the leftmost Limit Break square on the character sheet. Each dot of permanent Limit reduces the number of Limit points needed before the next Limit Break by one. Thus, a character who has two dots of permanent Limit will suffer from her Virtue Flaw when she gains eight points of normal Limit instead of 10. Consequently, as the Lunar's permanent Limit increases, she finds it increasingly easy to enter Limit Break, and if she remains in the Wyld, gain even more permanent Limit. Permanent Limit is the mechanism by which a Casteless is transformed into a chimera.

Lunars themselves are divided on how to define a chimera, but for mechanical purposes, a Lunar becomes a chimera when he gains 10 points of permanent Limit and is therefore in a permanent Limit Break condition. At that point, the character is no longer playable. The Silver Pact, however, is ignorant of even the concept of Limit and so must judge whether a Moonchild has become a chimera based on her actions and the number of mutations and obvious derangements she carries. Thus, an individual Lunar may choose to view Casteless with significantly fewer than 10 points of permanent Limit as irretrievably lost to the Wyld. Generally, after a Casteless has gained between four and six points of permanent Limit, he finds it impossible to conceal the extent of his Wyld taint from other Lunars, who typically target him for euthanasia.

ADVANTAGES OF CASTELESSNESS

In comparison to the danger of chimerism, the advantages of remaining Casteless seem slim. Nevertheless, some Lunars reject tattooing and remain Casteless despite the risks. For instance, a Casteless might know the dangers of chimerism but believes the Silver Pact exaggerates the risks. A cautious Casteless, they argue, can reduce the risk of becoming chimera simply by minimizing the use of Lunar shapeshifting and by staying out of the Wyld zones. To such Casteless, moonsilver tattoos simply represent a conscious decision to sacrifice one form of Lunar flexibility (shifting castes) in order to gain flexibility in other areas (safer shapeshifting and the freedom to enter the Wyld at will). They don't dispute the advantages of accepting tattoos; they just think the decision should remain with the individual Lunar, and that the potential advantages of a shifting caste have never been fully explored.

The chief advantage of Castelessness is that the Casteless has the potential to use the anima power of any caste so long as he does so at the proper time. As a practical matter, all Casteless are effectively Changing Moons for 11 days, Full Moons for three days, Changing Moons again for another 11 days and finally No Moons for three days before the cycle begins again. Casteless also bear the No Moon Caste during Calibration and during the rare lunar eclipses. Although Casteless gain Limit from exposure to the light of the Full Moon (as do all Lunars), the Casteless do not risk Wyld taint from gaining Limit in this way, as long as they stay out of the Wyld itself.

THE CHIMERAE

The predator slinks low through the jungle brush, carefully staying downwind of his prey. Just ahead, in a clearing stands a young doe facing away from him, oblivious to the nearby leopard. Slowly, meticulously, he skulks forward until he gets within range. Even the fastest deer could not escape a charging leopard from this range. The leopard charges, a blur of motion heading towards the helpless doe, which does not react to the sudden sound of movement.

Even as the leopard rushes forward and begins its leap, the doe does not react. In the back of the predator's mind lights a tiny spark of suspicion. Surely the doe must hear him now. Why doesn't it try to run? The thought cannot overcome the predator's instinct, and he hurls himself through the air at his prey.

The leopard strikes true, landing on the doe's back with enough force to snap it like a twig. But something is wrong. The predator's claws do not rend the doe's flesh so much as... sink into it as though it were made of tar. And the doe does not collapse under the leopard's weight. Instead, she rises up on her hindquarters, lifting the predator up with her. As she does, the thin hairs on her back extend and writhe like tiny serpents, coiling around the leopard's mouth and midsection. Her hindquarters thicken and become the powerful legs of a bull. Her forelegs bend back upon themselves, shifting like quicksilver as they reach behind around to grasp the leopard in razor-sharp eagle talons. The doe's head rotates backwards like an owl to examine her catch, her delicate deer mouth spreading obscenely to reveal the silver shark's teeth within.

The leopard struggles vainly, its front legs now almost entirely sunk into what was once a doe's back. Now, an observer could not even guess which side of the creature the leopard faced. Mighty arms grasp the terrified predator. Two large eyes open on a patch of bare skin to inspect the trapped beast. Suddenly, the entire area of skin beneath the leopard splits open, and the creature's viscera twist outward like tentacles, further ensnaring the leopard and drawing him inside the creature's body. The creature's ribs writhe

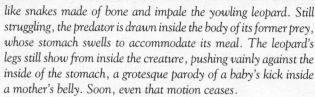

like snakes made of bone and impale the yowling leopard. Still struggling, the predator is drawn inside the body of its former prey, whose stomach swells to accommodate its meal. The leopard's legs still show from inside the creature, pushing vainly against the inside of the stomach, a grotesque parody of a baby's kick inside a mother's belly. Soon, even that motion ceases.

The creature bends forward once more and lands on four legs. Slowly, it shrinks in size as it digests both the heart's blood and the body of its former predator. Soon, the creature looks exactly like the leopard it devoured. Then, satisfied that it has mastered the predator's form, it lets out an unearthly howl, a sound nothing borne of Creation could ever make. Tensing, the chimera forces Essence through its body, and to the perfect form of a common spotted leopard, adds the wings of a great eagle. The chimera leaps into the air and takes to the sky. The true predator continues its hunt.

The Lunar Exalted are among the most terrifying beings in Creation. But what do the monsters fear? Other monsters. For the Lunar Exalted, one of the most dangerous and frightening enemies to encounter is the chimera, once a fellow Lunar, now twisted by the Wyld into an insane, shapeless monstrosity that considers its fellow Moonchildren its favorite prey.

BECOMING A CHIMERA

Only a Casteless Lunar can become a chimera. Lunar tattoos completely protect their wearers from all Wyld mutation effects, including chimerism. While individual members of the Silver Pact may view a Casteless Lunar with excessive Wyld mutations as a chimera and try to kill her, a true chimera is a Casteless Lunar who accumulated 10 points of permanent Limit and fell into a state of permanent Limit Break. At any point up to then, the Lunar can stop her slide into madness by receiving moonsilver tattoos, assuming she can get them. As a practical matter, however, most Lunars treat Wyld-tainted Casteless as lost causes somewhere around five points of permanent Limit, by which point the afflicted Lunar is barely recognizable as having once been human.

When a Casteless reaches seven points of permanent Limit, she completely loses her human and animal true forms. From that point on, she can assume those forms as a standard shapeshifting action, but can no longer treat them as true forms for any purpose. Her ability to assume her war form is unaffected, and many Casteless this close to chimerism choose to remain in their war forms constantly (to the extent that the war form can even be recognized beneath the Lunar's abundant mutations).

Beginning at the eight-point level, the Lunar suffers from constant shifting and undulating of her flesh, which no longer totally responds to her control. Although the Lunar can still adopt any form in her library, this disturbingly random movement of her body gives her away as something other than what she appears to be. Any character can spot this fluidity of flesh if her player succeeds at a (Perception + Awareness)

roll. Accordingly, if the Lunar wishes to maintain a form without giving herself away, she must concentrate fully on maintaining her physical integrity. While doing so, the Lunar can take no action other than a standard move action.

At the nine-point level, the Lunar loses the capacity to regain Essence normally through rest. Even while asleep, her form shifts and changes too much to permit the true rest needed for natural Essence recovery. The character can still regain Essence from any manse to which she is attuned. Fortunately for her (and unfortunately for any creature who crosses her path), the Lunar now gains access to a new method of Essence recovery. Whenever the Lunar totally consumes a living creature, she regains a number of Essence motes equal to the creature's total health levels. If the creature devoured was sentient, she gains Essence equal to twice its health levels. If the creature was an Essence user, such as an Exalt or a materialized god, the Lunar regains Essence equal to twice her victim's total health levels, *plus* any motes remaining in the victim's personal (but not peripheral) Essence pool. Acting on a cannibalistic urge requires the player to roll the Lunar's Compassion and get no successes. If the Compassion roll yields any successes, the Lunar may only devour a sentient being by spending a Willpower point and gaining a point of Limit. Lunars who have the Cannibalism Wyld derangement (see pp. 209-210) fail this Compassion roll automatically. Finally, at the nine-point level, the Lunar's previous Motivation is replaced with a new one: "Survive at all costs."

At 10 points of permanent Limit, the Lunar becomes a chimera and is no longer a playable character (assuming the Storyteller has not already ruled the character unplayable). Its sole purpose in life is to hunt, eat and remain in the Wyld, venturing outside only to prey on Lunars and other Essence users. Although the chimera can choose to acquire Wyld mutations at will, the chimera never again gains a mutation simply due to shapeshifting or being in the Wyld. The chimera is part of the Wyld, and the Wyld knows its own.

BENEFITS OF CHIMERISM

Becoming a chimera offers no benefits that outweigh the condition's serious drawbacks. The chimerae themselves might disagree, but then, chimerae are utterly insane. Nevertheless, the condition does confer some powers that make chimerae even more dangerous to their Lunar kin. Most significantly, a chimera can temporarily gain the benefits of any positive mutation as a reflexive action. The acquired mutation lasts for a scene: taking the mutation costs motes of Essence equal to its bonus point cost times three.

Additionally, the chimerae have access to a number of specialized Knacks that enable them to make better use of their infinitely protean flesh. A character who acquires five or more points of permanent Limit can purchase these powers as normal Knacks, and chimerae under the control of the Storyteller might have any of them. A sample of these Knacks follows:

QUICKSILVER FORM
Prerequisites: 5+ permanent Limit

No cage can contain the chimera. As a simple action, the chimera can reduce its entire body into a viscous material that flows effortlessly according to his will. In this form, the chimera can flow through any opening, no matter how small, although very tiny openings may take a long time to pass through. While in this form, the chimera becomes more vulnerable to powerful blunt attacks than to cutting attacks. Treat lethal cutting damage as normal bashing damage, but double the pre-soak damage of all normal bashing attacks. Lethal damage that is not based on cutting attacks (fire, acid and the like) is treated normally; so is aggravated damage. Activating Quicksilver Form requires a commitment of five motes of Essence.

BODY OF ACID
Prerequisites: 5+ permanent Limit

The chimera can diffuse its stomach acids across its entire form at no harm to itself. The chimera gains an acidic touch that adds four lethal damage to all Martial Arts attacks the chimera makes and inflicts four lethal dice of damage to anyone who attempts to grapple it. The acid corrodes any natural material and destroys any clothing or possessions carried by the chimera not made of one of the magical materials. Activating Body of Acid requires the commitment of five motes of Essence.

ASSIMILATION OF THE PREY
Prerequisites: Body of Acid, Quicksilver Form

The chimera can make its body flow over and around its chosen prey, totally engulfing the victim. Once trapped within the chimera's body, the victim suffers six lethal damage every five ticks. This damage bypasses armor, since the chimera's internal digestive organs can flow around such protective gear. Victims who die within the chimera's body are considered to be totally digested. The chimera's body then harmlessly expels indigestible materials (metals, glass, magical materials).

The chimera must have Quicksilver Form active in order to use this power, but she can activate both Knacks reflexively at a cost of seven motes. If Quicksilver Form is already active, there is no mote cost to activate Assimilation of the Prey

BLASPHEMOUS OFFSPRING
Prerequisites: Assimilation of the Prey

After a chimera consumes a victim through Assimilation of the Prey, the chimera can then expel an amount of its own body matter and shape it into the form of the creature the chimera has just devoured. The offspring is not a true living creature, but an amalgamation of excess body mass mentally under the control of the chimera. The chimera can perceive through the offspring's senses and can direct its movements. While controlling the offspring, the chimera has access to all the creature's normal instincts, memories and natural abilities (but not actual Abilities, Charms or other magical powers). However, if the chimera attempts to act on its own and also direct the offspring, the chimera suffers flurry penalties based on the total number of actions taken with *both* bodies.

Alternatively, the chimera can temporarily release control of the offspring, which will act as if it were the original creature and, if sentient, actually believe that it is the original creature. The chimera can reassert control over the offspring at any time, and the offspring will never voluntarily move more than a mile away from its creator.

Only Charms or stunts can possibly tell the difference between an offspring and the creature it mimics. Creating an animal offspring requires the commitment of six motes of Essence during the offspring's existence. Creating a human offspring requires the commitment of 10 motes and the expenditure of one Willpower point. A human offspring can duplicate anything the original was wearing not made of a magical material by shaping excess skin into the appropriate cloth or material. The chimera can only create an offspring based on an animal or a person, but not a demon, god, ghost or other totally supernatural creature. The offspring dies when the Essence commitment ends and vice versa.

GROTESQUE PSEUDOPODIA
Prerequisites: Quicksilver Form

The chimera makes some part of its body grow massively in size, as flesh, tendons and strange, tumorous growths stretch the affected body part into one or more massive, tentacle-like pseudopodia. These enable the chimera to make ranged Martial Arts attacks. While this Knack is active, the affected limb becomes a disgusting conglomeration of protoplasmic matter, and the chimera cannot hold anything in its hand during the instant of the attack. Accordingly, this Knack can only be uses to facilitate unarmed attacks. The possible effects depend on how many motes the chimera expends per action:

• **1 Mote:** The chimera extends one limb up to (permanent Essence x 2) yards as an instant, reflexive action. The chimera may extend its neck to make a ranged bite attack, extend an existing limb or cause an additional limb to sprout from its body, striking at its target and then returning to the body.

GROTESK PSEUDOPODIA					
Name	Speed	Accuracy	Damage	Defense	Rate
Pseudopod Strike	4	+2	+4B (or +9B)	+3	3

- **2 Motes:** The chimera can stretch one limb (Essence x 5) yards to make an attack. Other potential uses include reaching the roof of a building and grabbing hold before pulling up the rest of its body.
- **4 Motes:** The chimera can imbue its ranged Martial Arts attacks with great velocity and force, adding +5 to its damage on a single unarmed attack.

DEFENSE OF MEANINGLESS SHAPE

Prerequisites: Grotesque Pseudopodia

The chimera can instantly transform its entire body into a glutinous substance that retains its general shape but allows physical attacks to pass through it without harm. The effect is instant and reflexive, costing four motes and one Willpower point. This Knack offers a perfect defense against physical attacks, but carries the Temperance Flaw of Invulnerability. This Knack does not stop elemental or pure Essence attacks, or attacks using weapons that bear the Overpowering tag—the chimera *splashes* when struck with such weapons.

PERPETUAL REGENERATION

Prerequisites: Defense of Meaningless Shape, Essence 5

The chimera can apply the regenerative healing benefits of its war form to any shape it wears. See the description of Deadly Beastman Transformation, pages 136-137.

PERFECT REGENERATION

Prerequisites: Perpetual Regeneration, Essence 6

Not even the most sagacious Lunars suspect that some of their chimera foes are so dangerous because of centuries of experience, centuries often gained while the chimera was thought already to be dead. This Knack makes a chimera as close to immortal as anything in Creation besides a god or the Fair Folk.

The chimera's regeneration continues even after the creature is dead. Only burning every part of the corpse can release its Exaltation. If so much as a fingernail or even a few fresh drops of blood escape the fire, then the chimera slowly regenerates, bit by bit, until its reconstituted body returns to life. The chimera's Essence naturally collects in the largest remaining body part: splitting the chimera in two will not cause the body parts to create two chimerae. The amount of time this regeneration takes depends on how much of the body escaped destruction. As a guideline, a chimera whose corpse remains largely intact can return to life within a week, while one that must regenerate from a single drop of blood takes more than a year.

ECHINNA THE FACELESS, THE DEMON HUNTRESS OF THORNS

Echinna, the Demon Huntress of Thorns, is a sample Lunar chimera. It is unusually powerful for its age: A pack of young Lunars will need all their skills and ingenuity to put Echinna down.

Echinna was a Lunar who Exalted about 200 years ago. Unfortunately, she Exalted near Thorns, then a strong Realm tributary with a large Dragon-Blooded contingent. The Wyld Hunt chased the young Casteless into a Wyld zone just south of Thorns and fenced her in with magical wards. She stayed there until the coming of the Mask of Winters destroyed the barriers that trapped her in the Wyld. Echinna's imprisonment in the Wyld turned her into a chimera more than a century ago.

Only a few months after the Deathlord's forces took the city, Echinna left her—its—Wyld zone. Its maddened rampage took it into Thorns. The chimera single-handedly slew one deathknight and put down innumerable zombies (as well as just as many cowering citizens) before the Mask of Winters himself entered the fray. Surprisingly, he did not raise his weapon against the malleable monster. Instead, he called out Echinna's name as if he knew it and, with powerful Charms, he subdued the chimera. Then, the Deathlord walked boldly up to the chimera, kissed it on its misshapen forehead and whispered something in its ear. After that brief encounter, Echinna left Thorns without further incident, heading southeast into the jungles. Only one of his deathknights was close enough to hear what the Deathlord said, and even she could only make out a single name: Ma-Ha-Suchi.

Caste: None
Anima Banner: A constantly shifting conglomeration of different animal features
Attributes: Strength 5, Dexterity 4, Stamina 5; Charisma 3, Manipulation 3 Appearance 2; Perception 3, Intelligence 3, Wits 5
Virtues: Compassion 1, Conviction 3, Temperance 2, Valor 3
Abilities: Athletics 3, Awareness 3, Dodge 5, Integrity 2, Investigation 2, Martial Arts 4 (Pseudopodia +2), Melee 2, Presence 2 (Intimidation +2), Resistance 4, Stealth 4, Survival 4
Charms: First Strength Excellency, First Dexterity Excellency, First Stamina Excellency, Instinctive Strength Unity, Instinctive Dexterity Unity, Blood in the Wind, Bruise-Relief Method, Burrowing Devil Strike, Claws of the Silver Moon, Graceful Crane Stance, Impressions of Strength (Ogre's Loving Caress), Instinct Driven Beast Method, Lodestone Reckoning Manner, Moonsilver Stomach Conversion, Ox-Body Technique (x3), Relentless Lunar Fury, Secure Cat Stepping, Shell-Crushing Atemi, Wasp Sting Blur, Wyld-Sensing Instincts
Knacks: Grotesque Pseudopodia, Defense of Meaningless Shape, Impossible Body Rearrangement, Prey's Skin Disguise, Quicksilver Form, Mountainous Spirit Expression, Twin-Faced Hero
Permanent Wyld Mutations: Claws, Double-Jointed, Heart's Blood Addiction, Hideous Maw, Hooves, Prehensile Body Hair, Wings, Wyld Addiction
Join Battle: 8
Attacks:
Clinch: Speed 6, Accuracy 10, Damage 5B, Defense -, Rate 1

Kick (Hooves): Speed 5, Accuracy 10, Damage 10B, Defense -2 (PDV 3), Rate 2
Punch (Claws): Speed 5, Accuracy 8, Damage 5L, Defense +2 (PDV 5), Rate 3
Hideous Maw Bite: Speed 5, Accuracy 9, Damage 10L, Defense -, Rate 1
Pseudopod Strike: Speed 4, Accuracy 10, Damage 9B (or 14B), Defense +3 (PDV 6), Rate 3
Soak: 2L/5B
Health Levels: -0/-1/-1/-1/-1/-1/-1/-1/-2/-2/-2/-2/-2/-2/Incap (+6 dying levels)
Dodge DV: 6   **Willpower:** 7
Essence: 3
Personal Essence: 17   **Peripheral Essence:** 38
Derangements: Cannibalism (Debility), Mood Swings (Deformity), Wyld Addiction
Other Notes: None

WYLD MUTATIONS

Whenever the Wyld-powered unnatural mental attack triggered by a Casteless Lunar's shapeshifting exceeds his Dodge Mental Defense Values, the Lunar gains a mutation whose severity depends on the amount by which the attack exceeded the Mental Defense Value. When the Lunar gains a mutation, his player must roll the Lunar's Willpower + Essence, with an internal penalty equal to the amount by which the attack exceeded his Mental Defense Value. If the roll succeeds, the character gains a positive mutation (pox, affliction, blight, abomination). If the roll fails, the mutation is entirely negative (deficiency, debility, deformity). If the roll botches, the mutation is negative, *and* the player has an additional two mutation points to spend.

If a player is forced to purchase a mutation for his character, he must spend his mutation points on the most expensive type he can afford, with any extra mutations points lost. Thus, the more mutation points the Lunar gets from the Wyld attack, the more serious the negative mutation will be. When a Casteless gains a Wyld mutation, its effects must be incorporated into the Lunar's true forms if they possibly can be. A Lunar whose true form is a shark and who gains the Claws pox will not necessarily have claws in her shark form, since it has no hands, but she may develop claw-like spurs on the end of her fins, which can grant the same mechanical benefits. The Storyteller has the final say on how specific mutations affect the Lunar's true forms. A mutated Lunar can conceal her mutations by taking any form other than a true form. However, doing so adds one mote to the cost to change shape for each mutation the Lunar possesses that she wants to suppress.

In addition to the mutations described in **Exalted**, pages 288-290, you can find more mutations in **The Compass of Celestial Directions: The Wyld**. Some new mutations are described below, as are some previously listed mutations that players might find useful when designing Deadly Beastman Transformation forms (see pp. 136-137).

POXES

Poxes are the least severe mutations and are the easiest to conceal. If not exactly positive, they at least cause no real harm. Each pox costs one mutation point.

Hooves: The character's lower legs are replaced with hooves more appropriate for a horse, a goat, a boar or some other, similar creature. The character adds two bashing damage to his kicks. If the pox is taken a second time, its effects are identical to the Great Hooves affliction.

Serpentine Tongue: The character's tongue becomes long and forked like a snake's, and he unconsciously flicks it out every few minutes. The tongue is remarkably sensitive, and a character with this pox ignores the normal -2 external penalty for fighting invisible opponents.

Third Eye: The character has a third eye located on her forehead, just above her other two. The character gains a +1 bonus on all Awareness rolls. The third eye can be concealed normally.

Wolf's Pace: The character's legs become longer and contain more power. Often, they take on a digitigrade shape similar to that of a dog or deer. Add two to the character's Dexterity for the purpose of calculating movement during combat, and add two to the character's Strength for the purposes of jumping distances. The character adds one die to single rolls representing competitive running. In long-term movement (see **Exalted**, p. 264), the character may move as quickly as a drawn carriage.

This mutation may be taken multiple times. Each purchase stacks the mutation's benefits, but if it is taken more than once it can never be hidden. See *Gazelle's Pace* and *Cheetah's Pace*.

DEFICIENCIES

Deficiencies are the simplest negative mutations and are the easiest to conceal. In addition to the deficiencies found on page 288 of **Exalted**, new deficiencies are listed below. Each deficiency costs one mutation point.

Disgusting Scent: The character perpetually reeks of a foul odor such as rotting meat, raw sewage or simply skunk spray. No amount of cleaning can remove this stench, which inflicts a -2 external penalty on all Social rolls where the target of the roll is able to smell the character.

Disturbing Voice: The character's voice has some strange quality to it that most people find highly disturbing. For example, Ma-Ha-Suchi has this deficiency, which takes the form of a strange "silver bell" quality to his voice. The character suffers a -2 internal penalty on all Social rolls that involve the use of his voice.

Second Mouth: The character has a second mouth somewhere on his body. This mouth has no abilities other than speech, but its personality is separate from and usually antagonistic to the character. The second mouth is invariably under Storyteller control. When the mouth is closed, it resembles a small scar. Often, the mouth remains silent and closed when the character is around others, preventing him from proving the mouth's existence. The mouth also speaks with the character's voice, and it often says things when no one is watching it to get the character into trouble. The mouth has no teeth and cannot attack in any way. Any damage inflicted on the mouth is also inflicted directly on the character.

AFFLICTIONS

Afflictions are more noticeable but generally still useful mutations. In addition to the afflictions found on **Exalted**, page 289, new afflictions are listed below. Each affliction costs two mutation points.

Chakra Eye: This affliction provides all the benefits of the Third Eye pox but also allows the character to detect dematerialized spirits. To do this, the player rolls (Perception + Awareness) with a difficulty of the spirit's permanent Essence. However, the eye never blinks, and so attempts to conceal it cause discomfort for the character, inflicting a -1 internal penalty on all actions while the eye remains covered. If the character already has the Third Eye pox, then Chakra Eye can be purchased for only one additional mutation point. If this affliction is purchased a second time, its benefits and drawbacks are identical to the Lidless Demon Eye blight.

Gazelle's Pace: This affliction is equivalent to taking the Wolf's Pace pox twice. For long distance travel, the character can move overland as quickly as a horse. However, the character cannot possibly hide this mutation—his legs don't look remotely human.

Great Hooves: The character's legs turn into hooves per the Hooves pox. These powerful hooves inflict +2 damage to kicks, and all kicking attacks inflict lethal damage.

Scorpion's Tail: This affliction duplicates the Tail pox found on page 288 of **Exalted**. However, whatever the tail's form, it ends in a sharp pointed barb. The tail is long enough for the character to attack in any direction, but it cannot be concealed absent stunts or Charms. If the

Scorpion's Tail affliction is purchased a second time (or once as a blight), the tail's attack is considered piercing. Many mutants with this affliction also have the Toxin mutation (see **Exalted**, p. 289).

Talons/Tusks/Horns: (Revised from **Exalted**, p. 289.) The character sports dangerous talons, tusks, horns or some other hard growth that can be used as a natural weapon, inflicting lethal damage through Martial Arts attacks. Depending on the growths' locations or natures, treat them as punch or kick attacks that inflict lethal damage two greater than normal (i.e., a "punch" deals two lethal damage, the "kick" five lethal damage.) They remain natural weapons and cannot be disarmed, but they can be cut off with a crippling attack. This mutation cannot be stacked or hidden.

Thick Skin: The character's skin becomes denser and heavier than the Fur/Feathers/Leaves pox. It might be thick and horny like rhinoceros hide, it could be covered in bark and knots or have heavy, crocodilian scales and bony nodules. The character gains 2L/2B soak. If a character gains the Fur/Feathers/Leaves/Scales pox twice, replace it with this affliction.

DEBILITIES

These mutations are more obvious, with more serious drawbacks. In addition to the debilities found on page 289 of **Exalted**, new debilities are listed below. Each debility costs two mutation points.

Heart's Blood Addiction: Only the Lunar Exalted can suffer this debility. The character becomes obsessed with gaining new forms. When the character encounters a new species that is not currently in his heart's blood library, his player must roll the character's Temperance. If the roll fails, the Lunar feels compelled to seek out a specimen of the new species and take its heart's blood. Until he does so, the obsession nags at the Lunar, inflicting a cumulative -1 internal penalty to all rolls for every day he goes without satisfying his hunger. The Lunar can ignore the internal penalty for one scene by spending a point of Willpower.

BLIGHTS

Blights are extremely serious mutations whose positive benefits barely outweigh their drawbacks. In addition to the blights found on **Exalted**, page 289, new blights are listed below. Each blight costs four mutation points.

Acidic Pustules: The character's body is covered with disgusting pustules. Whenever the character suffers damage from a hand-to-hand attack, the pus from these repulsive growths can splash back on the attacker, inflicting acid damage. For every point of damage suffered by the character, regardless of type, roll one die of lethal damage against the attacker and anyone else within five yards, subtracting soak as normal.

Cheetah's Pace: This blight is equivalent to taking the Wolf's Pace pox three times. For long distance travel, this blight provides the speed of a simple horse relay. The mutation alters a human recipient's entire body: when running at full speed, including Dash actions, the character must go to all fours. This is not compatible with carrying weapons ready for use, or any other activity that requires hands; when the character stops running, she must spend the normal amount of time to draw weapons or otherwise prepare to use her hands again (typically a Miscellaneous Action or a Join Battle roll, as circumstances warrant).

Hideous Maw: The character has a second mouth somewhere on her body, most commonly on her stomach. This mouth must be used for eating, and the character can no longer eat through her normal mouth. The Hideous Maw is at least one foot wide (and may be larger if the character is a Lunar or otherwise capable of shapeshifting) and ringed with sharp teeth. Some Wyld mutants with this blight also gain the Tentacles blight (**Exalted**, p. 289), with the tentacles taking the form of viscera exploding from the mutant's body while the maw is open. The effects are otherwise identical to the Tentacles blight… just more disgusting.

Lidless Demon Eye: This blight is identical to the Chakra Eye affliction discussed previously, except that the eye glows with an unearthly green light that makes stealth impossible while the eye is exposed. The Lidless Demon Eye confers all of the benefits and drawbacks of the Chakra Eye except as follows. First, the Lidless Demon Eye can automatically perceive invisible and dematerialized creatures without the need for a roll. Second, the character can detect the use of Essence and magic as if he had used the Charm All-Encompassing Sorcerer's Sight (see **Exalted,** p. 222). Finally, attempting to cover the eye sufficiently to conceal its light is quite painful for the character, inflicting a -3 internal penalty on all actions while the light of the Lidless Demon Eye is concealed.

Prehensile Body Hair: The character's body hair is long and shaggy, although it does not look like actual fur as in the case of the Fur pox (see **Exalted**, p. 288). The character can cause hair anywhere on his body to stretch up to one yard and entangle a nearby target. Mechanically, doing so adds 3 to the character's Strength for purposes of maintaining a grapple. When the character does not manipulate his body hair, he still looks extremely hirsute, and his body hair tends to move on its own randomly; the hair does not stretch beyond its normal length unless the character wishes. The character's hairy body makes constricting clothing uncomfortable, though, increasing Fatigue and Mobility penalties for armor by +1 each.

Serpentine Hair: The character's hair has been replaced with dozens of writhing snakes. The snakes do not have independent brain function, for each one remains part of the character. However, each snake can extend up to three yards away from the character to strike a target. The snakes' bites are poisonous, using the Traits listed for coral snake venom (see **Exalted**, p. 131).

Name	Speed	Accuracy	Damage	Defense	Rate
Hideous Maw Bite	5	+1	+5L	n/a	1
Scorpion's Tail	5	+2	+2L	+2	2
Serpentine Hair	4	+3	+2L	+2	4

DEFORMITIES

Deformities are extremely serious mutations whose drawbacks make it nearly impossible for the Lunar to function in any civilized setting. Indeed, some deformities make survival itself a problem. In addition to the deformities found on pages 289-290 of **Exalted**, new deformities are listed below. Each deformity costs four mutation points.

Creature of Darkness: The Wyld has so infused the poor character that Charms bearing the Holy keyword treat him as a creature of darkness, just as the Fair Folk. The character can never use any Charm or other effect that includes the Holy quality.

Magical Plague Carrier: This deformity can only be taken by a character who has previously taken the Plague Carrier deformity outlined in **Exalted**, page 290. Instead of carrying a mundane plague, the character becomes a vector for a magical disease of some kind. Magical diseases seem particularly common among the Wyld-tainted, and many savants think that a mundane disease carried by someone exposed to the Wyld may itself be just as vulnerable to mutation as the creature who suffers from it. A few of the more common magical Wyld diseases are outlined on pages 211-213.

ABOMINATIONS

Abominations are unquestionably the most severe form of mutation. They often make it difficult or impossible for the Lunar to function anywhere in Creation. Even Wyld barbarian tribes fear people who carry an abomination. In most cases, only a stunt or Charms could conceal an abomination. In addition to the abominations found on page 290 of **Exalted**, new abominations are listed below. Each abomination costs six mutation points.

Serpent's Body: The character's legs fuse and stretch into a long, serpentine body, 15-20 feet long. The character gains a +4 Dexterity bonus only for calculating movement rates. The character also gains a +4 bonus on all grappling-related rolls when he uses his tail to constrict his foe. However, the character suffers a -3 internal penalty on all actions other than movement actions for which legs are essential, most notably jumping.

Spider Legs: This abomination causes the character to sprout four enormous spider legs from his back. Its effects resemble the Multiple Limbs abomination (see **Exalted,** p. 290), except that the spider legs do not confer a -1 reduction in flurry penalties. Instead, the character gains the ability to climb any surface that is not completely frictionless, without

any need for a roll. The character may not climb up objects that are not strong enough to support his weight, but he can hang upside down from a ceiling without difficulty. This abomination also grants a +4 bonus to the (Strength + Athletics) pool for determining how far or how high a character can jump, and a character with spider legs can fall a distance equal to twice his vertical jumping distance and land without injury.

Terrifying Mane: The character has a long mane of hair that can move according to her will and can extend up to 10 yards. The character can form multiple hair "tentacles" but is subject to the normal penalty for multiple actions no matter how many tentacles she fashions. These hair tentacles are strong enough to support the character's weight, easily allowing her to climb walls or brachiate through trees using only her hair to support her. The tentacles have the same Strength and Dexterity as the character herself. When the character does not actively control her hair, it tends to move about on its own, although it does not grow past its normal length unless the character wishes.

WYLD-INDUCED DERANGEMENTS

Whenever a Casteless Lunar shifts into a human form, including her human true form, she risks gaining a derangement instead of a physical mutation. Derangements can be more or less powerful, being rated as deficiencies, debilities or deformities. Unless stated otherwise, the effects of a derangement are constant, but a character can resist a derangement for one scene by spending a point of Willpower. This is considered natural influence and does not result in Limit gain. A number of Wyld-induced derangements can be found in **The Compass of Celestial Direction: The Wyld**. Also, the following mutations described in **Exalted** may be taken as either a physical mutation or a derangement: Mood Swings, Delusions and Wyld Addiction. Additional derangements include the following:

CANNIBALISM

A character with this derangement fixates on the idea of eating human flesh. He has no physical need to do so (unless he has the Diet debility—see **Exalted**, p. 289). Rather, he is fascinated by the very idea of violating the taboo of eating his own kind.

Deficiency: Whenever the character has an opportunity to taste human flesh, his player rolls the character's Temperance. On a failed roll, the character must give in to his urge

or spend a point of Willpower to resist. At the Storyteller's discretion, the Temperance roll may suffer internal penalties if, for example, the character has little chance of getting caught or punished.

Debility: The Temperance roll automatically suffers a -1 internal penalty *or* the character may not spend Willpower to resist the compulsion.

Deformity: The Temperance roll automatically suffers a -2 internal penalty *and* the character may not spend Willpower to resist the compulsion. "Opportunities to taste human flesh" include moments when the character might commit murder with little chance of being caught.

MEGALOMANIA

A character suffering from Megalomania is overcome by a powerful sense of his own superiority and fitness to lead others. Severe Megalomania often includes the delusion that one is a famous, powerful figure such as the Empress, the Mask of Winters or Luna.

Deficiency: When the character encounters people who do not accede to his commands or who demonstrate greater leadership abilities than himself, his player rolls Compassion. On a failed roll, the character develops a strong dislike for any person who undermines the character's sense of superiority. A botch drives the character into an immediate homicidal rage. These effects last for one scene, though the character may resist them by spending a Willpower point.

Debility: The Compassion roll automatically suffers a -1 internal penalty *or* the character may not spend Willpower to resist the compulsion. In addition, the effects last for a full day.

Deformity: The Compassion roll suffers a -2 internal penalty *and* the character may not spend Willpower to resist the compulsion. The effects last until the character is persuaded through Social rolls to forgive the person who failed to recognize his superiority. Otherwise, the effect with regard to that particular person is permanent.

PHOBIAS

Phobias consist of irrational, overpowering fears of certain phenomena. Virtually anything can become the subject of a phobia, from cats to enclosed spaces to the number 13. Low-level phobias typically trigger a strong aversion to the object of the phobia. Higher-level phobias result in panic attacks or even catatonia. Characters with Valor-related Virtue Flaws may not take this derangement.

Deficiency: When the character encounters the object of her fear, her player rolls the character's Valor. On a failed roll, the character must avoid the object of her fear at all costs. If forced to confront the object of her fear, she suffers a -2 internal penalty on all actions while in proximity to the fear stimulus. The character can ignore this penalty for a scene by spending a Willpower point.

Debility: At this level, the penalty on the Valor roll is -2 *or* the character may not spend Willpower to ignore the phobia.

Deformity: At this level, the penalty on the Valor roll is -4 *and* the character may not spend Willpower to ignore the phobia.

The listed internal penalties to the Valor roll assume that the object of the character's phobia is an item or situation rarely encountered or easily avoided: small pets, clowns, bee stings, old people, Anathema. Reduce the internal penalties by 1 if the object of a phobia is fairly common or hard to avoid: fire, illness, the dark, enclosed spaces, horses, storms.

SEXUAL ADDICTION

A character suffering from Sexual Addiction feels the need to engage in sexual activity at any opportunity. Charismatic or manipulative characters often engage in elaborate plots to lure a multitude of partners into bed. Less socially adroit characters often become serial rapists.

Deficiency: Whenever the character encounters a person who has Appearance of 3 or higher and whom he finds sexually compatible, his player must roll the character's Temperance. On a failed roll, the character becomes obsessed with bedding his target and suffers a -3 internal penalty on all actions until he has done so (or finds a new target for his lust). On a botch, the character loses any inhibitions he might have about nonconsensual sex. The character can spend a point of Willpower to ignore the initial need for a Temperance roll, but if the player makes the roll and fails it, thereafter, the character can only spend Willpower to ignore the internal penalty for a scene.

Debility: The Temperance roll suffers a -1 internal penalty.

Deformity: The Temperance roll suffers a -2 internal penalty, *and* the character cannot spend Willpower to resist at any stage.

SOCIOPATHIC DETACHMENT

A character who suffers from Sociopathic Detachment finds it difficult, if not impossible, to relate compassion-ately or even honestly with other people. She knows that other people have needs and feelings, but perceives them only as weaknesses to exploit. Characters with Compassion- or Temperance-related Virtue Flaws may not take this derangement.

Deficiency: A character with this derangement suffers a -1 internal penalty on all Compassion rolls and all Temperance rolls, and also loses one channel in each of those Virtues for purposes of channeling Virtues with Willpower.

Debility: The character suffers a -2 internal penalty on all Compassion rolls and Temperance rolls and loses the ability to channel one of those two Virtues. He still loses one channel in the other Virtue.

Deformity: The character suffers a -3 penalty on all Compassion rolls and Temperance rolls. He completely loses the ability to channel both of those Virtues.

MAGICAL DISEASES

Magical diseases are illnesses with supernatural properties. Many, if not most, such diseases result from a diseased person entering a Wyld zone: The transforming power of the Wyld may affect the disease instead of, or in addition to, the carrier. The disease then becomes a sort of communicable Wyld effect that can pass outside the Wyld zone to anyone exposed to the carrier. Other magical diseases may come from demesnes or other powerful supernatural forces.

Most such diseases have a relatively short duration. Infected people either recover and develop immunity, or they die, as with conventional diseases. Some unfortunates become magical plague carriers due to gaining the deformity of the same name (see p. 209). Such plague carriers never succumb to the effects of the disease they carry. Indeed, a carrier often never recognizes his condition. Most chimerae with this deformity are astute enough to realize it, although most also don't really seem to care.

Wyld-tainted magical diseases follow the same general rules as those outlined for mundane diseases (see **Exalted**, p. 350), subject to the following changes. First, Exalted can contract magical diseases, but they still retain a greater immunity when compared to mortals. Dragon-Blooded gain a +1 bonus to the (Stamina + Resistance) roll to resist the

disease's virulence, while Lunars and Sidereals gain a +2 bonus and Solars and Abyssals gain a +3 bonus.

The rules for treated and untreated morbidity function as they do for mundane diseases. However, the difficulty for mundane treatment of these diseases is usually so high that only Exalted armed with Medicine-related Charms have any realistic chance of treating them. These rules apply only to normal contagion and not to Charms that directly induce supernatural diseases, such as Citrine Poxes of Contagion Style martial arts (see **Scroll of the Monk**, pp. 124-129). Magical diseases carry the following Traits.

Virulence: The difficulty of the (Stamina + Resistance) roll for a character who has been exposed to the disease.

Incubation: The amount of time it takes for an infected character to show symptoms of the disease.

Diagnosis: The difficulty of any (Intelligence + Medicine) roll to identify the disease and devise a treatment regimen.

Difficulty to Treat (Mundane/Magical): The difficulty of any rolls (whether through mundane healing techniques or those augmented by Charms or magical effects) to heal an infected character.

Morbidity: The difficulty of an infected character's (Stamina + Resistance) roll to avoid dying from the disease without medical treatment.

Treated Morbidity: The difficulty of an infected character's (Stamina + Resistance) roll to avoid dying from the disease after successful medical treatment.

GREEN RAGE

Green Rage induces uncontrollable, psychopathic fury in its victims, along with compulsive cannibalism. Victims of Green Rage attack any living thing they encounter in a frenzy, but they preferentially pursue other humans and primates, the only two creatures who can contract the disease.

Green Rage has three stages. When a character first succumbs to the disease, he quickly loses his ability to stomach any food other than raw meat, which he can digest easily. After 24 hours without treatment, the character slips into Stage Two, in which the character's Intelligence drops by two points (to a minimum of 1) and he develops a craving for human flesh. At this stage, the character can still fight off the cravings if his player succeeds at a Compassion roll with a -2 internal penalty or spends one Willpower point per scene of resistance.

After four days or after the character has eaten human flesh, whichever comes first, the character enters Stage Three. At that point, his Intelligence drops to 1 if it hasn't already, but he gains +1 to his Strength and Dexterity due to a frenzied burst of energy. At that point, the character cannot resist his cannibalistic urges by any means save a cure.

Victims of Green Rage do not feed on other victims of the disease. When Green Rage sweeps through an area, therefore, the most common response is simply to wall up the victims together until everyone in the quarantine zone dies of starvation.

Vector: Savants believe that Green Rage entered Creation when a rabid animal wandered into the Wyld. The rabies itself mutated into Green Rage. The disease is transmitted only through bite, mercifully enough—but then, it's a rare victim of a Green Rage attack who escapes his attacker and lives long enough to develop the disease.

Treatment: There is no known mundane cure for Green Rage. The magical treatment difficulty listed below refers for victims suffering from the First Stage of Green Rage. Second Stage inflicts a +2 difficulty to the roll, while Third Stage inflicts a + 4 difficulty. If a victim is cured, he immediately loses his extra dots in Strength and Dexterity but regains one point of Intelligence. Any additional lost Intelligence points return at the rate of one per day.

Virulence: 6
Incubation: (Stamina) hours
Diagnosis: 3
Difficulty to Treat (Mundane/Magical): no cure/4
Untreated Morbidity: 6   **Treated Morbidity:** 2

GRINNING FOOL DEATH

This deadly illness is one of the more common strains of Drunken Moth Sickness, a magical disease that alters the victim's behavior. In the case of Grinning Fool Death, the victim feels an uncontrollable urge to laugh hysterically. Out of combat, the character laughs constantly as long as he stays conscious, taking one level of bashing damage every hour and fainting automatically whenever the accumulating damage fills his Incapacitated health box. Without the use of stunts or Charms, this bashing damage cannot heal while the character remains conscious. The laughter also inflicts a -2 internal penalty on all actions the character takes, and stealth becomes completely impossible. In combat, the character must devote one action on every tick in which he acts to laughing. This means that every combat action becomes at least a two-action flurry with the second action suffering a -3 penalty. It also means that the Defense Value penalty for any combat actions the character takes increase by one. If a character dies while under the influence of this disease, his face contorts into a hideous grinning rictus that not even the most skilled mortician in Sijan can remove.

An infected character can suppress the impulse to laugh for one minute by spending a point of Willpower (or for one action in combat). On each subsequent action, the infected character may either use a simple Charm, use a Combo or spend at least half her non-reflexive actions serving the disease's purpose. (This last assumes that the character uses a flurry, and the "half" rounds up. If the character takes just one action, it is spent laughing.)

Vector: Grinning Fool Death sometimes infects victims who have eaten Wyld-tainted fruit. Once the disease finds its way into Creation, however, the disease can pass to anyone who listens to an infected person laugh for more than a few minutes. A potential victim's player must roll whenever he first hears an infected person laugh, and the player must roll again in every new scene in which the character is exposed to the hideous, insane laughter. At the Storyteller's discretion, a potential victim who is exposed to a large number of infected people at once may suffer penalties to the Virulence roll.

Treatment: Grinning Fool Death is an exceedingly difficult disease to treat, because anyone who hears an infected person risks infection himself. Fortunately, the disease itself grants a certain amount of immunity to victims who survive it. If someone who contracts Grinning Fool Death and survives is exposed to it again, the difficulty of the Virulence roll drops to 3. After surviving the disease twice, the patient becomes permanently immune. The most common treatment involves binding and gagging the patient, locking him into a soundproof room and hoping he can ride the disease out. Some savants report anecdotal evidence that exposing an infected person to scenes of grotesque horror and brutality can "shock the patient" out of the disease. In particular, one Wood-aspected Cynis physician insists that he cured several children of Grinning Fool Death by forcing them to watch as he tortured their mother.

Virulence: 4
Incubation: Immediate
Diagnosis: 3
Difficulty to Treat (Mundane/Magical): 7/4
Untreated Morbidity: 6   **Treated Morbidity:** 2

WHITE SUN SICKNESS

Originally a form of malaria, White Sun Sickness appeared when a small Wyld zone expanded to encompass a Southern swamp, and the mosquitoes within mutated into a new and deadly form. The chief symptoms of White Sun Sickness are high fever accompanied by hallucinations. The disease itself attacks the victim's natural Essence, and the effect of the hallucinations is represented by an internal penalty on all actions equal to the victim's permanent Essence. As such, the disease presents greater danger to infected Exalted than to mortals.

The effects of the disease are also more pernicious for Essence users because the illness taints their very Essence supply. When a victim uses a Charm or some other Essence-fueled effect, the immediate Essence cost increases by one mote. The next Essence expenditure costs two extra motes, the third three motes, and so forth. For every day

that the Essence user goes without spending any Essence at all, the total extra mote cost drops by five motes, but otherwise, it can increase to infinity or until the character receives treatment.

Finally, Exalted who suffer from White Sun Sickness gain Limit at twice the normal rate, a coincidental effect of the Wyld's interaction with the Great Curse. Fortunately, White Sun Sickness is rarely lethal.

Vector: White Sun Sickness spreads through the bite of the white mosquito, a Wyld-tainted breed of mosquito that has spread all over the South. White mosquitoes look like normal mosquitoes except for their pale carapaces. White Sun mosquitoes are also much hardier than normal mosquitoes and can survive quite easily outside the swampy habitat of normal mosquitoes.

Treatment: The immediate treatment for a sufferer of White Sun Sickness is simply to keep him warm (to help break his fever) and restrained (to keep him from hurting himself and others while affected by a hallucination). Burning incense or citronella near a victim also seems to help with the affliction.

Virulence: 5
Incubation: 3-5 days
Diagnosis: 3
Difficulty to Treat (Mundane/Magical): 3/6
Untreated Morbidity: 5   **Treated Morbidity:** 2

CHAPTER SEVEN
STORYTELLING

Similar to the **Exalted** Storytelling section, this chapter offers guidance for you to share stories about reincarnated demigods. Unlike Solars, the Children of the Moon shape themselves in the image of the world as often as they mold Creation into their own image. Lunars may be the deadliest predators ever to walk the face of Creation, but their stories are as complicated by love, hate and a desire to understand their purpose in life as those of anyone. The goal of these pages is to help you make those stories into your own personal legends. If you haven't read the Storytelling chapter of **Exalted** recently, you can get a lot of ideas by referring back to it. Then come back here for tips, tricks and information more specific to running a Lunar series.

PLAYERS, TOO

Presumably, you picked up this **Manual of Exalted Power** because you want to run a game of Lunar heroes and heroines. However, **Exalted** is a shared experience, and this chapter contains nothing secret. Players are encouraged

to peruse this section along with rest of the book. Ideally, that will help you run the **Exalted** game that you and your players will enjoy.

A REMINDER

This book contains all of the rules required to add Lunar characters to a game of **Exalted**. The default way that Lunars interact with Creation is described throughout this book. Nevertheless, it is worth opening with this important reminder. Before any discussion of the rules of the game, Storytellers should always keep two cardinal laws of play in mind:

Rule 1: Have Fun. This is a game, and it's supposed to be entertaining for all parties involved. If you don't have fun, stop and do something else.

Rule 2: If you don't like it, change it. This is also known as the Golden Rule. Nothing is more important than Rule 2, so players and Storytellers may freely customize the setting and rules for their own games. Players should note that the Storyteller is the final arbiter of all rules.

GETTING STARTED

As a Storyteller, decide what kind of game you would enjoy running. If you aren't having a good time, then your players are doomed to a lackluster experience at best. Try to come up with more than one idea, in case the first one doesn't work out. Hopefully, the core **Exalted** book and the six chapters preceding this one have already inspired you with exciting ideas for a game about Luna's Chosen. You may also want to take a look at some of those suggested resources listed in the **Exalted** introduction (p. 19).

If you have conceived of a singular idea that is just too good to pass up, you should still consider some potential variations that your players might enjoy. Very often, a series doesn't go the way the Storyteller imagines. Players make unexpected choices; Storytellers get new ideas. So, take your series premise, twist it around and see what else you can do with it.

Say that you have thought of a way that someone could funnel the boundless energy of the Wyld into repairing Creation, simultaneously destroying the deathly shadowlands and circumventing the threat of chaos for a long time to come. You may want to mull over ways that this procedure could go terribly wrong. Doing so prepares you to present suitably great challenges to the characters who seek to accomplish this feat. It also prepares you for the possibility that some of your players may feel that a sugar-laden happy ending is out of theme for an epic game. How do your players' characters come by the knowledge to perform this procedure you imagine? What if they decide that the idea presents a terrible risk that they are not willing to take? Perhaps the world may indeed be rid of the canker of shadowlands, but the very laws of Creation might change forever. Maybe the process will take root and spread the walls of Creation millions of miles in every direction, expanding the world beyond all previous imaginings. Keeping variations in mind gives you and your players a greater range of options.

TALK IT OVER

Next, sit down with your players and have a group chat about what everyone wants to get out of the game. Tell them what you have come up with, but listen to what they have to say, too. Do they want to start in the underbelly of a city such as Nexus or Chiaroscuro as gritty street rats, maybe even literally so? Perhaps they want to play powerful barbarian warlords who emerge from the Wyld to sack the Realm, pillage its warehouses of jade, seize its mighty artifacts and turn its elegant nobles into harems. Are the characters loyal to the Silver Pact or steadfastly outside of its strictures

despite the inherent danger of being a Casteless? Perhaps they joined the Silver Pact, but have since discovered that they have irreconcilable differences with it. Can the Pact actually control a half-dozen Celestial Exalted who join together with some unified purpose?

The fact is that your players' characters represent a not-insignificant portion of all of the Lunar Exalted in Creation. As one of the largest close-knit groups of Celestial Exalted in your series, it is virtually impossible for these characters *not* to change the world in big ways. If you don't take this into consideration from the start, you may well be surprised by the heights of epic power your players' characters achieve and be ill prepared to handle the massive transformations they bring to the world around them.

TWO VISIONS, ONE GAME

Unless you are really lucky, or perfectly in tune with your group, chances are that you have your game vision, and some of your players are onboard for it, but at least one player thinks outside the boundaries of your series. Provided people are willing to work together, this isn't necessarily a bad thing. First, see if you can merge aspects of the ideas together into one larger context. Maybe you want to run a game about Lunars taking over the Realm, but one of your players really wants to belong to a Nexus street gang. Talk to the player about having him play an urban Lunar who encounters one of the early assaults by invading warlords and joins them. Divergent concepts often are much less troublesome than they initially seem and can be easily rolled into a larger general idea.

If you wanted to run a game about harnessing the potential of the Wyld to fix the world, but your players want to sack the Realm, then uniting your visions might prove more difficult. Nevertheless, take a look at how you might combine such ideas to create a greater story. You might begin your series with the Lunar characters invading the outlying satrapies of the Realm, and present them with evidence that the very fabric of the world is disintegrating along with the social order that they disrupt. The characters might discover that these reality engines were once powered with manses held by the satraps whose strongholds the characters have crushed. Or turn it around: The characters find a way to repair Creation, but it requires hundreds of Manses; and with the Dynastic Houses descending into civil war, the Realm will never implement the plan. Particularly if the troupe contains a No Moon, they could set out to conquer ever more powerful manses within the Realm in order to boost the effects of the reality engines to their greatest possible level. By combining your competing visions, you have created an interesting vessel with which to explore the concept of how order might be built from chaos.

INITIAL QUESTIONS

Before you begin your Lunar Exalted series, you and your players should answer some basic questions about the characters, the settings and the rules. To begin, reference the questions on pages 260-261 of **Exalted**. The more attention you give them, the stronger your game is likely to be. Next, consider these additional questions, which pertain especially to Lunars:

• Why did the characters Exalt as Lunars? Do they directly fit into the plans of the Silver Lady, or do they merely fit into her general design for the Lunar Exaltation? As with all Exalts, their patron has no direct control over them. Do the characters rebel against Luna even as they once fought in the gods' rebellion against the Primordials? Perhaps they see the Silver Lady as mother figure worthy of universal devotion and seek to raise her priesthood above that of the Immaculate Order?

• The Children of the Moon instinctively feel some sense of stewardship, even as Luna feels devotion to the Primordial Gaia. How do the characters' stewardships fit together? Do they share the same wards, or will it be a challenge for each of them to protect her own charge without hampering the efforts of her fellow Lunars? Hopefully, if the characters share any territory they can come to an accord, but what if other Children of the Moon are not so amiable? Will battles over conflicting stewardship rights cause rifts within the Silver Pact?

• What roles will the Lunar characters' Solar mates play? Have the Children of the Moon and their mates Exalted so far from each other that they may never meet, much less have a meaningful interaction? Even if this is the case, what happens if the Lunars gain earth-shaking influence and power that no one can ignore? Perhaps the Lunars Exalted during the same five-year period marking the Solar return and have naturally been drawn together again? Do the characters remember their First Age mates? Do they regard them with cautious fear, everlasting love or burning hatred?

• How much time, if any, have the characters spent in the Wyld? How has this altered their perceptions of Creation? Can they adjust to a world with rules and natural order?

• What are the characters' relationships with the Silver Pact? Do some of them remain close to their mentors? Have all of the characters rejected the wisdom of their elders? What are the consequences the characters face for doing so?

• What goals do the characters share? If they have nothing in common, then why do they working together? Are all of them under the control of a singularly powerful No Moon sorcerer? Are these goals righteous or selfish in nature? How many people must die to accomplish these goals?

CHANGING THE RULES

Lunar Exalted are extremely powerful individuals, easily capable of dominating the world around them. Nonetheless, for centuries they have been thwarted by the incomparable power of the Realm Defense Grid, and now, the returned Solars threaten to renew the golden hegemony they enjoyed in the First Age. The strong sense of duty the Lunars feel, which drives them to defend Creation against the endless sea of invaders found in the Wyld, is also partly responsible for their lack of success in seizing the center of power in Creation. But maybe that isn't the game you want to run?

The rules of the game are a set of guidelines, designed to give you and your players a framework within which to explore the awesome stories that **Exalted** offers. The rules are subject to change, though, according to the needs of the stories you plan to run. As noted on page 261 of **Exalted**, direct changes to the rules should be considered carefully with an eye toward the interlocking nature of the game's rules and setting. If you are comfortable changing the game's rules, though, then anything is possible.

Example: Conrad is a Storyteller who dislikes the degree to which Casteless are susceptible to the Wyld. He revises this for his game, allowing Casteless to change shapes twice per day without adding any dice to the roll to see whether they suffer Wyld mutation. He figures this will allow a Lunar to safely change to a useful shape and return to her true form once per day, but that it doesn't eliminate the threat for Casteless who continue to shift.

KEEPING CHARACTERS UNIQUE

This topic is also discussed in the Storytelling chapter of **Exalted**, but some players may feel that having three castes rather than five makes it more difficult to differentiate their characters. Certainly, if you have more than three players in your game, then at least two of their Lunar characters must share the same caste. Of course, some players may consider the Casteless as an option, but there is little doubt that the Casteless will face a tougher time than their tattooed companions. Some players may relish the opportunity for just such a challenge. As the **Exalted** storytelling chapter suggests, however, there is much more to a character than her caste. Two characters may share the same caste yet be very different in every other way.

Example: Brent's character Crimson Bear is a Full Moon Caste with a focus on immense strength and a grappling style of martial arts. His massive form plays into his habit of intimidating foes into fleeing battle rather than forcing him to fight. Though he is a powerful warrior, Crimson Bear tries to be a healer, and Brent made sure to give him a lot of dots in Medicine. Bunnie's character Elasis is also a Full Moon Caste, but she grew up in the jungles of the Southeast. She relies on speed and stealth, wielding a poisoned javelin with the deadly sureness of a serpent. Sometimes, she is a bit too quick on the attack, having learned the hard way that the first strike often wins the day.

Don't overlook the usefulness of spirit shape and Knacks when seeking to accentuate the differences between characters. Returning to our example: Giving Crimson Bear the spirit shape of a reddish-brown bear seems fitting, and it sets him further apart from the green mamba form of Elasis.

GAME STYLES

The core **Exalted** book discusses a number of play styles (see pp. 262-263), and many of those work well for Lunar games. This section discusses how to adjust those styles for use with Lunar games and offers some expanded styles particularly applicable to the Children of the Moon.

STYLES REMIX

"'Vanilla **Exalted**" can work for Lunar characters as easily as for Solars. The heroes of the Moon fight the Scarlet Empire, build their own power bases in the Threshold and eventually converge on the Realm to seize power. Interesting variations arise when you ponder how the Lunars might interact with the resurgent Solars—especially in the long run. Start with the Lunars and Solars renewing their ancient partnership.

Option One: The Solar Exalted might take full advantage of their return and successfully reestablish the Solar Deliberative. Given that only half of the Solar Essences remain uncorrupted by the Yozis and the Neverborn, however, the reborn Chosen of the Sun might depend more heavily on the Lunars for help than they did during the First Age. Due to their greater numbers, the Children of Luna might withstand the overwhelming charisma of the Solars and forge a somewhat more equal society this time.

Option Two: The Silver Pact contains so much of the remaining power of elder Exalts that perhaps a Lunar Deliberative rules the dawning new Age. How long can they keep control in the face of the Solars' inherent inclination toward perfection and natural talent for leadership? Lunars in the Silver Pact have their own plans for Creation. Will they work the Solars into their plans or play second fiddle again? How far will the Lunars go to stay free of the overwhelming destiny of the Solars? It's "'Vanilla' **Exalted**"—but the Lunars are the heroes, not the arriviste Solars.

Option Three: The heroes of the Moon and Sun do *not* unite. If the Solars want to restore their ancient world empire and the Silver Pact wants a fluid, ever-changing patchwork of competing states based on the Thousand Streams River, they must come into conflict. Perhaps the Solars take the Realm while the Lunars seize the Threshold. The cycle begins anew… but instead of the Dragon-Blooded, the Silver Pact faces the threat of resurgent Solars, going mad again to become the new villains.

You can come up with more twists and variations, too. Despite the name, "'Vanilla' **Exalted**" can still have many flavors.

"A Land Once Divided Must Unite" might be one of the hardest styles to portray with Lunars, but it is certainly not impossible. While the Children of the Moon are probably forced to gravitate toward political power from the edges of the Threshold, their shapeshifting Knacks are invaluable tools in intrigues meant to seize a throne, and their fierce capacity for combat will dominate most battlefields. Solars newly coming into their own, and Dragon-Blooded already deeply entrenched in the halls of power, are likely to represent the greatest competition in the arena of the Mandate of Heaven.

"And I'll Form the Head!" comes easily to a Lunar Exalt game. The Children of the Moon are not limited to

artifacts alone when it comes to achieving absurd feats of Creation-warping. With the right Knacks, Lunars might become monstrous behemoths fighting for supremacy while wading through the towers of Chiaroscuro or the Imperial City like so many blades of grass. In this style of game, it can readily be assumed that the Lunars carried innumerable artifacts with them when they fled the Usurpation. With the remarkable properties of moonsilver, you might even allow multiple Lunars with warstriders to join together into a single monstrous creation with one of them literally forming the head.

"Outlander" immediately suggests one of the realms where Lunars already shine above all other Exalted, the Wyld. Casteless characters are a poor choice in this style of play, because their susceptibility to the Wyld is a serious impairment when one is constantly faced with it. Other Lunars are eminently qualified to play in such a region, though. Such a game might even serve as an extended prelude for some other style, or an interlude within one.

"Invasion!" works well with a Lunar Exalted game, particularly if you assume that the otherworldly threat comes from the Wyld. Many Children of the Moon took up arms against the Fair Folk in order to keep the Usurpation from letting Creation fall to utterly dissolution by chaos. These Stewards, and those allied to them, hold the edges of the world and cannot fail to play a great part in any scenario wherein the Wyld pours through the ramparts of Creation. On the other hand, you could approach this scenario from the other side. What if the Lunar characters are the source of the invasion, leading one or more of the great tribal nations in conquest? How do their barbaric armies fare against the crack legions of Lookshy and the Realm? What if they take down the Realm only to have the Fair Folk launch their own invasion?

Factions in Conflict

The house of the silver moon is not a shiny happy place, and this style draws from its internal conflicts. Even during the First Age, the Silver Pact was not united in purpose. Some Lunars with a political bent saw the Pact as a tool for their individual agendas. Militant Moonchildren thought to wield its membership as a weapon against the insurgency of the Wyld. A handful of No Moons treated the Pact as little more than a research group composed of Lunar colleagues.

The separate groups within the Silver Pact are really very small, given that the entirety of Lunar population is merely 300 in number. Nonetheless, the Children of the Moon are Celestial Exalted, and this means that they wield considerable power. When a single Lunar can destroy an army, the potential of 20 or more Moonchildren working together is stupendous to consider. Such assemblies helped the sorcerer Salina weave the initiations of sorcery into the fabric of Creation and crafted the secrets of moonsilver tattoos. They have created numerous new societies of humankind and defeated innumerable invasion attempts from the Wyld.

However, the Silver Pact is no more unified now than it was 2,000 years ago. At least eight elder Lunars dating from the First Age still exist—and for some of them, their sanity is as questionable as their motives. Ma-Ha-Suchi nearly became a chimera, and now, his armies of twisted beastmen harry the Scavenger Lands in preparation for its conquest. Raksi jealously hoards the secrets of the City of Sorcery and revels in cannibalism. Leviathan and Tamuz claim vast tracts of untamed Creation as their own yet remain remarkably inactive, at least as far as anyone can tell. Rain Deathflyer and Silver Python created arguably the most successful of the Thousand Streams, the kingdom of Halta, but now, they seem content to defend it as their private shared territory. Magnificent Jaguar and Lilith have but recently awakened or returned to human ways, and no one can guess what they will do next.

The Silver Pact consists of five factions: the Crossroads Society, the Seneschals of the Sun Kings, the Swords of Luna, the Wardens of Gaia and the Winding Path. The decisions that your players make regarding which faction they want to support will immediately and regularly shape the nature of your game. If every player's character belongs to the same faction, then they may seriously shift the future of the Silver Pact in that direction. Should the group split between more than one faction, they may move the Pact toward greater unity (they might even form a "perfect circle" of all five factions) or, conversely, sharply highlight its divisions.

The Crossroads Society

This faction takes credit for the creation of the moonsilver tattoos, which saved Lunar Exalted from dissolution by the Wyld. Crossroads members can wield significant influence over the rest of Lunar society, thanks to their proficiency at sorcery and magical means of communication. As a living repository of First Age lore, the Crossroads Society may present one of the best chances of regaining Creation's past glories. The characters in your game might realize this and join with the faction they see as sure winners in the Time of Tumult. Alternatively, they might discover evidence of the Crossroads Society's treachery and finally gain some well-deserved justice. What will the characters do if the people most capable of creating Wyld-protecting tattoos also turn out to have betrayed their own kind in pursuit of power? Even if such information never comes to light, some Lunars are angry that the Society seems to tacitly support the cruel excesses of Raksi.

Seneschals of the Sun Kings

The return of the Solars is sure to give this faction new prominence in the coming days. Idealistic Lunars may latch onto the reborn Lawgivers, confident that the Chosen of the Unconquered Sun will save Creation before it is torn apart. More practical Children of the Moon may simply find little to admire in a Silver Pact leadership whose outward accomplishments are difficult to see and marvel at the swift rise of the Sun Kings. On the other hand, the Solars of the First

Age became mad despots whose excesses virtually demanded the Usurpation. Why should things turn out differently this time? The characters might see the return of the Sun Kings as a dangerous threat and act to thwart Lunars who cannot resist the ancient Celestial bonds.

SWORDS OF LUNA

The politics of this faction sometimes seem to be the simplest: Creation will fall to the Wyld unless the Lunars defend it vigilantly, and little else matters. Given their propensity to assume stewardship over the world around them, this position comes naturally to many Lunars. The scope of this task might give pause to some Moonchildren. When the existence of the world is at stake, what (and who) would a hero sacrifice to save it? Can you trust someone who considers you expendable? On the other hand, many Silver Pact members take the Swords of Luna somewhat for granted. They will forever battle the Fair Folk at the edges of the world and never win ultimate peace. No Moon sorcerers of the Crossroads Society might feel that it is fine to leave the dirty fighting on the front to the Swords of Luna. Meanwhile, they are free to design a weapon that will bring a permanent end to the depredations of the Wyld or perhaps merely to break into the Imperial Manse and seize control over the Realm Defense Grid.

WARDENS OF GAIA

This faction is at once the most protective of the natural world, and the most likely to experiment with it. Rain Deathflyer and Silver Python are the most prominent advocates of shaping human civilization so that it stays in harmony with nature. Holding forth the Republic of Halta as an example of what can be achieved, this pair enjoys considerable support in the Silver Pact. Young Lunars who stem from a culture that lives in tune with the wilderness, whether from a barbarian tribe or a kingdom with an enlightened shamanic tradition, generally gravitate to this group. On the other hand, the characters may abhor the disruptions of the natural order created by the Wardens' breeding programs. Humans living in harmony with beast shouldn't equate to humans breeding with beasts. One sub-faction of the Wardens follows Ma-Ha-Suchi and seeks to destroy urbanized civilization altogether. The Lunar warlord may prove successful in taking down the Dragon-Blooded Realm, but can a wilderness dotted with overgrown ruins stand against the onslaught of the Fair Folk or the armies of the Deathlords?

WINDING PATH

While the Wardens experiment with the shape of the world, the Winding Path faction seeks to shape its social groups. Sometimes, their goals may seem similar, but the Winding Path Stewards care more about the people of the world than its untamed beasts. Young Lunars are often drawn to this faction specifically because of its human-centric leanings. Unfortunately, the elders of the faction are generally obsessed with the Thousand Streams River. Given the great social powers a Changing Moon elder can bring to bear, young Lunars may spend years serving the goals of the Winding Path before they ever realize just how many times they have been deceived. Some Moonchildren turn to revenge at being tricked, while others never fall prey to their schemes in the first place. Swords of Luna in particular often see little difference between the jaded masters of the Winding Path and conniving Sidereals.

CELESTIAL POLITICS

A game with a political style need not limit itself to the Silver Pact and its factions. Lunar Exalted do not grow

up steeped in the incestuous politics of the Realm's Dragon-Blooded, and they don't possess the supernatural leadership qualities of the Lawgivers. Nonetheless, the Lunars are so powerful that their actions are sure to reach the ears of various gods in the Celestial City of Yu-Shan.

Most of the Exalted have much less contact with Heaven than they used to. The Sidereals nestle within the Bureau of Destiny, of course, but the gods of the other Celestial bureaus seem less than enthusiastic about working with the Dragon-Blooded. The Solars have yet to achieve such power that Heaven must treat with them once more; the Abyssals, of course, are abominations against Heaven. But the Lunars… as the Lunars spread their influence through the Threshold, they have worshipful populations to pique the gods' interest, while their battles to defend Creation have not gone unnoticed.

In these times, Lunars who consort with the gods have much to gain. The Bureau of Seasons is technically under the auspices of Luna. Many of its functionaries might consider aiding a Moonchild, if only to curry favor with the Silver Lady. Gods within the Bureau of Nature sometimes feel as though they owe some favor to the Silver Pact, particularly the Swords of Luna, for protecting their dominions against destruction by the Wyld. Indeed, Lunars sometimes gain intelligence that lets them regain lost stretches of Creation from the very gods who once claimed those territories as their own.

The relationship between Ma-Ha-Suchi and Amoth City-Smiter suggest possibilities for darker and deadlier tales of divine politics. Amoth is a powerful god in the Bureau of Humanity, whose dominion is the ruins of civilization. The destruction wrought by the Usurpation and Great Contagion propelled him to his current high position in the Bureau. Amoth hopes that Ma-Ha-Suchi and other Lunars of his ilk can ultimately ensure his control of the Bureau. If the goals of Ma-Ha-Suchi are suspect, then those of the City-Smiter are dangerously clear. A game of intrigue could also reveal secret contacts between ambitious Lunars and the Dragon-Blooded, a Sidereal faction, Abyssals or Deathlords. For the sake of power, some people will cut deals with anyone.

THE ELDERS ARE CRAZY

Even the No Moons of the Crossroads Society remain unaware of the sinister and subtle curses of the Neverborn. Nonetheless, the Great Curse works its malign influence upon the eldest Lunars as surely as it bent the virtues of First Age Solar Exalted. Young Lunars can see little sign of the fabled madness of the Lawgivers among the returning Solars, but it shows clearly enough in their own elders. The Curse does not instantly drive a new Exalt insane. Instead, its ironic impulses steadily wear away at the heart and soul of Creation's heroes. As such, newly Exalted Solars have yet to go mad, while the long years of damage done to ancient Chosen of the Moon might

only be "reset" by destroying the corrupt god-kings who rule the Silver Pact.

In this style of game, the Storyteller plays up the worst behaviors of the eldest Lunars, portraying a Silver Pact that has become nearly as rife with corrupt, ancient Exalts as the Solar Deliberative was. Depending upon the tastes of the players, the canonical elders can be milked for a lot of insane awfulness. Trying to learn the secrets of sorcery might mean joining in Raksi's cruel debaucheries, including being forced to engage in cannibalism. What monstrous experiments does she perform in the broken halls of Sperimin? Ma-Ha-Suchi mates with beasts and fosters a beastman cult that seeks to reduce all of Creation to overgrown ruins such as lie in nearby Rathess. He takes the disappearance of the Scarlet Empress as a sign that the time to destroy the Dragon-Blooded and their rotten Realm has come. Already he has incited the Arczeckhi hordes to invade the Hundred Kingdoms, on a scale not seen for nearly three centuries. Perhaps he is nearly a chimera, and in his heart, he wants the Wyld to wash away the world while he dives howling into its embrace. Leviathan rules the Western Ocean as its greatest predator, killing anyone who intrudes on his territory. Even Tamuz seems driven by inexplicable wants: He preaches the Thousand Streams River philosophy yet plans his future godhood as the Great Messiah of the Delzahn.

What terrible havoc will the eldest Lunars wreak upon Creation? How many hapless victims will die as they carve the world into personal territories? With the Solars but newly returned, the Dragon-Blooded hovering on the brink of civil war and the Sidereals embroiled in the petty politics of Yu-Shan, what force can hope to stand against the warlords of the Fickle Lady? Even if the Bronze Faction offered to help destroy the mad elders of the Silver Pact, could your characters trust that they wouldn't be thrown on the same funeral pyre? Will you somehow imprison the Essences of these Lunar despots, or will you risk having to fight them again and again? What will you do when the last No Moon to know the secrets of forging moonsilver tattoos is slain? What happens when the Fair Folk learn that their greatest enemies no longer stand in the way?

THE WAR TO END ALL WARS

The sea of chaos surrounding Creation is infinite in scope. In the true Wyld, everything is possible and nothing is constant. If the world built by the Primordials has existed for thousands of years, what is that but a blink of an eye to things for which time has no meaning? Lunar heroes who realize the endless nature of their enemies find the idea daunting. This style of game bears similarities to the "Invasion!" style but assumes an immensely larger scale.

Some possibility within the true Wyld moves closer to Creation and takes shape. A swarm of Fair Folk or behemoths forms that is literally many times larger than Creation itself. The world is engulfed like a chip of wood before a tsunami. You might draw inspiration from the Norse legends of Ragnarök, as the characters desperately fight to give the world some future chance of rebirth. Perhaps clever No Moons manage to open one or more portals into Elsewhere, contacting the Great Maker Autochthon, who provides a great ark to sail the darkness, bearing the rescued remnants of Creation and waiting for a new universe to coalesce from the chaos. Those who fail to escape struggle to survive for as long as possible in a world beaten by the whims of chaos until it wears away to nothing. Perhaps some fragment of their existence will pass on to the next world as a grain of pollen flies in the wind.

When running a game like this, it is important to do two things. First, let your players know that you intend to tell an apocalyptic tale that will end the world. Secondly, make the game offer the possibilities of significant victories that can still be grabbed from the jaws of certain and crushing defeat. The players' characters should be the ones to open the portals to the ark of Autochthon where they herd the last children of Gaia. Perhaps the characters even stage a daring raid on the Jade Pleasure Dome to tear the Incarnae away from the Games of Divinity so that they might bring light to a new era in the future. When a character dies, she should fall in the performance of a mighty deed, which can only happen because of her sacrifice. Perhaps she gives her last drop of blood to ensure that her fellow hunters manage to take the heart of a tremendous behemoth, whose strength is then turned against the Fair Folk. Maybe she gives her life to the engines of the Realm Defense Grid, as they are fired one last time to give the Lunars enough respite to open the portals to the ark of Autochthon before the Sword of Creation is broken forever. With the sure knowledge that the world is soon to end, the characters are freed from the petty concerns of life and inspired to the greatest heights of heroism.

HUMANITY DIES

In this variation of the epic threat to the world, the Deathlords release the Second Great Contagion and it deals a death blow to the human race. Luckily, Luna planned for this eventuality, having once witnessed Autochthon and other Primordials causing mass extinctions. The Silver Lady designed her Exalts to be able to restore humankind. When the last human dies, the Lunar Essences are left without a proper human host. As a failsafe, they Exalt animals who automatically assume human shape as their alternate true forms. The newly Exalted Lunars are hard put to survive the onslaught of the Underworld, to be sure, but for a time their every child becomes so important to destiny that she Exalts as a Lunar, Sidereal or Solar. Once humankind establishes a foothold again, the thin traces of Dragon-Blood may even have a chance to reappear.

The resulting Age is sure to make the Time of Tumult look like a calm day in the park, but this is a chance for the Lunars to shine beyond all other Exalted. Are the Deathlords

surprised by the self-induced onslaught of newly dead that invade the Underworld? What happens when the ancestor cults realize they no longer have anyone to sustain them? Can 300 Lunar Exalts who control all of the artifacts of humankind manage to thwart a new invasion by the Wyld long enough to repopulate humanity? What other races might gain the favor of the gods, and what might become of the Bureau of Humanity? What will a new humanity, which is truly a pure product of the Thousand Streams River, be like? With the ultimate necessity of Lunars clearly demonstrated to the world, how will other Exalted adapt?

Even if you plan to run this type of series, you might explore the innumerable stories found in the early stages of the catastrophe, when the Deathlords and Fair Folk first strike. Can the Lunars stop the Second Contagion? What will they do when they realize that they cannot stop it? If the masses of the world are destined to die anyway, how many of them will the Lunars ritually hunt in order to preserve their heart's blood?

THE CHANGING MOON SOCIETY

This game style assumes that once upon a time, there was a sixth faction of Moonchildren, which held that the acts of the Silver Pact were heresy against Luna. According to the Changing Moon Society, the Silver Lady intended Lunars to stay "casteless" as their natural state. During the First Age, powerful Chosen of Luna sought to enjoy a singular blessing of the Silver Lady for all time rather than constantly moving between phases. After that, young Lunars endured trials created by the Silver Pact to test which "caste" was most suitable to a particular Exalt. Socially ostracized by the Silver Pact, the Changing Moon Society was relegated to obscurity. For centuries, the halls of the Deliberative saw nothing but the Casted Lunars, and the world forgot about the Changing Moon Society.

When the Usurpation drove all Lunars into exile and the Wyld warped their shapes to a degree never seen before, the Changing Moon Society blamed the manipulations of the Silver Pact for their plight. If Luna's design had been left alone, then her Chosen would have prevailed. Or so the Society members claimed. In the end, they all succumbed to chimerism or died in angry conflicts with the Silver Pact. Even their name was co-opted as that of the new caste pieced together from the fragments of the lost castes. When a Lunar happens to recall some bit of memory about the Changing Moons, she is likely to confuse it for the caste she knows now rather than some fanatical secret society that was nearly forgotten even in its own time.

Occasionally, though, a young Lunar remembers the truth. There aren't many of them, but these Exalts refuse to accept the teachings of the Silver Pact. Indeed, most of them steadfastly avoid members of the Pact. How far they have come depends upon the needs of your series. You might want to explore the rise of a new Exalted faction with your players, as their characters remember the truth and rebel against the

Silver Pact's "heretical" practices. Will the young Lunars survive a faction of elders who feel threatened? Perhaps the Fickle Lady finally takes their side?

Alternatively, you might want the Changing Moon Society both to realize the long-hidden truth and successfully do something about it. Perhaps they can offer a method of tattooing that protects against the Wyld but does not give a Lunar a caste. Presumably, they achieve such a design by modifying techniques stolen from the Silver Pact. Maybe they eschew the moonsilver tattoos altogether and resurrect ancient Knacks that once protected them from the Wyld by tying their natures more closely to the protean Silver Lady. So long as they activate the Flowing Quicksilver Knack immediately whenever changing shapes threatens to cause Wyld mutation, they can throw off the unnatural influence of the Wyld by assuming a form other than whatever they first attempted. For instance, a Lunar might try to become a wolf, but quickly take the form of a raven instead when he feels the Wyld rise to twist the result.

FLOWING QUICKSILVER KNACK

This Knack enables a Casteless Lunar to avoid Wyld mutation. Whenever the result of a Wyld Taint roll generates more successes than the character's Dodge Mental Defense Value, the player can avoid the resulting mutation by immediately having the character take a different shape. Changing to the new shape operates as normal, including any Essence or Willpower cost for the effect, except that the immediate assumption of the new shape does not trigger a new taint roll. For extra shapeshifting fun, have the Storyteller pick the new shape at random from the Lunar's repertoire of heart's blood. Creative use of the unexpected form might count as a stunt.

If you want to really ramp up the antagonism between the Silver Pact and the Changing Moon Society, you might assume that the Society's members do more than just offer an alternative to the moonsilver tattoos. Perhaps they even offer a way to escape one's caste. The Shattered Silver Cage Knack must be willingly learned by a Lunar. Learning this permanent Knack immediately breaks the moonsilver tattoos that bind her to a caste, and her caste is shed along with the shards. If the Lunar is tattooed again, she loses the Knack and must pay experience points to "learn" it again.

Among Lunars touched by the Wyld, even crazier ideas occur to explain the puzzle of Lunar castes. One deranged Moonchild claims that "Casteless" are the fourth caste and chimerae are the fifth. Or perhaps they represent the sixth and seventh castes? Neither the Changing Moon Society nor the Silver Pact wants this sort of idea to take root, however.

If the Lunar's madness cannot be cured, she is likely to be killed to prevent her from encouraging others to risk becoming chimerae. What if she is right, though? Perhaps her theory falls short—what if there are 28 Lunar castes, one for each night of the month?

LOCATION, LOCATION, LOCATION

As the **Exalted** storytelling chapter points out, Creation is *huge*. The area shown on the map within the inside cover of Exalted reaches more than 13,000 miles from the East to West and more than 8,000 miles from the North to South, and a larger portion of that is covered by land than in our world. Beyond the edges of the map, however, Creation continues into the elemental wildernesses of the Wyld. Chosen of the Moon might be found anywhere within that vast expanse, but the nature of Lunar Exaltation makes them more likely to appear in certain regions.

THE TRIBES OF CREATION

The Exaltations designed by the Silver Lady seek out mortals who possess an inherently significant destiny, feel a sense of stewardship toward some part of the world and have proven survival instincts. While these features might apply to heroic figures throughout Creation, these Exaltations show a subtle bias toward the tough, self-reliant warriors of barbarian tribes; such champions come closest to the state of humanity when the Incarnae first Exalted their heroes.

Exalted briefly describes the populations of Creation in every quarter of the world (pp. 49-67). The extremely civilized nature of the Blessed Isle renders it an unlikely place for Lunar Exaltation, and the Wyld Hunt usually ensures that the few exceptions die quickly. Every other quarter of the world is home to at least one great tribal culture, and such groups have the greatest chance to spawn the epic heroes who Exalt as Lunars. Most No Moons believe this happens by the Silver Lady's design, but a few Lunar sages suggest that the success of the Thousand Streams River bears some responsibility. The following section provides a brief overview of the most renowned (or infamous) tribes of Creation. Details of these tribes may be found in various **Exalted** supplements, such as all five volumes of **The Compass of Terrestrial Directions**. These tribes are generally suitable as origins for Lunar Exalted characters, or as a source of followers and allies.

THE EAST

The Arczeckhi Horde is the scourge of the Scavenger Lands and the most persistent threat to the civilized East. Arczeckhi are commonly assumed to be a race of Wyld-tainted humans, clearly marked by their fanged mouths, red eyes, coarse fur, tufted ears and short, bandy legs that prevent them from riding horses. Arczeckhi religious beliefs insist that only the strong are "real," and this leads to a remarkable lack of conscience regarding outsiders. Arczeckhi who breed with humans always produce more Arczeckhi, which makes the idea of conquest rapes particularly terrifying.

The Forest People consist of many tribes who live deep in the Eastern woods. Some mark their territory by carving the trunks of great trees, while others live in the high boughs of the forest and never touch the ground. The Wyld has influenced many of the forest tribes, and they share green or brown skin with dark hair that is often mossy in color. Stealth, hunting and gathering are daily parts of life, and outsiders are rarely welcomed.

Hill Tribes are not always what civilized people imagine when they talk of barbarians. Yet, the wild regions of the River Province are home to numerous native groups who stand outside of urban society. These tribes usually follow an animistic religion and speak some dialect of Riverspeak. They do not farm, and often resort to raiding local territories unless they are violently repelled.

The Linowan and the **Haltans** are locked in interminable warfare, fighting over the great Northeastern forests. The Linowan have a loose alliance with the Realm, although they eschew the Immaculate faith in favor of various gods of river, sky and woodland. Their homeland covers a vast stretch of riverside meadows and ancient deciduous forests. The Haltans hold the great redwood forests east of Linowan, spending their lives high in the trees safe from the Fair Folk who prowl the ground below. Halta is arguably one of the most successful of the Thousand Streams River projects, for its people harmonize the natural redwood environment with their amazing arboreal cities. This conflict has reached epic proportion, with the Bull of the North allying with the Haltans and the Realm losing five legions trying to honor its alliance with the Linowan.

The Marukani Clans roam the plains south of Lookshy. The Marukani are renowned throughout Creation as unparalleled horsemen. The clans share a central trade city known as Celeren, and the Marukani's recognized leaders are chosen by popular approval from the various clan elders. The Marukani are allied with Lookshy and threatened by the malign forces of Thorns. More information about the Marukani can be found in the **Compass of Terrestrial Directions, Vol. 1: The Scavenger Lands**.

The Ten Tribes of the Oak live in a region on the Eastern edge of the Scavenger Lands. The ancestors of the Ten Tribes originally inhabited Sperimin, the City of Sorcerers that Raksi has claimed for her own. Fleeing the fall of their homeland, they made a pact with the forest god Elder Oak. A century ago, Elder Oak encouraged the Tribes to assault the logging community of Farhold. Unbeknownst to the Ten Tribes, their patron has abandoned them for the prayers and sacrifices of the people of Farhold and a Full Moon Lunar named Dark Eyes hopes to supplant Elder Oak's influence. The Ten Tribes are named Red Scars, Get of the Tigress, Devil Braids, Green Shadow, Axe of Judgment, Bone Faces, Wolf Eyes, Endless Branch, Sky Runners and Nine Ravens.

THE SOUTH

The Delzahn are the most powerful and numerous of the Southern tribes. They control the city-state of Chiaroscuro and vast stretches of the desert. The Delzahn are divided between those who support the Tri-Khan's rule of Chiaroscuro and those who live as nomads astride camels and horses. The tribe has taboos against warfare against other tribesmen, but the growing friction within the tribe ensures that their customary ritual duels become more frequent and more deadly. Delzahn prophecies speak of the coming of the Kha-Khan, who will descend from Heaven to unite the tribes. The Lunar elder Tamuz is the source of this legend, but any god or Exalt who fits the description might prosper as the Delzahn messiah if the elder were to disappear.

The Dune People are ghostly white albinos who travel by night to avoid the deadly touch of the sun. The Dune People's tribal tongue sounds like the rasping of serpents slithering across the sand, perhaps a result of their ancient pact with the Lunar Ka-Koshu and his snakemen. As if their appearance and voices weren't terrifying enough, the Dune People hunt other humans, drink their blood and sleep beneath the sand using hollowed out human femurs as breathing tubes. Many of their tools and weapons are crafted from human bone and ligaments, while manskin tapestries record their history in elaborate pictographs.

The Jackal Tribes are home to the outcasts of the Southeast. Whether plagued by vermin, disease or ancient spirit-curses, those whom the other Southeastern societies have driven out the Jackal Tribes open their arms to. Traditional garb in the Jackal Tribes includes the red scarves of lepers. Towns in the regions frequented by the tribes customarily leave some food and valuables at their outskirts whenever scarlet-masked riders approach, because no one wants to suffer the plagues of the outcast tribesmen. The Jackal Tribes also possess the greatest number of trained prides of simhata in Creation, employing these fast, vicious creatures for transport and battle.

THE WEST

The Island Tribes inhabit one or more of the hundreds of volcanic islands found throughout the Southwest. They sail swift outrigger canoes on lightning raids against the Wavecrest Archipelago and each other. Island tribesmen are quick to forge pacts with spirits of the sea, storms, fish and shore, and live by the strictures of innumerable spiritual taboos. The islanders go to sea dressed in elaborate battle armor, complete with carved shells bound with copper and decorated with brilliant tropical bird feathers. Besides engaging in raids on other isles, the island tribes are inveterate pirates.

The Pelagothropes are tainted by the Wyld such that they can breathe water and air alike. They often have long webbed feet, light scales, skin ranging from bleached corpse-white to sapphire and hair of green or blue. Given their natural facility with the sea, they make particularly dangerous pirates.

THE NORTH

The Haslanti tribes are another relatively successful experiment of the Thousand Streams River. They have bonded together to form what is arguably the most powerful nation in the North. Haslanti towns are built to endure the harshest winters and to prosper in the warmer months. The Haslanti League is known for its use of hot-air flying boats and iceships that sail across the Northern ice on steel runners.

Icewalkers are the most common nomads in the North. They follow the great herd animals across the frozen landscape throughout the year. The icewalkers' lives centers around a totemic beast, and the most powerful of these tribes are the Elk and Mammoth tribes. Icewalkers fear and hate unnatural things, and kill Wyld-tainted barbarians whenever they can. In the past decade, much of the icewalker culture has fallen under the sway of the Solar warlord Yurgen Kaneko, the Bull of the North. Under his leadership, they have united to threaten lands to the East, West and South as never before.

Tear Eaters are fervent ancestor worshipers who have joined in service to the Northern Deathlords. Only about two dozen clans comprise the Tear Eaters, and they travel from one shadowland to the next, engaging in raids along the way. These tribesmen are extremely devout, practicing solemn funeral rites in honor of their ghostly ancestors according to the interpretations of their necromantic shamans.

The Varajtul are feared and hated throughout the North, for they are ferocious cannibals. Certainly tainted by the Wyld, these barbarians are covered in fur of white, gray or light-blue and reach heights of eight feet. Their jaws and teeth are strong enough to crack human bone. Occasionally, the Varajtul take in humans who are outcast from other tribes due to Wyld mutation.

TRAVEL

Given the vast size of Creation, travel can consume a lot of time. As consummate shapeshifters, Lunars have innate ways to travel faster than most mundane methods. With the proper heart's blood, a Lunar can become a fish swimming downriver, a horse cantering across the land or a falcon flying through the air. Unless hampered by slower companions, a Child of the Moon is usually capable of moving much faster than other beings.

Typical bird shapes might be used to travel 20 to 50 miles per hour for up to 10 hours in a single day. Normally, birds can't press their speed to its limit over long distances and rarely travel more than 100 to 200 miles in a day. A Lunar in a hurry might push it for a day or so, but she must inevitably tire and slow down. Some particularly swift fish shapes can achieve speeds up to 50 miles per hour for brief spurts, but eight miles an hour is a better estimate of sustained speed over distance for a creature such as a salmon. Similarly, while a wolf might reach a speed of nearly 35 miles an hour over a short hunting distance, wolves can only make 60 miles a day for extended travel. To represent a Lunar in horse form, use the standard horse rate shown in **Exalted** on page 264 and add the +1/8 "exceptional" and +1/8 "enduring" modifiers.

The innumerable species of Creation are too varied to address in complete detail. Storytellers can research real-life animals should a Lunar's mode of transport become important to the series. Remember that a beast can only maintain its maximum speed for a short time. Look for figures regarding sustained speed, particularly those reported by field observers studying naturalism. Creation also contains mythic creatures that do not exist in the real world, but their speeds are generally comparable to some real creature. Choose a beast you find comparable, and go with what works. **Exalted** is a game of epic fantasy, so a few miles here or there won't make much difference, so long as you aren't letting characters zip across Creation as though it were a linen closet. Creation is huge, and too much speed diminishes its mythic quality.

DISTANCE AND COMMUNICATION

Exalted discusses numerous methods of distance travel and communication. Lunar Exalted benefit from access to shapeshifting Knacks and various spells and Charms, which speed their movement or allow them to communicate over vast distances. Members of the Silver Pact particularly try to keep in touch with each other so that they might respond to Creation-wide threats and try to coordinate responses as a group.

The Realm's heliograph towers are Creation's quickest non-magical means of rapid communication. The Moonchildren cannot build anything similar, of course, but the mortals of the Southeast achieve similar results using signal drums. Native performers can encode a message into patterns they play upon large drums. The sound reaches to the next village where another drummer repeats the message for someone in the next village to hear, and so forth. Provided the region enjoys some measure of cooperation, or the message is too important not to transmit, drum signals can spread information almost as swiftly as the Realm's heliograph system, albeit not so subtly. Anyone who understands the tribal codes (a "language" characters can acquire through their Linguistics Ability) can decipher the message beating on the wind.

THE IMPORTANCE OF SUPPLY

Even the most unskilled Lunar is an amateur hunter. Because of the Lunars' spirit shapes and those forms provided by their heart's blood, in addition to their natural favor for the skills of survival, the Lunars rarely starve. If a region contains anything edible, a Lunar can probably find it and eat it. Carnivorous forms can hunt; herbivorous forms may feed upon plants humans would scarcely find edible, such as a reindeer eating lichen in the North or a camel browsing throne-trees in the South. If the Lunar travels with an army, this feature doesn't protect his troops. However, each mouth that doesn't have to be fed is one less burden on his people. With luck, a Moonchild might even return with food that some portion of his human troops can eat.

NAVAL POWER

The Lunar Exalted aren't normally any better at ship-building or navigation than anyone else. They often have an edge when things go wrong, though. Many Lunars learn to assume one or more shapes of sea creatures. As such, they can afford to sink enemy vessels and seize their waterlogged possessions from the deeps. Similarly, they can expect to survive nearly any sea voyage regardless of threats that face their ship. Most sea creatures cannot actually descend to the greatest depths, however, so Lunars who want to truly master the sea must usually master more than one heart's blood from within it.

CHARACTER CONNECTIONS

As discussed in the **Exalted** Storytelling chapter, the Storyteller should decide whether the characters meet during the first session or already know one another when the game begins. Games that begin with characters already having common threads among them are often stronger and possess greater internal consistency. However, doing so definitely requires some extra work on the part of the Storyteller and the players before the series begins. Usually, the best way to handle this is to ask players what connections their characters have to each other before the game begins. Even a vague connection can lend plausibility to the idea of the group acting together throughout the rest of the series.

Example: Brent's character is an Exalted Haslanti warrior. He met Bunnie's character, who grew up in a Diamond Hearth mining camp, when he escorted a caravan of merchants representing the interests of a Council Oligarch. The two haven't seen each other in years and are surprised to meet again in a war council discussing a massive increase in raids by the Fair Folk. One of the other councilors seems strangely familiar, and during a drunken bout of boasting after dinner, the three Lunars suddenly realize that they have an ancient heritage in common. The next morning, after a private discussion stretching deep into the early hours, the three of them vow to rid the area of its Fair Folk foes. The Thousand Streams River of the Haslanti has three new heroes, whether the people know it yet or not.

LUNAR PACKS

Just as the Solar Exalted are often drawn together due to connections between their previous incarnations, so do the Lunars share attractions based upon previous lives. The Lunars of the First Age seldom formed long-lasting partnerships comparable to Solar circles. In part, this stemmed from lack of interest, but they were also divided by outside influences. Some Moonchildren fell under the sway of their Solar partners and suffered incalculable abuse. Others despaired of the situation and retreated to the edges of the Wyld, cutting themselves off from the rotting heart of civilization and warring endlessly against the invasions of the Fair Folk. A few tried to forge the Silver Pact into a political entity

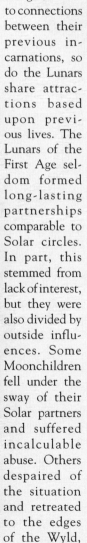

that could contest against Solar excesses. A handful of the Moonchildren gave in to their instincts and retreated from civilization altogether.

Nonetheless, First Age Lunars formed many personal friendships, squad loyalties and factional alliances during the Primordial War and subsequent lifetimes. Young Lunars may feel a sense of strong recognition toward another Chosen of Luna without understanding why. Sharing the fragments of memories left from previous lives may resurrect friendships, loves or rivalries from centuries long gone. Storytellers can use past-life connection as an additional tool to explain why characters form a pack, if such tools are necessary. Try not to rely upon it as a crutch, though, because connections the characters made in their current lifetime are probably more relevant to the events of your series.

LUNARS AND SOLARS

Some groups may want to run mixed series, wherein some players portray Solar characters while others play Lunar characters. While lesser Exalted such as the Dragon-Blooded may prove problematic simply because of the large power differences between them, Solars and Lunars are closer in might. The Incarnae designed the Solars as the most powerful kind of Exalted, just because the Unconquered Sun is the most powerful god. Nevertheless, the Silver Lady is the second greatest of the Celestial Incarnae, and her Chosen are mighty indeed. In particular, she gave her Chosen their shapeshifting powers, which no Solar can ever achieve—not greater than the Lawgivers, just different. Lunars' innate Attributes form the root of powerful Charms, as well. Once you consider such Backgrounds as Solar Bond, it is easy to see that the two Exalt types can work well together. Indeed, they clearly did so during the Primordial War.

Playing a Solar in a Lunar series or a Lunar in a Solar series is not a *right*, however. If your Storyteller wants to run a series with a specific focus, then demanding to bring in the odd-man-out Exalt type may cause problems for the entire game. If the Storyteller tries to craft a series about how the Cult of the Illuminated trains and manipulates a circle of young Solars, then introducing a Lunar might disrupt the plot. While some Illuminated members might allow Lunars to join, a story that centers on the Cult isn't *about* the Children of the Moon in the same way it's about the Lawgivers. Conversely, if your Storyteller wants to run an extremely challenging game where your Lunars risk their lives and sanity to unriddle a plot of the Fair Folk in the Deep Wyld, a Solar character will have problems. Sure, a starting Solar character can have Charms that protect against Wyld mutation—but making sure their ally doesn't grow a second head can still take time from the Lunar characters' pursuing the real plot. Players and Storytellers should both make sure their characters fit the series, and the series fits the characters people want to play.

CREATING A SERIES

You may wish to read through the section on Creating a Series (**Exalted**, pp. 269-270). When you create a series, one of the most important steps is to develop the area of Creation where the action takes place. Due to the potential power that characters can achieve, games of **Exalted** can easily grow quite large in scale, but every good game at least requires a starting point. If you think big from the beginning, then you may find that your setting holds up to the epic adventures of your group as the game progresses. The following section presents a number of special cases to consider for Lunars.

THOUSAND STREAMS RIVER

Chapter Two: A Better World discusses this concept in great detail, in case your characters want to create their own Thousand Stream culture experiment. If you want to explore this part of Lunar culture, then you should make sure that you develop an area the characters can influence. Unless you specifically want to play up conflict with other Lunars, you should probably keep the area free from current Lunar influence. The region could have been the subject of a previous experiment, whose Lunar architect was slain by a Wyld Hunt, letting the characters take over an experiment already in progress. Alternatively, the area might contain primitive tribes whom a group of young Lunars could easily manipulate, but building an elaborate civilization will take hundreds of years. On the other hand, you could increase the difficulty of the challenge by encouraging the Moonchildren to rework an area that is already civilized or a group that has already fallen under the sway of other Exalted. Some Silver Pact elders would like to free the icewalkers from the influence of the Bull of the North, for example.

WYLD NATION

The Wyld includes "islands of stability," separated from Creation but protected from the Wyld's ceaseless chaos by reality engines or other potent forces. Such places possess some degree of "normalcy" (though enough Wyld energy might have leaked in to make them look quite peculiar). Lunars might use them as bases for their fights against the Wyld or even as independent nation-states not subject to the powers of Creation. Such an island of stability must surely attract the hostile attentions of the Fair Folk and other being, but presumably, the devices that protect the place's integrity also offer some defense against the denizens of the Wyld. How *much* protection they offer can depend on the needs of the story. The mystic barriers might not hamper sentient Wyld creatures at all, making raids a common occurrence. Alternatively, the barriers might be nigh invulnerable to the Wyld, yet one of the engines could fail at an inopportune moment or perhaps fall prey to sabotage. Maybe the Fair Folk cannot penetrate the defenses, so they must seduce a Lunar into working their will, perhaps as a chimera?

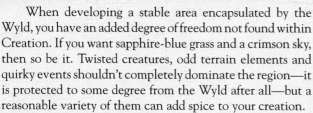

When developing a stable area encapsulated by the Wyld, you have an added degree of freedom not found within Creation. If you want sapphire-blue grass and a crimson sky, then so be it. Twisted creatures, odd terrain elements and quirky events shouldn't completely dominate the region—it is protected to some degree from the Wyld after all—but a reasonable variety of them can add spice to your creation.

Another option the "Wyld nation" offers is the ability to destroy your setting without destroying the entirety of Creation. If the Lunars lose their battles or make bad choices, then the Fair Folk might overrun the Lunars' haven in the Wyld. As the Princes of Chaos sweep across the borders, their minions wreck the intricate reality engines and overturn the pillars inlaid with moonsilver wards. The war has been lost, and the Lunars must retreat to Creation. In classic anime style, they are sure to want revenge and have likely learned valuable lessons in the meantime.

PILLAGE AND RUN

When the Lunars fled Creation, what did they take with them? Many of the Solar tombs seem to have a dearth of the immensely powerful artifacts one might expect to find there. While a good number of these were probably destroyed or taken by the Dragon-Blooded and the Sidereals of the Bronze Faction, surely the chosen of Luna spirited some artifacts away. Who better to know the secrets of the mighty artifacts forged by their Solar mates? Artifacts demand Essence for attunement, and sometimes require hearthstones to power. Lunars would find orichalcum artifacts particularly draining, due to the double cost of attunement. As such, the Swords of Luna or Crossroads Society might stash artifacts in hidden locations for quick retrieval when they are needed. When the Great Contagion struck and the Fair Folk hordes poured across the ramparts of Creation, those who knew the locations of these stockpiles were slain.

As the Storyteller, you might add one or more of these artifact stockpiles to your series. In one sense, they make a sort of thematic replacement for the Solar tombs. Carefully hidden, likely trapped against tampering and potentially inhabited by Fair Folk invaders or other creatures, artifact stockpiles provide a source of challenging adventure with the potential for great reward. You can also look at them as potential story hooks. What incredible tomes of forgotten knowledge might lie buried in lost memory crystals from the First Age? What if there was an odd orichalcum device inlaid with black jade that once served as an emergency measure for the Solar Deliberative in case the Realm Defense Grid fell into the wrong hands? Who else might know about this hypothetical key, and what if they knew the moment it returned to Creation? Perhaps the stockpile contains a number of inactive reality engines meant to replace those along the borders of Creation in case some were lost or destroyed. Such a hoard could even be used to create a new pocket of stability in the Wyld if you wanted to create a new Wyld nation.

THE WYLD

For a book that mentions the Wyld so often, it might seem as though this text doesn't tell you much about it. Chapter Six: The Casteless and the Chimerae discusses Lunars and their relation to the Wyld, but Storytellers and players are directed to **The Compass of Celestial Directions, Vol. 2: The Wyld** for comprehensive information about the roiling sea of chaos that surrounds Creation.

TIMING

Because of such factors as the Casteless, a game that focuses on Lunars shall probably take greater notice of the calendar than other **Exalted** games. Devout followers of the Silver Lady, such as Ma-Ha-Suchi, are also likely to pay close attention to the phases of the moon.

THE LUNAR CALENDAR

Obviously, the sun defines the divisions of time that matter most for human affairs, the day and the year. The passage of the Silver Lady through the sky provides the third important division of time; the calendars of every culture in Creation take note of her cycles.

The Realm calendar divides the 425 days of the year into 15 months of 28 days length, with each day consisting of 25 hours. The first day of each month is the new moon, with the half-moon falling on the eighth and 22nd evenings of the month and the full moon falling on the night of the 15th day. Following the last month of the year are the five days of Calibration, whose dark nights are moonless and starless. Although the first day of each year is also moonless, the return of the stars clearly marks the night of the first new moon as separate from the Calibration holiday that ends the previous year.

Each month consists of four weeks of seven days, with the days named respectively for the Celestial Incarnae: Sunday, Moonday, Marsday, Mercuryday, Jupiterday, Venusday and, finally, Saturnday. The crescent of the moon first shows on the second day of each month, which is always a Moonday. Each week of the year also has a dedicated god.

The movements of the celestial figures are not always as static and predictable as suggested by the calendar, however. At times, Luna and the Unconquered Sun arrange for an eclipse of the sun or moon. The starless nights of Calibration occasionally see a rogue star wandering strangely through the sky and sometimes falling to the earth. Seers pay special attention to these signs and scrutinize them for special meaning.

LUNA, THE MOON AND THE WYLD

Luna shines her brightest, as a full moon in the sky, precisely when the tides of the Wyld surge at their strongest. Before the weave of Creation swept the sea of chaos away, the Primordials warred with the Fair Folk themselves. The Primordials shaped Creation in part as a fortress to protect them while they played the Games of Divinity, and set the

Unconquered Sun to walk Creation's bounds. With this peerless warrior defending Creation, what purpose could Luna then have served?

Beings such as the Primordials, possessed of 20 or more souls, do not think as mortals do. Perhaps the Primordials saw that a sea of endless possibility could eventually spawn some threat their Unconquered Sun could not defeat. Thus, they designed Luna to possess the heart of the Wyld within her, so that she could adapt to its movements and repel it. Of course, she was not a creature of the Wyld herself, so her endless conflicts with the tides of chaos evolved into a cycle. When the Wyld presses most strongly against the world, Luna grows commensurately powerful, and her nature demands that she push back the surge of chaos. When the Wyld recedes, Luna diminishes, and it is then that she searches the tamed shores of Creation for the things left behind, as they are sometimes a source of primordial wisdom. Or at least, that's the most common theory among Lunar theologians.

PLAYING IN THE PAST

While the vast world of **Exalted** provides innumerable story opportunities, it also sports a rich history. You may want to run a series set in a period of time long past. From the raging war against the Primordials to the doom of the Great Contagion, the Lunars have fought as the Stewards of Creation. These are legends worthy of exploration.

THE PRIMORDIAL WAR

Though its outcome is already determined—unless you decide to change it for your game—the Primordial War is full of opportunities for massive battles against seemingly insurmountable odds. If one assumes the existence of 25 Primordials (matching the 25 constellations of Fate—but the number truly is arbitrary), each possessed of at least 20 component souls, then the Exalted necessarily had to defeat no fewer than 500 creatures, each with the power of a Third Circle demon. Given that the Yozis have reputedly become less than they were, those beings might have been even more challenging. How did the Exalted manage to kill

THE LOST CASTES

In the First Age, there were three other castes, whose fragments were welded together to create the current-day Changing Moon Caste.

• The **Waxing Moons** were Luna's chosen priests and courtiers. They were blessed with incredible beauty, remarkable grace and subtle powers of illusion. The Caste Attributes for the Waxing Moons were Charisma, Manipulation and Appearance.

Anima Effects: As his action, a Waxing Moon Exalt could channel 10 motes of Essence through his anima. He then glowed with the silvery light of his goddess Luna and illuminated the area for (Permanent Essence x 5) yards around him as brightly as it were a gibbous moon night. For the remainder of the scene, or until he chose to let the effect dissipate, he gained additional lethal and bashing soak equal to his Essence against attack by all creatures of the Wyld. In addition, when his anima was active, he could also add his Essence to the minimum number of dice he rolled for any attack made against such creatures (meaning that, in most cases, he would roll a minimum number of dice equal to twice his Essence). This effect came into play automatically once the Lunar spent 11 or more motes of Peripheral Essence. For purposes of this anima effect, "creatures of the Wyld" included Fair Folk, chimerae, Fae-Blooded and beings with more than five points of Wyld mutations (each pox counted as 1 point, afflictions 2, blights 4, and abominations 6).

• The **Half Moons** were observers and tacticians with a talent for seeing through others' plots and leading their allies out of danger. The Half Moons were equally adept at creating strategies to deceive their enemies. The Caste Attributes for the Half Moons were Charisma, Perception and Intelligence.

Anima Effects: The Half Moons' anima power cost five motes, and granted them extra dice, equal to their permanent Essence, to all Initiative rolls (such as Join Battle, Join Debate, Join War) and to rolls to detect unexpected attacks, for the remainder of the scene. This power was automatically activated whenever the Lunar's anima was filled by 11 or more Peripheral Essence.

• The **Waning Moons** were tricksters and spies, blessed with unnatural stealth. They used guile and shape-shifting prowess to slip in and out of enemy fortifications and sow discord among their foes. The Caste Attributes for the Waning Moons were Dexterity, Manipulation and Wits.

Anima Effects: The Waning Moons' anima granted them the ability to masquerade as someone else without need for the ritual hunt or heart's blood. The Waning Moon anima effect was identical to that of the modern Changing Moon Caste.

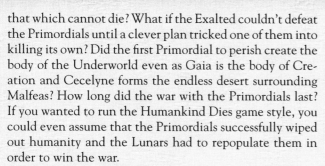

that which cannot die? What if the Exalted couldn't defeat the Primordials until a clever plan tricked one of them into killing its own? Did the first Primordial to perish create the body of the Underworld even as Gaia is the body of Creation and Cecelyne forms the endless desert surrounding Malfeas? How long did the war with the Primordials last? If you wanted to run the Humankind Dies game style, you could even assume that the Primordials successfully wiped out humanity and the Lunars had to repopulate them in order to win the war.

What were the Primordials like before they became Yozis and Neverborn? They created the world and the gods, and then retired to Yu-Shan. But what did they do on the occasions they chose to stop playing the Games of Divinity? Evidence suggests that they "played" with Creation, rearranging or destroying mountains and people as though they were a collection of children's toys. Of all the Primordials, only Gaia and Autochthon seemed to have anything resembling humane regard for their Creations. Of course, this could be nothing but propaganda woven by the winning side. If this primal Usurpation was *just* a case of ambitious underlings knocking off their bosses to take their place, and the first Exalted were just dupes or mercenaries, the setting assumes a darker tone.

The scope of terrains you can explore here is staggering. If you assume that the Primordial War began with an ambush within Yu-Shan itself, then you can portray epic battles in the streets of Heaven. Maybe the gods were initially afraid to confront the Primordials directly and they sought somehow to cut the massive spirit sanctum of Yu-Shan free and send it catapulting into Elsewhere. Perhaps the war began with the attempt to break into Heaven, with a circle or two of Exalts capturing and holding each of Yu-Shan's gates while the Exalted armies fought their way to their targets. Some of the Primordials certainly escaped to wreak havoc upon Creation: A legend says that great portions of it were burned away. Might all have been lost without the brave sacrifice of those who stood at the gates of Heaven? What if the vengeful Primordials had escaped into the Wyld and offered to help the Fair Folk destroy their Creation? How many terrible species did the Primordials create during the war, setting them upon the armies of the Exalted and their Dragon King allies? How many of these escaped into hidden passageways beneath the earth? (It is known that *something* terrible slinks through the deepest tunnels below Gethamane.) What if one of the Primordials slipped through the trap somehow? What might she be doing now?

THE FIRST AGE

Of all the Exalted, Lunars have changed the most since the First Age. In one sense, this is to be expected—the ultimate shapeshifters were created to adapt. On the other hand, the Lunars have also lost the most through the tragedies wrought by the Neverborn's Great Curse upon

their murderers. In the First Age, the Chosen of Luna did not yet bear the moonsilver tattoos, but neither were the Casteless subject to the ever-present threat of dissolving into chimerae.

Without a doubt, the Lawgivers dominated the First Age. Nonetheless, Lunar Exalted held powerful positions and achieved great things. At the height of the First Age, Leviathan held the position of High Admiral of the Realm, acknowledged as master of the water-borne fleets of the world. The Solar master Salina owed much of her success in her great working to her Lunar allies. Though the First Age is commonly portrayed as a golden era of peace turned rotten by the corruption of the Solars, conflicts worthy of Lunar attention certainly occurred. A game run during the early First Age might feature Lunar Exalted hunting down the remnants of the Primordials' misshapen armies. Any period of that long Age could focus on one of the many attempts the Fair Folk made to invade. Chosen of Luna were also forced to carry out military actions against wayward Dragon-Blooded daimyos from time to time—or perhaps the first Solars to go mad. The High First Age was punctuated with literally world-shaking wars of godlike heroes and followed by the sunset decadence of the Old Realm, when Lunar heroes were forced to operate under the eyes of demented Solar tyrants.

As the Usurpation begins, players can explore the option that maybe the Lunars *weren't* all innocent bystanders…. How *does* one pull off the murder of 300 insane, nigh-omnipotent god-kings? During the Usurpation, hard choices confront the Chosen of Luna. Unless you plan to change history, those who stand firmly with their Solar mates are ultimately slain. Lunars who flee into the Wyld may have survived the onslaught of the Sidereals and Dragon-Blooded, but those Lunars did not escape unscathed. Those Lunars of the Waxing Moon, Waning Moon and Half Moon Castes perished or lost their castes. The Casteless warped beyond recognition, joining the frightful ranks of the chimerae.

THE SHOGUNATE

The seven centuries of the Shogunate were not a pleasant time for Lunars. The Sidereal masters of the Usurpation instituted the Wyld Hunt, and Dragon-Blooded hordes hunted down and killed whatever Lunars they could find. Most Lunars kept to the edges of the Threshold, walking the border between Creation and the Wyld. Sometimes, an angry Lunar would lead a great war band against the Shogunate, perhaps even conquering the province of a daimyo who offended her. Sadly, the armies of the Shogun still retained large portions of the First Age military structure, and such invasions inevitably led to crippling defeat for the Lunar once the Shogunate felt sufficiently threatened to risk its most precious weapons.

Stealthier Lunars often managed to slip in and out of the Dragon-Blooded lands with relative impunity.

Generally, they avoided the Blessed Isle, where it was easiest to get caught, but little else was off limits. The Thousand Streams River took shape throughout this period, laying the seeds of new civilizations.

THE GREAT CONTAGION

Combined with the Fair Folk invasion, the Great Contagion nearly took out the entire human race. Nine-tenths of Creation died from the plague itself, and the survivors faced a seemingly endless assault by the denizens of the Wyld. Stories told during the Great Contagion and the subsequent invasion are certainly filled with opportunities for epic battles and tragic loss. This is one of the times when Lunars really shine. What great battles do your characters fight? Though the Realm does not know of them, your own Exaltation will remember—and so will the Fair Folk who realize the bitter price you cost them. What revenge might they plan for your next incarnation? Did any of your companions become chimerae? Are you still drawn together?

EXPERIENCE

The following section discusses the connection between Experience and Backgrounds. It also gives a list of the Ex-perience cost of raising various Traits within the game. In addition, Lunars have reduced training time for Favored Attributes, and that is discussed as well.

BACKGROUNDS AND EXPERIENCE

The core **Exalted** book gives rules for purchasing starting Backgrounds, but does not discuss how to raise a character's Backgrounds once play has begun. Storytellers are encouraged to consider one of the following two methods for this, depending upon their personal preferences and what works for their games:

Method 1: Backgrounds Cost Experience. Backgrounds may be raised at the cost of three experience points per new dot (the same cost as a specialty). Thus, raising Allies from four to five dots would cost an Exalt three experience points. Storytellers should generally let players recover experience invested in this fashion if story circumstances force the character to lose dots in a Background. Such protection should not be absolute—dumb moves should have consequences—but players shouldn't be afraid of permanent losses merely at a whim, either. If the story demands that a character gain a Background in play without having the necessary experience, she must spend at least half of all experience points on the Background until she is no longer in debt. For example, if Seven Devils Clever raids a Lunar tomb and gains a moonsilver daiklave, but doesn't have six experience points banked, then she would still gain the daiklave but would need to invest the experience as soon as possible or lose the daiklave to story development (perhaps it is stolen by a sneaky Wyld Hunt scout).

Method 2: Backgrounds Are "Free." Backgrounds do not cost any Experience to raise, but they may only be raised with the explicit permission of the Storyteller. The Storyteller may only allow the increase (or loss) of Backgrounds when dictated by the story of the game. Although Backgrounds gained under this method are "free," they must still be earned via in-character play. For Seven Devils Clever to gain an ancient moonsilver daiklave, she might delve into a tomb, while building a mercenary unit requires active recruitment and campaigning. The downside is that "free" Backgrounds may be lost just as easily as they're gained.

Neither of these procedures is inherently better than the other, so Storytellers are encouraged to use whichever method proves best for their game. Neither method obviates the fact that the character must earn the Background in play. One method simply requires that players invest experience in Backgrounds just as they do in other Traits. Because this assures tracking of the relative value of Background points gained after the start of the game, Method 1 is popular with Storytellers of shared games with large player bases (such as Internet chat games or organized play groups).

LUNAR EXALTED EXPERIENCE

Except as noted in this section, Lunars gain experience, spend it and train for new Traits at the same rates that Solars do. **Exalted**, pages 272-275, covers the rules for gaining experience, using it to increase Traits and training your character. The accompanying "Lunar Experience Cost" table gives appropriate costs and training times for Lunar characters, when they differ from the core book's values.

LUNAR EXPERIENCE COST

Trait	Cost	Training Times
Attribute	current rating x 4	(rating) months
Caste/Favored Attribute	current rating x 3	(current rating x 2) weeks
Caste/Favored Charm	10	(Min. Attribute) days
Out-of-Caste Charm	12	(Min. Attribute + Min. Essence) days
New Spell (Caste/Favored)	10	(spell circle) weeks
New Spell (Out-of-Caste)	12	(spell circle) weeks
Essence	current rating x 9	(rating) months
New Knack	11	1 month

INDEX

B

Backgrounds 99, 106-112
   Allies 106-107
   Artifact 107
   Backing 107
   Command 108
   Cult 108
   Familiar 108
   Followers 108
   Heart's Blood 109
   Influence 108
   Manse 108
   Mentor 108-109
   Reputation 109-110
   Solar Bond 110-111
   Taboo 111
   Tattoo Artifact 111-112
barbarian 15, 32, 224-226
   Arczeckhi 224
   Delzahn 225
   Dune People 225
   forest people 225
   Haltans 225
   Haslanti 226
hill tribes 225
icewalkers 226
island tribes 225
Jackal Tribes 225
   Linowan 225
   Marukani 225
   pelagothropes 225
   Tear Eaters 226
   Ten Tribes 225
   Varajtul 226
beastmen 15, 29, 86, 90

C

caste 15, 28-29, 97,
   112-118, 230
   Changing Moon 15, 115-116,
     230
Full Moon 15, 113-114
Half Moon 22, 97, 115-116,
     230
No Moon 15, 29, 117-118
Waning Moon 22, 97, 115-116,
     230
Waxing Moon 22, 26-27, 29, 34,
     97, 115-116, 230

Casteless 15, 119-120,
     200-202
character creation 95-103
   bonus points table 103
   character creation
     table 102-103
Charms 99-100, 138-196
   Appearance 176-177
   Charisma 163-170
   Dexterity 149-155
   General 140-142
   Intelligence 186-190
   Lunar Hero Style 151-152,
     194-196
   Manipulation 171-176
   Perception 177-186
   Stamina 155-163
   Strength 142-148
   Wits 190-194
chimera 15, 30, 35, 202-206
   Echinna 205-206
Claw-speak 36, 112
Culottes Society see Slacks of the
     Sun Kings

G

Great Curse 25, 121-123

H

heart's blood 15, 109
   addiction 208

I

Ingosh Silverclaws 30, 31-32, 34

J

Jodhpurs of Luna see Speedo of Gaia

K

Knacks 15, 131-138, 204-205

L

Leviathan 52-53
lexicon 15-16
Lilith 53

M

Ma-Ha-Suchi 53-54

magical diseases 211-213
mate 15, 20, 110-111

R

Rain Deathflyer 54-55
Raksi 55

S

sacred hunt 128-129
Silver Pact 15, 19-56
   Crossroads Society 15, 23, 43-45,
     139, 220
   Seneschals of the
     Sun Kings 15, 23, 45-46,
     220-221
   Swords of Luna 16, 23-24,
     46-47, 221
   Wardens of Gaia 16, 24,
     47-48, 221
   Winding Path 16, 24,
     48-50, 221
Silver Python 54-55
Silver Way 15-16, 38-43
Slacks of the Sun
   Kings see Jodhpurs of Luna
Speedo of Gaia see Winding Pants
spirit shape 16, 98, 114, 116,
     117, 120, 127
Steward 16, 22

T

Tamuz 55-56
tattoos 28, 36, 11-112,
     129-130
Tell 16, 98, 112, 121, 130
Thousand Streams
   River 16, 59-92
true form 16, 121, 126-128

U

Unblooded 16, 33, 35-36,
     199-202

W

war form 16, 128, 136-138
Winding Pants see lost forever
Wyld mutation 101, 206-210